P9-CQK-827

THE
MEDIEVAL
WORLD VIEW

Bernard of Chartres used to compare us to dwarfs perched on the shoulders of giants. He pointed out that we see more and farther than our predecessors, not because we have keener vision or greater height, but because we are lifted up and borne aloft on their gigantic stature.

John of Salisbury (c.1115–80)
Metalogicon

THE MEDIEVAL WORLD VIEW

An Introduction

William R. Cook and Ronald B. Herzman

STATE UNIVERSITY OF NEW YORK, GENESEO

New York   Oxford

OXFORD UNIVERSITY PRESS

1983

Copyright © 1983 by Oxford University Press, Inc.

LIBRARY OF CONGRESS CATALOGING IN PUBLICATION DATA

Cook, William R. (William Robert), 1943–
  The medieval world view.

  Bibliography: p.
  Includes index.
  1. Civilization, Medieval. I. Herzman,
Ronald B. II. Title.
CB351.C58   940.1   81–16775
ISBN 0–19–503089–3   AACR2
ISBN 0–19–503090–7 (pbk.)

Printing (last digit): 9 8 7 6 5 4 3 2 1

Printed in the United States of America

65730

Bonaventure: The Soul's Journey Into God: The Tree of Life, The Life of St. Francis translated by Ewert Cousins, © 1978 by the Missionary Society of St. Paul the Apostle in the State of New York.

Gregory the Great, *Pastoral Care* (Ancient Christian Writers Series Vol. 11) translated by Henry Davis, S. J., © 1950, 1978 by Johannes Quasten and Rose Mary L. Plumpe.

Used by Permission of Paulist Press.

Penguin Books, Ltd.: Augustine, *Concerning the City of God Against the Pagans*, translated by Henry Bettenson, 1972, pp. 1091, 652, 859, 547–548, 549–550, 553, 596, 875, 213.

Augustine, *Confessions*, translated by R. S. Pine-Coffin, 1961, pp. 168, 121–123, 21, 177–178, 107–108.

Bede, *A History of the English Church and People*, translated by Leo Sherley-Price, 1955, pp. 86–87, 77, 69, 85, 236–37.

Early Christian Writings, translated by Maxwell Staniforth, 1968.

Gregory of Tours, *The History of the Franks*, translated by Lewis Thorpe, 1974, pp. 107–8, 167–8, 154, 143–44.

Ovid, *The Metamorphoses*, translated by Mary M. Innes, 1955.

Two Lives of Charlemagne, translated by Lewis Thorpe, pp. 81, 79, 74, 82, 141, 142, 64–65, 71–72.

Vergil, *Aeneid*, translated by W. F. Jackson Knight, 1956.

Reprinted by permission of Penguin Books Ltd.

The University of Pennsylvania Press: *The Burgundian Code*, translated by Katherine Fisher Drew. Philadelphia: University of Pennsylvania Press, 1949.

The First Crusade, edited by Edward Peters. Philadelphia: University of Pennsylvania Press, 1971.

The Lombard Laws, translated by Katherine Fisher Drew. Philadelphia: University of Pennsylvania Press, 1973.

Monks, Bishops and Pagans: Christian Culture in Gaul and Italy, 500–700, edited by Edward Peters. Philadelphia: University of Pennsylvania Press, 1975.

Prentice-Hall, Inc.: Brian Tierney, *The Crisis of Church & State 1050–1300*. © 1964 by Prentice-Hall, Inc. Published by Prentice-Hall, Inc., Englewood Cliffs, New Jersey 07632.

Random House, Inc., Alfred A. Knopf, Inc.: *The Basic Works of Cicero*, edited by Moses Hadas. Random House, 1951.

The Complete Works of Tacitus, edited by Moses Hadas and translated by Alfred John Church and William Jackson Brodribb. Random House, 1942.

Brian Tierney, *The Middle Ages: Sources of Medieval History*, 3rd edition. Knopf, 1978.

Vergil's Works, translated by J. W. Mackail. Random House, 1950.

Regnery Gateway, Inc.: *The Letters of Saint Bernard of Clairvaux*, translated and edited by B. S. James. Copyright © 1953 by Regnery Gateway, Chicago. Reprinted by permission of the publisher.

For Ellen
And for Paul, Suzanne, and Edward

ACKNOWLEDGMENTS

For us, it is appropriate that in writing a book about a period whose achievements were institutional as well as individual we should incur debts not only to many individuals but to institutions as well. It is a pleasure to acknowledge these debts, and so to acknowledge the degree to which this book is a collaboration in ways other than the obvious one.

It began when we put together a very rough draft in preparation for a course we team-taught in the summer of 1975, "The Age of Dante." Before flying to Italy with our students, we had exactly one week to prepare them, many with little or no medieval background, for what they would be reading and seeing. The encouragement we received from this battlefield experiment—in fact, one colleague named it the boot camp of the mind—helped sustain us in the many subsequent drafts. From first to last, these drafts have been subject to the exacting scrutiny of our students, and we have been fortunate that many of them both at SUNY Geneseo and at Attica Correctional Facility have taught their teachers through their comments and support. We thank three in particular, and they must stand for many others: Mike Benton, Wes Kennison, and Gerry Twomey. Teachers, colleagues, and friends have also been generous with their help and encouragement as the book has taken shape. We would like to thank Brian Tierney, David Herlihy, David Bevington, Giles Constable, John Fleming,

Karen Pelz, William Stephany, David Sundelson, Susan Mosher Stuard, Richard Emmerson, and Pamela Sheingorn.

We would like to express our gratitude to the National Humanities Faculty, its former director Edwin Delattre and its former Associate Director Garry Rosenblatt. As NHF faculty visitors and advisors, we had the opportunity to try out many of our ideas to audiences in colleges and schools around the country.

Grants from the National Endowment for the Humanities enabled us to prepare to write later drafts. As NEH fellows-in-residence (Cook at Harvard University during the 1976–77 academic year; Herzman at the University of Chicago, 1978–1979), we had the opportunity to do a good deal of reading and thinking about the book, especially in those areas where we were conscious of the biggest gaps. The current Chairman of the Endowment, William J. Bennett, has enthusiastically supported this and other Cook-Herzman enterprises.

Many of the ideas in the book were presented in earlier versions at monasteries throughout the country. Here too we have been students as well as teachers, and have learned from these occasions much of what we know about monasticism. We have learned the most from our friends and neighbors at the Abbey of the Genesee, and owe a special debt of gratitude to Abbot John Eudes Bamberger and the community there. We would also like to thank the monks of St. Joseph's Abbey, Spencer, Massachusetts; Holy Spirit Abbey, Conyers, Georgia; Mepkin Abbey, Moncks Corner, South Carolina. At all these we were given exactly the welcome that Benedict prescribes, "with all the attention charity inspires." Our debt to the monastic tradition would not be paid unless we also mentioned Dom Jean Leclercq, who gave us encouragement and wisdom when both were much needed.

The medieval conference at Western Michigan University in Kalamazoo has now become an annual springtime pilgrimage for literally hundreds of medievalists. Papers we have given there jointly and separately over the last ten years have clarified our thinking about a number of topics treated in the book. Equally important, the conference has provided a unique setting for testing ideas, by fostering conversation with medievalists from every discipline. The fact that increasing numbers of us routinely think in interdisciplinary terms owes a great deal to this institution.

In its final form the book owes much to the care of Oxford University Press. The detailed and perceptive comments of Edward Peters and the useful suggestions of Thomas Burns, readers for the press, were incorporated, as much as possible, into the final version. Melanie Miller, our copy-editor, amazed us with her attention to detail. Nancy Lane, our editor, has been invaluable both for her skill and her enthusiasm for this project. Help was provided here at home by a grant from the Genesee Foundation for typing the manuscript. We would also like to thank Marie Henry and Laurie Scherner for typing large parts of it.

Our personal debts, like our professional ones, are legion. We have received encouragement and support from non-medievalist colleagues and from friends and families. Our families have always shown interest in this undertaking; and friends have contributed to this book more than they know. Ellen Ferens Herzman has spent many years putting up with the fanaticism and eccentricities generated by this book on *two* medievalists—a feat all the more heroic in that she had only bargained for one. Gratefully, we dedicate the book to her. The other part of the dedication, to our children, also suggests something of the way in which this book is not only a collaboration between colleagues and friends, but between families as well. In this, we recognize our extreme good fortune.

CONTENTS

Introduction   xvii

TIME LINE: 14 A.D.–1375 A.D.   xxv

PART ONE: Foundations of The Middle Ages

CHAPTER ONE: The Bible   3
CHAPTER TWO: The Classical Heritage   29
CHAPTER THREE: Early Christianity   50
CHAPTER FOUR: The Latin Fathers:
Jerome and Augustine   79

PART TWO: The Early Middle Ages

CHAPTER FIVE: The Transition from
Ancient to Medieval   115
CHAPTER SIX: Monasticism   166
CHAPTER SEVEN: The Carolingian Empire
and Its Aftermath   179

PART THREE: The High Middle Ages

CHAPTER EIGHT: Church, State, and Society   225
CHAPTER NINE: The Renaissance of the
    Twelfth Century   262
CHAPTER TEN: Francis of Assisi and
    the Mendicants   294

Conclusion   317
Notes   321
Bibliography   333
Index   353

INTRODUCTION

This book began as our response to the problems encountered by undergraduate students trying to understand the Middle Ages. As any teacher who must deal with a period remote from our own knows, the Middle Ages presents special problems to students, who for the most part are unaware of its quite different intellectual, aesthetic, institutional, and spiritual presuppositions. The twelfth-century epic *Song of Roland* is a literary work of a very high order; it is also an extremely useful document with which to teach the ideals of feudalism and the spirit of the Crusades. Students opening the *Song of Roland* for the first time, however, discover early on the disconcerting fact that Charlemagne is over two hundred years old. Even if their immediate response to this detail is not to close the book, so long as their only standards of decorum are modern ones, they will not take the work seriously, refusing to believe that a culture that has no respect for "reality" has anything to say to them. To understand and appreciate the work, they first need to understand how exaggeration is a technique used to give prominence to what is most important in medieval documents, whether they be works of literature or art.

Any teacher of the Middle Ages could provide a hundred similar examples, and it is for this reason that we have attempted to present the presuppositions of medieval society in a systematic fashion, by integrating texts and photographs into our exploration of the medieval world view. Thus the book can be used to understand and appreciate the Middle Ages from the inside, that is, as the people of the Middle Ages saw themselves. Perhaps more important, after reading the book a student will have some sense of how to approach any medieval literary text, artistic monument, historical document, or musical work in a more meaningful way. Although this is a relatively modest undertaking insofar as we are not offering a comprehensive new interpretation of the Middle Ages—though surely elements of our interpretation will not be everyone's—it is at least in one sense original: we know of no other book that attempts the same thing. Therefore it is useful to state at the outset some of our own presuppositions.

The most fundamental of these is that we are attempting to reconstruct important elements of the Middle Ages, in the phrase we have already used, "from the inside." To do this we emphasize the differences between that age and our own. The document most important for understanding the period is, of course, the Bible, a work necessary not only for understanding specifically religious subjects but for law, art, literature, and music as well. We approach the Bible from the standpoint of medieval exegesis rather than modern criticism. The chapter on the Bible, therefore, not only explains what the Bible is, but exphasizes those sections that were most frequently used in the Middle Ages, and gives clues, developed in subsequent chapters such as the one on Augustine, that explain how the Bible was read. It is likewise necessary to understand the contribution of Greece and Rome to the literature, art, or law of the Middle Ages. But the classical writers known and valued then were not necessarily those known and valued today. And so on, down a rather extensive list of differences between medieval and modern culture.

Our second presupposition follows from the first. To present the major developments of the Middle Ages in a somewhat systematic way, we have seen the need to deal with a very complex period as a unity. There are dangers in this which we think it would be wise to anticipate. We ourselves of course do not think that the danger lies simply in faulty interpretations—

though here we are obviously open to judgment—so much as it lies in being incomplete. In summarizing a phenomenon as complex as, say, feudalism, or a figure as monumental as Augustine, we understand too well that this trap is all but unavoidable. The risk we run of oversimplification, however, must be weighed against the primary goal of the book: to present that sense of the Middle Ages as a whole necessary to make any work of medieval culture intelligible to a modern student. We think that understanding the nature of feudalism or the place of Augustine can be aided by their placement within the larger context which the book develops. Equally significant, this context provides the starting point for a more detailed study of the particular figures and movements presented in the book. Genuinely valuable scholarly contributions to most aspects of the Middle Ages abound; we have listed many of the more important and more readily accessible of these in our bibliography. The problem with them from a student's point of view is that the best are rarely written as introductions. Because these works are usually written not only by experts but for experts as well, much of their value will be lost to students who do not have some sense of the period.

Perhaps the difference between what one sees as an expert and what one needs to see as a beginning student also allows us to talk intelligibly about the allusive and problematic question of what kind of unity really does exist in the thousand-year period we call the Middle Ages. Can this unity, which we presuppose, really be said to exist? Clearly the differences between Augustine and Aquinas, Beowulf and Dante (or even Chaucer and Dante), or a Merovingian tribal king and Louis IX are enormous; and to ignore or to underestimate them is to ignore the actual texture of medieval religion, poetry, and society. Those who argue against imposing a superficial unity on the Middle Ages perceive rightly the ever-present danger of reducing them to a Platonic model existing only in the mind of the scholar.

But it is also true that however great the differences between Augustine and Aquinas, they have many of the same concerns;

for example, both deal with the relationship between human reason and divine revelation. Whatever different conclusions they come to, they still have more in common with each other than they have with modern philosophers, for whom this relationship has ceased to be a primary concern. Literature provides similar examples of kinship. A Chaucer scholar easily recognizes enormous differences between Chaucer and Dante, differences in tone, temperament, and technique. But a modern student coming to either author for the first time needs to know that each work is structured according to the ideal of a medieval pilgrimage, a literal journey that is a sign of a spiritual transformation; that similarity alone shows that Chaucer has more in common with Dante than either author has with Beckett or Kafka. Even the changes themselves, all the changes that occurred in the thousand-year period between antiquity and the fifteenth century, can only be understood by first recognizing how they all take place in a culture given a degree of homogeneity by the intellectual revolutions of subsequent times. To anyone familiar with the period, let alone to a scholar familiar with its political institutions, a Merovingian warrior-king seems to have almost nothing in common with a thirteenth-century king who presides over a legal and bureaucratic structure and who has a firm theoretical conception of the state. But even these differences will be grossly misinterpreted by the modern student to whom the whole idea of kingship is utterly foreign, something our own more sophisticated age need not take seriously. For example, on the surface a Germanic warrior-king like Clovis appears to be radically different from a king like Louis IX of France (1228–1270). However, both perceived themselves as Christian kings modeled on biblical figures and both quite consciously, albeit differently, recognized their debt to the model of the emperors of Rome. In other words, when looked at from a distance, from the vantage point provided by the twentieth century, the people of the Middle Ages do indeed share a great deal. But the more scholars immerse themselves in the period, the more likely they are to take these differences between medieval and modern for granted, moving on to those discriminations within the period that are their real concern. This book takes the long view, the view that emphasizes the differences between medieval and modern, and hence the unity within the Middle Ages.

Moreover, it is our strong belief that such a holistic approach as we attempt is aided by an affinity between the various medieval disciplines far stronger than any that connect them in our own time. One example may suggest what the text itself demonstrates more convincingly. One of the significant differences between the medieval and modern world is that modern men and women are constantly searching for and discovering new truths, while truth in medieval society was perceived as having been discovered in the past. Because of this perception there is throughout the period an iconography—a symbolic code by which figures and events can be identified—that remains relatively constant. Saint Peter, to use an obvious and well-known example, is almost always pictured holding keys, a kind of shorthand referring to the text of Matthew's Gospel (Matt. 16:18) in which Christ gives Peter the keys of His Kingdom. Some knowledge of this iconography is necessary not only to understand theological writings and saints' lives but also sculpture, political writings, and literature.

There has been a long-standing and almost continuous debate over the precise dates for the beginning and the end of the Middle Ages, testimony to the problem inherent in any attempt to classify the past with exactness. Figures like Ambrose and Augustine, however influential they were to become for the entire Middle Ages, belong nonetheless to the world of late antiquity. Figures like Boethius and Gregory the Great, however much they draw from the ancient world, are usually classified as founders of the Middle Ages. Though this classification is somewhat arbitrary, it is nevertheless useful, and it is the one that we have adopted. We see the Middle Ages beginning with these so-called founders, the intellectual lights of that period that used to be dismissed as the Dark Ages and now is more often called the early Middle Ages, the period stretching from the sixth century to the beginning of the twelfth-century renaissance. Therefore the division of the book is threefold.

Part One treats the antecedents of the Middle Ages, the classical and Christian backgrounds of medieval culture, ending with the monumental figure of Augustine. Part Two deals with the early Middle Ages, beginning with the disintegration of the Roman Empire, including the Germanic invasions, the sixth- and seventh-century founders, the renaissance associated with the figure of Charlemagne, and ending about the middle of the eleventh century. Part Three, the High Middle Ages, includes material from this point until 1300.

Although references to the late Middle Ages, especially to Chaucer and Dante, are made throughout the work, the book does not deal per se with events and works after 1300, not because this date is our candidate for the end of the Middle Ages, but rather because the basic elements that continue to characterize medieval civilization are all developed by then: the mendicants, Gothic architecture, Scholasticism, nation-states, and so on. The fourteenth century alters, questions, and even in certain instances rejects these elements; however, nothing really replaces them. The book consequently provides students with what is needed to read a late medieval author such as Chaucer, appreciate the iconography of a fifteenth-century Burgundian manuscript illumination, or grasp what happens to the papacy during its exile in Avignon. Changes in style and substance come with the Italian Renaissance. The extent of these changes has also been much debated, but more recent scholarship has emphasized that along with them there are fundamental areas of continuity. Thus the material we have assembled here would not be an inappropriate introduction to the Renaissance, though this is not one of the principal aims of the book.

It will be obvious to the reader that equal division does not mean equal proportion. The longest section is the first, the background to the Middle Ages. At first this might seem to be a distortion, since the period that is slighted, the high Middle Ages, is the period of the greatest accomplishments—of Dante, of the Gothic cathedrals, of the great legal systems and the scholastic philosophers.

There is a story we have heard that is probably only partly apocryphal about a course in English history from the Norman Conquest in 1066 to the battle of Bosworth Field in 1485. As the story goes, the instructor intended to begin with a few days of background. Those few days of background somehow turned into a few weeks of background. Those few weeks somehow managed to engulf the whole course, so that by Thanksgiving the teacher was still trying frantically to reach 1066. It was probably an excellent course, but not the one that was originally planned. We would like to assure our readers that our emphasis on the earlier periods is not a sign that we have fallen into this trap, but is rather our deliberate attempt to help teachers and students to avoid it. We have concentrated on the origins to let students and teachers get on with the business of studying the major accomplishments, accomplishments that can best be understood once students have the background necessary to move directly to primary sources.

The quotation from Bernard of Chartres that provides the epigraph for the book is meant to be suggestive rather than programmatic, a useful entry into the text. We have tried to take into account its implications in the structure of our work by reminding the reader that the Middle Ages not only owed an enormous debt to the past—to its classical, Christian, and Germanic antecedents—but that it was in fact conscious of this debt as well. In the structure of the book, no less than for the thinkers of the Middle Ages, there is a constant backward glance to the achievements of the past.

Moreover, each phase of medieval culture was dependent on the achievements of the more immediate past as well as its pre-medieval foundations: it is impossible to understand the renaissance of the twelfth century without an understanding of those elements of the classical past that they rediscovered and reinterpreted. But it is also impossible to understand the twelfth-century renaissance without an appreciation of the Carolingian Renaissance of the early ninth century. In other words, classical and Carolingian writers can both be considered giants on whose shoulders the thinkers of the twelfth-century renaissance rest. Our attempt to emphasize both the giants who existed before the Middle Ages and the giants who existed within the period itself is a thread which runs through each chapter, and which helps give coherence to our reading of the Middle Ages.

Time Line: 14 A.D.–1375 A.D.

0 —	Death of Augustus 14
50 —	Crucifixion of Jesus c.30
	Persecution of Nero 64
	Death of Saint Paul c.65
100 —	Reign of Trajan 98–117
150 —	Martyrdom of Saint Ignatius 107
	Martyrdom of Saint Polycarp 155
	Tertullian born c.160–220
	Reign of Marcus Aurelius 161–180
200 —	Origen born c.185–254
250 —	Saint Antony (251–356) becomes a monk 269
300 —	REIGN OF DIOCLETIAN 284–305
	REIGN OF CONSTANTINE 312–37
	Edict of Milan 313
	Council of Nicaea 325
	Saint Ambrose born c.340–97
	Saint Jerome born c.342–420
350 —	Saint Augustine born c.354–430
	John Cassian born c.360–435
	Beginning of the Goths' permanent settlement in the Roman Empire 378
	Reign of Theodosius I 379–95
	Council of Constantinople 381
400 —	Sack of Rome by the Goths 410
	Council of Ephesus 431
	PONTIFICATE OF LEO I 440–61

450 —	Council of Chalcedon 451
	End of the Roman Empire in the West 476
	Saint Benedict of Nursia born 480–547
	Reign of Theodoric the Ostrogoth 493–526
500 —	Conversion of the Franks c.500
	Boethius (b. c.480) executed 524
	Publication of the Justinian Code 529
550 —	Gregory of Tours born 539–94
	PONTIFICATE OF GREGORY I 590–604
	Pope Gregory I sends mission
600 —	to England 597
650 —	Synod of Whitby 663–64
700 —	Venerable Bede born 673–735
	Beowulf written c.725
	Battle of Tours 732
	Alcuin born c.735–804
	Saint Benedict of Aniane born c.750–821
750 —	Pepin crowned King of the Franks
	by Saint Boniface 751
	REIGN OF CHARLEMAGNE 768–814
	Birth of Einhard c.770–840
800 —	Coronation of Charlemagne as Roman Emperor 800
	John Scotus Eruigena born c.810–75
	REIGN OF LOUIS THE PIOUS 814–40
	Death of Einhard 840
850 —	Pontificate of Nicholas I 858–67
	Reign of Alfred the Great, King of Wessex 871–99
900 —	Founding of Cluny Monastery 910
950 —	REIGN OF OTTO I 936–73
1000 —	Pontificate of Sylvester II (Gerbert) 999–1003
	Saint Anselm born c.1033–1109
1050 —	Pontificate of Leo IX 1049–54
	Norman conquest of England 1066
	PONTIFICATE OF GREGORY VII 1073–85
	Peter Abelard born 1079–1142
	Bernard of Clairvaux born c.1090–1153

Founding of La Grande Chartreuse Monastery   1084

First Crusade   1095

Founding of Cîteaux Monastery   1098

1100 — Peter Lombard born   c.1100–60

Revolt of the Commune of Laon   1112

Song of Roland written   c.1125

Joachim of Fiore born   c.1132–1202

Decretum written   c.1140

1150 — Second Crusade   1147

Reign of Holy Roman Emperor Frederick Barbarossa   1152–90

Reign of Henry II of England   1154–89

Martyrdom of Thomas à Becket   1170   (b.1118)

Saint Dominic born   c.1170–1221

Reign of King Philip Augustus of France   1180–1223

Saint Francis of Assisi born   c.1182–1226

Third Crusade   1190

Chartres Cathedral begun   1194

1200 — PONTIFICATE OF INNOCENT III   1198–1216

Fourth Crusade   1204

Fourth Lateran Council   1215

Reign of Holy Roman Emperor Frederick II   1220–50

Amiens Cathedral begun   1220

Saint Bonaventure born   1221–74

Saint Thomas born   c.1224–74

1250 — Dante born   1265–1321

Institution of the Feast of Corpus Christi   1264

Giotto born   c.1266–1337

Romance of the Rose written   c.1285

PONTIFICATE OF BONIFACE VIII   1294–1303

1300 — William of Ockham born   1300–49

Petrarch born   1304–74

John Wyclif born   c.1328–84

Hundred Years War begins   1337–1453

1350 — Geoffrey Chaucer born   c.1340–1400

Piers Plowman written   c.1370

Sir Gawain and the Green Knight written   c.1375

PART ONE

Foundations
of the
Middle Ages

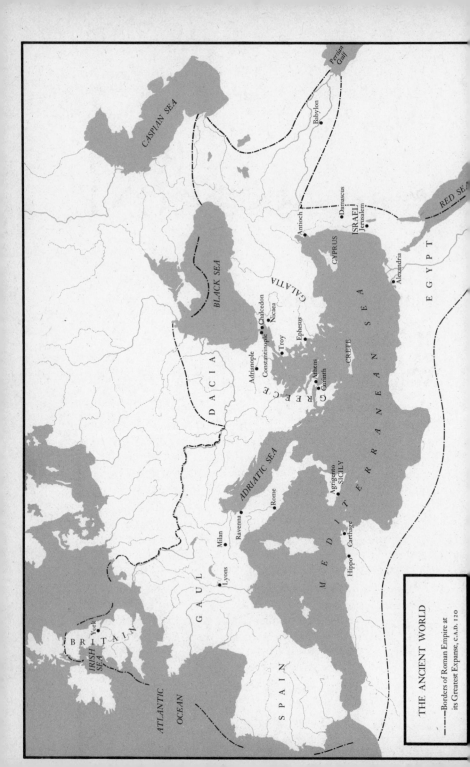

THE ANCIENT WORLD

- - - - Borders of Roman Empire at
its Greatest Expanse, c.A.D. 120

CASPIAN SEA

Persian Gulf

Babylon

RED SEA

Damascus

Antioch

ISRAEL
Jerusalem

CYPRUS

Alexandria

EGYPT

BLACK SEA

GALATIA

Chalcedon
Constantinople Nicaea

Adrianople

DACIA

Troy

Ephesus

Athens

Corinth

GREECE

CRETE

M E D I T E R R A N E A N   S E A

ADRIATIC SEA

Rome

Agrigento
SICILY

Ravenna

Milan

Carthage

Hippo

Lyons

GAUL

York

BRITAIN

IRISH
SEA

ATLANTIC
OCEAN

SPAIN

CHAPTER ONE

The Bible

The Bible was far and away the most influential and important book for the Middle Ages. Three fourths of the Bible is made up of the Old Testament, the writings of the Hebrews. But when students and scholars set out to study the Middle Ages, they often pay far less attention to the Old Testament than they do to the influence of classical antiquity and of early Christianity, let alone the New Testament. When Jerome translated the Bible into Latin in the fourth century in the version that became standard for the Middle Ages, he translated the Old Testament as well as the New, including what today are referred to as the Old Testament Apocrypha. And these Old Testament books were hardly ignored in the Middle Ages. They were read, commented upon, and depicted in art, though usually in what was perceived as their relationship to the New Testament. Thus a brief survey of the kinds of documents that make up the Old Testament is of great value to an understanding of the Middle Ages.[1]

The Old Testament was written over a much longer time than the New; perhaps seven hundred years separate the earliest from the latest document, and some of the stories existed either orally or in writing long before they reached the form in which they have been handed down. The Old Testament consists of legends, historical narrative, laws, poetry, allegory, prophecy, songs, and wise sayings. The first five books of the Old Testament (Genesis, Exodus, Leviticus, Numbers, Deuteronomy) are called the Law (English), the Torah (Hebrew), or the Pentateuch (Greek). These present, often in symbolic terms, the story of creation, the fall of man, the choosing of the Hebrews by God, and their history until the death of Moses. Many of the most familiar Bible stories are contained in these books: Adam and Eve, Cain and Abel, Noah, the Tower of Babel, Abraham, Isaac, Jacob, Joseph, the bondage in Egypt, the exodus into Palestine, the Ten Commandments. Much of these books is taken up with legal material and precise ritual. Although this ritual material is more or less ignored by Christians today, it captured the interest of medieval writers, and several long allegorical commentaries on the details of ritual and law were composed and widely known. The next two books, Joshua and Judges, tell the story of the conquest of the the Promised Land from the native inhabitants, the Canaanites. Perhaps the most famous stories in these books are Joshua at the battle of Jericho, and Samson and Delilah. These books were seen as especially relevant to the Crusades, wars fought with the aim of conquering the Promised Land again. Imagery from Joshua and Judges pervades Crusade chronicles; the epitaph of the man who conquered Jerusalem in the First Crusade refers to him as another Joshua. More subtly, the theory of causation in Joshua and Judges—warriors will triumph in battle only if they act morally—is used to explain victories and losses in battle in the Crusades.

After the short book of Ruth come eight books, more or less historical in their orientation, that tell the story of the founding, flourishing, division, conquest, and restoration of the Hebrew monarchy. The First and Second Books of Kings (in modern translations often called the First and Second Books of Samuel) tell of the annointing of Saul as king, the shepherd

David's defeat of the Philistine giant Goliath, the civil war between David and Saul, and the victories and prosperity of David's reign after Saul had been killed in battle. The Third Book of Kings (or First Book of Kings in modern translation) tells of the most wealthy and wise of all the Hebrew Kings— Solomon—who, at the end of his life, turned away from the Hebrew God Yahweh (sometimes written Jehovah). It then goes on to tell of the split between the north and south (respectively the kingdoms of Israel and Judah) after Solomon's death. The House of David ruled the south from Jerusalem while a succession of families attempted to rule in the north, eventually building a capital at Samaria. The Fourth Book of Kings continues to tell of the split and the falling away from the worship of Yahweh in both kingdoms, especially the northern one. It also describes the destruction of the northern kingdom by the Assyrians in 722–21 B.C. and the destruction of the southern kingdom by the Babylonians in 587–86 B.C.; it was with the fall of Jerusalem in 587–86 B.C. that thousands of Hebrews were forced into exile in Babylonian territory. There is no book that gives a narrative of events of the exile, but the books of Ezra and Nehemiah tell of the return of the exiles, the rebuilding of the Temple and the city walls, and the institution of religious reforms. After the restoration of the Temple in 516 B.C., the Jews remained governed by foreigners but generally were allowed to practice their religion undisturbed. From this time till about 169 B.C., there are no narrative accounts in the Old Testament. However, when the Greeks tried to enforce religious uniformity on the Hebrews around the time of 160 B.C., there was a rebellion of the Jews led by Judas Maccabaeus that was successful in winning de facto freedom. The story of this revolt is narrated in the First and Second Books of the Maccabees. After the revolt, there is no more historical narrative in the Old Testament.

In addition to these books, there are two other categories of documents in the Old Testament. One is a series of works of literature called the Writings, which provide models of conduct, advice, edifying stories, and magnificent poetry. The other is prophecy, of which there are sixteen books. Old Testament literary works were favorite sources of wisdom in the Middle Ages and were frequently commented upon by medieval writers. These include the Book of Job, a long narrative poem about a good man who lost all his earthly possessions in a test of his faith. Job was seen as a prefiguration of Christ in the Middle Ages, thanks largely to the long Commentary on the Book of Job written by Pope Gregory I. Perhaps the best-loved book of the Old Testament in the Middle Ages was the Psalms, a series of one hundred fifty songs, which were believed to have been written by King David. These songs express the widest variety of moods and attitudes, ranging from battle songs, songs of thanksgiving, wedding songs, and laments to hymns of praise. Some sing of the love of the faithful for God while others cry out for the annihilation of their enemies. For example, one can contrast the two texts below:

> Happy indeed is the man
> who follows not the counsel of the wicked;
> nor lingers in the way of sinners
> nor sits in the company of scorners,
> but whose delight is the law of the Lord
> and who ponders his law day and night.
>
> (Ps. 1:1–2)

. . .

> O God, break the teeth in their mouths,
> tear out the fangs of these wild beasts, O Lord!
> Let them vanish like water that runs away:
> let them wither like grass that is trodden underfoot:
> let them be like the snail that dissolves into slime:
> like a woman's miscarriage that never sees the sun.
>
> Before they put forth their thorns, like a bramble,
> let them be swept away, green wood or dry!
> The just shall rejoice at the sight of vengeance;
> they shall bathe their feet in the blood of the wicked.
> "Truly," men shall say, "the just are rewarded.
> Truly there is a God who does justice on earth."
>
> Ps. 57:7–12)

It is important to remember how familiar medieval people were with the Psalms. The Rule of St. Benedict prescribed that the entire Psalter was to be sung in church by all monks each week, and in secular churches also the Psalms were sung often.

The books of Ecclesiastes, Wisdom of Solomon, Ecclesiasticus (or the Wisdom of Jesus Son of Sirach), and Proverbs are full of pieces of wisdom and practical advice. A few examples from the Book of Proverbs will illustrate the richness and variety of advice:

Only the wise are strong. (24:5)

Send a fool on thy errand, thou hast a lame journey, and mischief brewing for thee. (26:6)

Like a dog at his vomit, the fool goes back ever to his own folly. (26:11)

Do not flatter thyself with hopes of tomorrow. (27:1)

Wisdom comes of reproof, comes of the rod; leave a child to go its own way, and a mother's care is wasted. (29:15)

These and hundreds of other bits of wisdom were both practical guides to daily living and important philosophical principles in the Middle Ages. The Song of Songs (Song of Solomon) is a poem that celebrates physical beauty and sexual relationships between a bride and bridegroom. In the Middle Ages this was one of the most commented-upon books, perhaps because it was treated allegorically, with Christ as the bridegroom and the Church as his bride.

The last major category of Old Testament literature is the prophets, those who are raised up by God to tell people, especially the leaders, of their faults and warn them of the consequences if they continue to sin, and who also predict what is to come in both the near and distant future. This group of sixteen books consists of four so-called major prophets (Isaiah, Jeremiah, Ezekiel, and Daniel) and twelve minor prophets (Hosea, Joel, Amos, Obadiah, Jonah, Micah, Nahum, Habakkuk, Zephaniah, Haggai, Zechariah, and Malachi). This division into major and minor does not indicate quality but rather length of the book and its arrangement in Scripture.

Although the writings of the prophets stretch out over several hundred years, the most important prophetic literature was written at the time of the disintegration of the kingdom of Judah and its destruction by the Babylonians. Many texts from these prophets were either quoted directly or clearly alluded to in the New Testament, especially in Matthew's Gospel. Two examples will show how important some of these texts are to New Testament writers and to all subsequent Christian writers. For example, the following text from Isaiah is quoted by all four evangelists as a prophecy of the ministry of John the Baptist:

> A cry, there, out in the wilderness,
> Make way for the Lord's coming;
> a straight road for our God through the desert!
> Bridged every valley must be,
> every mountain and hill levelled;
> windings cut straight,
> and the rough paths paced;
> the Lord's glory is to be revealed
> for all mankind to witness;
> it is his own decree.   (Isa. 40:3–5)

In the Gospels and Paul's Epistles, it is emphasized that Christ was a direct descendent of King David. The expectation of a savior coming from the House of David is predicted by several prophets, including Jeremiah:

> Nay, a time is coming, the Lord says,
> when I will raise up, from the stock of David, a faithful
>   scion at last.
> The land shall have a king to reign over it,
> and reign over it wisely, giving just sentence and due award.
> When that time comes, Juda shall find deliverance,
> none shall disturb Israel's rest;
> and the name given to this king shall be
> The Lord vindicates us.   (Jer. 23:5–6)

It is important to say something about form as well as content in the Old Testament since the imagery of the Hebrew writers permeates the Middle Ages. They usually did not speak in abstractions but rather their language was extremely vivid. They spoke in quite precise and detailed metaphor, as in the following Psalm:

He who dwells in the shelter of the Most High
and abides in the shade of the Almighty
says to the Lord: "My refuge,
my stronghold, my God in whom I trust."

It is he who will free you from the snare
of the fowler who seeks to destroy you;
he will conceal you with his pinions
and under his wings you will find refuge.

You will not fear the terror of the night
nor the arrow that flies by day,
nor the plague that prowls in the darkness
nor the scourge that lays waste at noon.

A thousand may fall at your side,
ten thousand fall at your right,
you, it will never approach;
his faithfulness is buckler and shield.

Your eyes have only to look
to see how the wicked are repaid,
you who have said: "Lord, my refuge!"
and have made the Most High your dwelling.

Upon you no evil shall fall,
no plague approach where you dwell.
For you has he commanded his angels,
to keep you in all your ways.

They shall bear you upon their hands
lest you strike your foot against a stone.
On the lion and the viper you will tread
and trample the young lion and the dragon.

> Since he clings to me in love, I will free him;
> protect him for he knows my name.
> When he calls I shall answer: "I am with you."
> I will save him in distress and give him glory.
>
> With length of life I will content him;
> I shall let him see my saving power.   (Ps. 90)

It is important to note how personally God is spoken of and in what concrete terms—"my stronghold," "his wings," and so on. Furthermore, the descriptions of God's power are vivid. God would rescue a man from hurting his foot on a rock, for in ancient times that would mean not being able to farm or harvest, and thus possibly starvation. This same passage is used by the devil in Matthew 4:6 and Luke 4:11 to tempt Christ. Finally, texts like this were often depicted in medieval art, such as the statues of Christ standing on a lion and a viper, symbolizing enemies of the Church. This Psalm was one of the best known in the Middle Ages since the Benedictine Rule prescribed its singing every day at the office of compline.

The New Testament is much shorter than the Old, much less varied in its literary forms, and written within a span of less than one hundred years. It consists of four Gospels; the Acts of the Apostles, an account of the early Church; thirteen letters attributed to Paul; the anonymous epistle to the Hebrews, believed in the Middle Ages to have been written by Paul; letters attributed to James, Peter, John, and Jude; and the Apocalypse or Book of Revelation attributed to John.

The Gospels are perhaps the most familiar part of the New Testament because they contain the stories of the life and teachings of Jesus Christ. However, these are not biographies in the sense that a historian would write a biography today. The authors of the Gospels are presenting highly theologized pictures of Christ and are more interested in presenting readers with an understanding of the meaning of Jesus than a chronicle of his activities. The Gospels are divided into two groups: the synoptics (Matthew, Mark, and Luke) and John. Though there are many elements common to all four, this division is useful. The synoptic Gospels, of which Mark is the earliest,

Sculpture from the south porch of Chartres Cathedral. 13th Century. This sculpture puts into stone the image of Christ trampling the lion and the dragon from Psalm 90.

share many stories and points of view that are not present in John. They have basically the same chronology of events; they describe the Last Supper and the institution of the Eucharist; in them Christ speaks primarily in parables. Nonetheless, there are also differences. For example, Mark has no account of the nativity while Matthew and Luke each describe Christ's birth, although with some differences between them. Each has a somewhat different perspective on the meaning of Christ's life and teachings.

Matthew's is the Gospel of fulfillment. Quoting the Old Testament well over a hundred times, he constantly emphasizes how Christ fulfills and completes the revelation of God in the Old Testament. All the evangelists develop this theme somewhat, but Matthew far exceeds the others. Consider the following passages from the nativity narrative:

> And this was the manner of Christ's birth. His mother Mary was espoused to Joseph, but they had not yet come together, when she was found to be with child, by the power of the Holy Ghost. Whereupon her husband Joseph (for he was a right-minded man, and would not have her put to open shame) was for sending her away in secret. But hardly had this thought come to his mind, when an angel of the Lord appeared to him in a dream, and said, Joseph, son of David, do not be afraid to take thy wife Mary to thyself, for it is by the power of the Holy Ghost that she has conceived this child; and she will bear a son, whom thou shalt call Jesus, for he is to save his people from their sins. All this was so ordained to fulfil the word which the Lord spoke by his prophet: Behold, the virgin shall be with child, and shall bear a son, and they shall call him Emmanuel (which means, God with us). (1:18–23)

> He [Joseph] rose up, therefore, while it was still night, and took the child and his mother with him, and withdrew into Egypt, where he remained until the death of Herod, in fulfillment of the word which the Lord spoke by his prophet, I called my son out of Egypt. (2:14–15)

> Meanwhile, when he found that the wise men had played him false, Herod was angry beyond measure; he sent and made

away with all the male children in Bethlehem and in all its neighborhood, of two years old and less, reckoning the time by the careful enquiry which he had made of the wise men. It was then that the word spoken by the prophet Jeremy [Jeremiah] was fulfilled: A voice was heard in Rama, lamentation and great mourning; it was Rachel weeping for her children, and she would not be comforted, because none is left. (2:16–18)

Perhaps this theme of Matthew can best be summarized by a text from the Sermon on the Mount: "Do not think that I have come to set aside the law and the prophets; I have not come to set them aside, but to bring them to perfection." (5:17)

Luke, who was probably the best educated of the evangelists and best acquainted with the way the Greeks wrote history, gives a particularly beautiful literary work. Some principal themes are the universal message of Christ—Matthew by contrast was writing primarily for Jews—the exaltation of the lowly and poor, the importance of Mary, and the significance of Christ as a man of prayer and solitude. In his nativity narrative (the most developed and the one still most familiar to Christians from its reading in churches at Christmas), Luke stresses the universal message of Christ in a song attributed to the prophet Simeon:

> Ruler of all, now dost thou let thy servant go in peace,
> according to thy word;
> for my own eyes have seen
> that saving power of thine which thou hast prepared
> in the sight of all nations.
> This is the light which shall give revelation to the Gentiles,
> this is the glory of thy people Israel.   (2:29–32)

The exaltation of the poor and the importance of Mary are both present in the song of Mary:

> And Mary said, My soul magnifies the Lord;
> my spirit has found joy in God, who is my Saviour,
> because he has looked graciously upon
> the lowliness of his handmaid.
> Behold, from this day forward

all generations will count me blessed;
because he who is mighty, he whose name is holy,
has wrought for me his wonders.
He has mercy upon those who fear him,
from generation to generation;
he has done valiantly with the strength of his arm,
driving the proud astray in the conceit of their hearts;
he has put down the mighty from their seat,
and exalted the lowly;
he has filled the hungry with good things,
and sent the rich away empty-handed.
He has protected his servant Israel,
keeping his merciful design in remembrance,
according to the promise he made to our forefathers,
Abraham and his posterity for evermore.   (1:46–55)

Two short passages illustrate the theme of Christ as a man of prayer:

> It was at this time that he went out on the mountain-side, and passed the whole night offering prayer to God . . . (6:12)

> There was a time when he had gone apart to pray, and his disciples were with him . . . (9:18)

Luke also emphasizes repentance and forgiveness, illustrated by the stories of the Prodigal Son and of the repentant thief who was crucified with Christ. Luke continues his history of the Church following Christ's earthly ministry in the book called Acts of the Apostles.

John's Gospel is different from the other three. It contains only one parable, and Christ speaks in a more sophisticated and philosophical way. Furthermore, the chronology differs from the synoptic Gospels. For example, Christ is crucified on the Passover in John and thus is identified with the sacrificial lamb while in the synoptics it was the Last Supper that took place on the Passover and the crucifixion was the day afterward. There are several important themes in John, two of which appear in the opening verses. Christ is associated with light, and Christ is called the Word, who is shown to have been active in the works of creation:

At the beginning of time the Word already was; and God had the Word abiding with him, and the Word was God. He abode, at the beginning of time, with God. It was through him that all things came into being, and without him came nothing that has come to be. In him there was life, and that life was the light of men. And the light shines in darkness, a darkness which was not able to master it. (1:1–5)

Christ's identification with the paschal victim (the lamb sacrificed in commemoration of God's plague "passing over" the Hebrews when they were in Egypt) is clear in John:

Next day, John saw Jesus coming towards him; and he said, Look this is the Lamb of God; look, this is he who takes away the sin of the world. (1:29)

According to John, Jesus' legs are not broken at the crucifixion, thus fulfilling a text in Leviticus that said that no bone of the paschal lamb was to be broken.

John's only parable is the famous one of Christ as the Good Shepherd, identifying Christ with the Messiah described by the prophets. This text is important for understanding early representations in art of Christ as the Good Shepherd as well as allusions in later medieval literature.

I am the good shepherd. The good shepherd lays down his life for his sheep, whereas the hireling, who is no shepherd, and does not claim the sheep as his own, abandons the sheep and takes to flight as soon as he sees the wolf coming, and so the wolf harries the sheep and scatters them. The hireling, then, takes to flight because he is only a hireling, because he has no concern over the sheep. I am the good shepherd; my sheep are known to me and know me; just as I am known to my Father, and know him. (10:11–15)

John carefully distinguishes between the letter and the spirit —the literal and the spiritual. In fact, one of the literary devices John employs is to have the Pharisees and even sometimes Jesus' friends take his spiritual pronouncements literally. The famous "bread of life" passage illustrates the Johannine distinction between the letter, which is temporal, and the spirit, which is eternal. Christ has just fed the five thousand with five loaves and two fishes, and the crowds have followed him:

So they said to him, Why then, what miracle canst thou do? We must see it before we trust thee; what canst thou effect? Our fathers had manna to eat in the desert; as the scripture says, He gave them bread out of heaven to eat. Jesus said to them, Believe me when I tell you this; the bread that comes from heaven is not what Moses gave you. The real bread from heaven is given only by the Father. God's gift of bread comes down from heaven and gives life to the whole world. Then, Lord, they said, give us this bread all the while. But Jesus told them, It is I who am the bread of life; he who comes to me will never be hungry, he who has faith in me will never know thirst. (But you, as I have told you, though you have seen me, do not believe in me.) All that the Father has entrusted to me will come to me, and him who comes to me I will never cast out. It is the will of him who sent me, not my own will, that I have come down from heaven to do; and he who sent me would have me keep without loss, and raise up at the last day, all he has entrusted to me. (6:30–39)

Believe me when I tell you this; the man who has faith in me enjoys eternal life. It is I who am the bread of life. Your fathers, who ate manna in the desert, died none the less; the bread which comes down from heaven is such that he who eats of it never dies. I myself am the living bread that has come down from heaven. If anyone eats of this bread, he shall live for ever. And now, what is this bread which I am to give? It is my flesh, given for the life of the world. (6:47–52)

One thing that the four Gospels do have in common, however, is that they all indicate some special place for Peter among Jesus' followers. Three passages in particular became important to the Middle Ages since the popes were seen as the successors of Peter and based their claims to power on Christ's words to Peter:

Then Jesus came into the neighborhood of Caesarea Philippi; and there he asked his disciples, What do men say of the Son of Man? Who do they think he is? Some say John the Baptist, they told him, others Elias, other again, Jeremy or one of the prophets. Jesus said to them, And what of you? Who do you say that I am? Then Simon Peter answered, Thou art the Christ, the Son of the living God. And Jesus answered him, Blessed art thou, Simon son of Jona; it is not flesh and blood, it is my Father in heaven that has revealed this to thee. And I tell thee this in my turn, that thou art Peter, and it is upon this rock that I will build my church; and the gates of hell shall not prevail against it; and I will give to thee the keys of the kingdom of heaven; and whatever thou shalt bind on earth shall be bound in heaven; and whatever thou shalt loose on earth shall be loosed in heaven. (Matt. 16:13–19)

And the Lord said, Simon, Simon, behold, Satan has claimed power over you all, so that he can sift you like wheat: but I have prayed for thee, that thy faith may not fail; when, after a while, thou hast come back to me, it is for thee to be the support of thy brethren. (Luke 22:31–32)

And when they had eaten, Jesus said to Simon Peter, Simon, son of John, dost thou care for me more than these others? Yes, Lord, he told him, thou knowest well that I love thee. And he said to him, Feed my lambs. And again, a second time, he asked him, Simon, son of John, dost thou care for me? Yes, Lord, he told him, thou knowest well that I love thee. He said to him, Tend my shearlings. Then he asked him a third question, Simon, son of John, dost thou love me? Peter was deeply moved when he was asked a third time, Dost thou love me? and said to him, Lord, thou knowest all things; thou canst tell that I love thee. Jesus said to him, Feed my sheep. (John 21:15–18)

The Acts of the Apostles, attributed to Luke, is a continuation of his Gospel, beginning with the Ascension of Christ to heaven and then narrating important events in the first years of the Church. It tells of the Christian community in Jerusalem following Christ's earthly ministry, the stoning of the first Christian martyr, Stephen, the conversion of Paul, the missions of Paul to the Gentiles, and the establishment of gentile (non-Jewish) Christianity. One of the most important stories in Acts is Pentecost, the descent of the Holy Spirit:

> When the day of Pentecost came round, while they were all gathered together in unity of purpose, all at once a sound came from heaven like that of a strong wind blowing, and filled the whole house where they were sitting. Then appeared to them what seemed to be tongues of fire, which parted and came to rest on each of them; and they were all filled with the Holy Spirit, and began to speak in strange languages, as the Spirit gave utterance to each. (Acts 2:1–4)

It can be argued that Luke's Gospel is about God the Son and the Acts is the story of God the Holy Spirit come at Pentecost to guide the early Church.

In some ways the Epistles of Paul are the most important part of the New Testament for the Middle Ages. While the Gospels provided most of the stories and images for medieval art, Paul provided the basis for the development of Christian theology. Augustine, clearly the most influential theologian for the Middle Ages and beyond, was especially reliant on him. Paul had been a rigid, legalistic Jew who persecuted early Christians; he had looked on approvingly at the stoning of Saint Stephen. However, according to Acts, he underwent a miraculous conversion, the model for later conversion stories, (e.g. Antony and Augustine) while on the road to Damascus:

> Saul [Paul's name before his conversion], with every breath he drew, still threatened the disciples of the Lord with massacre; and now he went to the high priest and asked him for letters of commendation to the synagogues at Damascus, so that he could arrest all those he found there, men and women, who belonged to the way, and bring them back to Jerusalem. Then, on his journey, when he was nearly at Damascus, a light from heaven shone suddenly about him. He fell to the ground, and heard a voice saying to him, Saul, Saul, why dost thou persecute me? Who art thou, Lord? he asked. And he said, I am Jesus, whom Saul persecutes. This is a thankless task of thine, kicking against the goad. And he, dazed and trembling, asked, Lord, what wilt thou have me do? Then the Lord said to him, Rise up, and go into the city, and there thou shalt be told what thy work is. (Acts 9:1–7)

Paul saw his mission as preaching the gospel of Jesus Christ to non-Jews, and spent years traveling primarily in the eastern Mediterranean, establishing Christian communities and writing them letters. He is believed to have died in the persecution of Nero in Rome, which began after the fire of A.D. 64.

Paul stresses the necessity of faith. Since the Middle Ages has often been called with some justification the "Age of Faith," it should be obvious that this emphasis was to become a key part of medieval theology. The following text will make the primacy of faith clear:

> What has become, then, of thy pride? No room has been left for it. On what principle? The principle which depends on observances? No, the principle which depends on faith; our contention is, that a man is justified by faith apart from the observances of the law. Is God the God of the Jews only? Is he not the God of the Gentiles too? Of the Gentiles too, assuredly; there is only one God, who will justify the circumcised man if he learns to believe, and the Gentile because he believes.
>
> Does that mean that we are using faith to rob the law of its force? No, we are setting the law on its right footing. (Rom. 3:27–31)

Although Paul never suggests that human knowledge is of no value, the proper value of study and human knowledge is to lead a person to God:

> The knowledge of God is clear to their minds; God himself has made it clear to them; from the foundations of the world men have caught sight of his invisible nature, his eternal power and his divineness, as they are known through his creatures. (Rom. 1:19–20)

For medieval theories of art, literature, music, science, and knowledge in general, there is no more important scriptural passage than this one. Augustine cites it constantly, and virtually every other great medieval thinker also uses it.

Paul's deep spirituality is sometimes misunderstood to mean

that he rejected as evil worldly things or human flesh. One must consider Paul's own words about the material world and about man:

> This is my assurance, this is what my conscience tells me in the name of our Lord Jesus, that there is nothing which is unclean in itself; it is only when a man believes a thing to be unclean that it becomes unclean for him. (Rom. 14:14)

A great deal of medieval political theory derives either directly from Paul or indirectly from Paul through Augustine. Paul writes:

> Every soul must be submissive to its lawful superiors; authority comes from God only, and all authorities that hold sway are of his ordinance. Thus the man who opposes authority is a rebel against the ordinance of God, and rebels secure their own condemnation. A good conscience has no need to go in fear of the magistrate, as a bad conscience does. If thou wouldst be free from the fear of authority, do right, and thou shalt win its approval; the magistrate is God's minister, working for thy good. Only if thou doest wrong, needst thou be afraid; it is not for nothing that he bears the sword; he is God's minister still, to inflict punishment on the wrongdoer. Thou must needs, then, be submissive, not only for fear of punishment, but in conscience. It is for this same reason that you pay taxes; magistrates are in God's service, and must give all their time to it. (Rom. 13:1–6)

Even medieval attitudes toward women derived to a great extent from Paul:

> And here is something you must know. The head to which a wife is united is her husband, just as the head to which every man is united is Christ; so, too, the head to which Christ is united is God. (1 Cor. 11:3)

> A man has no need to veil his head; he is God's image, the pride of his creation, whereas the wife is the pride of her husband. (The woman takes her origin from the man, not the man from

the woman; and indeed, it was not man that was created for woman's sake, but woman for man's.) And for that reason the woman ought to have authority over the head, for the angel's sake. (Not that, in the Lord's service, man has his place apart from woman, or woman hers apart from man; if woman takes her origin from man, man equally comes to birth through woman. And indeed all things have their origin in God.) (1 Cor. 11:7–12)

One should notice not only the subordinate place in which Paul put women, essentially accepting the conventions of his society, but also their new *importance* within Christianity.

As a Jew, Paul was thoroughly familiar with the Old Testament, and he often uses Old Testament stories in his letters. He sees Old Testament events as foreshadowings of things that occurred in the time of Christ: "That gospel, promised long ago by means of his prophets in the holy scriptures, tells us of his Son." (Rom. 1:2) This Pauline typology is absolutely essential to understanding the way medieval people viewed the entire Old Testament. The following text shows how events of the Jews' exodus from Egypt become a foreshadowing of things to come:

Let me remind you, brethren, of this. Our fathers were hidden, all of them, under the cloud, and found a path, all of them, through the sea; all alike, in the cloud and in the sea, were baptized into Moses' fellowship. They all ate the same prophetic food, and all drank the same prophetic drink, watered by the same prophetic rock which bore them company, the rock that was Christ. And for all that, God was ill pleased with most of them; see how they were laid low in the wilderness. It is we that were foreshadowed in these events. We were not to set our hearts, as some of them set their hearts, on forbidden things. You were not to turn idolatrous, as some of them did; so we read, The People sat down to eat and drink and rose up to take their pleasure. We were not to commit fornication, as some of them committed fornication, when twenty-three thousand of them were killed in one day. We were not to try the patience of Christ, as some of them tried it, the men who were slain by the serpents; nor were you to complain, as some of them complained, till the destroying angel slew them. When all this happened to them, it was a symbol; the record of it was written as a warning to us, in whom history has reached its fulfillment; and it means that he who thinks he stands firmly should beware of a fall. (1 Cor. 10:1–12)

This text shows the relationship between the passing through the Red Sea and Christian baptism, as well as that between the feeding of the Hebrews in the desert and the Eucharist. Paul sees the primary significance of the Old Testament as symbolic and directly relevant to his own time. He does not deny its literal truth but simply believes that this is not the primary level of meaning. The following text from Paul's Epistle to the Galatians makes this point clearer:

Tell me, you who are so eager to have the law for your master, have you never read the law? You will find it written there, that Abraham had two sons; one had a slave for his mother, and one a free woman. The child of the slave was born in the course of nature; the free woman's, by the power of God's promise. All that is an allegory; the two women stand for the two dispensations. Agar stands for the old dispensation, which brings up its children to bondage, the dispensation which comes to us from mount Sinai. Mount Sinai, in Arabia, has the same meaning in the allegory as Jerusalem, the Jerusalem which exists here and now; an enslaved city, whose children are slaves. Whereas our mother is the heavenly Jerusalem, a city of freedom. (4:21–26)

One of the most difficult but important connections between the Old and New Testament made by Paul comes in Romans 5. Here he talks of Christ coming as a second Adam to undo the sin of the first:

It was through one man that guilt came into the world; and since death came owing to guilt, death was handed on to all mankind by one man. (All alike were guilty men; there was guilt in the world before ever the law of Moses was given. Now, it is only where there is a law to transgress that guilt is imputed, and yet we see death reigning in the world from

Adam's time to the time of Moses, over men who were not themselves guilty of transgressing a law, as Adam was.) In this, Adam was the type of him who was to come. Only, the grace which came to us was out of all proportion to the fault. If this one man's fault brought death on a whole multitude, all the more lavish was God's grace, shewn to a whole multitude, that free gift he made us in the grace brought by one man, Jesus Christ. The extent of the gift is not as if it followed a single guilty act; the sentence which brought us condemnation arose out of one man's action, whereas the pardon that brings us acquittal arises out of a multitude of faults. And if death began its reign through one man, owing to one man's fault, more fruitful still is the grace, the gift of justification, which bids men enjoy a reign of life through one man, Jesus Christ. (5:12–16)

This image of Christ as the new Adam can be seen in all facets of medieval culture. In many paintings of the crucifixion, for example, there is the skull of Adam at the foot of the Cross. A famous legend of the Middle Ages had the Cross of Christ made from the tree in the garden of Eden from which Adam has sinned; thus as one tree brought sin, so did that same tree bring life through the sacrifice of Christ.

Of the non-Pauline Epistles, only one will be discussed here —the anonymous Epistle to the Hebrews. It is important because it deals with the concept of Christ as priest, in particular as perpetual priest in the order of Melchizedek (a priest-king who meets Abraham in Genesis and is mentioned again in Psalm 109:4: "You are a priest forever, a priest like Melchizedek of old").

The purpose for which any high priest is chosen from among his fellow-men, and made a representative of men in their dealings with God, is to offer gifts and sacrifices in expiation of their sins. He is qualified for this by being able to feel for them when they are ignorant and make mistakes, since he, too, is all beset with humiliations, and, for that reason, must needs present sin-offerings for himself, just as he does for the people. His vocation comes from God, as Aaron's did; nobody can take on himself such a privilege as this. So it is with Christ. He did not

Sculpture in the interior of Reims Cathedral. 13th Century. Melchizedek gives bread and wine to Abraham. The visual depiction suggests connections between the bread and wine described in Genesis and holy communion: Melchizedek giving food to Abraham prefigures Christ giving spiritual food to the Church.

raise himself to the dignity of the high priesthood; it was God that raised him to it, when he said, Thou art my Son, I have begotten thee this day, and so, elsewhere, Thou are a priest for ever, in the line of Melchisedech. Christ, during his earthly life, offered prayer and entreaty to the God who could save him from death, not without a piercing cry, not without tears; yet with such piety as won him a hearing. Son of God though he was, he learned obedience in the school of suffering, and now, his full achievement reached, he wins eternal salvation for all those who render obedience to him. A high priest in the line of Melchisedech, so God has called him. (Heb. 5:1–10)

It was this Melchisedech, king of Salem, and priest of the most high God, who met Abraham and blessed him on his way home, after the defeat of the kings; and to him Abraham gave a tenth of his spoils. Observe, in the first place, that his name means, the king of justice; and further that he is king of Salem, that is, of peace. That is all; no name of father or mother, no pedigree, no date of birth or of death; there he stands, eternally, a priest, the true figure of the Son of God. (Heb. 7:1–3)

Now, there could be no need for a fresh priest to arise, accredited with Melchisedech's priesthood, not with Aaron's, if the Levitical priesthood had brought fulfilment. And it is on the Levitical priesthood that the law given to God's people is founded. When the priesthood is altered, the law, necessarily, is altered with it. (Heb. 7:11–12).

This identification of Christ with Melchizedek, both priest and king, is important because Melchizedek becomes an important prefiguration of Christ in medieval art and the liturgy. Furthermore, Christ as priest and king becomes an important element in the development of theories of spiritual and royal authority.

The last book of the Bible, and to many the most puzzling, is the Book of Revelation or the Apocalypse. It is basically the description of a vision in which the author, believed in the Middle Ages to be John the Apostle (though it is now attributed to a different author with the same name), is given prophetic foresight of the last days of the world. It is full of vivid descriptions of the last days and of the kingdom of God in symbolic form. The Apocalypse was extremely important in the Middle Ages; from it were taken many common Christian representations in art and literature. One must remember that medieval people especially in very bad times or among the lower classes, looked for the immediate end of the world and the establishment of God's eternal reign, and the imagery of the Apocalypse is particularly appropriate to those times. The following passages will illustrate the characteristics of this book:

> Then a vision came to me; I saw a door in heaven, standing open. And the same voice, which I had heard speaking to me before, loud as the call of a trumpet, said to me, Come up to my side, and I will shew thee what must find, after this, its due accomplishment. And all at once I was in a trance, and saw where a throne stood in heaven, and one sat there enthroned. He who sat there bore the semblance of a jewel, jasper or sardius, and there was a rainbow about the throne, like a vision of emerald. Round it were twenty-four seats, and on these sat twenty-four elders, clothed in white garments, with crowns of gold on their heads. Lightnings came out from the throne, and mutterings, and thunders, and before it burned seven lamps, which are the seven spirits of God; facing it was a whole sea of glass, like crystal. And in the midst, where the throne was, round the throne itself, were four living figures, that had eyes everywhere to see before them and behind them. The first figure was that of a lion, the second that of an ox, the third had a man's look, and the fourth was that of an eagle in flight. Each of the four figures had six wings, with eyes everywhere looking outwards and inwards. (Rev. 5:1–8)

One thing to notice is the importance of numbers; certainly number symbolism is not unique to Revelation in Scripture, but it seems more abundant and more complicated here than anywhere else. Seven is a number of completeness, echoing the days of creation; the twenty-four elders represent the twelve of the Old (tribes of Israel) and the twelve of the New (the apostles). The description of the four living creatures comes from chapter one of Ezekiel. By the end of the second century, theologians had interpreted them as symbols of the evangelists, and so it was for the rest of the Middle Ages: Mark the lion, Luke the ox, Matthew the man, and John the eagle. There are innumerable representations of this scene in medieval art, most familiarly perhaps above the central portal of the Cathedral of Chartres.

Portal sculpture, Church of Saint Trophime, Arles, France. Twelfth century. Christ is presented in glory, surrounded by the four beasts described in Revelation 4. From the 2nd Century, they were understood to represent the four evangelists, clear here because each holds a book. Below are the twelve apostles.

Near the end of Revelation, there is a description of heaven, the New Jerusalem:

And now an angel came and spoke to me, one of those seven who bear the seven cups charged with the seven last plagues. Come with me, he said, and I will shew thee that bride, whose bridegroom is the Lamb. And he carried me off in a trance to a great mountain, high up, and there shewed me the holy city Jerusalem, as it came down, sent by God, from heaven, clothed in God's glory. The light that shone over it was bright as any precious stone, as the jasper when it is most like crystal; and a great wall was raised high all round it, with twelve gates, and

twelve angels at the gates, and the names of the twelve tribes
of Israel carved on the lintels; three gates on the east, three on
the north, three on the south, three on the west. The city wall,
too, had twelve foundation-stones; and these, too, bore names,
those of the Lamb's twelve apostles. The angel who was speaking to me had a rod of gold for a rule, to measure the city,
and its gates, and its wall. The city lies foursquare, the same
in its length as in its breadth, and when he measured it with
his rod, he counted twelve thousand furlongs. Length and
breadth and height are everywhere equal. And when he
measured its wall, he counted a hundred and forty-four cu-
bits, reckoned by the measure of a man, that is, of an angel.
The fashioning of its wall was of jasper, but the city itself was
pure gold, that seemed to have the purity of glass. And the
foundations of the city wall were worked in every kind of
precious stone. The first foundation was a jasper, the second
a sapphire, the third a chalcedony, the fourth an emerald; the
fifth a sardonyx, the sixth a sardius, the seventh a chrysolite,
the eighth a beryl; the ninth a topaz, the tenth a chrysoprase,
the eleventh a jacynth, the twelfth an amethyst. And the twelve
gates were twelve single pearls, one pearl for each gate; and the
street of the city was of pure gold, that seemed like trans-
parent glass. (21:9–21)

This long and elaborate description of the heavenly Jerusalem
again illustrating the importance of numbers and the highly
symbolic language of the book is of great importance in medieval art. The description of heaven as the New Jerusalem and
the concept that all men are pilgrims seeking to end their
journey in eternal rest as citizens of that city are governing
metaphors in medieval literature and theology (e.g. in the
writings of Augustine and Dante).

There are many "gospels" and "apocalypses" that were
written in the first Christian centuries but not included in
Scripture; these make up the New Testament Apocrypha. In
them are many stories not found in the canonical books of the
New Testament that were immensely popular in the Middle
Ages, and were important as sources of medieval literature and
art. Among the most important works of this type are those
that deal with the life of the Virgin Mary and the earliest
stories of her Assumption into heaven.

CHAPTER TWO

The Classical Heritage

When modern scholars divide European history into segments for convenience of study, the usual division is ancient, medieval, and modern, with ancient further subdivided into Greek and Roman. Scholars living in the time of the Middle Ages of course saw no such divisions. They could not have seen themselves coming in the middle of two ages, which is what the etymology of the word "medieval" suggests—a word generally used only since the eighteenth century. More important, in many crucial ways they did not see any distinct break between themselves and their classical forebears. In fact, elements from classical antiquity were taken over, modified, and used to such an extent that in some ways the legacy of classical antiquity is as important to the Middle Ages as the Judaeo-Christian heritage.

The ancient Greeks were the "inventors" of more aspects of Western civilization than any other people. We credit them with creating drama, both tragedy and comedy; historical writing, especially the examples of Herodotus and Thucydides; democracy as it evolved in Athens; many types of poetry, from the Homeric epics to Sapphic lyrics to the odes of Pindar; styles of monumental architecture—the Doric, Ionic, and Corinthian orders; and several branches of philosophy, including political philosophy, ethics, and much of what is now classified as natural science. This is a staggering list. But in some ways the single most important legacy of Ancient Greece to Western civilization generally and the Middle Ages in particular is the influence of its two greatest philosophers, Plato and Aristotle.

Plato (c.427–347 B.C.) and Artistotle (384–22 B.C.) lived in Athens within a generation of each other; Aristotle was Plato's student, although he wrote more in reaction to his teacher than as a continuation of Plato's thought. Much as he departed from the doctrine of his master, however, the two shared a number of important presuppositions about the nature of philosophical inquiry. Perhaps the most important of these is that both wrote in opposition to a prevalent philosophical skepticism, that is, to a mode of philosophical inquiry that held that truth was ultimately relative and that human reason was at best a faulty guide for answering questions about the nature of reality. For both Plato and Aristotle the doctrine that truth is relative was philosophically untenable, so much so that it is not inaccurate to view the thought of both men as an extended critique of philosophical relativism. This alone made both thinkers extremely congenial to the philosophers of the Middle Ages, who believed that truth existed and that, within certain limits, it was knowable. It is hardly surprising then that the two most influential figures in the entire history of Western philosophy should likewise be the most influential to the portion called the Middle Ages. The historian David Knowles has described this influence in especially emphatic terms. Speaking of the twelfth and thirteenth centuries in particular, he says that "it is possible to say that almost all the leading ideas of medieval philosophy, with the partial exception of that branch of it later known as natural theology, were identical with, or were directly derived from, ideas put into currency at Athens between 450 and 300 B.C."[1]

The philosophy of Plato has become a model for all subsequent philosophies that find reality in a realm beyond the senses. By positing the doctrine of "forms" or "ideas" he answered the question of what abiding reality might exist beyond the seemingly endless flux of the world of things. This doctrine asserted that any individual object existing in this world was only an appearance, an approximation to the real exemplar, or "form," which existed in a world beyond the senses. Since true reality exists in a supra-sensible world, everything that exists in the sensible realm is merely its reflection. Analogously, in the realm of ethics, he was concerned with the same problem —how to account for stability in a world of seeming change. He asked what constant reality might lie behind any individual action that could be considered good or just. Behind these individual actions he saw timeless ideas of "the good" and of "justice," of which individual actions were the dim reflections. Thus he is, both in his metaphysics and his ethics, "the father of those who have held that Soul or Spirit or Mind is the only reality, of those who regard all movements and activity as ultimately intellectual, of those who find the true life of the human spirit in an upward striving toward the Divine."[2] Plato was not only concerned with the unchangeable and unchanging reality that gives meaning to the flux of existence, but also with the relationship between the world of the senses and the world of ideas, that is, with the process by which one might move from the world of the senses to the world of intelligible reality. He was thus the father of a tradition of mystical ascent to God subsequently developed by such Neoplatonists as Plotinus and Pseudo-Dionysius, and later incorporated into the large body of mystical writing in the Middle Ages.

Ideas that can be traced back to Plato formed the fabric of philosophical thought in the Middle Ages, so much so that the entire period can be described philosophically as Platonic. What must be kept in mind, however, is that this influence, profound and all-pervasive as it unquestionably was, was largely indirect, transmitted to the Middle Ages through the pagan Neoplatonists of late antiquity and through Christian Neoplatonic writers such as Augustine and Pseudo-Dionysius. Little of Plato himself was directly known. Of the twenty-six

Platonic dialogues, only one, the *Timaeus*, was known to Western Europe during most of the Middle Ages; and that dialogue, dealing as it does with the creation of the universe and its mathematical form, was in some ways not typical (although it was of great importance, especially to the twelfth-century school of Neoplatonist philosophers connected with the school of Chartres). Later in the Middle Ages two more dialogues, the *Meno* and the *Phaedo*, came to be known. But Plato's influence was profound even where he was no more than a name, a wellspring from which philosophers, theologians, and mystical writers continued to draw.

Aristotle, like Plato, formulated a system that described the nature of reality and dealt with the problem of change, but his approach was significantly different. If Plato is the philosopher of the realm of the ideal, Aristotle is the philosopher of everyday experience. For Aristotle, philosophy begins in the realm of sense experience, and his analysis of the nature of being remains within the realm of experience. From the senses, he argued, the mind is able to apprehend the essence of a thing— that which makes a thing what it is—through a process of abstraction. He postulated that all being, which can be known first through the senses and then understood by the mind through the process of abstraction, can be understood as a combination of "matter" and "form." Matter is the element that gives a substance its individuality; form is the element that gives it universality. In other words, it is the form of a substance that determines what species, or general classification, a given substance belongs to. The form of a substance would determine, for example, that a certain object is a chair, the matter would determine that it is *this* particular chair. The relationship between matter and form was used by Aristotle to account for the multiplicity in the visible world—the same problem of things coming into existence and going out of existence which caused Plato to formulate the doctrine of ideas. If this relationship between matter and form is properly understood, then it can be seen that

if things are regarded not as being but as becoming or changing, then matter is the potential element, susceptible of a multiplicity of forms in succession, whereas form is the actuality; the relationship between matter and form, potentiality and actuality, therefore, extends over the whole range of being from prime or pure matter, which cannot be perceived and which has no independent existence, to pure form which is the last and purest matter to come into being at the other end of the scale.[3]

These distinctions between matter and form, potentiality and actuality, became the keystones of Thomas Aquinas's philosophy of being in the thirteenth century, especially in seeking to define God, to list God's qualities, and to delineate the distinctions between creator and created.

Other areas where Aristotle's thought has especial importance in the Middle Ages, chosen from the almost unthinkably large range of his accomplishments, are in the realms of ethics, political theory, logic, and science. In ethics and political theory, Aristotle begins with experience, with the observation of people in their relationships with each other. In ethics, his definition of virtue remained influential in the Middle Ages and well beyond. Virtue for Aristotle is defined as the mean between two extremes, between an excess and a defect. The virtue of hope, for example, would consist in avoiding the excess of foolish confidence and the defect of despair. One of the many medieval thinkers to make direct use of this definition was Dante, who uses it in his treatment of the hoarders and the wasters in the *Inferno*. Aristotle's political theory had a tremendous impact in medieval Europe beginning in the thirteenth century. His belief that man is by nature a political animal (i.e. one who lives in an organized society) and that the state is a positive force in bringing about the good life rather than only being a necessary evil whose purpose is to punish criminals had a great impact in both the theory and practice of statecraft; Aristotle's view of the state provided ammunition to secular rulers against claims of ecclesiastical interference and supremacy, and was a major element in the defeat of the idea of a universal Christian monarchy ruled by the pope. Thomas Aquinas's political writings were also directly derived from Aristotelian principles. Aristotle's system of formal logic was taken over by twelfth- and thirteenth-century writers seeking

Detail of a painting of the glorification of Thomas Aquinas by
Francesco Traini(?). 14th Century. Santa Caterina, Pisa. In this detail, Aristotle is portrayed showing his books to Thomas Aquinas,
thus indicating Thomas's indebtedness to the man often simply
called "The Philosopher" in the Middle Ages.

to order and synthesize centuries of tradition and a huge number of texts that often seemed to contradict one another. The great twelfth-century compilation of church law, which remained authoritative for centuries, was organized according to principles of Aristotelian logic; and works of theological synthesis such as the *Summa Theologiae* of Thomas Aquinas were only possible because of the reintroduction of Aristotelian logic.

Aristotle's scientific works were accepted as correct; and although some minor adjustments to and improvements on Aristotle's description of the natural world were made during the Middle Ages, his basic principles—such as that of a geocentric universe in which the heavenly bodies circled the earth embedded in crystalline spheres that were moved by the *primum mobile* (the outermost of these spheres)—remained unchallenged in the Middle Ages. Aristotle's emphasis on discovering the final cause of events—that is, their ultimate purpose—remained the central concern of scientists in the medieval period, thus limiting the scope of scientific inquiry and subordinating science to theology because all discussion of the final cause of anything led toward God, the creator of all. Though not the only scientist revered in the Middle Ages (the astronomer Ptolemy and the physician Galen were both important), Aristotle was the unchallengeable authority in the fields of astronomy, physics, and biology.

For much of the Middle Ages, Aristotle, like Plato, was not known directly. Some of his logic was translated by Boethius about A.D. 500; but for the most part, his own works were not known to Western Europe from the eighth to the twelfth century. Compared to Plato, his influence was relatively minor until his works became known through Latin translations; from then on, Aristotle's influence was enormous. It is often argued in fact that the change from an essentially Platonic philosophic perspective to an essentially Aristotelian one is the crucial turning point in the history of medieval speculative thought. What must be kept in mind in describing this change, however, is that the Aristotelian system was more an addition to than a substitution for Platonism. Even in such an Aristotelian thinker as Thomas Aquinas, Platonic elements remain large and significant.

What was true of Plato and Aristotle in the Middle Ages was also true of most of the other achievements of the Greeks: they were not known first hand. Medieval writers venerated Homer—Dante calls him the sovereign poet—but none of the writers who praised him had ever read more than the few lines of the *Iliad* or the *Odyssey* that had been quoted by Latin writers like Cicero. They knew Homer by reputation, and they knew the story of Troy from the Latin prose versions of two writers known as Dares and Dictys (the version of Dares probably came from the sixth century A.D., that of Dictys from the fourth century A.D.). Furthermore, it was through Latin examples that so many of the other poetic forms developed by the Greeks were known to the Middle Ages. Catullus, Horace, and Ovid provided models for the lyric, rather than Pindar or Sappho. The tradegies of Aeschylus, Sophocles, and Euripides, and the comedies of Aristophanes and Menander were also unknown; for the Middle Ages the models of classical drama came principally from the tragedies of Seneca and the comedies of Terence. The models for the writing of history came not from Herodotus and Thucydides but from Sallust, Livy, and the biographer Suetonius. As the Romans had primarily borrowed and modified the Corinthian order of architecture from the Greeks, it was that decorative order that was best known in the Middle Ages. Since one can say that most of the Greek influence on the medieval period came from Roman adaptations of the Greek originals, a major legacy of Rome to the medieval world and beyond was the transmission and transformation of the achievements of the Greeks.

If one considers those Roman writers whose influence was significant, the list would vary depending on which part of the Middle Ages was examined. But it would be a long list, consisting of most of those authors who are now studied by students of Roman literature and also consisting of writers such as Lucan and Statius—no longer widely studied in our own time but who were extremely influential to medieval writers. If one were forced to choose from among them, Cicero, Vergil, and

Ovid would be most indicative of the types and range of the influence of the Latin classics on the Middle Ages. All three, men of genius worth studying for their own sake as well as for their subsequent influence, are thorough students of Greek models.

Cicero was a writer and political figure of the first century B.C. Both in form and content his writings were more studied and imitated than any other prose author. He was considered the master of Latin rhetoric, and thus his mode of expression was a model for students in monastic and cathedral schools, who learned Latin by a conscious imitation of classical models. Anyone who became a professed monk or a university student was exposed to Cicero; and even where the influence of his thought was not significant, his sentence structure and his manner of expression were assimilated by the educated clerics of the Middle Ages. However, he was important for more than his prose style. His stoic philosophy, adapted from the philosophical school that originated in Athens in the third century B.C., spoke of the need for humanity to conform to natural laws. This philosophy provided support for the Christian concept of natural law and for Christian ideas about the family of humanity. To give one example of this aspect of Ciceronian influence, his writings on friendship served directly as models for twelfth-century writings on monastic friendship; Aelred of Rievaulx's work, *On Spiritual Friendship*, was modeled on Cicero's treatise *On Friendship*.

The following passage is from "The Dream of Scipio," a fragment of a longer work by Cicero entitled *On the Republic*. Although most of the text of *On the Republic* was lost to the Middle Ages, the fragment concerning Scipio's dream survived as an independent work, together with a commentary by the fourth-century writer Macrobius, and was among Cicero's most influential writings. In this passage, the Roman patriot Scipio Africanus takes his grandson to "a certain place in heaven . . . assigned to all who have preserved, or assisted, or improved their country, where they are to enjoy an endless duration of happiness."[4] The grandfather uses this as an opportunity to inculcate a love of virtue in his grandson:

"Consequently, should you renounce hope of returning to this place where eminent and excellent men find their reward, of what worth is that human glory which can scarcely extend to a small part of a single year? If, then, you shall determine to look on high and contemplate this mansion and eternal abode, you will neither give yourself to the gossip of the vulgar nor place your hope of well-being on rewards that man can bestow. Virtue herself, by her own charms, should draw you to true honor . . ."

When he had finished I said: "Truly, Africanus, if the path to heaven lies open to those who have deserved well of their country, though from my childhood I have ever trod in your and my father's footsteps without disgracing your glory, yet now, with so noble a prize set before me, I shall strive with much more diligence."

"Do so strive," replied he, "and do not consider yourself, but your body, to be mortal. For you are not the being which this corporeal figure evinces; but the soul of every man is the man, and not the form which may be delineated with a finger. Know also that you are a god, if a god is that which lives, perceives, remembers, foresees, and which rules, governs, and moves the body over which it is set, just as the supreme God rules the universe. Just as the eternal God moves the universe, which is in part mortal, so does an everlasting soul move the corruptible body."[5]

A heavenly abode as the reward for virtue and the belief that the soul is immortal are two obvious concerns in this passage that were easily absorbed into the medieval Christian universe. In its original context, Cicero is referring specifically to political virtue—he is discussing the reward of the good statesman—but thinkers in the Middle Ages would interpret the passage more broadly, that is, as applying to virtue in general. The dream vision, the dream as a mode of illumination, anticipates scores of dream-vision poems in the Middle Ages. (Macrobius's commentary itself was one of the most important sources for the interpretation of various kinds of dreams, their natures, sources, and significance.) The setting of Scipio's dream, the heavens, as a vantage point from which to view the earth and its strife and as a place to compare the harmony that exists above with the chaos below, also became something of a medieval common-place. As one example of the continuing influence of this work, Chaucer, writing at the end of the fourteenth century, draws directly from the "Dream of Scipio" at the beginning of the *Parliament of Foules*.

The second writer is Vergil (70–19 B.C.), a poet who lived during the reign of Augustus. His epic poem, the *Aeneid*, itself modeled on the *Iliad* and the *Odyssey* of Homer, was both in form and content as much a model for poetry in the Middle Ages as the writings of Cicero were for prose. The poem describes the journey of Aeneas from the ruins of Troy to the shores of Italy, where he begins the foundation of Rome. His journey to Rome includes his stop at Carthage, where he re-counts the fall of Troy (Books 2 and 3) and has a tragic love affair with the Carthaginian queen Dido (Book 4), and his trip through the underworld to see his father (Book 6). Both of these episodes exercised great influence on the imagination of the writers of the Middle Ages. Dido became an important character in medieval literary history and beyond. The trip to the underworld was a direct model for Dante, whose *Inferno* uses the geography, setting, and characters of Vergil's under-world. In Dante's political treatise, *De Monarchia*, the *Aeneid* is likewise his most frequently quoted authority and provides key proofs for his ideas of relationship between ecclesiastical and temporal authorities. The following passage from the *Aeneid* (Book 6), the meeting of Aeneas and Dido in the under-world, illustrates the conflict between private desires and public duty that is at the heart of the poem:

> Among them was Phoenician Dido, who was roaming in the broad wood with her wound still fresh upon her. Troy's hero found himself near to her and as soon as he recognized her dimly through the shadows, like one who early in the month sees or thinks that he sees the moon rising through the clouds, his tears fell and he spoke to her in the sweet accents of love: "O Dido, unhappy Dido, was the news, then, true which was brought to me, that you had perished, had taken the sword, and trodden the path to its end? Ah, could I have been the cause of your death? By the stars, by the high Gods, I swear

by any truth there may be in the depths of the earth, that it was not by my own will, your Majesty, that I departed your shores; but rather was I imperiously forced by that same divine direction which compels me now to pass through the shadows in this world of crumbling decay under deepest night; and I could not have known that my leaving you would have caused you so terrible a grief. Stay your step and withdraw not from my sight. Whom do you seek to escape? My speaking to you now is the last indulgence which fate can give me." By such words Aeneas tried to soften her, and invited tears. But in her the anger blazed and grimly she glared, holding her gaze averted and fixed on the ground; she was no more moved by what Aeneas had begun to say than if she had been hard flint or a standing block of Parian marble. At length she flung herself away, and, in hatred still, fled back into the shadows offered her by the wood, where Sychaeus, her husband in former days, had sympathy for her distress and matched his love to hers. Aeneas was shocked by her unjust fate; and as she went long gazed after her with tearful eyes and pity for her in his heart.[6]

The journey of Aeneas to his true home had strong resonances with the medieval Christian concept of pilgrimage. Augustine's spiritual autobiography, the *Confessions*, moves from Carthage to Rome, perhaps in direct and conscious imitation of the journey of Aeneas. In the Middle Ages, continuing a tradition developed in late antiquity, commentaries were written of the *Aeneid* that allegorized the journey of Aeneas as the journey of the soul seeking wisdom. Among the most important of these medieval commentaries was that of Bernardus Silvestris, writing in the twelfth century. These commentaries contributed to Vergil's enormous reputation as a sage in the Middle Ages. He was regarded as a prophet as well, a pagan who anticipated the truths of Christianity, in large part because of a Christian interpretation of the following passage from his fourth *Eclogue*.

Now is come the last age of Cumaean prophecy: the great cycle of periods is born anew. Now returns the Maid, returns the reign of Saturn: now from high heaven a new generation comes down. Yet do thou at that boy's birth, in whom the iron race will begin to cease, and the golden to arise all over the world, holy Lucina, be gracious; now thine own Apollo reigns. And in thy consulate, in thine, O Pollio, shall this glorious age enter, and the great months begin their march: under thy rule what traces of our guilt yet remain, vanishing shall free earth ever from alarm?[7]

In the Middle Ages, people were sure they recognized a prophecy of Christ's incarnation in this passage. Furthermore, the fact that he was writing at the time of Augustus, in whose reign Christ was born, supported this interpretation. It was regarded as no mere coincidence.

The third writer is Ovid (43 B.C.–A.D. 17), who also lived during the reign of Augustus. It was his version of the stories and legends of the gods and heroes of classical mythology that came down to the Middle Ages and beyond, allowing them to become part of the storehouse of imaginative topics for subsequent literature. His long narrative poem, the *Metamorphoses*, tells the stories of the classical gods and heroes from creation to his own time, linking them together through the theme of change. For example, in the story of the rape of Europa, Jove changes from his divine form to a bull in order to seduce the maiden Europa more easily. The story of Pygmalion, from Book 10 of the *Metamorphoses*, was as popular to the Middle Ages as it has continued to be in our own time:

When Pygmalion saw these women, living such wicked lives, he was revolted by the many faults which nature implanted in the female sex, and long lived a bachelor existence, without any wife to share his home. But meanwhile, with marvelous artistry, he skilfully carved a snowy ivory statue. He made it lovlier than any woman born, and fell in love with his own creation. The statue had all the appearance of a real girl, so that it seemed to be alive, to want to move, did not modesty forbid. So cleverly did his art conceal its art. Pygmalion gazed in wonder, and in his heart there rose a passionate love for this image of a human form. . . .

The festival of Venus, which is celebrated with the greatest pomp all through Cyprus, was now in progress, and heifers, their horns gilded for the occasion, had fallen at the altar as the axe struck their snowy necks. Smoke was rising from the incense, when Pygmalion, having made his offering, stood by the altar and timidly prayed, saying: "If you gods can give all things, may I have as my wife, I pray—" he did not dare to say: "the ivory maiden," but finished: "one like the ivory maiden." However, golden Venus, present at her festival in person, understood what his prayers meant, and as a sign that the gods were kindly disposed, the flames burned up three times, shooting a tongue of fire into the air. When Pygmalion returned home, he made straight for the statue of the girl he loved, leaned over the couch, and kissed her. She seemed warm: he laid his lips on hers again, and touched her breast with his hands—at his touch the ivory lost its hardness, and grew soft; his fingers made an imprint on the yielding surface, just as the wax of Hymettus melts in the sun and, worked by men's fingers, is fashioned into many different shapes, and made fit for use by being used. The lover stood, amazed, afraid of being mistaken, his joy tempered with doubt, and again and again stroked the object of his prayers. It was indeed a human body! The veins throbbed as he pressed them with his thumb. Then Pygmalion of Paphos was eloquent in his thanks to Venus. At long last he pressed his lips upon living lips, and the girl felt the kisses he gave her, and blushed. Timidly raising her eyes, she saw her lover and the light of day together.[8]

With Ovid, thinkers of the Middle Ages were forced to wrestle with the problem of whether stories that were obviously not literally true were dangerous or whether they were valuable. Could the story of Pygmalion, let alone the stories of Jove and his amorous adventures, hold anything of value for a medieval Christian? Although Ovid, and other writers of imaginative literature as well, were regarded in some quarters as highly suspect, they were defended by the concept of the "beautiful lie," the idea that a poet weaves an outer coat that, however fanciful, covers an inner truth. False stories could teach true doctrine. Though the debate itself continued throughout the Middle Ages, the defense allowed imaginative literature to be written and enjoyed in the Middle Ages. When a story such as Pygmalion was retold in the Middle Ages—as it was at the end of the long allegorical poem called the *Romance of the Rose* (c.1285)—it was often utilized for purposes quite different from the original. Sometimes the stories were moralized and given explicitly Christian meanings; sometimes they were given contemporary applications by writers who saw in them meaning for their own time, just as Ovid himself took stories and legends that originally came from the Greeks and made them applicable to his age. Although writers felt free to make these stories their own, and the purpose of the stories might have been changed, an awareness of the basic stories of classical mythology themselves was simply assumed by poets in the Middle Ages (and beyond at least as far as the nineteenth century); authors such as Jean de Meun (author of the second part of the *Romance of the Rose*), Dante, and Chaucer drew freely from Ovid in their own poetry. Ovid's work, like Vergil's, was also the subject of allegorical commentaries.

In the Middle Ages, as in classical times, historical writing was also considered a branch of literature; and like the other literary genres discussed above, the language and themes of Roman historical writing were taken over by the historical writers of the Middle Ages. While today many scholars consider Tacitus (c. A.D. 55–c.120) as the greatest historian of Rome, he was almost unknown in the Middle Ages. Livy (59 B.C.–A.D. 17), the great historian writing in the Age of Augustus, was highly respected in the Middle Ages although he became more important to the republican writers of the Renaissance. However, two other Roman historians were quite well known and imitated. The first is the imperial biographer Suetonius (c. A.D. 69–c.140). Despite his scandalous stories of the emperors, his twelve imperial biographies were important models for medieval secular biography, most noticeably Einhard's biography of Charlemagne. The other historian of great importance is Sallust (86–34 B.C.), a contemporary of Cicero whose two extant works have strong moral overtones. This is precisely the reason Sallust was so popular in the Middle Ages, for history was perceived as a branch of ethics whose purpose was to teach moral lessons and to provide positive and negative exemplars. The tendency of modern historians to avoid moral judgments and not to assign praise or blame would have been totally foreign to medieval writers of history as well as to ancient writers like Sallust. Furthermore, ethics was considered to be a part of the study of rhetoric in ancient Rome and the Middle Ages. Thus, the literary conventions of history did not encourage simple narrative of literal truth but rather allowed and encouraged some rearrangement and embellishment of the facts in order to make the moral clear. These elements of ancient historiography combined with elements of biblical historical writing in the Middle Ages to allow for exaggeration and distortion of the facts (as contemporary historians perceive them). Because of our modern, more "scientific" and "objective" view of history, many nineteenth- and twentieth-century writers have tended to disparage medieval historical writings; only if we recognize the purposes and conventions of those texts, can we appreciate the greatness of someone like the Venerable Bede or Geoffrey of Monmouth.

Sallust and Suetonius were contemporaries of many of the events they wrote about and even eyewitnesses to some of them. The belief that contemporary history was the most creative and the most useful form of historical writing existed in the ancient world and became the most important type of medieval historical writing. Even writers such as the Venerable Bede and Gregory of Tours, who began in the distant past, usually brought their works to the present and concentrated on events of their own times.

A second important legacy from Rome to the medieval world was its law. Although the Greeks had theorized extensively about the nature of law, the science of jurisprudence was really invented during the growing complexity of the late Roman Republic. One of the products of this new science was a carefully defined concept of the state. Furthermore, philosophers of the same period, borrowing from the Greeks, developed a highly sophisticated theory of natural law. During the period of the Roman Empire, the largest and most complex state that had yet existed, it was necessary that the numerous laws of the Empire be codified, that is, ordered and organized so that they could be a unifying factor in an empire that stretched from the Irish Sea to the Persian Gulf. Ironically, the greatest law codes were compiled as the Empire was breaking up. Ultimately, the most important codification of Roman law occurred after the fall of the Empire in the West. Commissioned by the Byzantine Emperor Justinian (r. 527–65), it remained the basis of Byzantine law for almost a thousand years. This code contained not only a great number of laws but also commentaries on the law by the greatest Roman jurists. For several centuries the Justinian Code was unknown in the West, although the less complete fifth-century Theodosian Code was used extensively by early medieval kings. In the twelfth century, the Code of Justinian was rediscovered in the West. From that time on, emperors quoted directly from it in objecting to ecclesiastical authority; kings used it as a model for constructing their own legal systems; church lawyers were inspired to codify the law of the Church, the canon law. Much of the language of early parliamentary documents in England and elsewhere was drawn from Roman law; even the common law system in England owes much more to Roman law than has sometimes been acknowledged. The medieval dependence on Roman law is an important legacy of the Middle Ages to modern times; in the nineteenth century, the Justinian Code was used as a model both in Europe and America.

A third legacy from Rome was the idea of empire. Rome was neither the first power to have a large empire nor the first to consider the benefits of a world governed from one center. Alexander the Great had conquered much of the world and had talked of the universal brotherhood of man. However, it was the Romans who built on this notion and who passed it on. And most important, it was the Romans who institutionalized it. Alexander's empire was his personal conquest; when he died the empire was divided. The Romans ruled a vast empire from the late republican period (first century B.C.) until the disintegration of the Empire in the West (in the fifth century A.D.). Thus an idea was combined with a process of institutionalization. The Romans in fact considered ruling as their chief skill and as their destiny. The ideal of Rome as ruler is nowhere better exemplified than in Book 6 of Vergil's *Aeneid*.

Consider what Aeneas's father says to his son during the visit to the underworld, when Aeneas comes to learn his own destiny and hence the destiny of Rome:

> Others, for so I can well believe, shall hammer forth more delicately a breathing likeness out of bronze, coax living faces from the marble, plead causes with more skill, plot with their gauge the movement of the sky, and tell the rising of the constellations. But you, Roman, must remember that you have to guide the nations by your authority, for this is to be your skill, to graft tradition onto peace, to show mercy to the conquered, and to wage war until the haughty are brought low.[9]

This is of course more a statement of the ideal of Roman rule than its reality, but it was a passage known, quoted, and believed in the Middle Ages, an ideal that no one was ready to dismiss lightly.

The concept of empire far outlived the reality of a unified Mediterranean world. In the East, the Byzantine emperors in Constaninople regarded themselves as the heirs of the Empire, seeing their city as a new (and Christian) Rome. However, with the rise of Charlemagne, the Empire was reconstituted in the West into what is called the *Holy* Roman Empire. It appeared for a time that the emperors in the West who succeeded Charlemagne would continue to be rulers in fact as well as in theory, but this did not come to be. However, long after the Empire ceased to be the most important political power in Western Europe, people still looked to the emperor as the de jure head of the West. Dante placed his hopes in the reestablishment of the Empire's authority in the West in his treatise *De Monarchia*, written sometime after 1300; in the *Inferno*, he placed Brutus and Cassius on either side of Judas at the bottom of hell because they had assassinated the first emperor, Julius Caesar, and thus had tried to subvert Rome's destiny to rule. In the middle of the fourteenth century, long after the emperors had ceased to be a major political factor, a famous fresco by the painter Andrea da Firenze depicted the emperor as the highest political authority in the West. The actual boundaries of the Holy Roman Empire changed often

Cross of the Holy Roman Emperor Lothar. 9th Century. Aachen,
West Germany. This medieval imperial cross contains a cameo
of the Roman Emperor Augustus (d. A.D. 14). Its position on an
imperial cross suggests the continuity between the Empire of
ancient Rome and the reconstituted Empire begun by Lothar's
grandfather Charlemagne.

in the Middle Ages, but the Empire lasted in some form until 1806. In the East, after the fall of Constantinople in 1453, the rulers in Moscow claimed to be heirs of the Roman imperial tradition and saw Moscow as the third Rome; they even took the title of the emperors—caesar, or in Russian, czar.

A fourth legacy from Rome is the Latin language; for as we have already implied in our discussion of Cicero, Vergil, Ovid, and the Roman historians, Latin remained a living language throughout the Middle Ages, an area in which scholars simply took for granted a continuity with the classical past. Indeed, Latin served as the international language of the Middle Ages. It was the language of the Church and thus of virtually all religious writing, including the liturgy. It was the language of the universities and the schools, and thus of all philosophical writing. (In the later Middle Ages, students in the Oxford colleges were fined if they were caught speaking anything but Latin within the college precincts.) It was the language of literature, at least until the late Middle Ages when there was a shift to the vernacular languages—Jean de Meun wrote in French, Dante in Italian, Chaucer in English. Though learned by imitation from models of Roman prose and poetry, Latin continued to change throughout the Middle Ages. Vocabulary changed as many Germanic words were incorporated into the language; and style, syntax, and grammar changed as well. (The influence, moreover, was reciprocal; Latin style, syntax, and vocabulary also influenced the vernacular languages.) Yet these very changes were a sign of the vitality of the language, allowing for the expression of what was most highly unique and original in medieval culture, from early Christian hymns up to the writings of Thomas Aquinas. As in so many areas, medieval people borrowed language from classical antiquity but adapted it to their own needs. It can be argued that it was the revival of classical Latin as the ideal in the Renaissance that gradually turned Latin into an artificial language. In trying to eliminate all postclassical accretions and imitate Cicero directly in their own writings (rather than learning from Cicero), Renaissance humanists in fact contributed to its demise.

The achievements of biblical and classical thinkers took place independently of one another. For example, the Greek historian Herodotus traveled throughout the Near East, writing extensively about the Egyptians and Persians while hardly mentioning the Jews. Yet by the time he made his journey, the Pentateuch was complete, and the prophecies of Isaiah and Jeremiah were already recorded. By the time of Augustus, there were Jewish settlements throughout the Mediterranean, and the Old Testament had been translated into Greek. Nevertheless, writers like Vergil remained largely ignorant of Jewish history and literature. However, with the spread of Christianity beginning with Saint Paul, the two cultures began to interact with one another; Paul himself was a Jew, a Christian, Greek-educated, and a Roman citizen. In philosophy, in the concept of empire, in literature, law, language, art, and architecture, the classical heritage is one of the wellsprings of medieval culture. The next two chapters will examine the spread and development of Christianity by emphasizing the beginnings of the interaction of biblical and classical cultures and values.

CHAPTER THREE

Early Christianity

By the middle of the fifth century, Christianity was the dominant religion of the Roman Empire. Doctrine was rather well defined through the actions of synods and especially four great councils. The Church had attained great wealth, and its leaders were among the most important persons of the Empire. By this time there was also a rich body of Christian tradition preserved in liturgy, art, and stories of its holy men and women. To understand this extraordinary growth and development, we need to go back to the infancy of Christianity.

The Beginnings of Christianity

We know about the earliest Christians primarily from two sources—the Acts of the Apostles and the letters of Paul. Together they present a picture of both doctrinal and institutional development in the years immediately after Christ's earthly ministry. Immediately after Jesus' Passion and resurrection, there were few who accepted him as the son of God; Acts suggests that they may not have been more than 120 in all. Yet within just a few years, several thousand Jews in and around Jerusalem came to believe that Jesus was the Messiah. With the conversion and apostleship of Paul (c.A.D. 33) came the spread of Christianity among the Gentiles (non-Jews) in the eastern Mediterranean. Paul began his Christian ministry preaching Christ to the Jews; but when he found that his teachings were not accepted by most Jews, he acted accordingly:

> "It was necessary," they [Paul and his fellow missionaries] said, "that the word of God should be declared to you [the Jews] first. But since you reject it and thus condemn yourselves as unworthy of eternal life, we now turn to the Gentiles. For these are our instructions from the Lord: "I have appointed you to be a light for the Gentiles, and a means of salvation to the earth's farthest bounds." (Acts 13:46–47)

Paul taught these gentile Christian converts that they were not bound by Jewish laws such as those concerning circumcision and dietary regulations. By the end of the first century A.D., Christianity was no longer centered in Palestine, although this is in large part because of the Romans' destruction of Jerusalem in A.D. 70 after a Jewish revolt against Roman rule. Most Christians by the year 100 were Gentiles.

This predominantly gentile Church (the Greek word *ecclesia* means "assembly") soon completely broke away from Judaism and became a separate religion. This is of the greatest significance in Christian history, for Christ was a Jew, and all his earliest followers were Jews who adhered to the laws of the Old Testament. With the advent of Paul's gentile mission, there were Jewish Christians who adhered to the Law and gentile Christians who were free from it. By 100, the two religions, Judaism and Christianity, were almost completely separated; and one finds in some Christian writings of that time the beginnings of anti-Semitism. This anti-Jewish attitude became firmly implanted in Christianity and was an important element in the Church throughout the Middle Ages and far beyond. One early passage that indicates the beginnings of anti-Semitism is found in the letter of Saint Ignatius of Antioch (martyred 107) to the Magnesians:

> . . . So lay aside the old good-for-nothing leaven [of the Old Testament], now grown stale and sour, and change to the new, which is Jesus Christ. . . . To profess Jesus Christ while continuing to follow Jewish customs is an absurdity. The Christian faith does not look to Judaism, but Judaism looks to Christianity, in which every other race and tongue that confesses a belief in God has now been comprehended.[1]

Despite the separation from Judaism, Christians continued to accept the Old Testament, although they followed Paul in giving a specifically Christian meaning to it, that is, they saw the events of the Old Testament in terms of their relationship to Christianity.

Perhaps even in Paul's lifetime, there were some converts to Christianity who attempted to combine their new religion with a philosophy that had developed in the eastern part of the Roman Empire called Gnosticism. Although not all Gnostics held identical beliefs, there are certain general conceptions common to them. The basic tenet of Gnosticism is the complete opposition between the material and spiritual realms; Gnostics saw all material things as intrinsically evil and all spiritual things as intrinsically good. Thus the Gnostic view of the story of creation in Genesis was that it is about an evil god or a rebellious spirit since it is the story of the making of evil things. Gnostics interpreted the New Testament to be about a pure spirit who only *appeared* to be human. Obviously, Gnostic interpretations of Scripture were seen by most Christians as dangerous and misleading; and Gnostic interpretations were generally rejected by Christian communities. The rejection of Gnostic interpretations of Scripture, however, did not mean that the philosophy of Gnosticism disappeared from Christianity. In the fourth century, for example, the young Augustine, before his conversion to Christianity, was an adherent of a Gnostic group called the Manichees (after the Gnostic teacher

Mani). Some scholars have argued that some later forms of Christian asceticism were influenced by Gnostic views. And as late as the twelfth century, there was a major outbreak of Christian Gnosticism in southern France and northern Italy called the Albigensian (after the French city of Albi) or Cathar movement (from a Greek word meaning "the pure ones").

The Development of Church Offices

According to Acts of the Apostles, there were two offices in early Christian communities. One was that of teacher and preacher of the gospel—the priesthood; the other was that of administrator of the goods of the community—the diaconate or office of deacon. However, as Christian communities grew up in cities around the Mediterranean quite distant from one another, the problem of unity within a community became acute, especially when there were doctrinal differences due to Gnostic influence or simply differences of interpretations regarding certain tenets of the faith. At first, it was often possible to refer disputes to persons of great authority such as Paul. But how were differences to be resolved and unity preserved when the apostles were no longer alive?

One solution to the problem of unity within a community was to designate one priest as the spokesman for and arbiter within a community, and this chief priest would also appoint (later ordain) new priests. This official came to be called the bishop (in Greek, *episcopos*; hence words such as "episcopal" and "episcopacy"). Thus from the original twofold division of office came a threefold one—bishop, priest, deacon—and this remained and remains the basic structure of the ecclesiastical hierarchy.

The question of the source of episcopal authority and thus the bishops' claim to obedience arose, however, for these men had not received personal commissions from Christ as the apostles had. The answer to this question is the principle of apostolic succession, which was formulated by the end of the first century. Simply, this theory suggests that the authority conferred by Christ upon the apostles is passed on to properly chosen successors; that is, Christ created offices rather than merely giving authority to individuals. The bishops' claim to obedience is explicit in Ignatius of Antioch's letter to a Christian community in Asia Minor:

> Your obedience to your bishop, as though he were Jesus Christ, shows me plainly enough that yours is no worldly manner of life, but that of Jesus Christ Himself, who gave His life for us that faith in His death might save you from death. At the same time, however, essential as it is that you should never act independently of the bishop—as evidently you do not—you must also be no less submissive to your clergy [i.e. priests], and regard them as apostles of Jesus Christ our Hope, in whom we shall one day be found, if our lives are lived in Him. The deacons too, who serve the mysteries of Jesus Christ, must be men universally approved in every way; since they are not mere dispensers of meat and drink, but servants of the church of God, and therefore under obligation to guard themselves against any slur or imputation as strictly as they would against fire itself.[2]

It is clear from this document that the threefold division of office in the church has also been established by the beginning of the second century.

Some bishops came to be regarded as especially important because they were leaders of Christian communities first headed by apostles; thus their succession to the apostles was uniquely direct. In particular, the bishop of Rome (usually called the pope, from a Latin word meaning father, from the fifth century on) was so regarded because Peter and Paul were believed to have established and headed the Christian community there. And it must have seemed natural to look to Rome since it was the political center of the world. In addition, of all the apostolic sees (seats of bishops), Rome was the only one in the Latin-speaking West while there were three in the Greek East that were often at odds with one another. Sometimes other bishops would ask advice from the bishop of Rome because of the prestige of his office as the leading bishop of the Empire, the first among equals. As early as the latter part of the second century, we find a description of the special importance of the see of Rome in a treatise by Irenaeus, bishop of Lyons (d. c.200):

> But since it would be very long in such a volume as this to enumerate the successions of all the churches, I can by pointing out the tradition which that very great, oldest, and well-known Church, founded and established at Rome by those two most glorious apostles Peter and Paul, received from the apostles, and its faith known among men, which comes down to us through the successions of bishops, put to shame all of those who in any way, either through wicked self-conceit, or through vainglory, or through blind and evil opinion, gather as they should not. For every church must be in harmony with this Church because of its outstanding pre-eminence, that is, the faithful from everywhere, since the apostolic tradition is preserved in it by those from everywhere.[3]

By the fifth century, a full-fledged theory of papal jurisdictional supremacy emerged. Pope Leo I (the Great, r. 440–61) is perhaps most responsible for the so-called Petrine theory, the ultimate foundation of claims of papal supremacy. Leo argued from Matthew 16:18–19 that Peter received the power to govern the Church from Christ and that this power was inherited by Peter's successors. Peter was believed to have founded and led the Christian community in Rome, and thus the bishops of Rome were his successors. His claim was recognized by the Fourth Ecumenical Council (Council of Chalcedon) in 451: "Peter has spoken through Leo." Leo explained the meaning of Matthew 16:18–19 in a sermon preached on the third anniversary of his becoming pope:

> The dispensation of Truth therefore abides, and the blessed Peter persevering in the strength of the Rock, which he has received, has not abandoned the helm of the Church, which he undertook. For he was ordained before the rest in such a way that from his being called the Rock, from his being pronounced

the Foundation, from his being constituted the Doorkeeper of the kingdom of heaven, from his being set as the Umpire to bind and to loose, whose judgments shall retain their validity in heaven, from all these mystical titles we might know the nature of his association with Christ. And still today he more fully and effectually performs what is entrusted to him, and carries out every part of his duty and charge in Him and with Him, through Whom he has been glorified. And so if anything is rightly done and rightly decreed by us, if anything is won from the mercy of God by our daily supplications, it is of his works and merits whose power lives and whose authority prevails in his See. . . . For throughout the Church Peter daily says, "Thou art the Christ, the Son of the living God" (Mt 16:16), and every tongue which confessed the Lord, accepts the instruction his voice conveys.[4]

In some sense, this theory that Leo put forth is a specific application of the principle of apostolic succession, that is, the authority specifically conferred upon Peter by Christ is specifically conferred upon Peter's successors as leaders of the Roman Church. It is important to note that Leo was not claiming personal infallibility but rather universal jurisdiction in the Church. This means that he is the final voice in settling disputes among bishops, disputed elections to ecclesiastical offices, and other controversies.

Christian and Pagan

Almost all the earliest Christian converts had come from the lower strata of society, including many slaves. The instability of the Empire after A.D. 180 and a changing and generally more pessimistic world view developing in the late second and third centuries provided a context for the conversion of significant numbers of well-educated, upwardly mobile people to Christianity. Educated converts did not simply abandon all knowledge they had accumulated in pagan schools, and consequently they were often interested in defining the relationship between pagan learning and Christian revelation. Justin Martyr, toward the end of the second century, believed that much of the wisdom of the great pagan thinkers was compatible with Christian teaching. He even believed that men such as Socrates had some limited revelation from God and, like the great Old Testament figures, were "Christians before Christ."[5] It was in the center of Greek learning, Alexandria, that the study of pagan works and the tools of critical scholarship developed by the Greeks were put to the service of Christianity. The foundation had been prepared by a group of Greek-speaking Jewish philosophers, the most important of whom was Philo (20 B.C.–A.D. 50), who were concerned with reconciling Jewish tradition and Greek thought.

The most important Christian in these developments was Origen (d.254). Some of his theological speculations, such as his belief that at the end all people would be saved, led to controversies over his writings for centuries after his death. There were several condemnations of Origenism, partly because his followers often went beyond what he himself had said. Here, we shall be concerned with three facets of Origen's work that were influential in the development of Christian thought. First, he was a firm believer in the use of reason and hence the acquisition of pagan learning by Christians. Here is Origen's reply to a letter of praise from one of his students:

Thine ability is fit to make thee an accomplished Roman lawyer, or a Greek philosopher in some one of the schools esteemed reputable. But my desire has been that thou shouldest employ all the forces of thine ability on Christianity as thine end, and to this effect I would beseech thee to draw from Greek philosophy such things as are capable of being made encyclic or preparatory studies to Christianity, and from geometry and astronomy such things as will be useful for the exposition of Holy Scripture, in order that what the sons of the philosophers said about geometry and music and grammar and rhetoric and astronomy, that they are handmaidens of philosophy, we may say of philosophy in relation to Christianity.[6]

Second, Origen recognized the need for accurate texts and translations of Scripture. His use of the tools of textual criti-

Church of San Biagio, Agrigento, Sicily. 12th Century. This church was built directly upon the remains of a Greek temple of the 5th century B.C. dedicated to Demeter and Persephone, visually demonstrating that Christians built upon the foundations of classical antiquity. The foundation is easy to see here because the temple was bigger than the church.

cism was of great influence generally and upon writers such as Saint Jerome in particular. And third, Origen was a great interpreter of Scripture. He rejected simple literal readings, since as a scholar he recognized obvious historical discrepancies and impossibilities; rather, he emphasized the allegorical levels of interpretation as most important:

> There is something else that we must realize. The main aim of scripture is to reveal the coherent structure that exists at the spiritual level in terms both of events and injunctions. Wherever the Word [Christ] found that events on the historical plane corresponded with these mystical truths, he used them, concealing the deeper meaning from the multitude. But at those places in the account where the performance of particular ac-

tions as already recorded did not correspond with the pattern of things at the intellectual level, Scripture wove into the narrative, for the sake of the more mystical truths, things that never occurred—sometimes things which never could have occurred, sometimes things that could have but did not. . . .

It was not only in the relation of events before the coming of Christ that the Spirit arranged things in this way. Because he is the same Spirit and comes from the one God, he has acted in the same way with the gospels and the writings of the apostles. Even they contain a narrative that is not at all points straightforward; for woven into it are events which in the literal sense did not occur. Nor is the content of the law and commandments to be found in them entirely reasonable.[7]

The idea that Scripture, especially the Old Testament, contains allegory can be traced back to Paul. However, Origen created a rational, systematic approach to interpreting Scripture allegorically; and he goes farther than most church Fathers—a general term used to designate all major orthodox Christian writers before c.600—in admitting the possibility that even the New Testament contains material that is historically untrue. Later biblical commentators borrowed much from Origen in presenting their own theories of biblical exegesis. Both Jerome and Augustine used allegorical interpretations, often derived directly from Origen, but combined with a firm belief in the literal truth of Scripture.

Not all Christians shared Justin's and Origen's enthusiasm for pagan learning. A North African Latin-speaking Christian named Tertullian (d. c.220) believed that the truth of Scripture so excelled that of the pagan writings as to render the latter useless. He also argued that Christians should separate themselves as much as possible from pagan society in order not to be corrupted by it:

What has Athens to do with Jerusalem, the Academy with the Church? . . . We have no need for curiosity since Jesus Christ, nor for inquiry since the Gospel. . . . Tell me what is the sense of this itch for idle speculation? What does it prove, this useless affectation of a fastidious curiosity, notwithstanding the strong confidence of its assertions? It was highly appropriate that Thales, while his eyes were roaming the heavens in astronomical observation, should have tumbled into a well. This mishap may well serve to illustrate the fate of all who occupy themselves with the stupidities of philosophy.[8]

Tertullian went farther than his rejection of classical culture and seemed to reject reason itself in his famous phrase, "I believe because it is absurd."[9] Even in the very language of his condemnations, however, Tertullian used the satire and invective developed by pagan Latin writers, though he turned it against the pagans themselves. Later Latin writers such as Jerome, who was a major figure in the development of medieval Latin, followed Tertullian's example in borrowing from the style of pagan authors.

Tertullian and Origen, perhaps, represent the two extremes in their attitude toward the pagan world's achievements. Most of the writers influential for the Middle Ages, such as Jerome and Augustine, fall somewhere in between. And in various forms, the debate about the value of pagan learning for Christians continued throughout the Middle Ages. The question was central in disputes such as those between Bernard of Clairvaux and Peter Abelard in the twelfth century and between some Franciscan and Dominican theologians in the thirteenth.

Persecution and Triumph

The early Church faced persecution. Christ himself was put to death by a Roman governor at the insistence of the Jewish leadership in Jerusalem. The apostles and their followers in Jerusalem faced the possibility of persecution once they became numerous enough to be a perceived threat to Judaism by the religious leaders.

The first Christian martyr was the deacon Stephen, killed by the Jews c.35. This first martyr story is recorded by Luke in Acts of the Apostles:

> At [Stephen's preaching] they [the Jews] gave a great shout and stopped their ears. Then they made one rush at him and, flinging him out of the city, set about stoning him. . . . So they

stoned Stephen, and as they did so, he called out, "Lord Jesus, receive my spirit." Then he fell on his knees and cried aloud, "Lord, do not hold this sin against them," and with that he died. (Acts 7:57–60)

Stephen's last words are presented to remind the reader of Christ, who uttered similar words of forgiveness to his killers from the cross. James was the first of the apostles to be martyred, and that too took place in Jerusalem c.44.

The most famous of the early persecutions of Christians, and the first launched by a Roman emperor, took place during the reign of Nero. He had been accused by some of having started a great fire in Rome in the year 64 and needed a scapegoat. So he blamed the fire on the small, weak, and unpopular Christian community. The persecution was confined to Rome and was not an attempt to wipe out the infant religion. However, both Peter and Paul were probably martyred during this persecution, Peter in the circus of Nero in a place called the Vatican, where four hundred years later a great basilica was built in his honor.

For almost two hundred years after Nero, there were scattered Christian persecutions, but all were short-lived and local. Most occurred in response to local problems (a bad crop, for example, where the populace may have believed that the Roman gods were punishing them for tolerating nonbelievers in their midst) or because the Christians were so different from other Roman citizens. Christians generally refused to serve in the army, go to the cruel entertainments so popular with the masses, or sacrifice to the Roman gods (considered as much a patriotic as a religious act). Sometimes Christians were harrassed by being "rounded up" for questioning. Probably the attitude of the Emperor Trajan (r.98–117) was typical of imperial policy toward Christians in this period. In the following text, he is answering a provincial governor who had expressed concern about the Christian "problem":

> You have acted quite properly, Pliny, in examining the case of those Christians brought before you. Nothing definite can be laid down as a general rule. They should not be hunted out.

If accusations are made and they are found guilty, they must be punished. But remember that a man may expect pardon from repentance if he denies that he is a Christian, and proves this to your satisfaction, that is by worshipping our gods, however much you may have suspected him in the past. Anonymous lists should have no part in any charge made. That is a thoroughly bad practice, and not in accordance with the spirit of the age.[10]

Among the second-century martyrs was Ignatius of Antioch (d.107). In surviving letters, he suggests his willingness to die for his faith, his conviction that martyrdom was the surest way to heaven, and his recognition that to die for Christ was the closest possible imitation of Christ's own passion:

All the ends of the earth, all the kingdoms of the world would be of no profit to me; so far as I am concerned, to die in Jesus Christ is better than to be monarch of the earth's widest bounds. He who died for us is all that I seek; He who rose again for us is my whole desire. The pangs of birth are upon me; have patience with me, my brothers, and do not shut me out from life, do not wish me to be stillborn. Here is one who only longs to be God's; do not make a present of him to the world again, or delude him with the things of earth. Suffer me to attain to light, light pure and undefiled; for only when I am come thither shall I be truly a man. Leave me to imitate the Passion of my God.[11]

Another second-century martyr was Polycarp (d.155). An excellent account of his martyrdom survives, but perhaps the most important aspect of the text is the description of what the pious Christians did after his death:

So, after all, we did gather up his bones—more precious to us than jewels, and finer than pure gold—and we laid them to rest on a spot suitable for that purpose. There we shall assemble, as occasion allows, with glad rejoicings; and with the Lord's permission we shall celebrate the birthday of his martyrdom. It will serve both as a commemoration of all who have triumphed before, and as a training and a preparation for any whose crown may be still to come.[12]

This text suggests that as early as the second century there was interest in preserving the relics (physical remains) of a holy person and that the day of his death—his birthday in heaven—was celebrated. In the Middle Ages, the celebration of the feast days of the saints, especially the martyrs, and the veneration of relics were two of the most important forms of popular piety. Relics were much sought after—bought, given as gifts, and stolen. Relics were regarded as the means through which innumerable miracles were performed. Though there are many reasons for the development of cults of saints and relics, we can trace the roots back as far as the middle of the second century.

A saint is one who is in heaven and thus eternally in God's favor. From the first century, Christians who died a martyr's death were presumed to be in heaven, and the above text concerning Polycarp suggests that at least by the middle of the second century, it was regarded as useful to preserve and venerate their earthly remains. There was at this time no formal process of canonization (the process by which one was declared a saint); the fact of martyrdom was sufficient evidence for veneration. With the end of large-scale persecutions in the fourth century, the definition of sainthood was enlarged to include those who professed Christianity and lived an exemplary Christian life. This class of saints is called confessors. Until the twelfth century, canonization varied from one area to another, and local cults sprang up in virtually all cathedrals and monasteries. Declaring someone a saint usually amounted to little more than placing the saint's relics in a place to be venerated and proclaiming that person's sanctity. From the twelfth century until the present, canonization has been the prerogative of the pope, who collects evidence of sanctity and declares a person to be a saint throughout the Church.

In the year 250, a new type of persecution began under the Emperor Decius. He ordered all citizens of the Empire to sacrifice to the Roman deities under penalty of death. This decree was intended to wipe out Christianity. Fortunately for the Christians, this persecution was short-lived because Decius died in 251. However, a similar persecution was ordered by the

Emperor Valerian in 258, and it lasted until 261. Among the victims of these persecutions was the deacon Lawrence. His story and those of other martyrs remained popular throughout the Middle Ages, as evidenced by their frequent appearances in sculpture, painting, and stained glass. His life continued to be rewritten and embellished. Here, for example, is a version taken from Jacobus de Voragine's *Golden Legend*, an enormously popular thirteenth-century collection of saints' lives:

> In that same night Lawrence was again brought before Decius. Then Hippolytus wept, and cried out that he too was a Christian. But Lawrence said to him: "Do thou rather hide Christ within thee, and when I shall call, give heed and come!" Then every sort of torture was prepared for him, and Decius said to him: "Sacrifice to the gods, or thou shalt pass the night in torments!" And Lawrence answered: "My night hath no darkness: all things shine with light!" "Let an iron bed be brought," said Decius, "that this obstinate fellow may take his rest thereon!" Then the executioners stripped him and stretched him on a gridiron, passing him down with forks; and they heaped burning coals beneath. And Lawrence said to Valerian: "Know, wretched man, that these coals bring refreshment to me, and eternal punishment to thee! For the Lord well knows that being accused I have not denied him, that being put to the question I have confessed Christ, that being roasted I give thanks!" And with joyous mien he said to Decius: "Behold, wretch, that thou hast well cooked one side! Turn the other and eat!" And giving thanks, he said: "I thank Thee, O Lord, that I have been made worthy to enter Thy portals!" And so saying, he breathed his last.[13]

The genre of literature that recites the lives of saints is called hagiography (from the Greek *hagios*—"holy"—and *graphein*—"to write"). Hagiography was extraordinarily popular in the Middle Ages. The stories were colorfully written with much action and adventure. The heroes and villains were as easy to spot as they are today in white-hat/black-hat cowboy movies. These writings were not attempts to provide biographies of holy people but rather were attempts to edify, instruct in the virtues, and present idealized models for imita-

Martyrdom of Saint Eustace and his Family. Fresco, 14th Century. Monastery of Pomposa, Italy. Eustace, a Roman martyr, was put to death by being roasted inside a hollow bronze bull. Above the depiction of the martyrdom the souls of Eustace and his family ascend to heaven. Like so many other stories of Roman martyrs, this one is interesting for its ingenuity. This form of martyrdom is adapted from a form of torture found in classical Greek texts.

tion. The disregard for historical accuracy is obvious in the text above where the author has Decius as the emperor, then Valerian, then Decius again. Even a casual tourist visiting the churches and museums of Europe cannot fail to see evidence of the enormous popularity of the stories of the saints in the Middle Ages. However, interest in the lives was more than merely entertainment and edification for the masses. The greatest writers of the Middle Ages, among them Bernard of Clairvaux, Bonaventure, and Chaucer, also wrote or rewrote saints' lives. Of equal importance, these hagiographical conventions were often incorporated even into secular literary genres as well.

The growing Christian Church survived the persecutions of Decius and Valerian, and was generally left in peace during the next fifty years. In fact, it is known that there were some buildings constructed for Christian worship in the latter half of the third century. However, Emperor Diocletian (r.284–305), who did much to rebuild the Roman Empire, was concerned that the primary loyalty of Christians was not to the state, and began the most serious and wide-ranging persecutions in 303; they continued—with some interruptions—until his successor Constantine's Edict of Milan in 313. Thousands of Christians died in Diocletian's attempt to rid the empire of Christianity, and many books and pieces of church property were destroyed. Out of this persecution, too, came some of the Church's most famous martyrs, including Lucy, Margaret, Catherine of Alexandria, Vincent, and Sebastian. An account of one bishop's encounter with the persecutors, written by a contemporary, perhaps gives the best picture of what was involved:

> The magistrate Magnilianus said to him: "Are you Felix the bishop?"
>
> "I am," answered Bishop Felix.
>
> "Hand over whatever books or parchments you possess," said the magistrate Magnilianus.
>
> "I have them," answered Bishop Felix, "but I will not give them up."
>
> The magistrate Magnilianus said: "Hand the books over to be burned."
>
> "It would be better for me to be burned," answered Bishop Felix, "rather than the divine Scriptures. For it is better to obey God rather than men."
>
> The magistrate Magnilianus said: "The emperors' orders come before anything you say."
>
> Bishop Felix answered: "God's commands come before those of men."[14]

After Diocletian's retirement in 305, there was civil war among several claimants to the imperial title. Among them was

Constantine, son of one of Diocletian's caesars (assistant emperors). He was proclaimed emperor by his army in York, England, in 306; but he became effective ruler of the western half of the Empire only after defeating his rival Maxentius at the battle of Milvian Bridge on the outskirts of Rome in 312 and did not rule the entire Roman Empire until 323. According to tradition, on the eve of the battle, Constantine has a vision of the Cross and heard a voice telling him he would conquer by that sign. He had Christ's monogram marked on his soldiers' shields the next morning. Whatever the historical accuracy of this popular story, Constantine and his co-emperor issued the Edict of Milan in 313, which brought Diocletian's persecution to an end and granted toleration to all religions. In the years following the edict, Constantine came more and more to favor Christianity, although he was not baptized until just before his death in 337. Among his favors to Christianity were the proclamation of Sunday as a holiday, the elimination of branding on the face as punishment because humans are made in the image of God, the grant of exemptions from government service to the clergy, and gifts of buildings and property to the Church.

Although some historians have argued that Constantine's conversion to Christianity was politically motivated and perhaps even a political ploy, there seems to be no good reason to doubt the sincerity of his adherence to Christianity. But if Constantine had hoped that Christianity would cement his empire together, he realized soon after the Edict of Milan that there were serious divisions within the Church. One issue arose directly from the persecution of Diocletian. Unlike Felix, some clergy submitted Christian books to the Roman authorities to be burned, and some even sacrificed to pagan gods in order to escape execution. After the persecution, some of these priests and bishops wanted to take up their offices in the Church again. In North Africa, a dispute broke out because some Christians (who later came to be called Donatists, after Donatus, a bishop who replaced one of the "traitors") refused to recognize these "traitors" as priests and bishops. The bishop of Rome, a synod of bishops meeting in France, and Constantine himself (in 316, long before he was baptized) condemned Donatism; the emperor even used his imperial power to attempt to put an end to it. This is the first instance of an emperor using political authority to try to settle an essentially internal, theological controversy among Christians. Despite continued imperial support of the orthodox position, Donatism persisted in North Africa until the Moslem conquest in the seventh century. In the fifth century, the North African Bishop Augustine was a strong opponent of Donatism and wrote powerful treatises supporting the orthodox position.

The Donatist and orthodox views represented two competing beliefs concerning the nature of the Church. The Donatists perceived the Church to be a community of saints, the holy ones of God, and sinners were to be excluded. On the other hand, the orthodox position was based on a broader conception of the Church as a mixed body of saints and sinners, all benefiting from the community and the sacraments. Furthermore, the clergy were believed to administer the sacraments validly even if they were not of good character; ultimately it was Christ who administered the sacraments, and he could give grace in the sacraments even through unworthy agents. The victory for the orthodox position was of great importance to the development of the Church, whose membership for much of the medieval period consisted of virtually the entire population of Western Europe. However, on occasion, church reformers attacking clerical corruption in the Middle Ages came very close to the Donatist position. Among these are the eleventh-century reformer Cardinal Humbert and the fourteenth-century English theologian John Wyclif. A number of popular heresies in the Middle Ages also included Donatist tenets.

The Donatist problem was not, however, the most fundamental theological problem Constantine had to face. A priest from Alexandria named Arius (d.c.336) argued that Christ was not coeternal with the Father but rather with the first fruit of creation: "There was a time when he [Christ] was not." He emphasized distinctions between God and Father and God the Son and spoke of them as being of different "substance," a philosophical term best rendered in modern English as "essence" or "being." Encouraged by his ecclesiastical advisors, Constantine summoned a council of bishops, almost entirely from the Eastern part of the Empire, which met at Nicaea in Asia Minor in 325. Constantine himself presided over this gathering, now referred to as the First Ecumenical (from the Greek word meaning "the inhabited world") Council although he was not a baptized Christian at the time. The Council condemned Arianism and approved a statement concerning the proper relationship of God the Father to his Son probably suggested by Constantine himself although based on the advice of trusted bishops. This formula was incorporated into a statement of belief called the Nicene Creed (from the Latin *credere* meaning "to believe"). This creed received significant additions at the Second Ecumenical Council held at Constantinople in 381, incorporating a greater recognition of the Holy Spirit as part of the Godhead, and was later further added to in the West. Its final version is worth presenting here in its entirety. The creed is important not only for its condemnation of Arianism and strong proclamation of the Trinity, but also because in the Middle Ages it was incorporated into the Mass and thus was the principal declaration of belief made by the faithful in the West (the section containing the condemnation of Arianism is in italics). The Creed is divided into four parts; one concerns each member of the Trinity and the fourth concerns the Church.

> We believe in one God,
> the Father, the Almighty,
> maker of heaven and earth,
> of all that is, seen and unseen.
> We believe in one Lord, Jesus Christ,
> the only Son of God,
> eternally begotten of the Father,
> God from God, Light from Light,
> true God from true God,
> *begotten, not made,*
> *of one Being* [substance] *with the Father.*
> *Through him all things were made.*

For us men and for our salvation
he came down from heaven:
by the power of the Holy Spirit
he became incarnate from the Virgin Mary, and was made
    man.
For our sake, he was crucified under Pontius Pilate;
he suffered death and was buried.
On the third day he rose again in accordance with the
    Scriptures;
he ascended into heaven
and is seated at the right hand of the Father.
He will come again in glory to judge the living and the
    dead,
and his kingdom will have no end.
We believe in the Holy Spirit, the Lord, the giver of life,
who proceeds from the Father and the Son.
With the Father and the Son he is worshipped and
    glorified.
He has spoken through the Prophets.
We believe in one holy catholic and apostolic Church.
We acknowledge one baptism for the forgiveness of sins.
We look for the resurrection of the dead,
and the life of the world to come.
Amen.[15]

Many followers of Arius did not abandon their beliefs after Nicaea, and a significant number of bishops who signed the Nicene formula later reverted to Arianism. Constantine himself leaned toward Arianism after Nicaea and was baptized on his deathbed by an Arian bishop in 337. His three sons, who ruled from 337 to 361, were Arians; and there were brief periods when the Nicenes seemed to be in a minority and even faced persecution as heretics. Generally, Arianism was confined to the East; the Latin-speaking West was firmly Nicene. In the 360s and 370s the pendulum swung back toward the Nicene position; and the Second Ecumenical Council, meeting in Constantinople in 381, once again condemned Arianism. This was its death blow within the Roman Empire.

Arianism, however, was still to have a great impact on the history of the Church and the history of early medieval Europe. Between the two ecumenical councils that condemned Arianism, Christianity was taken for the first time to the Germanic Goths living outside the empire by the missionary Ulfilas (c.311–383), who had learned his Christianity from and was consecrated a bishop by an Arian. Thus Christianity was first taken to the Germans in its Arian form. Later, the Goths entered the Roman Empire and eventually occupied and ruled significant portions of it. The Germanic tribes of the Vandals, Burgundians, and Lombards also became Arian. Collectively, these tribes ruled most of the Western Roman Empire by 500; the Goths controlled most of Italy and Spain, the Vandals were in North Africa, and the Burgundians occupied part of Gaul (France). When considering the Germanic invasions, it is important to remember that the Germans were not only a political threat but a religious threat as well. Nicene bishops, including the bishop of Rome, found themselves surrounded by people whom they regarded as dangerous heretics. Some of the Germanic chieftains persecuted Nicene Christians. The sixth-century bishop Gregory of Tours recounts the story of a Nicene martyr in Arian Spain:

> About this time Trasamund began to persecute the Christians and by tortures and all sorts of executions forced the whole of Spain to accept the heresy of the Arian rite. It so happened that a young girl of strong religious convictions was dragged forward for this torment. She was extremely wealthy and according to the class-distinctions of this world she belonged to a noble senatorial family. What is nobler still than all this, she was strong in the Catholic faith and served Almighty God in a faultless way. . . .
>
> As she was dragged off to be re-baptized against her will and compelled to suffer immersion in the filthy font, she shouted: "I believe the Father with the Son and the Holy Ghost to be of one substance." As she said this she stained all the water with her blood, for her menstrual period began. Then she was submitted to a legal interrogation, and tortured by the rack, the flames and the pincers. Finally she was consecrated to Christ our Lord by having her head cut off.[16]

Only in the seventh century did Arianism disappear as the Germanic tribes gradually accepted the orthodox (Nicene) position on the relationship of the Father to the Son.

After Constantine, the Empire continued to be ruled by Christians except for the two-year reign of the Emperor Julian the Apostate (r.361–63). The importance of Constantine's conversion and the beginning of imperial support for Christianity after three centuries of neglect or persecution is hard to overestimate. Among the most immediate changes were the number and kind of converts. Until Constantine, Christians were a small minority but highly dedicated to their faith, as evidenced by the willingness of many to be martyred; when people became Christians, they obviously did not do so for any material advantages. But with imperial acceptance of Christianity, countless thousands converted because Christianity was the religion of the emperor and thus perhaps a good way to get ahead in the Empire. Those ready to die for the faith had to learn to deal with and accept many "lukewarm" Christians.

In fact, now that Christianity was a safe and even favored religion, now that martyrdom with rare exceptions was no longer possible, how could those deeply devoted Christians show their willingness to lose all for Christ, as the venerated martyrs had done? One reaction was the growth of asceticism (from the Greek word meaning "athletic training"), a vigorous self-denial of worldly pleasures, which was sometimes viewed as a kind of "daily martyrdom" (see ch. 6). The ascetic movement was not confined to men and women living as hermits or in monastic communities in the deserts of Egypt, Palestine, and Syria. In fourth-century Rome, for example, there were widows and unmarried women, often from prominent families, vowing celibacy and poverty, sometimes voluntarily living in poor and even squalid conditions.

Another significant change after Constantine occurred in the role of the bishop. The bishops began to wear insignia once used only by imperial civil servants, and they were often regarded by the emperor and others as the religious counterparts to imperial officials. Even the "throne" or *cathedra* that came to be used by bishops in their churches was modeled on the seat of high-ranking imperial officials. (The word "cathedral," meaning a church that is the seat of a bishop, derives from this piece of imperial regalia adapted to Christian use.) The bishops of Rome, of course, also adopted the imperial regalia; in addition, the pope began to use the title and privileges once held by the chief pagan priest of Rome—the *pontifex maximus*. The popes also sponsored large building projects, including the construction of churches on the spots where famous Christians had been martyred. Among these was the Church of St. Peter, built on the site of Nero's circus in the Vatican. The pope came to live in a palace called the Lateran, which was bequeathed by Constantine to the bishops of Rome. It was next to this palace that the cathedral of Rome, St. John in the Lateran, was built. For most of the Middle Ages, the residence of the pope was the Lateran palace. Only in the fifteenth century did the popes permanently move to another papal palace in the Vatican.

The Church began to acquire wealth from both imperial and private gifts. The fact that the bishop was the head of a wealthy corporate community added to the importance of the episcopal office. The control of wealth by the Christian clergy meant that they were important to the economy and governance of the Empire. This is one reason the emperors were so interested in the disputes within Christendom. We have already seen how Constantine became directly involved in what were essentially theological disputes both with the Donatist problem and with the Arian problem at the Council of Nicaea. On the other hand, bishops sometimes sought to exercise their spiritual authority over a Christian emperor to influence essentially political policy. The best example of this involves the Emperor Theodosius (d.395) and the bishop of Milan, Saint Ambrose (d.397). For political reasons Theodosius carried out a massacre in the Greek city of Thessalonica (modern Thessaloniki) in the year 390. When the emperor returned to Milan, his capital, Ambrose chastised him and forbade him to enter the cathedral of Milan until he did public penance for his sin. Theodosius did public penance. On another occasion, a group of zealous Christian monks had burned a synagogue in the Eastern part of the Empire; Theodosius ordered the local bishop to restore the synagogue with Church funds. Ambrose's biographer Paulinus recounts what happened upon the emperor's return to Milan:

Moreover, after he [Theodosius] had returned to Milan, he [Ambrose] preached on this very topic in the presence of the people, and the emperor was present in the church at the time. In this sermon he introduced the person of the Lord as speaking to the emperor: "I made you emperor from the lowest; I handed over to you the army of your enemy; I gave to you the supplies which he had prepared for his own army against you; I reduced your enemy into our power; I established one of your sons on the throne of the empire; I caused you to triumph without difficulty—and do you give triumphs to me over my enemies?" And the emperor said to him as he was descending the pulpit: "You spoke against us today, Bishop." But the bishop replied that he had not spoken against him but for him. Then the emperor: "Indeed, I issued a stern order against the bishop concerning the rebuilding of the synagogue. Moreover, the monks must be punished."[17]

Ambrose forced Theodosius to recall the order to rebuild the synagogue by refusing to celebrate mass until he received Theodosius's promise of obedience in this matter. This same Theodosius was the first emperor to persecute people who were not orthodox Christians, i.e. both heretics such as the Arians and pagans. In 391, he issued a decree that was designed to effectively prohibit paganism:

No person shall pollute himself with sacrificial animals; no person shall slaughter an innocent victim; no person shall approach the shrines, shall wander through the temples, or revere the images formed by mortal labour, lest he become guilty by divine and human laws. Judges shall also be bound by the general rule that if any of them should be devoted to profane rights and should enter a temple for the purpose of worship anywhere, either on a journey or in a city, he shall be immediately compelled to pay fifteen pounds of gold.[18]

Thus in less than a century Christianity had gone from a minority, persecuted religion to the official religion of the Roman Empire, the religion required of all public officials.

Throughout the Middle Ages, people were aware that the conversion of Constantine marked a (perhaps *the*) major change in the history of the Church. Reformers and critics of the Church often lamented that Constantine's favors to the Church and all the consequences of imperial favor had ultimately led to a corruption of Christian values and Christian ecclesiastical offices. For example, Dante, meeting avaricious popes in hell, moans: "Ah, Constantine, to how much evil gave birth, not thy conversion, but that dower the first rich father had from thee!"[19]

Similarly, here are the words of the important fifteenth-century Bohemian reformer John Hus:

> This [spiritual poison] was intimated when Emperor Constantine first enriched the Roman bishop, having given him estates; for a voice was heard from heaven saying: "Today poison has been poured into the Christian communion."[20]

A widely held belief in the Middle Ages was that Constantine actually conferred upon the pope the authority to govern the Western half of the Roman Empire; the legend was put in written form perhaps in the eighth century. This so-called Donation of Constantine was from time to time a major point of dispute between the Holy Roman Emperors and the popes. Elaborate theories of church-state relations relied on the donation. Some writers such as Dante denied the legality and thus the validity of the transferal of imperial power to the pope. However, it was not until the mid-fifteenth century that the Italian humanist Lorenzo Valla demonstrated authoritatively that the Donation of Constantine was a forgery.

A final dispute concerning the nature of Christ arose toward the end of the fourth century that led to the calling of the Third and Fourth Ecumenical Councils, the last councils to be concerned primarily with christological questions. Although the precise theological positions are complex, the crux of the dispute was the relationship of Christ's divinity to his humanity. One position, developed in Alexandria, argued that Christ was fully divine but did not have all human traits; in particular, Christ did not have the limitations of a human mind. More extreme adherents to this position, the Monophysites (from

Fresco of the Donation of Constantine. 13th Century. Church of Santi Quattro Coronati, Rome. In this depiction of the papal point of view, we see a humble and subordinate Constantine conferring the symbol of temporal rule upon Pope Sylvester I.

the Greek word meaning "one nature"), believed that Christ had only one complete nature, i.e. a complete divine but only an incomplete human nature. The opposing position came from Antioch but later was centered in Constantinople when its leading proponent Nestorius became bishop of that city. The essence of this position is that Christ had two completely separate natures, and adherents emphasized the importance of his human nature. Followers of this belief were called Nestorians. The Third Ecumenical Council in 431 at Ephesus condemned the Nestorian position by decreeing that Mary is the Mother of God; (the Nestorians had argued that Mary was the mother of the human nature of Christ but not mother of his divinity.) The Nestorians faced persecution and fled to the Persian Empire. In later centuries, Nestorian missionaries traveled to China where, especially in the thirteenth century, they were quite successful and established churches in Peking. When Marco Polo and some Franciscan missionaries arrived in China in the thirteenth century, they were surprised to find a rather flourishing albeit heretical Christian community there.

This christological controversy was not settled by the Council of Ephesus, since moderates and Monophysites still argued the rightness of their beliefs. A council at Ephesus in 449 upheld the Monophysite position over the objections of Pope Leo I. However, a new emperor summoned a council to Chalcedon in 451, now known as the Fourth Ecumenical Council. It denounced the Monophysite position as heretical and defined Christ as having two complete natures, human and divine, each retaining all its properties but indissolubly united at the Incarnation. As mentioned earlier, the Council of Chalcedon also recognized papal primacy, that "Peter had spoken through Leo."

Like the other heretical groups before, the Monophysites continued to exist, though almost exclusively in the Eastern part of the Roman Empire; they were particularly strong in Egypt. Monophysitism was a major divisive element in the Eastern Roman (Byzantine) Empire until all the strongholds of the Monophysites were captured by the Moslems in the seventh century. Several Monophysite churches exist today, including the Coptic church, the Jacobite church in Syria, and the Armenian church.

The development of the doctrine and institutions of Christianity, which has been the focus of this chapter, has demonstrated the interaction between classical and biblical culture. Taking place as it did primarily in the eastern Mediterranean, this interaction occurred within a Greek cultural and linguistic framework. A parallel interaction took place in the Latin-speaking West, a development which we will trace in the next chapter by an examination of its two greatest figures, Jerome and Augustine.

CHAPTER FOUR

The Latin Fathers:
Jerome and Augustine

With the exceptions of the writings of Tertullian and Cyprian (d.258), virtually all the Christian writings before the fourth century were in Greek, even in the western Mediterranean. It was only in the fourth and fifth centuries, as the Roman Empire became permanently divided between East and West, that a theological tradition developed in the Latin-speaking West.

The first major figure was Saint Jerome (c.342–420). Jerome grew up in Italy and studied in Rome where he was baptized and served as a secretary to Pope Damasus I. However, he lived most of his adult life in the Holy Land, in a monastery in Bethlehem. He was an important writer on asceticism, an influential biblical scholar (often drawing heavily from Origen), and a translator. Although there were Latin versions of Scripture before Jerome, it was he who retranslated most of both Testaments from their original languages into the version that became standard in the West for more than a thousand years. This translation is usually referred to as the Vulgate (from the Latin *vulgus* meaning "common"), because it was the Bible common to medieval Europe. Jerome's introductions to and commentaries on many books of the Bible also became standard starting points for biblical commentary in the Middle Ages. Anyone who has ever studied a foreign language can appreciate how a translator has to use certain metaphors and approximations of meaning. Jerome's choices as a translator determined how people understood and knew the Scriptures; and since his translations remained authoritative for so long, any errors he made were a part of the received biblical tradition in the West throughout the Middle Ages.

Jerome wrote several important works other than his biblical scholarship. Having been educated in the pagan classics like many other Christians, he was concerned with the proper relationship between them and Scripture. While his viewpoint does not remain entirely consistent from one mood or period to another, the overall tone is clear: classical writings can be used by Christians, though with caution and in a role subordinate to Scripture. Consider the following two passages from the writings of Jerome:

> While the old serpent was making me his plaything, about the middle of Lent, a deep-seated fever fell upon my weakened body, and while it destroyed my rest completely—the story seems hardly credible—it so wasted my unhappy frame that scarcely anything was left of me but skin and bone. Meantime preparations for my funeral went on; my body grew gradually colder, and the warmth of life lingered only in my throbbing breast. Suddenly I was caught up in the spirit and dragged before the judgment seat of the Judge; and here the light was so bright, and those who stood around were radiant, that I cast myself upon the ground and did not dare to look up. Asked who and what I was I replied: "I am a Christian." But He who presided said: "Thou liest, thou art a follower of Cicero and not of Christ. For where thy treasure is, there will thy heart be also." Instantly I became dumb, and amid the strokes of the lash—for He had ordered me to be scourged—I was tortured

most severely still by the fire of conscience, considering with myself that verse, "In the grave, who shall give thee thanks?" Yet for all that I began to cry and to bewail myself, saying, "Have mercy upon me, O Lord; have mercy upon me."[1]

He [Paul] had read in Deuteronomy the command given by the voice of the Lord that when a captive woman had had her head shaved, her eyebrows and all her hair cut off, and her nails pared, she might then be taken to wife. Is it surprising that I too, admiring the fairness of her form and the grace of her eloquence, desire to make that secular wisdom which is my captive and my handmaid, a matron of the true Israel? Or that shaving off and cutting away all in her that is dead whether this be idolatry, pleasure, error, or lust, I take her to myself clean and pure and beget by her servants for the Lord of Sabbaoth? My efforts promote the advantage of Christ's family, my so-called defilement with an alien increases the number of my fellow-servants. . . . Ezekiel shaves his head as a type of that Jerusalem which has been an harlot, in sign that whatever in her is devoid of sense and life must be removed.[2]

In other words, one is not to reject or ignore the wisdom of the Greeks or Romans, but must select only those elements from the classical heritage that are useful in one's attempt to achieve salvation.

Saint Augustine lived during the waning days of the Roman Empire in the West. Born in North Africa in 354, he traveled to Italy, and was converted to Christianity in 386 under the influence of Ambrose, bishop of Milan and an influential Christian writer. After Augustine's conversion, he became bishop of Hippo in North Africa; when he died in 430, Vandal invaders were closing in on the city. He was an educator, a polemicist, a pastor, and a preacher, in addition to being a prolific writer of theology and philosophy. The importance of the writings of Augustine to the Middle Ages and beyond cannot be overemphasized. He is one of the two or three most influential thinkers in all of Christian thought, and perhaps the seminal figure in determining the way the Middle Ages looked at reality. He wrote on almost every topic, and even to survey what he has done in any complete fashion would be impossible;

but by examining three of his important works, one can see something of both the breadth and depth of his influence. *On Christian Doctrine* contains his theory of how to read Scripture. The *Confessions* is his autobiography, the pattern of his conversion to Christianity. *The City of God* is an interpretation of all of history in terms of the struggle between the heavenly and the earthly, the city of God and the city of man.

To understand the influence of *On Christian Doctrine*, one must first recall what has been said about the absolute centrality of the Bible to the Middle Ages. If one judges by the influence the Bible has now, even to practicing Christians, one will underestimate its importance to medieval culture. Perhaps at no time in history has a culture been so influenced by a single book. Modern scholars will read a great many more books in the course of their careers than their medieval counterparts, the explosion of material in all fields being one of the significant cultural changes that has taken place since the Middle Ages. But those books that medieval scholars knew, they knew exceedingly well; and the book that they knew best was the Bible.

Not only was the Bible itself known in a way all but foreign to modern readers, but much of the scholarly writing in the Middle Ages consisted of commentary on its various parts. Many important works, such as Bernard of Clairvaux's sermons on the Song of Songs or Ambrose's commentary on the Gospel of Luke, to take two well-known examples, are exegeses of the Bible. Augustine himself wrote many such works. The last part of his *Confessions* is a commentary on the book of Genesis, and his longest work is a series of commentaries and sermons on the Psalms. The Bible, then, was known, studied, and commented upon. Many of its books considered most important were actually known by heart by the great scholars and thinkers. It was able to reach those who could not read as well as those who could, through preaching and through the visual arts. As modern scholars such as Emile Mâle have shown, most of the sculpture, stained glass, and painting of the Middle Ages was an examination and interpretation of biblical narrative.[3]

It follows from the importance of the Bible that Augustine's theory of how it is to be read would have resonances with many areas of reality not specifically connected to theology. *On Christian Doctrine* is an important document both to the history of ideas in general and the history of literary theory in particular, defining a literary aesthetic influential to the entire Middle Ages; Augustine presents a distinction at the beginning of Book 1 that provides a basis not only for subsequent arguments in this work but to his thought as a whole. He distinguishes between the use and enjoyment of any object:

> To enjoy something is to cling to it with love for its own sake. To use something, however, is to employ it in obtaining that which you love, provided that it is worthy of love. For an illicit use should be called rather a waste or an abuse. Suppose we were wanderers who could not live in blessedness except at home, miserable in our wandering and desiring to end it and to return to our native country. We would need vehicles for land and sea which could be used to help us reach our homeland, which is to be enjoyed. But if the amenities of the journey and the motion of the vehicles itself delighted us, and we were led to enjoy those things which we should use, we should not wish to end our journey quickly, and, entangled in a perverse sweetness, we should be alienated from our country, whose sweetness would make us blessed. Thus in this mortal life, wandering from God, if we should wish to return to our native country where we can be blessed we should use this world and not enjoy it, so that the "invisible things" of God "being understood from the things that are made" [Rom. 1:20] may be seen, that is, so that by means of corporal and temporal things we may comprehend the eternal and spiritual . . . .
>
> The things which are to be enjoyed are the Father, the Son, and the Holy Spirit, a single trinity, a certain supreme thing common to all who enjoy it.[4]

This quotation obviously has far-reaching implications in that it helps to explain the proper attitude toward anything whatsoever, whether it be money, property, sex, or God. To see this as the beginning of a theory of aesthetics, however, is perhaps not so obvious. Augustine believed that this attitude must also govern one's approach to language. Words too are to be used rather than enjoyed, which means that one must not see them as things in themselves, but as signs pointing to something else. In one sense of course this is obvious, in that words are referential. It would be self-defeating, when reading the word "horse," to concentrate on the word itself, rather than on the four-legged animal to which the word refers. But when reading Scripture, Augustine tells us, one is to go beyond merely seeing the object that the word refers to; one must see words themselves as pointing toward a spiritual truth that exists behind the physical reality. He is elaborating a theory of symbolism. In Scripture, the language is a means of leading the reader from the visible to the invisible. It is no accident that Augustine quotes Paul—"Invisible things are understood by the things that are made" (Rom. 1:20)—no less than six times throughout *On Christian Doctrine*. He tells us about both ways of seeing words as signs:

> There are two reasons why things written are not understood: they are obscured either by unknown or by ambiguous signs. For signs are either literal or figurative. They are called literal when they are used to designate those things on account of which they were instituted; thus we say *bos* [ox] when we mean an animal of a herd because all men using the Latin language call it by that name just as we do. Figurative signs occur when that thing which we designate by a literal sign is used to signify something else: thus we say "ox" and by that syllable understand the animal which is ordinarily designated by that word but again by that animal we understand an evangelist, as is signified in the scripture, according to the interpretation of the apostle, when it says, "Thou shalt not muzzle the ox that treadeth out the corn."[5]

Augustine believes, then, that discovering the spiritual meaning that the words of Scripture point toward is the task of the serious student of Scripture. Much of *On Christian Doctrine* is devoted to ways in which this is to be done. The qualities of mind that Augustine sees as necessary to this task are intertwined with the very quality of one's life; he is concerned with showing that understanding Scripture is always more than simply an academic study. To understand the spiritual meaning of Scripture, one must lead a life spiritually in accord with Scripture. In talking about how it is possible for one to misunderstand the spirit behind certain sections of the Old Testament, he tells us:

> Again caution must be exercised lest anyone think that those things in scripture which are neither vices nor crimes among the ancients because of the conditions of their times, even when such things are taken literally rather than figuratively, may be transferred to our own times and put in practice. Unless he is dominated by cupidity and seeks protection for it in the very scriptures by means of which it is to be overthrown, no one will do this. The wretched man does not realize that these things are so arranged for this purpose: that men of good hope may profitably see both that the customs which they disdain may have a good use and that the customs which they themselves embrace may be damnable if charity moves the first and cupidity accompanies the second.[6]

Augustine is saying that one's own cupidity is the biggest obstacle to understanding Scripture. His theory helps to explain why certain parts of Scripture seem obscure; until one is able to pierce beneath the veil of the story itself to see the spiritual truth it contains one may indeed think that much of the surface story of Scripture is strange and unintelligible. And Augustine wants the reader to know both the difficulty of that enterprise and the importance of devoting one's life to its completion.

A question that logically follows however is why Scripture should have been written in such seemingly obscure fashion. Why does God not present spiritual truth simply, rather than in the roundabout fashion that Augustine has described? His answer to this question is one of the most important sections of the work, and one of the most influential statements on aesthetics for the Middle Ages:

> But many and varied obscurities deceive those who read casually, understanding one thing instead of another; indeed, in certain places they do not find anything to interpret errone-

ously, so obscurely are certain sayings covered with a most dense mist. I do not doubt that this situation was provided by God to conquer pride by work and to combat disdain in our minds, to which those things which are easily discovered seem frequently to become worthless. For example, it may be said that there are holy and perfect men with whose lives and customs as an exemplar the Church of Christ is able to destroy all sorts of superstitions in those who come to it and to incorporate them into itself, men of good faith, true servants of God, who, putting aside the burden of the world, come to the holy laver of baptism and, ascending thence, conceive through the holy spirit, and produce the fruit of a twofold love of God and their neighbor. But why is it, I ask, that if anyone says this he delights his hearers less than if he had said the same thing in expounding that place in the canticle of canticles where it is said of the church, as she is praised as a beautiful woman, "Thy teeth are as flocks of sheep, that are shorn, which come up from the washing, all with twins, and there is none barren among them?" Does one learn anything else besides that which he learns when he hears the same thought expressed in plain words without similitude? Nevertheless, in a strange way, I contemplate the saints more pleasantly when I envisage them as the teeth of the church cutting off men from their errors and transferring them to her body after their hardness has been softened as if by being bitten and chewed. I recognize them most pleasantly as shorn sheep having put aside the burden of the world like so much fleece, and as ascending from the washing, which is baptism, all to create twins, which are the two precepts of love, and I see no one of them sterile of this holy fruit.[7]

This statement describes a movement from the visible to the invisible: Augustine makes it clear that the purpose of figurative language is not the pleasure to be gained in the language itself, but the intellectual truth to which the figurative language leads. The example he uses, by virtue of its jarring effect on a modern sensibility, reinforces this. The image takes the reader on a bizarre ride through the intestinal tract of a sheep, which can make sense only when one solves the intellectual puzzle it presents: how can *a* mean *b*? Augustine would claim that the reader gains intellectual satisfaction from the discovery of truth, which is a satisfaction separate from contemplation of truth itself; and the difficulty of the image increases the satisfaction. At the beginning of the above quotation Augustine states explicitly that those things which are easily gained are not greatly valued. Conversely, one values the intellectual truth behind what he calls a "most dense mist" precisely because of the work that one must put into uncovering it. This example may seem rather extreme, but it illustrates all the more forcefully a significant difference between medieval and modern aesthetic theory; the function of imagery to Augustine was not to arouse a spontaneous emotional attitude in observers, but rather to encourage them to "seek an abstract pattern of philosophical significance beneath the symbolic configuration."[8]

Augustine also treats the question of what sort of limits exist in the number of interpretations in a given scriptural passage:

> Whoever, therefore, thinks that he understands the divine Scriptures or any part of them so that it does not build the double love of God and of our neighbor does not understand it at all. Whoever finds a lesson there useful to the building of charity, even though he has not said what the author may be shown to have intended in that place, has not been deceived, nor is he lying in any way.[9]

This statement is hardly a *carte blanche* invitation to medieval symbol hunters. At the same time it is clearly open-ended, suggesting that even an author's intention is not so important as the promotion of the doctrine of charity.

One other section of *On Christian Doctrine* is worth quoting, because of its confirmation of the method just described. Augustine writes about the possible uses of classical culture:

> If those who are called philosophers, especially the Platonists, have said things which are indeed true and are well accommodated to our faith, they should not be feared: rather, what they have said should be taken from them as from unjust possessors and converted to our use. Just as the Egyptians had not only idols and grave burdens which the people of Israel detested and avoided, so also they had vases and ornaments of

gold and silver and clothing which the Israelites took with them
secretly when they fled, as if to put them to a better use. They
did not do this on their own authority but at God's command-
ment, while the Egyptians unwittingly supplied them with
things which they themselves did not use well. [Exod. 3:22;
11:2; 12:35] In the same way all the teachings of the pagans
contain not only simulated and superstitious imaginings and
grave burdens of unnecessary labor, which each one of us leaving the society of pagans under the leadership of Christ ought
to abominate and avoid, but also liberal disciplines more suited
to the uses of truth, and some most useful precepts concerning
morals. Even some truths concerning the worship of one God
are discovered among them. These are, as it were, their gold
and silver, which they did not institute themselves but dug up
from certain mines of divine providence, which is everywhere
infused, and perversely and injuriously abused in the worship
of demons.[10]

Here, Augustine reads the quotation from Exodus, "that they
are to claim gold and silver trinkets from their neighbor"
(2:11), according to his own allegorical method. So understood, it becomes an explanation of the proper attitude toward
pagan culture generally and, as such, becomes another important contribution to the much-debated question of what to
do with the classical culture inherited by the Middle Ages.
Augustine's answer, that one should take what is good, use it,
and leave the rest behind, describes what actually happens to
the culture of antiquity. One is justified in taking elements from
the pagan past because they contain truth that can be converted to Christian uses.

This explains why, for example, when a manuscript contains
an illumination of Cicero, he is pictured as a medieval monk,
thus being turned to Christian use. As modern readers with a
much more acute time-consciousness, our immediate reaction
is to see this transformation as simplistic and naive. But medieval
people really show a sensible and sophisticated attitude, once
one accepts their premise. They wished to show the relevance
of the past and so they see people and events as constantly
present, whether it be the portrayal of Cicero as a monk or of

Capital, Church of St. Austremoine. 12th Century. Issoire, France. This depiction of Christ carrying his cross shows Roman soldiers dressed as 12th Century knights in chain mail. Much Roman sculpture survived into the Middle Ages. This depiction was not due to ignorance of Roman dress, but rather represents an attempt to bring the past into the present and so make it meaningful to its audience.

an Old Testament prophet using fourteenth-century English place names in a mystery play. In medieval painting or sculpture, figures who lived at different places and times are often depicted together on the same surface. This juxtaposition is also a way of bringing past and present together, showing that thematic connections are more important than temporal differences. Our reaction—to see only their distortion of the past —is perhaps another kind of naivete, the opposite side of the coin from the medieval view. In some ways we have lost the ability to see the continuity between our age and the past, and as a result tend to stress the differences.

The *Confessions*, Augustine's autobiography, is one of the great autobiographies in the history of the West, as well as one of its great spiritual documents. But to understand it as a work seminally influential to the thought of the Middle Ages, it is necessary to explain differences between modern ideas of autobiography and Augustine's. We think of biography today as a description of events in a person's life, useful and important to the extent that they give a detailed account of what actually happened. Above all, a biography is supposed to be factually accurate and complete. To understand Augustine's idea of autobiography, however, these ideas are of less use than his principles of scriptural interpretation. He constructs the *Confessions* as a consciously articulated movement from the visible to the invisible. Just as in reading Scripture one is led to an inner truth more important than the visible means by which this truth is presented, the events of Augustine's life are less important than the pattern of conversion toward which these events lead. His portrayal of the facts of his life is a means to an end rather than an end in itself; and the end of the *Confessions* is Augustine's conversion, his turning away from self and toward God. The last several books of the *Confessions* are themselves scriptural exegeses, forming an explication of the beginning of the book of Genesis. Thus his conversion becomes the necessary condition for the proper understanding of Scripture. As *On Christian Doctrine* is a model for the understanding and interpretation of Scripture throughout the Middle Ages, so the *Confessions* is one of the most important models for the pattern of conversion, a pattern that exerted extraordinary influence on the thought of the Middle Ages.

The story of a person who turns away from self and toward God did not originate with Augustine. In fact, he relates in the *Confessions* how his own conversion was influenced by other famous conversion stories, that of Saint Antony of the Desert (251–356), written by Saint Athanasius (c.296–373), and the most famous conversion of the New Testament—Paul on the road to Damascus. In the following excerpt, a friend sees an opened copy of Paul's Epistles lying in Augustine's house and this leads him to talk about his own conversion, realizing that Augustine's interests are close to his own:

Eventually, he told us of the time when he and three of his companions were at Treves. One afternoon, while the emperor was watching the games in the circus, they went out to stroll in the gardens near the city walls. They became separated into two groups, Ponticianus and one of the others remaining together while the other two went off by themselves. As they wandered on, the second pair came to a house which was the home of some servants of yours, men poor in spirit, to whom the kingdom of heaven belongs. In the house they found a book containing the life of Antony. One of them began to read it and was so fascinated and thrilled by the story that even before he had finished reading he conceived the idea of taking upon himself the same kind of life and abandoning his career in the world—both he and his friend were officials in the service of the state—in order to become your servant. All at once he was filled with the love of holiness. Angry with himself and full of remorse, he looked at his friend and said, "What do we hope to gain by all the efforts we make? What are we looking for? What is our purpose in serving the state? Can we hope for anything better at court than to be the emperor's friends? Even so, surely our position would be precarious and exposed to much danger? We shall meet it at every turn, only to meet another danger which is greater still. And how long is it to be before we reach it? But if I wish, I can become the friend of God at this very moment."

After saying this he turned back to the book, labouring under the pain of the new life that was taking birth in him. He read on and in his heart, where you alone could see, a change was taking place. His mind was being divested of the world, as could presently be seen. For while he was reading, his heart leaping and turning in his breast, a cry broke from him as he saw the better course and determined to take it. Your servant now, he said to his friend, "I have torn myself free from all our ambitions and have decided to serve God. From this very moment, here and now, I shall start to serve Him. If you will not follow my lead, do not stand in my way." The other answered that he would stand by his comrade, for such service was glorious and the reward was great.[11]

This interlocking pattern of conversions—Augustine's own is influenced by his friend's, and his friend's is influenced by that of Antony of the Desert—helps to explain why the *Confessions* is such an important document to the Middle Ages. As the life of Antony was for Augustine's friend, and indirectly for Augustine himself, so was Augustine's for subsequent history. Augustine's preeminence cannot be explained simply on the grounds that he was a better writer than his predecessors. In titling the work *Confessions*, Augustine makes use of several senses of the word "confess." Most obviously, he uses the word to mean "these are my deeds—I confess that I have committed them." He also uses the word to mean "to bear witness," a sense it developed in the early Church through the deeds of those who bore witness to Christ.

His conversion makes him a witness and model for the future that parallels the conversion of paganism to Christianity in the late Empire. In other words, Augustine symbolizes what happened to the whole culture of late antiquity. A passage that suggests the sense of crisis and change in the whole culture has been elaborated by the literary critic Erich Auerbach in his book *Mimesis*.[12] In Book 6, Augustine narrates the story of his friend Alypius, who undergoes a kind of conversion, although it is a reverse conversion—away from God and toward self. Yet like Augustine's own conversion, we are presented here with a radical turning, one that overwhelms the whole being. His friend is taken to the gladiatorial shows and is overwhelmed with bloodlust:

But he did not abandon his career in the world, for his parents would not allow him to forget it. He went to Rome ahead of me to study law and there, strange to relate, he became obsessed with an extraordinary craving for gladiatorial shows. At first he detested these displays and refused to attend them. But one day during the season for this cruel and bloodthirsty sport he happened to meet some friends and fellow-students returning from their dinner. In a friendly way they brushed aside his resistance and his stubborn protests and carried him off to the arena.

"You may drag me there bodily," he protested, "but do you imagine that you can make me watch the show and give my mind to it? I shall be there, but it will be just as if I were not present, and I shall prove myself stronger than you or the games."

He did not manage to deter them by what he said, and perhaps the very reason why they took him with them was to discover whether he would be as good as his word. When they arrived at the arena, the place was seething with the lust for cruelty. They found seats as best they could and Alypius shut his eyes tightly, determined to have nothing to do with these atrocities. If only he had closed his ears as well! For an incident in the fight drew a great roar from the crowd, and this thrilled him so deeply that he could not contain his curiosity. Whatever had caused the uproar, he was confident that, if he saw it, he would find it repulsive and remain master of himself. So he opened his eyes, and his soul was stabbed with a wound more deadly than any which the gladiator, whom he was so anxious to see, had received in his body. He fell, and fell more pitifully than the man whose fall had drawn that roar of excitement from the crowd. The din had pierced his ears and forced him to open his eyes, laying his soul open to receive the wound which struck it down. This was presumption, not courage. The weakness of his soul was in relying upon itself instead of trusting in you.

When he saw the blood, it was as though he had drunk a deep draught of savage passion. Instead of turning away, he fixed his eyes upon the scene and drank in all its frenzy, unaware of what he was doing. He revelled in the wickedness of the fighting and was drunk with the fascination of bloodshed. He was no longer the man who had come to the arena, but

simply one of the crowd which he had joined, a fit companion
for his friends who had brought him.

Need I say more? He watched and cheered and grew hot
with excitement, and when he left the arena, he carried away
with him a diseased mind which would leave him no peace until
he came back again, no longer simply together with the friends
who had first dragged him there, but at their head, leading new
sheep to the slaughter. Yet you stretched out your almighty,
ever merciful hand, O God, and rescued him from this madness.
You taught him to trust in you, not in himself. But this was
much later.[13]

As the passage shows, Alypius does not concede to the forces
of evil little by little; he concedes completely, violently. The
completeness of the conversion reminds the reader of other
examples of the same type of turning: Peter's abrupt denial of
Christ in the Gospels, or Saul's conversion on the road to
Damascus. The passage embodies a pattern that is the exact
inverse of the *Confessions* as a whole. But more is implied than
simply a contrast to Augustine's own life. The reader is told at
the end of the passage that Alypius eventually returns to God,
and his defeat was a necessary first step toward his conversion.
He learned not to rely on himself; the triumph of a true conversion can come only when one has learned to rely on God.
As Auerbach rightly observes, Alypius is not merely a random
example whose pride in his own self-sufficiency is being
crushed; he is also a type of the entire rationalistic and individualistic culture of classical antiquity, a culture whose insuffici-
ency is also proved in the movement of the passage. In classical
Roman literature, rational self-discipline and moderation is
the ideal. A self-reliant individual should be able to keep from
intemperance by an act of the will. Individual self-reliance and
the sufficiency of pagan culture are both overwhelmed in this
passage. The pattern of Augustine's conversion suggests where
sufficiency is to be found: "Our hearts find no peace until they
rest in you."[14]

One can also see the *Confessions* as a particularly sophisticated example of the genre of hagiography. The story of how a
holy man or woman lived was, as we have seen, one of the

most popular genres in the Middle Ages, and the pattern of the saint's conversion from a life of sin to a life of virtue was very often its core. A popular example of such a conversion story can be seen in the life of Saint Pelagia, as it is told in the thirteenth-century collection called *The Golden Legend*:

Pelagia was the first among the women of Antioch for her wealth, for her beauty of form, for the pretentious splendour of her attire, and for her lewdness of mind and body. One day she was walking through the city, so bedizened that naught could be seen upon her but gold and silver and precious stones, and that wherever she went, she filled the air with the scent of her perfumes; and a great retinue of maids and youths, likewise richly adorned, surrounded her. On her way she met a certain holy father named Veronus, the bishop of Heliopolis (which is now called Damietta); and when he saw her, he began to weep bitterly, because she was more concerned with pleasing the world than he with pleasing God. He fell face downward upon the pavement, beat his brow upon the ground, watered the earth with his tears, and said: "Most high God, have mercy on me as a sinner, for the adornment contrived by a sinful woman for one day surpasses my labours of a lifetime! She has tricked herself out with the greatest care to catch the eyes of earthlings, whereas I, proposing to please Thee, by my negligence have failed to do so!" Then he said to those that were with him: "In truth I say to you that God will bring this woman forth against us in the day of judgement, for that she has arrayed herself so studiously to give pleasure to earthly lovers, while we have given so little care to pleasing our heavenly Spouse."

When he was saying these and other like things, he fell into a sleep, and in a vision saw a black and evil-smelling dove flying about his head as he celebrated the Mass; but when he turned to dismiss the catechumens, the dove disappeared. Then, after the Mass, it returned, and when the bishop washed it in a vessel of water, it came forth clean and white, and flew to such a height that it could no longer be seen. When he awakened, he went to the church to preach; and Pelagia, who was present, was so moved with compunction that she sent a messenger to him with a letter, saying: "To the holy bishop, the servant of Christ, Pelagia, the servant of the Devil. If thou wilt show thyself a true disciple of Christ, Who, as I have heard, came down from heaven for sinners, do thou deign to receive me, a sinner in sooth, but one who repents of her sins."

Three days later she gathered all her possessions and gave them to the poor. Then, some days thereafter, she fled in the night, unknown to all, and came to the Mount of Olives, where she took the garb of a hermit and dwelt in a narrow cell, serving God with fasting and self-denial.[15]

As this example shows, the saint's life was a genre that provided both popular entertainment and moral instruction, combining a vivid, entertaining (and sometimes sensational) surface with a clear and explicit moral. This combination helps explain why the conversion of a prostitute—a theme that goes back to the figure of Mary Magdalen in the Gospels—was such a popular story in the twelfth and thirteenth centuries.

The actual conversion scene in the *Confessions*, though more sophisticated and less sensational, contains essentially the same movement as the story of Pelagia:

I had much to say to you, my God, not in these very words but in this strain: Lord will you never be content? Must we always taste your vengeance? Forget the long record of our sins. For I felt that I was still the captive of my sins, and in my misery I kept crying, "How long shall I go on saying 'Tomorrow, tomorrow'? Why not now? Why not make an end of my ugly sins at this moment?"

I was asking myself these questions, weeping all the while with the most bitter sorrow in my heart, when all at once I heard the singing voice of a child in a nearby house. Whether it was the voice of a boy or girl I cannot say, but again and again it repeated the refrain, "Take it and read, take it and read." At this time I looked up, thinking hard whether there was any kind of game in which children used to chant words like these, but I could not remember ever hearing them before. I stemmed the flood of tears and stood up, telling myself that this could only be a divine command to open my book of scripture and read the first passage on which my eyes should fall. For I had heard the story of Antony, and I remembered how he happened to go into a church while the gospel was being read and had taken it as a counsel addressed to himself when he heard the words "go home and sell all that belongs to you. Give it to the poor, and so the treasure you have shall be in heaven; then come back and follow me." By this divine pronouncement he had at once been converted to you.

So I hurried back to the place where Alypius was sitting, for when I stood up to move away I had put down the book containing Paul's epistles. I seized it and opened it, and in silence I read the first passage on which my eyes fell: "Not in revelling and drunkenness, not in lust and wantonness, not in quarrels and rivalries. Rather, arm yourselves with the Lord Jesus Christ; spend no more thought on nature and nature's appetites" [Rom: 13:13–14]. I had no wish to read more and no need to do so. For in an instant, as I came to the end of the sentence, it was as though the light of confidence flooded into my heart and all the darkness of doubt was dispelled.[16]

Both to show Augustine's method and his subsequent influence, this passage is of exceptional importance. The meaning of the passage once again makes sense only when the reader moves beneath the surface to the substance: Augustine is trying to present his conversion in the strongest possible terms, to show how radical and complete was the turning away from himself and toward God. Once this is understood, the surface narrative makes more sense: it is a means to an end. Is it likely that events happened exactly as Augustine describes them? Did he really hear the voice? Did he really open up to the right page of Scripture? All the details that are most likely to strain the credulity of the modern reader are in one sense the wrong questions, questions of surface and not substance. These dramatic details are presented in such striking and memorable form in order to bring out the important substantial meaning.

The influence of the passage, and implicitly the influence of the *Confessions* as a whole, can be seen by the frequency with which the passage is referred to in subsequent works. It is used in literature as an icon—a definitive emblem—of radical conversion. In the fourteenth century Dante uses the language of Augustine's conversion in Canto 5 of the *Inferno*, the canto of the lustful. When Francesca da Rimini describes how it came

about that she subjected reason to desire and made a radical
turn from God toward herself, the language she uses is the
language of conversion, almost identical to the language of
Augustine. She too learns from a book; as Augustine finds the
right passage in Scripture, she finds the right passage in the
story of Lancelot:

> We read one day for pastime of Lancelot, how love con-
> strained him. We were alone and had no misgiving. Many
> times that reading drew our eyes together and changed the
> color in our faces, but one point alone it was that mastered
> us; when we read that the longed-for smile was kissed by so
> great a lover, he who never shall be parted from me, all trem-
> bling, kissed my mouth. A Galeotto [pander] was the book and
> he that wrote it; that day we read in it no farther.[17]

Thus Dante's poem is enriched for readers who understand
the implications of what modern critics would call a literary
allusion. This kind of literary influence, however, is much more
central to medieval literary art than to modern. It is a language
similar to the "language" of visual arts of the Middle Ages,
where there is also a code, a standard iconography, that remains
constant for hundreds of years. Anyone seeing a picture of a
person with a halo in a medieval painting would know it was a
saint—anyone that is, who knows the code, who understands
the conventional language where halo stands for saint. It is
such works as the *Confessions* that provide the iconography—
the language—for subsequent writers. To a much greater extent than is true in modern literature, medieval poetic language
is a language that is already charged with external meaning, a
language, as in the example from Dante above, where stories
that seem to have such immediate local references, and which
seem to us to be "realistic," are very often also charged with
the literary energies of previous stories. Unless one reads "icon-
ographically," large areas of meaning will be lost in the reading of medieval literature.

The proper interpretation of Scripture is a major concern
of the *Confessions* as well as of *On Christian Doctrine*. In an
important section he treats the relationship between the Old

Martyrdom of St. Sebastian. 14th Century. Museo dell'Opera del Duomo, Florence. St. Sebastian is identified by arrows, a symbol of his martyrdom. As the arrows identify Sebastian, so also can other saints be identified by symbolic devices. Understanding medieval art and literature frequently depends upon the identification of such devices.

and New Testaments. Augustine had been misled by the interpretations of the Manichees, one of whose arguments against Christianity was the absurdity of much that is contained in the Old Testament. It was not until he met Ambrose that he learned another, "correct" interpretation of the Old Testament:

> This man of God received me like a father and, as a bishop, told me how glad he was that I had come. My heart warmed to him, not at first as a teacher of truth, which I had quite despaired of finding in your church, but simply as a man who showed me kindness. I listened attentively when he preached to the people, though not with the proper intention; for my purpose was to judge for myself whether the reports of his powers were accurate, or whether eloquence flowed from him more, or less, readily than I had been told. So while I paid the closest attention to the words he used, I was quite uninterested in the subject matter, and was even contemptuous of it. I was delighted with his charming delivery, but although he was a more learned speaker than Faustus, he had not the same soothing and gratifying manner. I am speaking only of his style for, as to content, there could be no comparison between the two. Faustus had lost his way among the fallacies of Manicheism, while Ambrose most surely taught the doctrine of salvation. But your mercy is unknown to sinners such as I was then, though, step by step, unwittingly, I was coming closer to it.
>
> For although I did not trouble to take what Ambrose said to heart, but only to listen to the manner in which he said it—this being the only paltry interest that remained to me now that I had lost hope that man could find the path that led to you—nevertheless his meaning, which I tried to ignore, found its way into my mind together with his words, which I admired so much. I could not keep the two apart, and while I was all ears to seize upon his eloquence, I also began to sense the truth of what he said, though only gradually. First of all it struck me that it was, after all, possible to vindicate his arguments. I began to believe that the Catholic faith, which I had thought impossible to defend against the objections of the Manichees, might fairly be maintained, especially since I had heard one passage after another in the Old Testament figuratively explained. These passages had been death to me when I took them literally, but once I had heard them explained in

their spiritual meaning I began to blame myself for my despair, at least in so far as it had led me to suppose that it was quite impossible to counter people who hated the law and the prophets.[18]

According to Augustine, then, the Old Testament must be explained figuratively rather than literally, a process beginning with the perception that it cannot be understood in isolation from the New, as the Manichees claimed. Events in the Old Testament are to be understood as prefigurations of events in the New, completing their meaning by their relationship to events in the New. Augustine, unlike Origen, never denies that these events have historical importance in themselves; nor does he reduce them simply to allegories (he states this explicitly in Book 17 of the *City of God*). Nevertheless, they do point forward to events in the New Testament. Thus the Fall of Man in the Garden of Eden anticipates the temptations of Christ in the desert; the killing of Abel by Cain is an anticipation of the betrayal of Christ; the sacrifice of Isaac by his father Abraham likewise anticipates the sacrifice of Christ; David, as king and prophet in the Old Testament, anticipates the fullness of kingship and prophecy of Christ in the New. In each of these Old Testament prefigurations, there is a similarity to the event prefigured, but equally important, there are differences. In the story of Abraham and Isaac, for example, Abraham, the father of the Hebrew people, is analogous to God the Father, as Isaac is analogous to Christ the Son. Since Abraham is not God, this is only an analogy. The significant difference in the story of Abraham and Isaac as a prefiguration of the sacrifice of Christ is that at the last moment God intervenes and Isaac is not sacrificed; yet Christ does sacrifice himself for the sins of humanity. Insofar as the events in the Old Testament are similar to the events they prefigure, the history of salvation can be seen as a timeless whole; what is to come is in some sense present in what has been. Insofar as these events are different from what they prefigure, however, they show that the events of salvation history are in linear progression from the Old Testament to the New, from the creation to the last judgment.

Manuscript Illumination. Winchester Bible. 12th Century. The Beatus initials—that is, the first letter of the first psalm, from *Beatus vir*, or "Happy The Man"—are illuminated so as to suggest the relationship between David, who in the Middle Ages was believed to be the sole author of the Psalms, and Christ. In the loops of the first "B" David rescues the sheep from the bear and from the lion. In the second "B" Christ, the Good Shepherd, expels an evil spirit from the boy possessed by a demon (Mark 9:17), and Christ delivers souls from hell. Thus events in the life of David (I Kings 17:34, 37) prefigure events in the life of Christ, and also suggest that the Psalms themselves can be read in terms of prefiguration. (*The Dean and Chapter of Winchester Cathedral*)

Much of medieval biblical commentary consists of explaining the relationship between the Old and New Testaments. These commentaries are sophisticated, subtle, and extremely important. As a way of thinking, their influence can be found everywhere. The structure of the great medieval play cycles of the fourteenth and fifteenth centuries, for example, is based on this figural relationship; the plays begin with the creation and move toward the last judgment. Each play can be seen both as part of a linear progression and as microcosm of the whole of salvation history. Countless examples in medieval art embody the relationship between Old and New. In the great stained glass windows at Chartres, for example, the lancet windows under the south rose show the four evangelists, each seated on the shoulders of one of the Old Testament prophets. A visual counterpart to Bernard of Chartres's image of "dwarfs seated on the shoulders of giants" quoted at the beginning of the book, they are smaller, but they are also able to see farther.

Augustine's theory of history also begins with his interpretation of Scripture. Although he saw all human history as the universal story of salvation, a continuum from creation to the last judgment, he saw divisions within this story, the seven ages of history:

> Now if the epochs of history are reckoned as "days," following the apparent temporal scheme of Scripture, this Sabbath period will emerge more clearly as the seventh of those epochs. The first "day" is the first period, from Adam to the Flood; the second from the Flood to Abraham. Those correspond not by equality in the passage of time, but in respect of the number of generations, for there are found to be ten generations in each of those periods.
>
> From that time, in the scheme of the evangelist Matthew, there are three epochs, which take us down to the coming of Christ; one from Abraham to David, a second from David to the Exile in Babylon, and the third extending to the coming of Christ in the flesh. Thus we have a total of five periods. We are now in the sixth epoch, but that cannot be measured by the number of generations, because it is said, "It is not for you to know the dates: the Father has decided those by his own authority." After this present age God will rest, as it were, on the seventh day, and he will cause us, who are the seventh day, to find our rest in him.[19]

The implications of this way of looking at history are extremely far reaching. Most obviously, it reinforces in yet another way the importance of the Bible as a document central to medieval thought (and Augustine as one of its definitive interpreters), providing as it does the pattern for all human history. Second, by linking the days of creation to the ages of history, Augustine shows in this passage that God's direct action in history is present throughout time, as well as in its beginnings at creation. The relationship between the seven days of creation and the seven ages of history was in fact frequently and systematically elaborated by medieval thinkers, including Isidore of Seville at the beginning of the seventh century, the Venerable Bede in the eighth, and Bonaventure in the thirteenth. Third, according to this scheme, the medieval Christian lives in an old world. Man is now living in the sixth epoch, which begins with the coming of Christ at the Incarnation. The second coming of Christ at the last judgment will usher in the seventh and last age, the age of rest. As the passage clearly indicates, Augustine himself denies that it is possible to know how long the present age will endure, believing that attempts to calculate the precise dates of the end are misdirected and sinful.

Nevertheless, the belief in a world that is old and about to pass away with the second coming of Christ is always implicit in medieval thought, emerging explicitly from time to time especially at moments of catastrophe, upheaval, and unrest. Reflection on the chaos of such times caused people to believe that the signs of the end of the world and the second coming, which were predicted in the book of Revelation, were being fulfilled in the present, including the all-out conflict between the forces of good and evil, the appearance of the Antichrist, and the appearance of various beasts such as the one described in Revelation 11:7. Apocalypticism, as it is called, was not necessarily the province of radical and extreme thinkers. From the fifth century to the end of the Middle Ages and beyond, apocalyptic expectations were an important element in European religious and political life; in literature these expectations influenced such diverse but "orthodox" works as the *Song of Roland*, Dante's *Divine Comedy*, and *Piers Plowman*. The more radical reformers at the end of the Middle Ages (and throughout the Reformation as well) tended by contrast to believe in millinarianism. Interpreting the text of Revelation 20:1–10, which refers to a period of a thousand years, they posited the establishment of a thousand-year kingdom of peace, plenty, and goodness on earth that would precede the end. (Augustine had argued especially vigorously against millenial expectations, asserting that Revelation 21:1–10 did not refer to a literal thousand-year period, but rather symbolized the establishment of Christ's Church on earth from Pentecost to the second coming.)

Since history was a part of God's plan for salvation, it is not surprising that for Augustine the purpose of historical writing was never merely to present factual information. History should instruct and edify people and advance them toward salvation. The following passage, referring to parts of the Old Testament, indicates what makes good and bad history.

And there may be other explanations and better ones, that could be advanced, which would be in harmony, with the faith of this City. I would be prepared to say the same about all the other interpretations which can be put forward on this topic. Different suggestions may be made; but they must be checked by the standard of the harmonious unity of the Catholic faith. No one ought to imagine, however, that this account was written for no purpose, or that we are to look solely for a reliable historical record without any allegorical meaning, or, conversely, that those events are entirely unhistorical, and the language purely symbolical, or that, whatever may be the nature of the story it has no connection with prophecy about the Church. Surely it is only a twisted mind that would maintain that books which have been so scrupulously preserved for thousands of years, which have been safeguarded by such a concern for so well-ordered a transmission, that such books were written without serious purpose, or that we should consult them simply for historical facts? . . .

Thus, after two of Noah's sons had been blessed, and the middle son cursed, from then onwards down to Abraham, the record is silent about any righteous men who worshipped God with true devotion; and that covers a period of more than a thousand years. I am not inclined to suppose that such people did not exist, but if they were all mentioned the narrative

would become tedious, and would be more notable for historical accuracy than for prophetic foresight. Accordingly, the
writer of these holy Scriptures (or rather the spirit of God
through his agency) is concerned with those events which not
only constitute a narrative of past history but also give a
prophecy of things to come, though only those things which
concern the City of God.[20]

As has been suggested, this Augustinian theory of history,
based largely on the biblical tradition, fused with classical modes
of historical thought to form the basis for medieval historical
writing.

In scope and size, *City of God* is the most important of
Augustine's works, the work that exerts the largest influence on
the thought of the Middle Ages. On the surface, the *City of
God* seems to be a work about politics and history. However,
nothing better illustrates the inadequacy of applying modern
categories to medieval patterns of thought than this classification. The *City of God* was written in response to an event that
shook the foundations of the world of Augustine's time: the
sack of Rome by the Goths in 410, an unprecedented event that
meant that the most visible sign of countinuity and permanence
in civilization was in chaos. Everyone naturally sought explanations for this catastrophe. The one advanced by pagan intel-
lectuals of the time was that Rome fell because of the influence
of the Christians; this would never have happened, they argued,
had its citizens adhered to the pagan virtues and the pagan
gods. Augustine, responding to this charge, turns it around;
Rome fell not because it was too Christian, but because it was
not Christian enough. Augustine sees in moral terms what our
age would classify as a political issue, a classification that remains true throughout the Middle Ages. Such an attitude is
expressed as late as the Hundred Years War, for example, eight
centuries after Augustine; when the tide of battle began to
turn against the English, some blamed the inability of their
nobles to live up to the ideals of Christian knighthood.

Augustine argues throughout the *City of God* that if one
looks closely at the kind of society that Rome really is, one

will realize that it is not a commonwealth—that is, it is not a community acting with the interest of its citizens at heart. If one sees the city for what it is, one will see that change, flux, and devastation are its very nature:

> If, then, the home, every man's haven in the storms of life, affords no solid security, what shall one say of the civil community? The bigger a city is, the fuller it is of legal battles, civil and criminal, and the more frequent are wild and bloody seditions or civil wars. Even when the frays are over, there is never any freedom from fear.[21]

Cities such as Rome, by nature unable to endure permanently, are at best means to an end. Our life on earth is a pilgrimage to the only lasting city, the heavenly Jerusalem. The earthly city can provide only a temporary home for men and women as they go about the business of journeying toward their permanent home. This is the dichotomy that structures the entire work: the City of God, the heavenly Jerusalem of love; or the city of man, the earthly city of pride. Augustine borrows the ideal of citizenship from Roman political theory to describe the inhabitants of the two cities. If one is content to be a citizen of the earthly city, then one can do no more than accept the transient pleasures which that city offers. By contrast those who desire citizenship in the City of God understands that they are pilgrims on earth, and that the earthly city can only be used, never enjoyed for itself.

Augustine examines this dichotomy from a number of interrelated perspectives. Perhaps the most important of these is the way in which this same dichotomy operates within each of us:

> I have already stated in the foregoing books that God chose to make a single individual the starting-point of all mankind, and that his purpose in this was that the human race should not merely be united in a society by natural likeness, but should also be bound together by a kind of tie of kinship to form a harmonious unity, linked together by the "bond of peace." And this race would not have been destined for death, in re-

spect of its individual members, had not the first two human beings (of whom one was created from no one, and the other from him) incurred death as the reward of disobedience: and so heinous was their sin that man's nature suffered a change for the worse; and bondage to sin and inevitable death was the legacy handed on to their posterity.

Now the reign of death has held mankind in such utter subjection that they would all be driven headlong into that second death, which has no ending, as their well-deserved punishment, if some were not rescued from it by the undeserved grace of God. The result is that although there are many great peoples throughout the world, living under different customs in religion and morality and distinguished by a complex variety of languages, arms, and dress, it is still true that there have come into being only two main divisions, as we may call them, in human society: and we are justified in following the lead of our Scriptures and calling them two cities. There is, in fact, one city of men who choose to live by the standard of the flesh, another of those who choose to live by the standard of the spirit. The citizens of each of these desire their own kind of peace, and when they achieve their aim, that is the kind of peace in which they live. We need to examine first what is meant by living "by the rule of the flesh" and "by the rule of the spirit."[22]

The macrocosm of the state is a reflection of the microcosm of the individual. Political truth is linked to more fundamental truths: historical truth, since the fall of Adam and Eve is ultimately responsible for the struggle between flesh and spirit in each person, which Augustine describes by means of the dichotomy between the city of man and the City of God; and moral truth, since Adam's fall can be seen in each one of us, sons and daughters of Adam within whom the battle between flesh and spirit is being fought. Augustine sees the same fundamental reality governing areas that today belong to widely different realms of experience: history, psychology, morality.

For an understanding of what the words "flesh" and "spirit" mean, one must read in a spiritual, that is to say allegorical, way. Augustine goes on to define the meaning of the word "flesh" using direct textual criticism, by analyzing Paul's letters:

Thus the inspired Scripture uses the term "flesh" in many ways, and it would be tedious to collect and scrutinize them all. Our present purpose is to track down the meaning of "living by the rule of the flesh" (which is clearly a bad thing, though the natural substance of flesh is not an evil in itself); and to enable us to achieve this purpose, let us carefully examine the passage in St. Paul's Epistle to the Galatians where he says, "It is obvious that the works of the flesh are: such things as fornication, impurity, lust, idolatry, sorcery, enmity, quarrelsomeness, jealousy, animosity, dissention, party intrigue, envy, drunkenness, drunken orgies, and so on. I warned you before, and I warn you again, that those who behave in such ways will never have a place in God's kingdom."

A consideration of this whole passage of Paul's letter sufficient for the requirements of the present topic will enable us to answer the question of what is meant by "living by the rule of the flesh." For among "the works of the flesh" which he said were obvious, and which he listed and condemned, we find not only those concerned with sensual pleasure, like fornication, impurity, lust, drunkenness and drunken orgies, but also those which show faults of the mind, which have nothing to do with sensual indulgence. For anyone can see that devotion to idols, sorcery, enmity, quarrelsomeness, jealousy, animosity, party intrigue, envy—all these are faults of the mind, not of the body. Indeed, it may happen that a man refrains from sensual indulgence because of devotion to an idol, or because of the erroneous teaching of some sect; and yet even then, though such a man seems to restrain and suppress his carnal desires, he is convicted, on the authority of the Apostle, of living by the rule of the flesh; and it is the very fact of his abstention from fleshly indulgence that proves that he is engaged in "the works of the flesh."

Can anyone feel enmity except in the mind? Would anyone, speaking to an enemy, real or supposed, express himself by saying, "Your flesh is set against me," rather than "Your mind"? Finally, if anyone heard of "carnalities" (if there is such a word) he would undoubtedly attribute them to the carnal nature; and by the same token, no one doubts that animosities are concerned with the *animus*, with the mind. It follows that the reason why "the teacher of the Gentiles in faith and truth" gives the name of "works of the flesh" to those and similar failings is simply that he intends the word "flesh" to be taken as meaning "man" by the "part for whole" figure of speech.[23]

It is a matter of seeing correctly, which for Augustine means seeing that God is the end toward which all things should move:

> I have already said that two cities, different and mutually opposed, owe their existence to the fact that some men live by the standard of the flesh, others by the standard of the spirit. It can now be seen that we may also put it in this way: that some live by man's standard, others by God's. St. Paul puts it very plainly when he says to the Corinthians, "For since there is jealousy and quarrelling among you, are you not of the flesh, following human standards in your behaviour?" Therefore, to behave according to human standards is the same as to be 'of the flesh', because by 'the flesh', a part of man, man himself is meant.[24]

There are also close connections in the *City of God* with Augustine's pilgrimage from himself to God, which is the subject of the *Confessions*. The concept suggests the relationship that should exist between the City of God, which is above, and the life that we lead here below. He talks of this relationship in describing the historical origins of the two cities, moving from Adam's fall to the story of Cain and Abel:

> Scripture tells us that Cain founded a city, whereas Abel, as a pilgrim, did not found one. For the City of the saints is up above, although it produces citizens here below, and in their persons the City is on pilgrimage until the time of its kingdom comes. At that time it will assemble all those citzens as they rise again in their bodies; and then they will be given the promised kingdom, where with their Prince, "the king of ages," they will reign, world without end.[25]

Throughout subsequent history, followers of Cain are all those who think the city of man is permanent, all those who live according to the flesh. Followers of Abel are those pilgrims who recognize, in the words of the late-fourteenth-century English poet, Geoffrey Chaucer, that "Here is no home, here is but wilderness."

Augustine's influence on political theory in the Middle Ages is no less than his influence in aesthetics. Deeply influenced by Paul, he argues that the subjugation of humans to other humans, including the formation of government itself, is a result of sin:

> Now, as our Lord above says, "Everyone who commits sin is sin's slave," (John 8:34) and that is why, though many devout men are slaves to unrighteous masters, yet the masters they serve are not themselves free men; "for when a man is conquered by another he is also bound as a slave to his conqueror" (2 Peter 2:19). And obviously it is a happier lot to be slave to a human being than to a lust; and, in fact, the most pitiless domination that devastates the hearts of men, is that exercised by this very lust for domination, to mention no others. However, in that order of peace in which men are subordinate to other men, humility is as salutary for the servants as pride is harmful to the masters. And yet by nature, in the condition in which God created man, no man is the slave either of man or of sin. But it remains true that slavery as a punishment is also ordained by that law which enjoins the preservation of the order of nature, and forbids its disturbance; in fact, if nothing had been done to contravene that law, there would have been nothing to require the discipline of slavery as a punishment.[26]

Humans would have no need for government had it not been for the fall; government is thus a kind of punishment. This becomes more explicit when Augustine talks of the rule of the wicked, as in the following passage on the infamous Emperor Nero:

> Yet even to men like this the power of domination is not given except by the providence of God, when he decides that man's condition deserves such masters. God's statement on this point is clear, when the divine Wisdom says, "It is through me that kings rule, and through me that tyrants possess the land."[27]

This generally negative attitude toward the state became especially influential in the eleventh century when the papacy asserted itself vis-à-vis the major secular power of the time. Papal apologists argued for the inherent superiority of the Church over the state on the basis that the state is a result of sin while the Church on earth is a representation of the heavenly city to which all should aspire. Only with the revival of Aristotle in the thirteenth century did this view face a serious philosophical challenge.

PART TWO

The Early Middle Ages

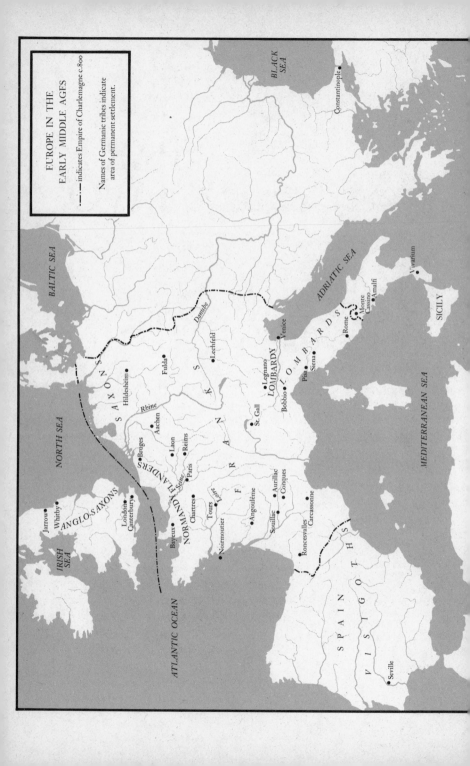

EUROPE IN THE
EARLY MIDDLE AGES

—·—·— indicates Empire of Charlemagne c.800

Names of Germanic tribes indicate
area of permanent settlement.

BLACK SEA

Constantinople

BALTIC SEA

ADRIATIC SEA

VIVARIUM

SICILY

NORTH SEA

Danube

Lechfeld

Venice

Monte Cassino

Amalfi

Rome

MEDITERRANEAN SEA

SAXONS

Fulda

Hildesheim

Rhine

Aachen

FRANKS

St. Gall

Legnano

LOMBARDY

Bobbio

Pisa

Siena

L O M B A R D S

IRISH SEA

Jarrow

Whitby

ANGLO-SAXONS

London

Canterbury

Bruges

FLANDERS

Laon

Reims

Seine

Paris

NORMANDY

Bayeux

Chartres

Tours

Loire

Noirmoutier

Angoulême

Souillac

Aurillac

Conques

Roncesvalles

Carcassonne

SPAIN

VISIGOTHS

VISIGOTHS

Seville

ATLANTIC OCEAN

CHAPTER FIVE

The Transition
from Ancient to Medieval

The first part of the book examined the Judaeo-Christian and Greco-Roman sources of medieval civilization and the beginnings of their contact and interaction, which took place within the context of the Roman Empire. However, only forty-six years after the death of Augustine, the Roman Empire no longer existed in the West, and the emerging Latin-Christian culture continued to develop without its strong institutional and psychological base. Furthermore, other cultural and social traditions began to interact with this Latin-Christian culture, especially those of the Germanic invaders but also those of the Celtic peoples, in particular the Irish. The transition from ancient Rome to the Middle Ages is one of the most important chapters in the development of Western civilization.

The End of the Roman Empire in the West

In his monumental *The Decline and Fall of the Roman Empire* (1776), Edward Gibbon declared that the second century A.D. was the best time to have been alive in all of history. Gibbon may have exaggerated, but there surely is much to support his position. An empire relatively free of foreign or domestic problems stretched from the wall of Hadrian—roughly the border between England and Scotland—to the Persian Gulf, encompassing the entire Mediterranean and parts of three continents. To those alive at the time, it may well have seemed that this huge empire and its way of life would last forever. Yet, beginning in 180, the Empire suffered through a century of political instability; and although in the next century the powerful Emperors Diocletian (r.284–305) and Constantine (r.312–37) carried out a reform, they failed to return the Empire to its unchallenged military position or its earlier quality of life. Following the death of Constantine, the story of the Empire in the West is one of almost constant defensive war and political disintegration, until in 476 its last emperor was deposed almost without notice or immediate impact.

In fact, the second century, Gibbon's age of prosperity and stability, was not without its unresolved problems. One of them was the method of imperial succession. In the first eighty years of that century, the emperors were all hand-picked successors of their sonless predecessors, all competent administrators and generals. However, Marcus Aurelius (d.180) chose to leave the Empire to his incompetent son Commodus, whose excesses, leading to his assassination, ushered in a century of political instability highlighted by frequent military coups. Moreover, Marcus Aurelius was forced to fight Germanic invaders along the Danube frontier; and though he was essentially successful, the Germans continued to exert pressure along that hard-to-defend northwestern border of the Empire until their large-scale migrations in the fourth century. A serious plague during Marcus Aurelius's reign had a significant impact on agriculture, trade, and the army. The resulting shortage of soldiers offered a temptation to the Germanic tribes to raid the Empire across the Rhine-Danube frontier, which was almost irresistable when combined with the fact that the Roman generals and their armies frequently left their border posts to march on Rome and claim the imperial title.

A century after Marcus Aurelius the Empire appeared to enter a new period of stability under Diocletian, a peasant who rose to power through the army. In his twenty-one-year reign, he was able to renew and reorder the Roman state. Because of the shortage of soldiers and the threat of generals desiring the imperial title, the army was reorganized; non-Roman citizens, including many Germans in the West, became its main element. The Empire was divided into two parts, with Diocletian and a "junior emperor" administering each of the two halves. To insure stability and production of necessary products, the emperor forced people to remain fixed in their professions and to train their children to succeed them; many farmers were required to remain on the land even if they could not make enough money to live. The Empire entered a new period in other ways as well: court ceremonies became more elaborate, and the emperor became a more remote figure, surrounded by eunuchs from the East. When he appeared in public, he wore jewel-encrusted clothes and shoes. Toward the end of his reign, Diocletian became convinced that Christianity was a serious obstacle to the consolidation of the Empire, and he carried out the great persecution described previously.

With the retirement of Diocletian in 305 came a struggle to determine his successor. In the West, the winner was decided at the Battle of Milvian Bridge in 312; it was Constantine. Although best known for his conversion to Christianity, he is also an important figure in the political history of the Empire, retaining Diocletian's reforms and making major changes in the structure of the army. Furthermore, he decided to build a splendid new city in the East in his own honor; choosing the site of the old Greek city of Byzantium near the entrance to the Black Sea, he erected Constantinople. By the end of the century, it had become the administrative capital of the Empire in the East, a new and a Christian Rome.

After the death of Constantine, there were no long periods of peace or stability in the Empire. It was invaded continuously, especially by the Germans. One of the most significant events of the fourth century was the showdown between the Germanic Goths and the imperial forces at Adrianople in modern Bulgaria in 378. The Emperor Valens was killed, and after the battle the Goths and later other Germanic tribes were pretty much able to live and loot within the borders of the Empire at will.

From Adrianople until the extinction of the western part of the Empire in 476, the German invasions and the brief but important invasion by the Huns under their brilliant leader Attila dominate imperial history. During this period, the city of Rome was sacked by Goths and Vandals; the Western emperors were often little more than puppets of German generals; violence and rapine were practiced by both German and Roman armies; and the Germans hired by Rome to fight other Germans often turned against their employers. It was a military, political, economic, and religious (recall that the Germans were either Arian Christians or pagans) crisis that the Empire could not solve. By the end of the fifth century, the Roman Empire existed only as an idea and a memory in the West. And although the sixth-century emperor in Constantinople, Justinian (r.527–65), tried to reconstitute the Roman Empire, gaining control of much of the western Mediterranean, his conquests were neither complete nor permanent. Byzantine power in the West eroded steadily after his death, and by 754 Byzantine territory in the West consisted only of parts of southern Italy and Sicily. Despite the fact that Byzantium retained a foothold in Italy until 1071, it played only a nominal role in the politics of the West after the mid-eighth century.

However, this does not mean that Byzantine civilization ceased to be important to the West culturally. In the tenth century, a Byzantine princess was regent for her son, the Holy Roman Emperor Otto III; and Byzantine craftsmen were major contributors to the cultural revival there known as the Ottonian Renaissance. Eleventh- and twelfth-century Byzantine artists executed magnificent mosaics in Sicily and Venice. Much thirteenth-century Italian painting is correctly described as Byzantine. A translation of the complete works of Aristotle was accomplished by Latin scholars working with Byzantine manuscripts in Constantinople in the mid-thirteenth century. These influences of East upon West, by no means complete, are representative of the almost continuous interaction and cross-fertilization between Byzantine East and Latin West.

Germanic Culture and Society

Many Germanic tribes appear and disappear in the records of the invasions; the most important are those that were the successors of the Romans as the rulers of the West. In the fifth century, the Vandals, who were Arian Christians, occupied Latin-speaking North Africa and came in constant conflict with its Catholic population. One should recall that Augustine's city of Hippo was under Vandal attack at the time of his death. The Byzantine Emperor Justinian defeated the Vandals, his first military campaign in the West. However, Byzantine rule lasted only about a century. By 700, the armies of Islam had dispossessed the Eastern Empire of North Africa; this conquest was permanent, bringing it into a cultural and religious sphere quite different from its earlier Roman-Christian heritage.

Most of the Iberian Peninsula came under the control of the Visigoths, Arian Christians who became Catholic in 587, probably for political reasons. Despite a reasonably high level of prosperity and cultural development in the seventh century, the kingdom fell quite rapidly to Moslem invaders from across the Mediterranean in 711–13. For three hundred years, all but small, isolated parts of the peninsula were Moslem. In the eleventh century, these surviving Christian regions took the offensive against Islam. This so-called *Reconquista* was successful in wresting most of the peninsula away from the Moslems within a century, although it was completed only with the conquest of Granada, the last Moslem stronghold, in 1492.

Britain, on the periphery of the Roman Empire, was abandoned in 410 when all available soldiers were needed closer to the heart of the Empire. Its Roman-Christian heritage was all but erased by the invasions, which had already begun before Roman withdrawal. Angles, Saxons, and Jutes (pagan Germanic tribes from the southern shore of the North Sea) raided and began to settle in England, eventually conquering all but the western and northern extremities of Britain. The Anglo-Saxons did not subdue the romanized Celtic Christian population easily, however. About 500, a Celtic military victory slowed the Anglo-Saxon conquest of Britain by perhaps as much as fifty years. Centuries later, stories of one of the Celtic leaders traditionally called King Arthur, mixed with Celtic folklore, became the primary source for authors of the romance (see ch. 9). The Anglo-Saxons did eventually defeat the Celtic Britons, and many of them fled to Cornwall and Wales where Christianity and their Celtic heritage and language survived. Modern Welsh is a direct descendant of the language of these Britons.

The Franks, who originally entered the Empire in the pay of Rome, came to rule the northern part of Gaul before 500. By the middle of the sixth century, they had wrested control of southwestern Gaul from the Visigoths and southeastern Gaul from the Burgundians, thus ruling what is now roughly France plus Germany west of the Rhine. The Franks were pagan until the baptism of their able King Clovis (d.511) as a Catholic. Although the Frankish kingdom suffered from interminable civil wars, often splitting into virtually independent kingdoms upon the death of a king, the dynasty of Clovis, the Merovingian dynasty, ruled at least in name until 751. From the mid-seventh century on, however, Merovingian kings were almost without exception feeble in both mind and body; and the rule of the kingdom soon passed de facto to the family that had made itself the heredity mayors of the palace, later called the Carolingians. It was the Carolingian mayor of the palace, Charles Martel, who defeated the Moslems at the important battle of Tours/Poitiers in 732–33; his son Pepin (whose son was Charlemagne), with papal approval, took the crown from the Merovingians in 751.

Odoacer, the German general who deposed the last Roman

emperor in Italy in 476, belonged to a small tribe. In 493, he was defeated in battle by Theodoric the Ostrogoth (d.526), who, despite his Arian Christianity, had the support of the Catholic emperors in Constantinople. Theodoric's court was centered in Ravenna, the last imperial capital in the West, and contained men of great genius, including Boethius and Cassiodorus. However, Ostrogothic rule in Italy did not long survive Theodoric; Justinian, investing enormous resources, conquered Italy through a series of destructive wars that severely damaged Italy's central economic and cultural position in the world. Despite Justinian's efforts, Byzantine rule lasted no longer than had the Ostrogothic; in 568, three years after his death, the Arian Lombards, invading Italy from the North, took virtually all of northern and central Italy save Ravenna and Rome. These Lombards, who eventually became Catholic while nevertheless remaining political enemies of both the pope and the Byzantine Empire, ruled most of Italy until 774, when Charlemagne took their iron crown for himself.

Not all Germans moved into the Roman Empire. To the east of the Rhine were Germanic peoples such as the Saxons and the Bavarians. They remained pagan until the eighth century when missionary activity in the first half of the century and Charlemagne's armies in the second brought Christianity and the culture that accompanied it. To the north, in Scandinavia, were other Germanic people, who remained pagan until some of them (the Vikings) invaded and settled in Britain and the Frankish kingdom, where they accepted Christianity in the ninth and tenth centuries. Shortly thereafter, missionaries brought Christianity to the inhabitants of Scandinavia itself.

The culture and society of the Germans and the ideas and institutions they brought with them into the Roman Empire are in some ways more difficult to describe with precision than the process of migration. Historians are hampered by the fact that Germanic cultures was not a written culture until it came into contact with the Roman world, and more especially with Christianity. Thus the earliest written records of the Germans come from Roman authors. As early as the second century A.D., they were described by the great Roman historian Tacitus.

Although he was more interested in teaching his own society moral lessons than objectively describing German customs and although he perceived the Germans in Roman terms, his descriptions are nonetheless useful. Here his comments describe the military character of Germanic society:

> To abandon your shield is the basest of crimes; nor may a man thus disgraced be present at the sacred rites, or enter their council; many, indeed, after escaping from battle, have ended their infamy with the halter.[1]

> They transact no public or private business without being armed. It is not, however, usual for anyone to wear arms till the state has recognized his power to use them. Then in the presence of the council, one of the chiefs, or the young man's father, or some kinsman, equips him with a shield and a spear.[2]

Tacitus also explains the personal relationship between a chieftain and his warriors:

> When they go into battle, it is a disgrace for a chief to be surpassed in valor, a disgrace for his followers not to equal the valor of the chief. And it is an infamy and a reproach for life to have survived the chief, and returned from the field. To defend, to protect him, to ascribe one's own brave deeds to his renown is the height of loyalty. The chief fights for victory; his vassals fight for their chief.[3]

This martial quality and sense of personal loyalty between chief and vassal became important elements of medieval society, elements vital to a proper understanding of such important literary works as *Beowulf* and the *Song of Roland* and to the kinds of relationships usually described as feudal.

The military character of Germanic society posed the same difficult problem of cultural assimilation that the conversion of Constantine had earlier, for Christianity in its origins was essentially pacifist. As late as the fourth century the most popular saints included men who refused to fight in the army or who left the military in order to pursue lives of holiness (for example, Saint Sebastian and Saint Martin of Tours). Although Ambrose condoned violence and Augustine developed a theory of the just war, the Church hardly glorified violence to the extent that the Germans did. When Germans like Clovis accepted Christianity, they saw Christ not as the Prince of Peace but as a warrior god; that is, to accept him in terms they understood, they interpreted his life and teachings in ways different from their original intent. During the time of the Germanic kingdoms, legends of warrior saints such as Saint George were created. Yet though the Church tolerated and sometimes even encouraged violence, as late as the tenth and eleventh centuries it organized peace movements to try to diminish the violence within Europe. Only in the twelfth century, the heyday of the Crusades, did the glorification of violence become a part of the Catholic tradition.

Germanic law differed in many essentials from Roman law. In particular, Germanic law was personal while Roman law was territorial. (A Lombard was judged by Lombard law no matter where he was—*who* a person was determined the law which governed him; a person within the boundaries of the Roman Empire was subject to Roman law no matter what ethnic group he belonged to—*where* a person was determined what law governed him.) The surviving law codes of the Germans—the codification and publication of law was itself a Roman borrowing, as was the Latin in which they were written—contain elements of both personality and territoriality, but ultimately the Roman principle won out.

The idea of the state was an integral part of Roman law and Roman political philosophy; the Germans however had no conception of the state. A Germanic king did not perceive himself as the ruler of all the people within a clearly defined territory but rather as the leader of a group of free warriors. The land a king controlled was treated as personal property and usually divided among his male heirs. It was centuries before the Roman idea of the state replaced the Germanic idea of kingship.

Germanic law allowed bloodfeuds; it permitted an injured family to seek revenge against the offender's family. Obviously, this was a custom that led to a great deal of violence, often escalating to become a serious problem of tribal unity and even survival. To mitigate this problem, the Germanic tribes, borrowing from the Roman system of fining a person for an offense, developed the *wergild*, the money value of a person that was to be paid to the injured family. The following selections from Rothair's Edict of 643, the earliest surviving laws of the Lombards, illustrates the use of the *wergild* alongside a more purely Roman system of fines:

> 49.   On cutting off noses. He who cuts off another man's nose shall pay half of that one's wergild as composition.
>
> 50.   On cutting off lips. He who cuts off another man's lip shall pay sixteen soldi as composition [compensation]. And if one, two or three teeth are thereby exposed, he shall pay twenty soldi as composition.[4]

Not every person's *wergild* was the same, as is clear from a list of penalties for murder in the early sixth-century Burgundian Code:

> Then the guilty party shall be compelled to pay to the relatives of the person killed half his wergild according to the status of the person: that is, if he shall have killed a noble of the highest class, we decree that the payment be set at one hundred fifty soldi, i.e., half his wergild; if a person of the middle class, one hundred soldi; if a person of the lowest class, seventy-five soldi.[5]

Germanic law was localized, putting much of the responsibility for justice on small groups—the family and the neighborhood in particular—to report crimes and to swear to a person's innocence. Out of this Germanic sense of local responsibility eventually come both the grand jury, a body to inquire and gather evidence, and the trial jury, a body to determine innocence and guilt. Both developed in medieval England.

On occasion, Germanic law called for trial by combat to determine guilt, or even trial by ordeal; for example, a suspect's guilt or innocence would be determined by requiring the suspect to hold a bar of red-hot iron until it burned the hand. If the burn healed, the person was innocent; if it did not, the person was guilty. These primitive methods of judgment survived in some parts of Europe until the thirteenth century, a time when Roman law was once again being studied. In literature, one finds trial by combat in the twelfth-century *Song of Roland.*

When the Germans entered the Empire, they not only brought their political and social institutions but also their languages and cultures. In areas where Roman influence remained the greatest—present-day Italy, France, and Spain—vernacular languages developed from Latin, although they were not unaffected by Germanic tongues. But in England, Germany, and Scandinavia the vernacular languages were and indeed still are Germanic. Thus the very medium of thought and expression in a large part of Europe in the Middle Ages—especially the later Middle Ages, when vernacular literature flourished—came from the Germans. In art, Germanic elements of style, especially the tendency toward abstraction, exerted a strong influence throughout the Middle Ages, the abstract quality of early medieval art contrasting with the more realistic art of the Roman Empire. The Germanic style, which is evident in such striking interlace designs as the treasure from the Anglo-Saxon Sutton Hoo burial ship, later blended with elements from the Celtic and classical traditions to produce much great manuscript illumination and sculpture of the Middle Ages. Stories from the heroic Germanic past, its gods and heroes, are another important transmission. These stories too blended with other traditions, as in the fruitful synthesis of pagan and Christian in Old English poetry, seen in such poems as *Beowulf*, "The Dream of the Rood," "The Wanderer," and "The Seafarer." Stories from Germanic mythology also became incorporated into such Christian literary forms as saints' lives. Even the modern English names for the days of the week come from Germanic mythology.

The Germanic peoples looked to their past to find a model for the way things should be. They believed that law, for example, had been perfect in their past but was obscure and corrupt in the present. Thus good law was to be discovered, not made. Although they sometimes allowed for new laws to be created by giving them a past, it was not until the revival of Roman law in the twelfth and thirteenth centuries that new laws could consciously be legislated. The idea that one had to find truth by looking to the past and stripping away modern accretions found resonances in both the Christian and classical traditions, in which people looked back to the Garden of Eden or the Golden Age. These three traditions thus reinforced one another in the Middle Ages. The decline of the world since the golden days is a concept of singular importance in medieval literature and historiography.

The collapse of the Roman Empire in the West ushered in a period of violence and chaos, a decline of culture and literacy, as well as other woes. The following text from a letter dated 473 of Sidonius Apollinaris, a Roman living in Gaul, suggests the experience of the Germanic invasions:

> There is a rumor that the Goths have moved their camp into Roman soil; we luckless Arvernians are always the gateway to such incursions, for we kindle our enemies' hatred in a special degree; the reason is, that their failure so far to make the channel of the Loire the boundary of their territories between the Atlantic and the Rhone is due, with Christ's help, solely to the barrier which we interpose. As for the surrounding country, its whole length and breadth has long since been swallowed up by the insatiate aggression of that threatening power. But we have little confidence that our reckless and dangerous courage will be supported by our hideously charred walls, our palisades of rotting stakes, our battlements worn by the breasts of many a sentinel; our only comfort is in the aid of the Rogations [prayers for deliverance said in procession] which we introduced on your advice.[6]

Sidonius's despair of victory without supernatural intervention is eloquent testimony to the effect of the invasions on the Roman population.

Perhaps the most famous statement of political and cultural decline following the destruction of the Roman Empire in the

West comes from the late sixth-century historian Gregory of Tours, himself of Roman lineage:

> A great many things keep happening, some of them good, some of them bad. The inhabitants of different countries keep quarreling fiercely with each other and kings go on losing their temper in the most furious way. Our churches are attacked by heretics and then protected by the Catholics; the faith of Christ burns bright in many men, but it remains lukewarm in others; no sooner are the church-buildings endowed by the faithful than they are stripped bare again by those who have no faith. However, no writer has come to the fore who has been sufficiently skilled in setting things down in an orderly fashion to be able to describe these events in prose or verse. In fact in the towns of Gaul the writing of literature has declined to the point where it has virtually disappeared altogether. Many people have complained about this, not once but time and time again. "What a poor period this is!" they have been heard to to say. "If among all our people there is not one man to be found who can write a book about what is happening today, the pursuit of letters is really dead in us!" I have often thought about these complaints and others like them. I have written this work to keep alive the memory of those dead and gone, and to bring them to the notice of future generations. My style is not very polished, and I have had to devote much of my space to the quarrels between the wicked and the righteous.[7]

Gregory vividly describes one example of the cruelty of the age, in this case inflicted upon the Franks by another Germanic tribe called the Thuringians:

> Hostages were exchanged and our Franks were ready to make peace with them. The Thuringians murdered the hostages in all sorts of different ways. They attacked our fellow-countrymen and stole their possessions. They hung our young men up to die in the trees by the muscles of their thighs. They put more than two hundred of our young women to death in the most barbarous way: they tied their arms round the necks of their horses, stampeded these animals in all directions by prodding them with goads, and so tore the girls to pieces; or else they stretched them out over the ruts of their roads, attached

their arms and legs to the ground with stakes, and then drove
heavily-laden carts over them again and again, until their bones
were all broken and their bodies could be thrown out for the
dogs and birds to feed on.[8]

As stark as the story of violence and destruction is, it is
equally important to realize that the Germanic kings were not
seeking to destroy Roman civilization so much as to make it
their own. Of course their perception of the Roman tradition
was through Germanic eyes; nevertheless, much of the change
that took place with the coming of the Germans was not intended to be destructive. For example, Clovis, the first Christian king of the Franks, sought to legitimize his authority by
receiving Roman titles from the emperor in Constantinople
and imitating imperial largesse:

> Letters reached Clovis from the Emperor Anastasius [of Con-
> stantinople] to confer the consulate on him. In St. Martin's
> church he stood clad in a purple tunic [the imperial color] and
> the military mantle, and he crowned himself with a diadem. He
> then rode out on his horse and with his own hand showered
> gold and silver coins among the people present all the way
> from the doorway of St. Martin's church to Tours cathedral.
> From that day on he was called Consul or Augustus.[9]

In the sixth century, the Merovingians created a myth that
traced the origins of the Franks back to Troy, giving themselves a common and thus equal ancestry with the Romans. In
the following text, the author makes clear Theodoric the
Ostrogoth's attempt to continue the traditions of Rome:

> He so governed two races at the same time, Romans and Goths,
> that although he himself was of the Arian sect, he nevertheless
> made no assault on the Catholic religion; he gave games in the
> circus and the amphitheatre, so that even by the Romans he
> was called a Trajan or a Valentinian, whose times he took as a
> model; and by the Goths, because of his edict, in which he es-
> tablished justice, he was judged to be in all respects their best
> king. Military service for the Romans he kept on the same

footing as under the emperors. He was generous with gifts and the distribution of grain, and although he had found the public treasury nothing but a haystack, by his efforts it was restored and made rich.[10]

One of the most important steps in the process of the integration of the Germans with those whom they conquered was their acceptance of orthodox Christianity. The change from Arianism to Catholicism was a turning point in the history of both the Visigoths and the Lombards, but even more important to the history of Europe were the conversions of the Franks and the Anglo-Saxons from paganism to Catholic Christianity. The conversion of the Franks was initiated by the conversion of their King Clovis, a story Gregory of Tours deliberately parallels to Constantine's conversion nearly two centuries earlier:

Finally war broke out against the Alamanni and in this conflict he [Clovis] was forced by necessity to accept what he had refused of his own free will. It so turned out that when the two armies met on the battlefield there was great slaughter and the troops of Clovis were rapidly being annihilated. He raised his eyes to heaven when he saw this, felt compunction in his heart and was moved to tears. "Jesus Christ," he said, "you who Clotild [Clovis's wife] maintains to be the Son of the living God, you who deign to give help to those in travail and victory to those who trust in you, in faith I beg the glory of your help. If you will give me victory over my enemies, and if I may have evidence of that miraculous power which the people dedicated to your name say that they have experienced, then I will believe in you and I will be baptized in your name. I have called upon my own gods, but, as I see only too clearly, they have no intention of helping me. I therefore cannot believe that they possess any power, for they do not come to the assistance of those who trust in them. I now call upon you. I want to believe in you, but I must first be saved from my enemies." Even as he said this the Alamanni turned their backs and began to run away. . . .

King Clovis asked that he might be baptized first by the Bishop [Remigius]. Like some new Constantine he stepped forward to the baptismal pool, ready to wash away the sores of his old leprosy and to be cleansed in flowing water from the sordid stains which he had borne so long. As he advanced for his baptism, the holy man of God addressed him in these pregnant words: "Bow your head in meekness, Sicamber. Worship what you have burnt, burn what you have been wont to worship."[11]

The mention of leprosy refers to a legend that Constantine was miraculously cured of the disease upon his baptism. Gregory's description of Clovis's baptism shows how ritual and splendor helped convert the Germans to Christianity:

The public squares were draped with coloured cloths, the churches were adorned with white hangings, the baptistry was prepared, sticks of incense gave off clouds of perfume, sweet-smelling candles gleamed bright and the holy place of baptism was filled with divine fragrance.[12]

The conversion of Clovis meant the conversion of the Franks: three thousand of Clovis's warriors were baptized the same day. The Roman population that the Franks governed was Christian, and thus the Franks had long been in contact with Christianity. But there was little or no instruction in the faith for most Franks; there were just mass baptisms. Therefore, their formal conversion did not immediately make the Franks thoroughly Christian; nor did it make them forsake their old gods, their sacred places, or their magic.

Paganism continued to exist in practice if not in name for centuries, especially in the countryside (in fact, the word "pagan" comes from the Latin word meaning "one who lives in the country"). Gradually, some elements of paganism became Christianized: pagan stories were given Christian interpretations; pagan holy places became the sites of Christian churches and shrines; many of the pagan divinities who were implored for protection were replaced by saints, some wholly ficticious, who became protectors in their place.

If this amalgamation of pagan and Christian occurred more or less haphazardly in the kingdom of the Franks, it was given a theoretical basis and papal approbation by Gregory the Great in a letter of 601 that he addressed to the missionaries he had sent to convert the Anglo-Saxons:

[We] have come to the conclusion that the temples of the idols among that people should on no account be destroyed. The idols are to be destroyed, but the temples themselves are to be aspersed with holy water, altars set up in them, and relics deposited there. For if these temples are well-built, they must be purified from the worship of demons and dedicated to the service of the true God. In this way, we hope that the people, seeing that their temples are not destroyed, may abandon their error and, flocking more readily to their accustomed resorts, may come to know and adore the true God. And since they have a custom of sacrificing many oxen to demons, let some other solemnity be substituted in its place, such as a day of Dedication or the Festivals of the holy martyrs whose relics are enshrined there. On such occasions they might well construct shelters of boughs for themselves around the churches that were once temples, and celebrate the solemnity with devout feasting. They are no longer to sacrifice beasts to the Devil, but they may kill them for food to the praise of God, and give thanks to the Giver of all gifts for the plenty they enjoy. If the people are allowed some worldly pleasures in this way, they will more readily come to desire the joys of the spirit. For it is certainly impossible to eradicate all errors from obstinate minds at one stroke, and whoever wishes to climb to a mountain top climbs gradually step by step, and not in one leap. It was in this way that the Lord revealed Himself to the Israelite people in Egypt, permitting the sacrifices formerly offered to the Devil to be offered thenceforward to Himself instead. So He bade them sacrifice beasts to Him, so that, once they became enlightened, they might abandon one element of sacrifice and retain another. For, while they were to offer the same beasts as before, they were to offer them to God instead of to idols, so that they would no longer be offering the same sacrifices.[13]

It would be difficult to overestimate the importance of this statement. We have already observed how non-Christian ideas of Greco-Roman culture were adapted to Christian use and how this practice was justified by men like Jerome and Augustine, but theirs was a rather different situation. Greco-Roman culture was the highly sophisticated culture of the Roman Empire where Christianity originated and grew. Gregory here allows customs and practices from a foreign, non-literate culture to be adapted to Christian use. This clearly aided further missionary activity to the Germans and later to non-Germanic peoples as well: even in the sixteenth century, Catholic missionaries to America and India based their work on the theory of conversion enunciated by Gregory almost a millenium earlier. Gregory's instructions also insured the survival of elements of pagan culture that would have otherwise been neglected or destroyed. A poem such as *Beowulf* probably survived because a pagan story had been Christianized. The traditional yule log ceremony still practiced in churches in England was originally a pagan Germanic custom.

Missionaries encountering Anglo-Saxon customs associated with purification after childbirth sent this question back to Pope Gregory shortly after their arrival: "How soon after childbirth may she [a mother] enter churches?"[14] The question itself is instructive, showing that the problems they encountered were as much concerned with daily activities and common practices as with matters of theology. Gregory's answer is also instructive:

> As to the interval that must elapse after childbirth before a woman may enter church, you are familiar with the Old Testament rule: that is, for a male child thirty-three days and for a female, sixty-six. But this is to be understood as an allegory, for were a woman to enter church and return thanks in the very hour of her delivery, she would do nothing wrong.[15]

One discovers from this text how the allegorical method of scriptural exegesis made popular in the West by Augustine gives someone like Gregory the opportunity to deal effectively and creatively with problems that arose in a world quite different from that of Palestine in biblical times and yet remain faithful to the belief in the inerrancy of Scripture.

The writings of the Venerable Bede (673–735), our main source for the conversion of England, show that the missionaries to England made use of art and ritual much as Remigius had done a hundred years earlier with Clovis and the Franks:

> But the monks were endowed with power from God, not from the Devil, and approached the king carrying a silver cross as their standard and the likeness of our Lord and Saviour painted on a board. First of all they offered prayer to God, singing a litany for the eternal salvation both of themselves and of those to whom and for whose sake they had come.[16]

Only after this ceremony did the missionaries preach the word of God to King Ethelbert of Kent.

Neither the dedication of missionaries nor the wisdom of Gregory the Great was sufficient to ensure immediate conversion. Ethelbert of Kent refused to force his subjects to become Christians. Traditional societies do not easily change their religion. Moreover, the Anglo-Saxon kingdoms often reverted to paganism after the death of a Christian king or in response to a disaster such as loss in battle or a bad crop. In fact, when Ethelbert of Kent died, he was succeeded by his pagan son. Gradually over the course of the seventh century, however, England became a Christian land. One reason for the ultimate success of Christianity was the continuing close link between the papacy and England. Until the Norman conquest in 1066, England's chief contact with the continent was not across the England Channel with the Frankish kingdom but directly with Rome. And even until the Protestant Reformation in the sixteenth century, there continued to be a special relationship between England and the papacy.

The papacy sent more than men to England; it also sent the material necessary to establish Christianity there:

> They [envoys from Rome] brought with them everything necessary for the worship and service of the Church, including sacred vessels, altar coverings, church ornaments, vestments for priests and clergy, relics of the holy Apostles and martyrs, and many books.[17]

It was important for the English church to learn not only the language of Christianity but also the form of the liturgy. Thus, a famous Roman cantor was sent to England:

> Benedict received Abbot John and conducted him to Britain, where he was to teach his monks the chant for the liturgical year as it was sung at Saint Peter's, Rome. In accordance with the Pope's instructions, Abbot John taught the cantors of the monastery the theory and practice of singing and reading aloud, and he put into writing all that was necessary for the proper observance of festivals throughout the year. This document is still preserved in this monastery, and many copies have been made for other places. John's instruction was not limited to the brethren of this monastery alone; for men who were proficient singers came from nearly all the monasteries of the province to hear him, and he received many invitations to teach elsewhere.[18]

The papacy continued to provide learned leaders for the infant English church:

> Theodore of Tarsus [c.602–90] was the first archbishop whom the entire Church of the English obeyed, and since, as I have observed, both he and Hadrian were men of learning both in sacred and in secular literature, they attracted a large number of students, into whose minds they poured the waters of wholesome knowledge day by day. In addition to instructing them in the holy Scriptures, they also taught their pupils poetry, astronomy, and the calculation of the church calendar. In proof of this, some of their students still alive today are as proficient in Latin and Greek as in their native tongue.[19]

With the coming of Christianity to England came Latin and to some extent even Greek culture. The Church established schools and libraries, giving England a sophisticated written culture. By the eighth century, English schools were probably the best in Europe, producing the Venerable Bede, arguably the greatest historian of the Middle Ages and the most learned man in Europe at the time, and Alcuin, chief architect of educational reform on the continent under Charlemagne.

England developed a thriving Latin culture; unlike other

Germanic kingdoms it also developed a written vernacular. The missionaries had brought not only a religion and a culture but also the vehicle for the transmission of the existing traditions of the Anglo-Saxons. The earliest surviving text in Anglo-Saxon is the laws of Ethelbert of Kent. Bede reproduces in his history a poem of Caedmon in Anglo-Saxon dating from 680. This written vernacular culture, flourishing throughout the Anglo-Saxon period, produced such poems as *Beowulf* and the "Dream of the Rood" and translations of such seminal Latin works as Boethius's *Consolation of Philosophy* and Gregory the Great's *Pastoral Care.*

Anglo-Saxon Christianity did not develop solely from the Roman tradition. Irish monks had arrived in the north of Britain in 565 with their own distinct form of Christianity, the product of a unique cultural synthesis. In the fifth century, Ireland, never a part of the Roman Empire, embraced Christianity, as legend has it thanks to the efforts of Saint Patrick. But Christianity in Ireland developed in some ways quite differently from Christianity inside the territory of the Empire. First, Latin, never spoken in Ireland, had to be learned in order to understand Christian culture (the Bible, the liturgy, the writings of the Fathers). Since Latin was always a scholarly language there, it was not subject to change as it was in those areas under the control of the Germans. Latin thus remained most classical in a part of the world that had never been subject to Rome. Second, Ireland, organized by clans, had no cities; thus there were no natural centers to establish bishops. Consequently, Ireland came to be organized monastically rather than episcopally, and bishops there were usually subordinate to their abbots. Third, a zealous and somewhat extreme asceticism was practiced by the Irish monks.

One peculiarity of this monastic Christianity was the peregrination: a monk would simply set off as a wanderer by land or sea, going where God took him. This literal exile from one's home, a symbol of life on earth as an exile from one's true home in heaven, is a partial explanation for Irish missionary activity in England and on the continent. The following text is from Jonas's life of Saint Columbanus (c.550–615), an important Irish missionary on the continent in the late seventh and early eighth centuries. It illustrates the close connection between exile and pilgrimage on the one hand and missionary activity on the other:

> After he had been many years in the cloister, he longed to go into strange lands, in obedience to the command which the Lord gave Abraham: "Get thee out of thy country, and from thy kindred, and from thy father's house, into a land that I will show thee." . . . Having collected a band of brethren, St. Columban asked the prayers of all, that he might be assisted in his coming journey, and that he might have their pious aid. So he started out in the twentieth year of his life, and under the guidance of Christ went to the seashore with twelve companions. Here they waited to see if the mercy of the Almighty would allow their purpose to succeed, and learned that the spirit of the all-merciful Judge was with them. So they embarked, and began the dangerous journey accross the channel and sailed quickly with a smooth sea and favorable wind to the coast of Brittany. Here they rested for a while to recover their strength and discussed their plans anxiously, until finally they decided to enter the land of [Merovingian] Gaul. They wanted zealously and shrewdly to inquire into the disposition of the inhabitants in order to remain longer if they found they could sow the seeds of salvation; or in case they found the hearts of the people in darkness, go on to the nearest nation.[20]

When these Celtic missionaries arrived in Britain, there were some serious conflicts between the two traditions—Roman and Irish—over such issues as the dating of Easter. The Synod of Whitby in 663–64 resolved all disputes in favor of the Roman practices, and gradually the Irish themselves began to adopt these customs. However, Celtic Christianity had a great impact upon the development of the Church in England. In addition to reinforcing the high level of scholarship brought from Rome, the Celtic style of manuscript illumination became the basis for the English style.

In the seventh century, Irish monks such as Columbanus went to the continent, sought to reform the Church, and built a series of monasteries as far south as Bobbio in Italy. These monasteries gradually accepted the Rule of St. Benedict; equally important, their strict asceticism and high level of scholarship influenced continental monasticism.

The Irish monks developed a unique penitential system. In the early Church adult baptism was the norm, and thus the question of how sins committed after baptism were forgiven was not a central pastoral issue. However, with the triumph of Christianity and the growth of the practice of infant baptism, forgiveness of sins committed after baptism became tremendously important. A general confession and absolution became common on the continent. In Irish monasticism, however, a system of private confession to a priest and his assignment of a specific penalty to the sinner was adopted. Books called penitentials, containing the proper penalties for a great variety of sins, were compiled for use by confessors. Here is an example of an assigned penalty:

> A [priest] or a deacon who commits natural fornication, having previously taken the vow of a monk, shall do penance for seven years. He shall ask pardon every hour; he shall perform a special fast during every week except in the fifty days (between Easter and Pentecost). . . . He shall at all times deplore his guilt from his inmost heart, and above all things he shall adopt an attitude of the readiest obedience. After a year and a half he shall take the Eucharist and come for the kiss of peace and sing psalms with his brethren, lest his soul perish utterly through lacking so long a time the celestial medicine.[21]

The following articles concerning negligence toward the consecrated host provide an insight into the great number of contingencies these penitentials deal with:

1. He who fails to guard the host carefully, and a mouse eats it, shall do penance for forty days.
2. But he who loses it in the church, that is, so that a part falls and is not found, twenty days. . . .
7. One who vomits the host because his stomach is overloaded with food, if he casts it into the fire, twenty days, but if not, forty days.

8. If, however, dogs consume this vomit, one hundred. . . .

19. He who acts with negligence towards the host, so that it dries up and is consumed by worms until it comes to nothing, shall do penance for three forty-day periods on bread and water.

20. If it is entire but if a worm is found in it, it shall be burned and the ashes shall be concealed beneath the altar, and he who neglected it shall make good his negligence with forty days [of penance].

21. If the host loses its taste and is discoloured, he shall keep a fast for twenty days; if it is stuck together, for seven days.[22]

One can see from the following articles how the Church in Ireland dealt with the details of daily life in terms of sin and punishment:

12. He who gives to anyone a liquor in which a mouse or a weasel is found dead shall do penance with three special fasts.

13. He who afterwards knows that he has tasted such a drink shall keep a special fast.

14. But if those little beasts are found in the flour or in any dry food or in porridge or in curdled milk, whatever is around their bodies shall be cast out, and all the rest shall be taken in good faith. . . .

18. Whoever eats or drinks what has been tainted by a household beast, namely, the cat, shall be healed with three special fasts.[23]

The Irish penitential system was adopted on the continent in the eighth and ninth centuries. It essentially remained an integral part of the Church's pastoral activity for the rest of the Middle Ages and is the direct ancestor of Catholic practice today. Great preachers of repentance in the Middle Ages, like Francis of Assisi, operated within the context of this system. When the system was abused—and it often was—the abuse was pointed out by reformers and poets such as Dante and Chaucer. Penance in virtually the form created by the Irish monks was defined as one of the seven sacraments of the Church before the end of the Middle Ages.

The Irish missionary zeal, which had brought them to both Britain and the continent, became integrated into Anglo-Saxon Christianity and was largely responsible for a succession of English missionary monks to the continent from the end of the seventh to the middle of the eighth century. Of these the most significant is Saint Boniface (680–754), a man extraordinarily important in the development of the medieval world for many reasons. First, he brought Christianity to the Germans east of the Rhine. Boniface had placed himself under the direct authority of the pope before embarking on his mission and thus brought the new church in Germany into the same kind of close relationship with Rome that England enjoyed. His approach to missionary work came out of the tradition Gregory the Great had established for missionaries to the Anglo-Saxons a century before. An English bishop sending advice to Boniface explains how to convert the Germans in a manner that was consistent with Gregory's admonition:

And so I have with affectionate good will taken pains to suggest to Your Prudence a few things that may show you how, according to my ideas, you may most readily overcome the resistance of those uncivilized people. Do not begin by arguing with them about the origin of their gods, false as those are, but let them affirm that some of them were begotten by others through the intercourse of male with female, so that you may at least prove that gods and goddesses born after the manner of men are men and not gods and, since they did not exist before, must have had a beginning. Then when they have been compelled to learn that their gods had a beginning since some were begotten by others, they must be asked in the same way whether they believe that the world had a begining or was always in existence without beginning. If it had a beginning, who created it? Certainly they can find no place where begotten gods could dwell before the universe was made. I mean by "universe" not merely this visible earth and sky, but the whole vast extent of space, and this the heathen can imagine too in their thoughts. But if they argue that the world always existed without beginning, you should strive to refute this and to convince them by many documents and arguments. . . . Do they think the gods are to be worshiped for the sake of temporal and immediate good or for future and eternal blessedness? If

for temporal things, let them tell in what respect the heathen
are better off than Christians. What gain do the heathen suppose accrues to their gods from their sacrifices, since the gods
already possess everything? Or why do the gods leave it in the
power of their subjects to say what kind of tribute shall be
paid? If they are lacking in such things, why do they not themselves choose more valuable ones? If they have plenty, then
there is no need to suppose that the gods can be pleased with
such offerings of victims.[24]

Thus, conversion was to begin with already existing beliefs; the
entire statement is based on the premise that the Germans
should be reasoned with rather than marched into the river
for mass baptisms like Clovis's warriors.

Although Boniface constantly struggled with pagan survivals
and revivals, and was martyred by pagans in Germany in 754,
Germany was essentially Christian by the time of his death.
What Boniface could not eradicate by word and example
Charlemagne destroyed in a series of wars by the end of the
century.

In 742, Boniface turned his attention to the Frankish kingdom. With papal support and the aid of a reform-minded
Carolingian mayor of the palace, he set out to reform the
Frankish church, placing it more firmly under papal control.
He realized that there were dangers in a reform sponsored and
enforced by a layman, but he also knew that without such
support the Church had little power to enforce its decrees.

Without the support of the Frankish prince I can neither govern the members of the Church nor defend the priests, clerks,
monks, and maids of God; nor can I, without orders from him
and the fear inspired by him, prevent the pagan rites and the
sacrilegious worship of idols in Germany.[25]

However, lay sponsorship and enforcement of ecclesiastical
reform meant a degree of lay control over the Church and
use of its property for secular ends.

The decrees of one Frankish synod supervised by Boniface
suggest the range of problems in the Church; these are par-

ticularly interesting in light of the fact that the Franks had by this time been Christian at least in name for almost two and a half centuries:

> We have decreed, according to the canons, that every bishop within his own diocese and with the help of the count, who is the defender of the Church, shall see to it that the people of God perform no pagan rites but reject and cast out all the foulness of the heathen, such as sacrifices to the dead, casting of lots, divinations, amulets and auguries, incantations, or offerings of animals, which foolish folk perform in the churches, according to the pagan custom, in the name of holy martyrs or confessors, thereby calling down the wrath of God and his saints, and also those sacrilegious fires which they call "Niedfeor," and whatever other pagan practices there may be.[26]

The close link forged between the papacy and the Franks largely through Boniface had enormous political consequences. In 751, Boniface anointed the Carolingian Pepin as king of the Franks on behalf of the pope. This special relationship between the new Frankish dynasty and the papacy led directly to the pope's coronation of Pepin's son Charlemagne as Roman Emperor in the year 800.

Gregory the Great and the Papacy

With the collapse of the Roman Empire in the West, the papacy found itself in a weak position because Western Europe was ruled either by heretics—Arians—or pagans. The popes were forced to look toward Constantinople for protection and support despite theological differences between East and West. When the Byzantine Emperor Justinian brought Italy under his rule, the bishops of Rome rejoiced. However, Justinian continued to support the claims of the bishop of Constantinople, in opposition to the papal claim of universal jurisdiction. Furthermore, Justinian's conquests were not permanent, for as we have seen, in 568 the Arian Lombards overran most of Italy; and Byzantine preoccupation with its northern and eastern borders precluded further significant military involvement in Italy.

At the end of the sixth century, in a period of papal impotence in Western Europe and of an unstable relationship between the papacy and the Byzantine Empire, came the pontificate of Gregory the Great (r.590–604), often called the founder of the medieval papacy. Gregory, a monk with a well-deserved reputation for holiness at the time of his election, accepted and, in fact, furthered Leo the Great's claims of papal authority. In a letter to the Bishop of Alexandria, he brought the three most important Petrine texts together to put forth the claim of universal papal jurisdiction:

> For who can be ignorant that holy Church has been made firm in the solidity of the Prince of the apostles, who derived his name from the firmness of his mind, so as to be called *Petrus* from *petra*. And to him it is said by the voice of the Truth, "To thee I will give the keys to the kingdom of heaven" (Mt. 16:19). And again it is said to him, "And when thou art converted, strengthen thy brethren" (Lk. 22:32). And once more, "Simon, son of Jonas, lovest thou me? Feed My sheep" (Jn. 21:17). Wherefore, though there are many apostles, yet with regard to the principality itself the See of the Prince of the apostles alone has grown strong in authority. . . . For he himself adorned the See to which he sent his disciple as evangelist. He himself established the See in which, though he was to leave it, he sat for seven years.[27]

Gregory had spent time in Constantinople as a papal ambassador before his election and had come to doubt that the papacy could count on imperial help. Thus his policy was to make the papacy independent of Byzantium. For example, he made peace with the Lombards without informing the emperor. He also took charge of provisioning and defending the city of Rome so that it would not be dependent upon an imperial army.

We have already seen how Gregory's missionaries in England assured papal influence there and later helped to strengthen papal authority throughout northern Europe through the work of men like Boniface. Related to his desire to spread Christianity was his concern for the education of people who were already at least nominally Christian. Concerned that his flock was worshipping images in church, the bishop of Marseilles had ordered their destruction. Gregory's prohibition of this order presents the theory of the use of art in Christian instruction that became standard in the Middle Ages:

> For to adore a picture is one thing, but to learn through the story of a picture what is to be adored is another. For what writing presents to readers, this a picture presents to the unlearned who behold it, since in it even the ignorant see what they ought to follow; in it the illiterate read. Hence and chiefly to the nations, a picture is instead of reading. And this ought to have been attended to especially by thee who livest among the nations, lest, while enflamed inconsiderately by a right zeal, thou shouldst breed offense to savage minds. And, seeing that antiquity has not without reason admitted the histories of saints to be painted in venerable places, if thou hadst seasoned zeal with discretion, thou mightest undoubtedly have obtained what thou were aiming at, and not scattered the collected flock but rather gathered together a scattered one; so the deserved renown of a shepherd might have distinguished thee, instead of the blame of being a scatterer lying upon thee.[28]

This statement of Gregory's—echoing once again the theme of moving from visible to invisible—became the dominant attitude of the Church toward art in the Middle Ages. Christian art flourished with little opposition before the Protestant Reformation of the sixteenth century, and richly decorated Romanesque abbeys and Gothic cathedrals were in a real sense the books of the laity.

Gregory's writings were of enormous importance for the Middle Ages. He was regarded as one of the four Latin doctors, along with Jerome, Ambrose, and Augustine. Perhaps his best-known work in the Middle Ages was the *Pastoral Care*, a standard manual of conduct for bishops and later for parish priests. As the title suggests, Christ and his representatives, the bishops, are seen as shepherds. This image, which Gregory employs

Mosaic from the tomb of Galla Placidia, Ravenna, Italy. 5th Century. The theme of Christ the Good Shepherd keeping watch over his flock becomes for Pope Gregory the Great the model for the clergy to imitate. (*Scala/Editorial Photocolor Archives*)

effectively in the letter quoted above, comes, of course, from the Gospels. The good shepherd was the most common depiction of Christ in the art of the catacombs and in churches built immediately following the conversion of Constantine. Bishops, as Christ's representatives on earth and as successors of the apostles, should be shepherds of their flocks in imitation of Christ the Good Shepherd. Gregory's achievement was to address the question of what it meant to be a good shepherd in a world quite different from that of the New Testament. Two passages from the *Pastoral Care* demonstrate Gregory's development of the pastoral image and its application to the episcopate:

> Further, there are some who investigate spiritual precepts with shrewd diligence, but in the life they live trample on what they

have penetrated by their understanding. They hasten to teach what they have learned, not by practice, but by study, and belie in their conduct what they teach by words. Hence it is that when the pastor walks through steep places, the flock following him comes to a precipice. Therefore, the Lord complains through the Prophet of the contemptible knowledge of pastors, saying "When you drank the clearest water, you troubled the rest with your feet. And my sheep were fed with that which you had trodden with your feet, and they drank what your feet had troubled" (Ezek. 34:18f). Evidently, the pastor drinks water that is most clear, when with a right understanding they imbibe the streams of truth, whereas to foul the water with the feet is to corrupt the studies of holy meditation by an evil life. The sheep, of course, drink of the water befouled by those feet, when the subjects do not follow the instruction which they hear, but imitate only the wicked examples which they see. While they thirst for the things said, but are perverted by the the things done, they imbibe mud with their draught as if they drank from polluted fountains of water. Consequently, too, it is written by the Prophet: "Bad priests are a snare of ruin to my people" (Hosea 5:1, 9:8).

The ruler should be discreet in keeping silence and profitable in speech, lest he utter what should be kept secret, or keep secret what should be uttered. For just as incautious speech leads men into error, so, too, unseasonable silence leaves in error those who might have been instructed. Often, indeed, incautious rulers, being afraid of losing human favour, fear to speak freely of what is right, and, in the words of the Truth, do not exercise the zeal of shepherds caring for the flock, but serve the role of mercenaries; for when the wolf appears, they flee and hide themselves in silence. Wherefore, the Lord reproves them through the Prophet, saying: "They are dumb dogs, not able to bark" (Isaiah 56:10).

Again he complains of them, saying: "You have not gone up to face the enemy, nor have you set up a wall for the house of Israel, to stand in battle in the day of the Lord" (Ezek. 13:5). Now, to rise up against the enemy is to oppose worldly powers with candid speech in defence of the flock. To stand in battle in the day of the Lord is to resist from love of justice evil men who contend against us. For if a shepherd feared to say what is right, what else is that but to have turned his back by not speaking? But when one places himself in front of the flock to defend them, he is obviously opposing a wall for the house of Israel against the enemy.[29]

The image of bishop and priest as shepherd remains central to theologians like Saint Bernard of Clairvaux in the twelfth century and John Wyclif in the fourteenth. And when poets held up the ideals of ecclesiastical office as a contrast to the wicked and greedy clergy of their own time, they turned to Gregory's *Pastoral Care.* Chaucer's description of his ideal priest, the Parson, in the *General Prologue to the Canterbury Tales*, used Gregory's description of a good shepherd almost verbatim. Dante criticized the popes in his own time with such phrases as "the lawless shepherd."

Gregory was also known throughout the Middle Ages for his great work of biblical exegesis, the *Moralia* on the Old Testament Book of Job. In it Augustine's approach to Scripture is made more accessible. The following passage illustrates the movement from visible to invisible, using the Old Testament figure Job as a prefiguration of Christ:

For when the light of a candle is kindled in the dark, the candle, which causes other objects to be seen, is first seen itself. And so, if we are truly endeavoring to behold the objects which are enlightened, it is necessary for us to open the eyes of our mind to that Lightening which gives them light. But it is this which shines forth in these very discourses of blessed Job, where the shades of allegory too have been driven away, as though the gloom of midnight had been dispelled, a bright light as it were flaming across them. As when it is said, "I know that my redeemer liveth, and in my flesh I shall see God." Paul had doubtless discovered this light in the night of history, when he said, "All were baptized in Moses in the cloud and in the sea, and all ate the same spiritual meat, and all drank the same spiritual drink. But they drank of the spiritual Rock that followed them, but the Rock was Christ." If then the Rock represented the redeemer, why should not the blessed Job suggest the type of Him, since he signified in his suffering Him whom he spoke of in his voice? And hence he is not improperly called "Job," that is to say "grieving," because he sets forth in his own person the image of Him, of Whom it is announced long before by Isaiah, that He Himself "bore our griefs." It should be further known, that our Redeemer has represented himself as one person with Holy Church, whom He has assumed to Himself. For it is said of Him, "Which is the head, even Christ." And again it is written of His church, "And the body of Christ, which is the Church." Blessed Job therefore who was more truly a type of Christ, since he prophesied of his passion, not by words only, but also by his sufferings, when he dwells on setting forth the Redeemer in his words and deeds, is sometimes suddenly turning to signify His body; in order that, as we believe Christ and his Church to be one person, we may behold this signified by the actions of a single man.[30]

In Gregory's *Dialogues*, a series of conversations about holy men and women, one book is devoted to the life of Saint Benedict. This work helped to set a pattern for later works of hagiography, together with Athanasius's life of Saint Antony and Augustine's *Confessions*, and helped to spread the fame of Benedict and his Rule (see ch. 6). Another of Gregory's achievements was his codification of Church liturgy and music. Perceiving the need for some unity in the order of Church services, he established a basic pattern for the liturgy and compiled chants appropriate for the various services and seasons. Although he probably wrote none of these himself, they, and others written later in the same style, have come to bear his name: Gregorian chant.

Gregory's writings became widely known almost immediately, his place as one of the great saints of the Church assured. But during the seventh century, his goal of papal independence from Byzantium remained unrealized. And it was more than a century before the papacy's influence north of the Alps encompassed more than the Anglo-Saxon kingdoms. One reason for the revival of Gregory's policies was the election of Gregory II in 715. This second Gregory, who had also lived in Constantinople before his election, chose his papal name purposefully; and his accomplishments made him a worthy successor to his namesake. It was he who commissioned Boniface to convert the Saxons and other Germanic peoples.

Gregory was an enthusiastic supporter of Benedictine monas-
ticism, and Boniface established the Rule of St. Benedict in
Germany and furthered its use in the Frankish kingdom.
Furthermore, Gregory severely rebuked the Byzantine Emperor
Leo III for his policy of iconoclasm, a policy that called for the
destruction of Christian art.

By the middle of the eighth century, the Germans and Franks
had close ties to Rome while Roman relations with Byzantium
continued to deteriorate. In 751, Pope Zacharias supported
Pepin's taking the Frankish crown. Two years later, with the
Lombards threatening Rome and the Byzantine emperor un-
willing to send help, Pope Stephen II called upon Pepin, who
successfully came to the defense of Rome. With the Frankish-
papal alliance, the papacy was never again dependent on the
emperor in Constantinople. Western Europe became politically,
culturally, and religiously independent of the East, through the
alliance of the Frankish monarchy and the papacy.

Intellectual Developments

Gregory of Tours was surely right when he described his age
as one of general educational and intellectual decline. However,
this should not be taken to mean that the era was without
writers of sophistication and influence. Gregory the Great is
only one of several writers in the three centuries following the
end of the Roman Empire in the West who can be called,
along with Jerome and Augustine, founders of the medieval
world view.

Boethius (c.480–524), statesman and philosopher, was minister to the Ostogothic King Theodoric, who ruled Italy from
493 to 526; but he fell into disfavor, lost his position, and later
lost his life when he was accused of plotting against Theodoric.
His most important work, the *Consolation of Philosophy*, is
one of the central documents of the early Middle Ages, a work
remaining influential throughout the Middle Ages and beyond.
More manuscripts of the *Consolation* survive than almost any
other work of the Middle Ages. It was translated into Old

English by King Alfred the Great, into German by Notker, into French by Jean de Meun, author of the *Romance of the Rose*, into Middle English by Geoffrey Chaucer, and into Early Modern English by Queen Elizabeth I. Scarcely an educated man from the sixth to the eighteenth centuries would have been without a deep knowledge and love of the work. In the late Middle Ages, the greater the writer, the more profound the effect of Boethius on his work. An understanding of the *Consolation* is almost essential for a proper understanding of Dante and Chaucer, for example.

His subject, as one surmises from the title, is the kind of consolation that philosophy can provide, a subject that no doubt springs from his experience as an exile and prisoner. But he did not feel himself to be under the immediate threat of death when he wrote the *Consolation*; that was to come later. He writes about the fall of a statesman from high position, and from his own fate he generalizes: the *Consolation* is about the instability of any man's fortune.

Both in external and internal structure the work was highly influential. The *Consolation* was written in five books, each consisting of alternating sections of verse and prose. (The five-book structure of Chaucer's *Troilus and Criseyde* is one example of a later work modeled on the *Consolation*.) The internal structure of the work is even more suggestive to later writers; it can be charted by the growth of the speaker, Boethius the exile and prisoner, as he laments his fate in Book 1, is educated by Lady Philosophy throughout the central books and has gained an understanding of the ways of God to men by Book 5. This movement from ignorance to knowledge resonates throughout the literature of the Middle Ages, establishing a pattern repeated over and over in narrative poetry. Lady Philosophy, comforting and enlightening Boethius, performs for him the very function that Dante's guides perform in the *Divine Comedy*. The seemingly overwhelming task of approaching the *Comedy* for the first time can be greatly simplified by seeing there the same pattern as in the *Consolation* —of a man moving from ignorance to knowledge. Dante the Pilgrim, no less than Boethius the exile, starts out by asking the wrong questions, begins to ask the right ones, and finally learns some answers. This movement is also the pattern of the saint's life, with its pattern of conversion from self to God. It is the pattern of the dream vision, in which the dreamer falls asleep and is enlightened by his dream. It is also the pattern of first person narratives such as *Piers the Plowman* and the pattern of quest romances such as *Sir Gawain and the Green Knight*. Even the writings of medieval mystics show the same movement of the speaker from ignorance to knowledge.

The *Consolation*'s most well known and most influential image is that of Fortune and Fortune's wheel. An important step in Boethius's education is to learn to move from contemplation of what changes to contemplation of what is permanent. Explaining to Boethius why he should not lament the loss of his earthly fame and possessions, Lady Philosophy says to him:

> "What is it, my friend, that has thrown you into grief and sorrow? Do you think you have encountered something new and different? You are wrong if you think that Fortune has changed toward you. This is her nature, the way she always behaves. She is changeable, and so in her relations with you she has merely done what she always does. This is the way she was when she flattered you and led you on with false happiness. You have merely discovered the two-faced nature of this blind goddess. Although she still hides herself from others, she is now wholly known to you. If you like her, abide by her conditions and do not complain. But if you hate her treachery, ignore her and her deceitful antics. Really, the misfortunes which are now such a cause of grief ought to be reasons for tranquility. For now she has deserted you, and no man can ever be secure until he has been forsaken by Fortune.
>
> "Do you think that your lost happiness is a precious thing? Can present good fortune be dear to you, even though you know you may lose it, and that the loss will bring sorrow? If you cannot keep her, and if it makes you miserable to lose her, what is Fortune but a promise of future distress? It is not enough to see what is present before our eyes; prudence demands that we look to the future. The double certainty of loss and consequent misery should prevent both the fear of her threats and the desire of her favors. Finally, once you have

submitted yourself to her chains, you ought to take calmly whatever she can do to you. If you were to wish for a law to control the comings and goings of your mistress, you would be unjust, and your impatience would merely aggravate a condition which you cannot change. If you hoist your sails in the wind, you will go where the wind blows you, not where you choose to go; if you put seeds in the ground, you must be prepared for lean as well as abundant years.

"You have put yourself in Fortune's power; now you must be content with the ways of your mistress. If you try to stop the force of her turning wheel, you are the most foolish man alive. If it should stop turning, it would cease to be Fortune's wheel."[31]

Fortune and her wheel express the proper medieval attitude toward worldly goods. Any worldly good, such as money or property, or any worldly pleasure, such as food or sex, is incapable of fully satisfying anyone because it is only partial. As the *Consolation* states at a later point:

"The good is defined as that which, once it is attained, relieves man of all further desires. This is the supreme good and contains within itself all other lesser goods. If it lacked anything at all, it would not be the highest good, because something would be missing, and this could still be desired."[32]

To see any of Fortune's goods—those subject to Fortune's wheel—as the highest good is to seriously misunderstand the nature of reality: what is subject to change is incapable of bringing full satisfaction. Or, to express this same idea in the language of Augustine, to put one's trust and hope in any worldly possessions is to mistake those things for ends that must rather be seen as means to an end. Whenever the wheel of Fortune appears in medieval art or medieval literature, it suggests these related concepts: the instability of all earthly possessions and the folly of putting one's trust in them. At the beginning of *Sir Gawain and the Green Knight*, the reference to Fortune's wheel, describing the fate of kingdoms to which Camelot is the successor, is meant as a reminder of the instability and mutability of all attempts at governance in our unstable world. Fortune's wheel is an image that dominates the structure of Chaucer's *Troilus and Criseyde*, whose movement from "wo to wele [happiness], and after out of joie" recreates one complete turning. The image is also responsible for medieval definitions of comedy and tragedy: when the wheel makes a downward turn, moving from good fortune to bad, it describes a tragedy; when the wheel makes an upward turn, moving from bad fortune to good, it is a comedy.

Boethius's education also consists of learning that one is responsible for one's actions. The problem of fate and free will is one of the crucial concerns of the Middle Ages and is explored at length in the *Consolation*. Lady Philosophy tells Boethius that humans have free will, but she adds that those who have been blinded by passion are unable to see clearly, and hence unable to choose clearly:

> "Human souls, however, are more free while they are in contemplation of the divine mind, and less free when they are joined to bodies, and still less free when they are bound to earthly fetters. They are in utter slavery when they lose possession of their reason and give themselves wholly to vice. For when they turn away their eyes from the light of supreme truth to mean and dark things, they are blinded by a cloud of ignorance and obsessed by vicious passions. By yielding and consenting to these passions, they worsen the slavery to which they have brought themselves and are, as it were, the captives of their own freedom. Nevertheless, God, who beholds all things from eternity, foresees all things in his providence and disposes each according to its predestined merits."[33]

This quotation contains the substance of the central problem. If God sees all things, and if whatever he forsees must take place, how can one's will really be free? If the outcome of human events does indeed depend on humans' free choices, the outcome must be uncertain, or as Boethius would put it, not necessary. If this is so, how can God forsee them? The answer to this dilemma begins in the perception of the radical difference between two ways of knowing, human and divine:

"This is an old difficulty about Providence," Philosophy answered. "It was raised by Cicero in his book on divination, and has for a long time been the subject of your investigation, but so far none of you had treated it with enough care and conviction. The cause of the obscurity which still surrounds the problem is that the process of human reason cannot comprehend the simplicity of divine foreknowledge. If in any way we could understand that, no further doubt would remain."[34]

The difference between what is above and what is below forms one of the major thematic concerns of the *Consolation*, and is responsible for some of its most memorable and influential imagery.

Then, as though she were making a new beginning, Philosophy explained: "The generation of all things, and the whole course of mutable natures and of what is in any way subject to change, take their causes, order, and forms from the unchanging mind of God. This divine mind established the manifold rules by which all things are governed while it remained in the secure castle of its own simplicity. When this government is regarded as belonging to the purity of the divine mind, it is called Providence; but when it is considered with reference to the things it governs, it has from very early times been called Fate. . . .

"Some things, however, which are subject to Providence are above the force of Fate and ungoverned by it. Consider the example of a number of spheres in orbit around the same central point: the innermost moves towards the simplicity of the center and becomes a kind of hinge about which the outer spheres circle; whereas the outermost, whirling in a wider orbit, tends to increase its orbit in space the farther it moves from the indivisible midpoint of the center. If, however, it is connected to the center, it is confined by the simplicity of the center and no longer tends to stray into space. In a like manner, whatever strays farthest from the divine mind is most entangled in the nets of Fate; conversely, the freer a thing is from Fate, the nearer it approaches the center of all things."[35]

This difference between divine and human knowledge leads to the conclusion that divine foreknowledge is not really foreknowledge at all; since God exists out of time, it is more accurately described simply as knowledge. What we see as past, present, and future is all present to God. The work uses this distinction to solve the problem of fate and free will. Lady Philosophy suggests that part of the problem is due to the limits of human reason.

A final way of suggesting the importance of Boethius to the Middle Ages is in the images from the *Consolation* that became commonplace in medieval literature. When Lady Philosophy first comes to Boethius, one of her complaints is that he has forgotten his "native country." He has, in other words, mistaken his life here on earth for his true home. This formulation, so close to the scriptural and Augustinian ideal of life as a pilgrimage, is repeated throughout the Middle Ages. In one of his short poems, Chaucer uses it practically word for word. Boethius's early questions about his condition are all so wide of the mark that Lady Philosophy is not convinced that he is even capable of understanding her wisdom. Returning his questions with a question, she implies that he may be too gross to understand a spiritual message:

> "Do you understand what I have told you," Philosophy asked, "have my words impressed you at all, or are you like the ass which cannot hear the lyre? Why are you crying? Speak out, don't hide what troubles you. If you want a doctor's help, you must uncover your wound."[36]

The image of the beast unable to respond to spiritual music remains highly charged throughout the Middle Ages. Another image in this passage is that of Lady Philosophy coming to Boethius as a physician to cure his malady. This has resonances with the New Testament, where Christ is portrayed as a spiritual physician. Throughout medieval literature, when doctors and medicine are mentioned, there is a good chance that the malady is not exclusively physical.

In the *Consolation of Philosophy* the character of Lady Philosophy is an example of personification allegory, the use of a human figure to represent an abstract idea. Another work making use of the same technique is Martianus Capella's *Mar-*

riage of Mercury and Philology (c.430), a work similar to the *Consolation* not only in form (it also uses alternating prose and verse sections), but in the extent of its influence. The work is a treatise on the seven liberal arts, personified as characters in a mythological story. Following a classical tradition that can be traced back as far as Isocrates in the fourth century B.C., Martianus divides the seven into groups: the trivium, consisting of grammar, rhetoric, and logic; and the quadrivium, consisting of music, astronomy, arithmetic, and geometry. The liberal arts appear at the marriage of Mercury and Philology as the handmaidens of Mercury; the marriage was traditionally taken to symbolize the union of eloquence and learning, that is, the union of the trivium and the quadrivium. For the next thousand years the work was to be one of the most widely read in Western Europe, insuring that the seven liberal arts became the educational core of the Middle Ages. Their position was further strengthened by the approval of Martianus's schema in the writings of Cassiodorus (c.485–580), an official at the court of Theodoric the Ostrogoth who later established a monastery where classical as well as Christian texts were studied and copied, and whose authority therefore commanded great respect in the early Middle Ages. The revival of the seven liberal arts became the key to the educational reforms of the Carolingian Renaissance in the eighth century. Their study (with emphasis on the trivium, and especially on grammar and rhetoric) was part of monastic education throughout the Middle Ages. They were central to the educational system developed in the cathedral schools in the twelfth century. From the time of the Carolingian Renaissance to the end of the Middle Ages, personifications of the liberal arts were also an important subject in art, their depiction on the facade of Chartres Cathedral being perhaps the best-known example.

We have already examined excerpts from the writings of the historians Gregory of Tours and Bede. Gregory (539–94), bishop of Tours, came from a Roman family and was an important advisor to the Merovingian kings. Though deploring much of their cruelty, he supported the Franks because of their orthodox Christianity. His long *History of the Franks*—about six hundred pages in the newest English translation—begins with creation but concentrates on the events of his own lifetime. The book is filled with palace intrigue, grotesque punishment, religious charlatans, miraculous cures, and rebellious monks and nuns. Gregory's narrative and descriptive powers maintain the reader's interest; in the final analysis, however, he lacks the clear organization and analytical skills of his Anglo-Saxon counterpart.

Bede (673–735) spent part of his childhood and all his adult life as a monk of Jarrow in the north of England. His *History of the English Church and People* is perhaps the most significant piece of historical writing in the entire medieval period. The work focuses on England from the time of the arrival of the Roman missionaries and magnificently unfolds the story of the establishment of Christianity there. His descriptions of the most important events such as the conversion of Ethelbert of Kent and the Synod of Whitby plus the sharply and sympathetically drawn portraits of kings, bishops, monks, and nuns are unforgettable. Bede was also the author of numerous works of science, biblical exegesis, and hagiography; and his writings were widely known throughout Europe in the Middle Ages. He is, for example, the only Englishman Dante places in his *Paradiso*.

The Visigothic kingdom also produced an author of the greatest importance—Isidore of Seville (560–636). He was the historian of the Visigoths and an important compiler of church law. But he is most famous for his encyclopedia, called the *Etymologies*. Isidore attempted no less than to assemble all human knowledge. Drawing mostly from classical Latin authors, he put together what became a standard reference work for the Middle Ages. The table of contents gives a sense of the work's scope.

Book I:	Grammar
Book II:	Rhetoric and Dialectic
Book III:	Arithmetic, Geometry, Music, Astronomy
Book IV:	Medicine
Book V:	Law; Divisions of Time and Chronology

Book VI:	Books of the Bible and Their Interpreters; Canons; Ecclesiastical Offices
Book VII:	God; Angels; Saints
Book VIII:	The Church and the Sects
Book IX:	Languages; Races; Kingdoms; the Army; Citizens; Kingship
Book X:	Etymological Word List
Book XI:	Men and Fabulous Monsters
Book XII:	Animals
Book XIII:	The Universe and its Parts
Book XIV:	The Earth and its Parts
Book XV:	Buildings and Lands
Book XVI:	Stones and Metals
Book XVII:	Agriculture and Botany
Book XVIII:	War; Games; Pastimes
Book XIX:	Ships; Building Materials; Dress
Book XX:	Food and Drink; Furniture[37]

The *Etymologies* was widely used for reference even where the Latin authors from whom Isidore derived his information survived; having so much in one book was convenient. For example, many of the fabulous creatures carved in the twelfth-century Church of Saint Mary Magdalen in Vézelay were originally described by the Roman nauralist Pliny, but they were probably known in Vézelay through Isidore. In some cases, Isidore's sources did not survive. Consequently he himself became an important source for the transmission of classical culture to the Middle Ages.

The *Etymologies* derives its name from the fact that Isidore gave the origins of the words and names he wrote about. The idea that the etymology of a word says something about the essence of the object or person it names remained a popular concept throughout the Middle Ages. The following example, fancifully explaining the origin and meaning of the name Gregory, comes from the thirteenth-century collection of saints' lives called the *Golden Legend*:

Gregory comes from *grex*, flock, and *gore*, preaching or speaking. Therefore, the name Gregory means preacher of the flock. Or, Gregory is the same as *egregorius* which comes from *egre-*

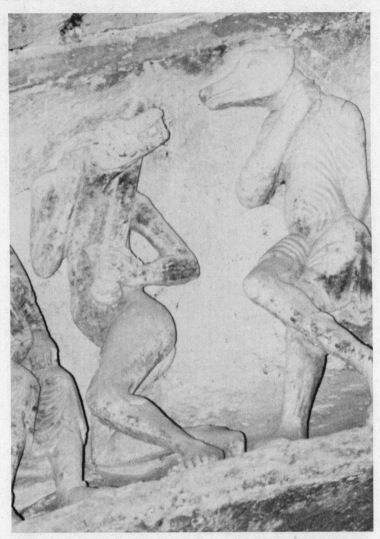

Detail of the tympanum from the Church of Mary Magdalen, Vézelay, France. Early 12th Century. The dog-headed men depicted here were originally described by the Roman writer Pliny. However, Isidore of Seville drew from Pliny, and the artist probably had Isidore rather than Pliny as his immediate source.

gius, and *gore*, a praiseworthy teacher or speaker. Or, in our language, Gregory means the watchful one, for he was watchful to himself, to the Lord, and to his flock; to himself in preserving his purity, to God in his contemplative life, to the flock in his industrious preaching. By means of these three anyone may merit the sight of God.[38]

One other author must be considered in any list of the influential writers of the period. He has become known as the Pseudo-Dionysius (fifth century), since in the Middle Ages the writings of this anonymous Greek-speaking monk were falsely attributed to Dionysius the Areopagite, an Athenian converted to Christianity by Paul according to Acts of the Apostles (17:34). In order to appreciate these writings and their influence, it is necessary first to discuss the origins of Christian mysticism.

Mysticism is based on the belief that the highest goal of humans is union with God through contemplation and that the achievement of this union is not dependent on their striving toward God so much as God's opening himself up to them. Direct contemplation of God is to be sought and found neither in intellectual activity nor by striving to learn and understand all that God has revealed, but rather by turning inward. People ready themselves for this direct contact by emptying themselves of any desires, activities, and predispositions that prevent them from attaining the total detachment in which God might make his presence known. The tradition of Christian mysticism in the Middle Ages can be traced back to the early Fathers such as Gregory of Nyssa (c.332–95), considered to be the founder of Christian mysticism, and back beyond that to those points in the scriptural tradition in which God directly made himself known. Thus Christ's apparition to Paul on the road to Damascus, together with Paul's statements that he journeyed to the third heaven (2 Cor. 12:2–4), become the most important icons of the mystical experience in the New Testament, just as Moses, seeing God directly on Mt. Sinai, becomes its exemplar in the Old. From the time of the Fathers the tradition then stretches forward through a whole line of thinkers and writers throughout the Middle Ages: Augustine, who devotes a great deal of his writings to the meaning of contemplation; the twelfth-century school of Saint Victor in Paris, whose most famous writers, Hugh and Richard, present the main tenets of Christian mystical tradition in both devotional and analytic terms; Bernard of Clairvaux, perhaps the most important and influential mystical writer of the Middle Ages; Bonaventure, who in the thirteenth century became the most important academic synthesizer of the tradition.

In the fifth century, most likely from Syria, came two mystical works of Pseudo-Dionysius. In Western Europe, Pseudo-Dionysius was an important figure not only because he was thought to be an exemplar of the mystical approach to God but also because of his speculative theology, first introduced in the West in the Latin translations of John Scotus Eruigena (c.810–c.75). Or perhaps it would be closer to the truth to say that his theological writings were thought to be another embodiment of his mystical gifts. The account of his life collected in the *Golden Legend* connects his life and his works as follows:

> It is said that Paul made known to him the things that he had seen when he was rapt to the third heaven, and this Dionysius himself seems to insinuate in several places. Hence he has written so aptly and clearly of the hierarchies of the angels, their orders, dispositions, and offices, that you would not think that he had learned this of another, but had himself been rapt to the third heaven, and had there viewed all these things.[39]

His description of the kinds and attributes of angels, in his work *The Celestial Hierarchies*, became standard for much of the Middle Ages, finding its way into such important later works as Bonaventure's *Mind's Road to God*, Dante's *Divine Comedy*, and the portals of many Gothic cathedrals. His description of the universe as an emanation from God allowed him to see in all creation vestiges of divine attributes, and he develops from this what comes to be called the doctrine of analogy. According to this doctrine, the reality of a given entity can be described in terms of the kind and amount of Divine Being it possesses. Pseudo-Dionysius was a most important channel through which this aspect of Neoplatonic thought was transmitted throughout the Middle Ages. This doctrine was enormously influential in the thought of the mystical tradition, but also in the thought of so unmystical a writer as Thomas Aquinas, who wrote commentaries on the works of Pseudo-Dionysius and who incorporated the doctrine of analogy into his *Summa*.

In *The Divine Names*, Pseudo-Dionysius describes the knowledge that can be obtained from reading Scripture and proceeds from there to talk about the relation of the universe to its creator:

> These mysteries we learn from the Divine Scriptures, and thou wilt find that in well-nigh all the utterances of the Sacred Writers the Divine Names refer in a Symbolical Revelation to Its beneficent Emanations. Wherefore, in almost all consideration of Divine things we see the supreme Godhead celebrated with holy praises as One and an Unity, through the simplicity and unity of Its supernatural indivisibility, from whence (as from an unifying power) we attain to unity, and through the supernal conjunction of our diverse and separate qualities are knit together each into a Godlike Oneness, and all together into a mutual Godly union. And It is called the Trinity because Its supernatural fecundity is revealed in a Three fold Personality, wherefrom all Fatherhood in heaven and on earth exists and draws Its name. And It is called the Universal Cause since all things came into being through Its bounty, whence all being springs; and It is called Wise and Fair because all things which keep their own nature uncorrupted are full of all Divine harmony and holy Beauty; and especially It is called Benevolent because, in one of Its Persons, It verily and wholly shared in our human lot, calling unto Itself and uplifting the low estate of man, wherefrom, in an ineffable manner, the simple Being of Jesus assumed a compound state, and the Eternal hath taken a temporal existence, and He who supernaturally transcends all the order of the natural world was born in our Human Nature without any change or confusion of His ultimate properties. And in all the other Divine enlightenments which the occult

Tradition of our inspired teachers hath, by mystic Interpretation, accordant with the Scriptures, bestowed upon us, we also have been initiated: apprehending these things in the present life (according to our powers), through the sacred veils of that loving kindness which in the Scriptures and the Hierarchical Traditions, enwrappeth spiritual truths in terms drawn from the world of sense, and the super-essential truths in terms drawn from Being, clothing with shapes and forms things which are shapeless and formless, and by a variety of separable symbols, fashioning manifold attributes of the imageless and supernatural Simplicity. But hereafter, when we are incorruptible and immortal and attain the blessed lot of being like unto Christ, then (as the Scripture saith), we shall be for ever with the Lord, fulfilled with His visible Theophany in holy contemplations, the which shall shine about us with radiant beams of glory (even as once of old it shone around the Disciples at the Divine Transfiguration); and so shall we, with our mind made passionless and spiritual, participate in a spiritual illumination from Him, and in an union transcending our mental faculties, and there, amidst the blinding blissful impulsions of His dazzling rays, we shall, in a diviner manner than at present, be like unto the heavenly Intelligences. For, as the infallible Scripture saith, we shall be equal to the angels and shall be the Sons of God, being Sons of the Resurrection. But at present we employ (so far as in us lies), appropriate symbols for things Divine; and then from these we press on upwards according to our powers to behold in simple unity the Truth perceived by spiritual contemplations, and leaving behind us all human notions of godlike things, we still the activities of our minds, and reach (so far as this may be) into the Super-Essential Ray, wherein all kinds of knowledge so have their pre-existent limits (in a transcendently inexpressible manner), that we cannot conceive nor utter It, nor in any wise contemplate the same, seeing that It surpasseth all things, and wholly exceeds our knowledge, and super-essentially contains beforehand (all conjoined within Itself) the bounds of all natural sciences and forces (while yet Its force is not circumscribed by any), and so possesses, beyond the celestial Intelligences, Its firmly fixed abode. For if all the branches of knowledge belong to things that have being, and if their limits have reference to the existing world, then that which is beyond all Being must also be transcendent above all knowledge.[40]

One can extract from this passage the core of Dionysius's thought. The created universe is a ladder that leads humans back to God. In this, Dionysius is clearly in the Pauline-Augustinian tradition, seeing the visible universe as a means to reach its invisible creator. Much of Dionysius's work, like that of Augustine, can be seen as a gloss on Romans 1:20; and this text is quoted, significantly, in *The Divine Names*. Within this framework, however, he emphasizes the radical and total separation between creature and creator. We have the traces of God through his creation; they should lead us back to God. But it is impossible to talk about God as he really is from what we know about these traces. We should be led to the contemplation of God as our ultimate goal, but this experience is not describable by humans while on earth. It is an experience that is so above anything here that it is both ineffable and incommunicable. Traces are left in the language we use, as Pseudo-Dionysius indicates by his concern in the passage with the words that attribute certain qualities to God; but the actual experience of God is even above language itself since, as he implies in the last sentence, language belongs to the existing world, the world of being, and "that which is beyond all being must be transcendent above all knowledge."

Perhaps the most important of those words attributable to God is "illumination." God is illumination, for we know from John's Gospel that Christ is the light of the world, coming into the world and dispelling the darkness. To the Middle Ages, light becomes a most important source of order and value here on earth; by the doctrine of analogy, the more a substance was infused with light, the more it resembled God as an image or shadow of its creator. Though the reality of God's illumination is above human comprehension, light, the substance that was considered the purest, is the most important trace that leads us back to Him. The influence of Dionysius's thought was limited during the Early Middle Ages, in part because his Latin translator Scotus Eruigena was also a figure of limited influence. But during the High Middle Ages the effect of this theology of light was extraordinarily great. As Otto von Simson says in *The Gothic Cathedral*, "for the twelfth and thirteenth centuries, light was the source and essence of all visual beauty."[41] This beauty was not a quality independent of or added to a substance's other qualities, but was rather an insight into a substance's very nature because it suggested the degree to which that substance partook of Being itself. Thus the luminosity that is the characteristic of medieval manuscript illuminations and stained glass windows: they are both attempts to recreate the celestial harmony. It also explains why, again in von Simson's words, "in the philosophical literature of the time, as in the courtly epic, no attributes are used more frequently to describe visual beauty than 'lucid', 'luminous', 'clear'."[42] Most important, it is a key to the aesthetic of the Gothic cathedral and to another "cathedral" in light, Dante's *Paradiso*. Light shining through the windows of the Gothic cathedral portrays a human attempt to recreate the celestial city; the opening lines of the *Paradiso* prepare the reader for the visions of light to follow: "The glory of Him who moves all things penetrates the universe and shines in one part more and in another less."[43]

The first attempt to translate these principles of light aesthetics into architectural form was made in the building of the Abbey Church of St. Denis, near Paris, under the direction of its famous abbot, Suger (c.1081–1151). It was believed in the Middle Ages that the Pseudo-Dionysius came to France and was martyred by beheading. After the beheading "at once the body of Dionysius stood erect, and took his head into his hands; and with an angel guiding it and a great light going before, it walked for two miles, from the place called Montmartre to the place where, by its own choice and by the providence of God, it now reposes."[44] That place, of course, was later the site of Suger's church; the relation between the place and the doctrine informing the building of the church was by no means accidental.

The period discussed in this chapter was clearly an end—but it was also a beginning. This period of destruction, chaos, and cultural decline was also one of creativity, synthesis, and even genius. The traditions that came together often clashed, bringing confusion and bloodshed. But the Roman Empire that disappeared in the West in 476 was not the empire of Augustus or of the second century; it was rather a totalitarian, oppressive, and inefficient empire whose demise was an opportunity to start over, to create a new civilization. Although that civilization did not begin to flourish until the reign of Charlemagne (r.768–814) or perhaps even later, without the experimentation, dedication, and inventiveness of people in the centuries following the collapse of the Empire it could never have come into being. More than most periods of history, this was indeed an age of transition, perhaps even *the* greatest age of transition in the history of Western civilization.

CHAPTER SIX

Monasticism

In about the year 269, an eighteen-year-old boy named Antony, a Christian raised in Egypt, entered a church. This entrance symbolically marks the beginning of Christian monasticism. The story is told in the famous life of Saint Antony (251–356) written by Saint Athanasius (c.296–373):

> He went into the church pondering these things, and just then it happened that the Gospel was being read, and he heard the Lord saying to the rich man, "If you would be perfect, go, sell what you possess and give to the poor, and you will have treasure in heaven." It was as if by God's design he held the saints in his recollection, and as if the passage were read on his account. Immediately Antony went out from the Lord's house and gave to the townspeople the possessions he had from his forebears.[1]

Soon Antony went to live in the desert; and although he returned to "the world" several times later in his life, he continued to live in solitude for the rest of his life—eighty-seven years! He lived alone in the desert most of that time, praying and supporting himself through manual labor. In his own lifetime he became famous for his holiness, and men came in large numbers to live near him in imitation. As mentioned in chapter three, this ascetic movement flourished after the end of Christian persecution, when Christianity became a favored religion. People now could become Christians who were less than devoted to it; consequently, many saw the kind of commitment that Antony made as a way of demonstrating the depth of their devotion now that martyrdom was no longer literally possible. Antony came to a similar understanding of his own life:

> When finally the persecution ended, and Peter the blessed bishop had made his witness, Antony departed and withdrew once again to the cell, and was there daily being martyred by his conscience, and doing battle in the contests of the faith. He subjected himself to an even greater and more strenuous asceticism, for he was always fasting, and he had clothing with hair on the interior and skin on the exterior that he kept until he died. He neither bathed his body with water for cleanliness, nor did he wash his feet at all, and he would not even consent to putting them in water unless it was necessary. Neither did anyone ever see him undressed—indeed, no one saw the body of Antony naked, except when he died and was buried.[2]

Throughout the Middle Ages people continued to regard the monastic vocation as a particularly high calling because of its imitation through asceticism of the martyrs of the church, and the documents of early monasticism were therefore treated with special reverence throughout the Middle Ages. Antony brought to Christian, and especially monastic, imagery the concept of life as an inward journey:

> But do not be afraid to hear about virtue, and do not be a stranger to the term. For it is not distant from us, nor does it stand external to us, but its realization lies in us, and the task is easy if only we shall will it. Now the Greeks leave home and traverse the sea in order to gain an education, but there is no need for us to go abroad on account of the Kingdom of

heaven, nor to cross the sea for virtue. For the Lord has told us before, the Kingdom of God is within you. All virtue needs, then, is our willing, since it is in us, and arises from us.[3]

This image of the inward journey is central to the writings of Augustine, all monastic literature of the Middle Ages, and a very great number of nonmonastic works as well.

Antony believed that a monk should deny himself earthly pleasures, perform physical labor, pray, and also remain in the same place:

> Just as fish die if they remain on dry land so monks, remaining away from their cells, or dwelling with men of the world, lose their determination to persevere in solitary prayer. Therefore, just as the fish should go back to the sea, so we must return to our cells, lest remaining outside we forget to watch over ourselves interiorly.[4]

Antony was not a scholar. He understood the need to read, of course, because the word of God was contained in the Bible. Yet Antony saw that God "wrote" another book as well:

> A certain philosopher asked St. Antony: "Father, how can you be so happy when you are deprived of the consolation of books?" Antony replied: "My book, O philosopher, is the nature of created things, and any time I want to read the words of God, the book is before me."[5]

This passage, closely related to the movement from visible to invisible expressed in Romans 1:19–20, describes the attitude toward nature that is dominant in Europe until the thirteenth century, and continues to be important long after that time. Although Antony was not a philosopher, his wisdom was said to exceed that of the great scholars of Alexandria. The following story illustrates this:

> Antony was also extremely wise. It was a marvel that although he had not learned letters, he was a shrewd and intelligent man. For example, once two Greek philosophers visited him,

thinking they would be able to put him to the test. He was in the outer mountain at the time, and knowing what the men were from their appearance, he went out to them and said through an interpreter, "Why did you go to so much trouble, you philosophers, to visit a foolish man?" When they responded that he was not foolish, but quite wise, he said to them, "If you came to a foolish man, your toil is superfluous, but if you consider me wise, become as I am, for we must imitate what is good. If I had come to you I would have imitated you; but since you came to me, become as I am; for I am a Christian." In amazement they withdrew, for they saw that even demons feared Antony.[6]

People wise in things of the spirit overcoming those of worldly wisdom can be seen in countless works of the Middle Ages. The hermit who dispenses true wisdom to the worldly-wise becomes an important figure in medieval literature, especially in stories of the knights of King Arthur's round table.

One of the difficulties inherent in the ruggedly individualistic monasticism of Antony and his followers was that the monks in the desert were deprived of the sacraments of the church since they were not priests. Furthermore, the desert was dangerous, especially to those who were ill or too old to provide for themselves. In the fourth century it thus became common for monks to gather together, living in communities that shared the liturgy, meals, and necessary labor. These monasteries did not supersede the hermit life; instead, two kinds of monasticism coexisted in the desert, and many of those who later became hermits began their monastic lives in a monastery.

Both kinds of monasticism spread first to the Holy Land and the East, but also eventually to the West as well, reaching the latter as early as the middle of the fourth century. From this period of coexistence between eremitical (hermit) and cenobitic (communal) monasticism came two important writers: Saint Basil (c.330–79), who described the way a monastery should work; and John Cassian (c.360–435), who recorded talks he had with monks in the Egyptian desert. Both of these writers were very important in the formation of Western monasticism. Benedict recommends in his Rule that monks read the lives of the saints, especially Antony, John Cassian, and Basil (ch. 73). The following passage from John Cassian's *Institutes* is of special importance. It suggests that a monk must be constantly vigilant against the sin of pride, a point that Benedict also stresses:

> Our eighth and last combat is against the spirit of pride, which evil, although it is the latest in our conflict with our faults and stands last on the list, yet in beginning and in the order of time is the first: an evil beast that is most savage and more dreadful than all the former ones, chiefly trying those who are perfect, and devouring with its dreadful bite those who have almost attained the consummation of virtue.
>
> And so it is most clearly established by instances and testimonies from Scripture that the mischief of pride, although it comes later in the order of combat, is yet earlier in origin, and is the beginning of all sins and faults: nor is it (like the other vices) simply fatal to the virtue opposite it (in this case, humility), but it is also at the same time destructive of *all* virtues: nor does it only tempt ordinary folk and small people, but chiefly those who already stand on the heights of valour.[7]

When Cassian refers to pride as the first sin, he is alluding to the story of the fall of Lucifer from among the angels. Pride becomes a particularly important monastic concern because the monk who gives up so much can easily come to believe himself superior to those who live in the world. It is an "occupational hazard" for one progressing toward perfection by ridding oneself of lust, gluttony, and sloth. Cassian wrote about the value of all the material sacrifices that a monk makes:

> Therefore fastings, vigils, meditation on the Scriptures, self-denial, and the abnegation of all possessions are not perfection, but aids to perfection: because the end of that science does not lie in these, but by means of these we arrive at the end. He will then practice these exercises to no purpose, who is contented with these as if they were the highest good, and had fixed the purpose of his heart simply on them, and does not extend his efforts toward reaching the end, on account of which these should be sought: for he possesses indeed the implements of his art, but is ignorant of the end.[8]

This distinction between means and ends is a familiar one. In this context Cassian warns that self-denial will be of no benefit unless it is a means to move toward God, together with prayer and the practice of virtue. This remains an important lesson to the monks of the Middle Ages. Cassian himself came to Western Europe and established two monasteries in southern Gaul. However, the state of monasticism was about as chaotic as the political situation, each monastery living under its own rule. Many monasteries flourished under a strong holy leader (called an abbot) and then floundered if there was no one to take his place. Some monasteries were quite lax while others had severe regulations.

In the sixth century there came a man who was to become the most important influence on Western monasticism from his own time till the present. His name is Saint Benedict of Nursia (480–547); his Rule, which was written for his own monks at Monte Cassino in southern Italy, eventually spread all over Latin Christendom. Benedict's life was told by Gregory the Great in Book 2 of his *Dialogues*. One of the most important saint's lives of the early Middle Ages, Gregory's life of Benedict was itself one of the most important reasons for the spread of the Rule. What follows is Gregory's description of one of Benedict's temptations after he gave up his study in Rome to become a hermit:

> A greater temptation of the flesh than he had ever experienced overtook the holy man. For the evil spirit brought back before the mind's eye a certain woman whom he had once seen. So intensely did the Tempter inflame his mind by the sight of that woman that he could hardly control his passion. He was overcome by sensuality, and almost considered leaving his solitary retreat. Then suddenly God graciously looked upon him and he returned to himself. Since he saw that thickets of nettles and thorn bushes were growing nearby, he stripped off his garments and flung himself naked upon those stinging thorns and burning nettles. He rolled about there for a long time, and came out with his whole body wounded by them. So through the wound of the skin he drew out from his body the wound of the mind by changing his lust to pain. Although

St. Benedict. Panel painting by Ambrogio Lorenzetti. 14th Century. Siena, Italy. This is not a portrait of the saint taken from life, but rather it suggests certain qualities for which he was known in the Middle Ages. As the father of western monasticism, he was always depicted as a wise and fatherly man. Generally, portraits in the Middle Ages present a person's spiritual qualities rather than a physical likeness. The haircut of Benedict, called the tonsure, is the sign that he is a cleric and thus subject to the law of the Church regulating clerical conduct.

he burned painfully on the outside, he had put out the forbidden flame within.[9]

After a rather unsuccessful attempt to reform a monastery that had asked for his help and an unsuccessful attempt to return to the solitary life of a hermit, Benedict tore down a pagan shrine and in its place founded a new monastery at Monte Cassino. There Benedict combined older monastic sources with his practical and commonsense approach to the cenobitic life to create the Benedictine Rule. In the preface he states the monk's and the monastery's prime purpose:

> And so we are going to establish a school for the service of the Lord. In founding it we hope to introduce nothing harsh or burdensome. But if a certain strictness results from the dictates of equity for the amendment of vices or the preservation of charity, do not be at once dismayed and fly from the way of salvation, whose entrance cannot but be narrow. For as we advance in the religious life and in faith, our hearts expand and we run the way of God's commandments with unspeakable sweetness of love. Thus, never departing from His school, but persevering in the monastery according to His teaching until death, we may by patience share in the sufferings of Christ and deserve to have a share also in His kingdom.[10]

The Rule called for a strong abbot in the monastery, almost unlimited in his powers and answerable only to God. However, the abbot could not act completely on his own:

> Whenever any important business has to be done in the monastery, let the Abbot call together the whole community and state the matter to be acted upon. Then, having heard the brethren's advice, let him turn the matter over in his own mind and do what he shall judge to be most expedient. The reason we have said that all should be called for counsel is that the Lord often reveals to the younger what is best.[11]

The monks were to take vows of poverty (though the community could own property corporately, no individual could own anything), obedience (to the abbot), chasity, stability (a monk was to live and die in the monastery and not leave except on monastic business), and conversion of manners (a monk was to strive continually for spiritual improvement). The principal activities of the monk were to pray and work, in Latin, *ora et labora*. Through the Rule of St. Benedict, manual labor was given a dignity it never had in Roman times. An elaborate schedule of services for prayer, called offices, was established in the Rule, beginning with vigils at about 2:30 A.M. and ending with compline at 6:30 or 7:00 P.M. In between were lauds, prime, tierce, sext, none, and vespers. At times when offices were not being said, the monks remained busy because

> Idleness is the enemy of the soul. Therefore the brethren should be occupied at certain times in manual labor, and again at fixed hours in sacred reading. To that end we think that the times for each may be prescribed as follows.
>
> From Easter until the Calends of October, when they come out from Prime in the morning let them labor at whatever is necessary until about the fourth hour, and from the fourth hour until about the sixth let them apply themselves to reading. After the sixth hour, having left the table, let them rest on their beds in perfect silence; or if anyone may perhaps want to read, let him read to himself in such a way as not to disturb anyone else. Let None be said rather early, at the middle of the eighth hour, and let them again do what work has to be done until Vespers.
>
> And if the circumstances of the place or their poverty should require that they themselves do the work of gathering the harvest, let them not be discontented; for then are they truly monks when they live by the labor of their hands, as did our Fathers and the Apostles. Let all things be done with moderation, however, for the sake of the faint-hearted.[12]

A monk's day alternated between times of communal prayer, manual labor, and rest. The interweaving of these was a way to see all activity as God-centered and thus as a kind of prayer. Furthermore, the monastic day conformed to nature. The office of vigils, sung at night, had the theme of waiting for the Lord. The office of lauds, at daybreak, celebrated the coming of the Lord, symbolized by the light. The office of vespers, coming at the end of the working day as the sun was setting, was an office of Thanksgiving.

Study was not a main element of the monk's life for Benedict, although each monk was expected to be literate and had an obligation to read an entire book during Lent. Monte Cassino was first and foremost a place to win salvation rather than a place to advance knowledge of the world.

One of the necessary conditions for living the prescribed life of prayer was silence:

> Therefore, since the spirit of silence is so important, permission to speak should rarely be granted even to perfect disciples, even though it be for good, holy, edifying conversation; for it is written, "In much speaking you will not escape sin," and in another place, "Death and life are in the power of the tongue."
>
> But as for coarse jests and idle words or words that move to laughter, these we condemn everywhere with a perpetual ban, and for such conversation we do not permit a disciple to open his mouth.[13]

Food, drink, shelter, and clothing were all provided for the monk at the discretion of the abbot, but Benedict certainly intended a minimum of food and plain clothing:

> We think it sufficient for the daily dinner, whether at the sixth or the ninth hour, that every table have two cooked dishes, on account of individual infirmities, so that he who for some reason cannot eat of the one may make his meal of the other. Therefore let two cooked dishes suffice for all the brethren; and if any fruit or fresh vegetables are available, let a third dish be added.
>
> But if it happens that the work was heavier, it shall lie within the Abbot's discretion and power, should it be expedient, to add something to the fare. Above all things, however, over-indulgence must be avoided and a monk must never be overtaken by indigestion; for there is nothing so opposed to the Christian character as over-indulgence, according to Our

Lord's words, "See to it that your hearts be not burdened with over-indulgence."

. . . We believe that a hemina of wine a day is sufficient for each. But those to whom God gives the strength to abstain should know that they will receive a special reward.

If the circumstances of the place, or the work, or the heat of summer require a greater measure, the Superior shall use his judgment in the matter, taking care always that there be no occasion for surfeit or drunkenness. We read, it is true, that wine is by no means a drink for monks; but since the monks of our day cannot be persuaded of this, let us at least agree to drink sparingly and not to satiety, because "wine makes even the wise fall away." . . .

We believe, however, that in ordinary places the following dress is sufficient for each monk: a tunic, a cowl (thick and woolly for winter, thin or worn for summer), a scapular for work, stockings and shoes to cover the feet.

The monks should not complain about the color or the coarseness of any of these things, but be content with what can be found in the district where they live and can be purchased cheaply. . . .

And in order that this vice of private ownership may be cut out by the roots, the Abbot should provide all the necessary articles: cowl, tunic, stockings, shoes, girdle, knife, pen, needle, handkerchief, tablets; that all pretext of need may be taken away.[14]

Benedict wrote this Rule only for Monte Cassino, never envisioning the founding of an order. However, the cult of Benedict spread rapidly; and the Rule became the norm for monastic life in England and was firmly established in Germany and Gaul in the eighth century. In the ninth century the Rule became universal in Latin Christendom, making it the most important document in the history of Western monasticism. There were two primary reasons for its success. One was the popularity of the cult of Saint Benedict largely due to the writings of Pope Gregory the Great. Second was the genius of the Rule itself. It provided a stable structure with a strong abbot, and it provided a synthesis of the older desert tradition with a new moderation. The combination of moderation and strictness in Benedict's attitude toward the monks drinking wine, quoted above, is a good example of this synthesis.

Although the Rule became the constitution of hundreds, indeed thousands, of monasteries for both men and women, like all constitutions it had to be interpreted and adapted to conditions quite different from sixth century Italy. In two obvious examples, it was clear that the clothing regulations would not be adequate for a cold climate, and in some parts of northern Europe, wine was nonexistent. Thus, in the spirit of the Rule itself, different customs developed throughout Western Europe within the context of Benedictine monasticism. Some of the customaries from the tenth and eleventh centuries survive, but it is clear that the establishment of a pluralism within the tradition began as soon as the Rule spread from Monte Cassino.

Although in the eleventh, twelfth, and thirteenth centuries new monastic orders were formed that did not live under the Rule, it did continue to be the fundamental law in hundreds of Benedictine houses (black monks) and Cistercian houses (white monks, a reform of the Benedictines established in 1098). Men and women in all walks of life in the Middle Ages knew the basic tenets of the Rule; thus there are many allusions to it in medieval literature. One immediately thinks of the Monk in the *General Prologue* to Chaucer's *Canterbury Tales*, who takes the tenets of the Rule and systematically turns them upside down.

Despite the overwhelming importance of Benedict for Western monasticism, his was not the only influence. Were one to ask nonmedievalists to describe a medieval monk, they would probably picture a scholar-scribe seated at his workbench preserving the texts of classical antiquity. That would be right in part; yet neither the desert fathers nor Benedict envisioned the monk primarily as a scholar. Such an emphasis on scholarship was the work of monks like Cassiodorus (c.485–580), who established two monasteries at Vivarium where monks attempted to combine pagan and Christian learning. Scholarly zeal in the monastic tradition also comes from another source, Irish monasticism.

Although monks were people who removed themselves from

Church of Ste. Foi, Conques, France. 12th Century. This church is one of the finest surviving examples of monastic architecture (French Embassy Press and Information Division).

the mainstream of medieval society, monasticism, paradoxically, permeated that society. Because of their value to the monastic vocation, both classical and early Christian writings were preserved in monasteries; the earliest surviving manuscripts of both were copied by monks. It was in the monasteries of early medieval Europe that the first fully Christian culture developed—that is, in a monastic setting all was subordinated to the search for God and the achievement of salvation. With the brief exception of the reign of Charlemagne, monastic schools had a virtual monopoly on education until the middle of the twelfth century. Finally, many men who either were themselves monks or who were educated in monasteries served secular rulers, became bishops, or even were elected pope, thus bringing monastic culture out of the cloister and into the world.

CHAPTER SEVEN

The Carolingian Empire and Its Aftermath

Charlemagne

The anointing of Pepin as king of the Franks by Boniface on behalf of the pope in 751 was an important turning point in the history of the Middle Ages, for the papal-Frankish alliance was reaffirmed and sealed by a series of events in the following half century, the most famous of which was the coronation of Pepin's son Charlemagne (Charles the Great) as Roman Emperor. The name Charlemagne is one of the best known of the entire Middle Ages and deservedly so. He ruled the Franks from 768 to 814, and during that time conquered northern Italy from the Lombards and much territory to the east of the Franks from the Saxons, Bavarians, and Avars. Charlemagne's empire thus consisted of virtually all of Western Christian continental Europe. However, Charlemagne was much more than a successful conqueror; his concept of empire and his sponsorship of a program of educational reform, often called the Carolingian Renaissance, make his reign the most important of any ruler in early medieval history. Charlemagne became a figure celebrated in song and legend, revered as a warrior and a saint.

The papacy did not wait long to call upon the new Frankish king Pepin for help, for the Lombards threatened Rome in 753. Pepin came, defeated the Lombards, and in 756 "donated" the conquered territory to the papacy. It is possible that Pepin knew of the forged Donation of Constantine (see ch. 3). If not, it came into existence shortly after the Donation of Pepin.

Pepin divided his kingdom between his two sons; when Carloman died in 771, Charlemagne became sole ruler of the Franks. He was a great warrior who conquered the Lombards and took their crown for himself, fought a long and ultimately successful series of wars with the Saxons, virtually destroyed the Hunnic Avars on his eastern frontier, and waged war with some modest success against the Moslems in Spain.

By the end of the 780s, Charlemagne, in part under the influence of his trusted advisors, had begun to develop a concept of a Christian empire of which he was the head. He clearly perceived himself as the defender of the Church and quite naturally issued decrees on matters of ecclesiastical policy and even doctrine, which he expected to be obeyed by clerics and laity alike. It is no accident that his nickname at court was David after the great Hebrew king. In his famous *Admonitio Generalis* of 789, he likened himself to another Old Testament king, Josias, the great religious reformer (2 Kings 22ff.). In this decree, he used pastoral language reminiscent of Gregory the Great when describing the functions of the clergy:

> Accordingly it has pleased us to solicit your efforts, O pastors of the churches of Christ and leaders of His flock and distinguished luminaries of the world, to strive to lead the people of God to the pastures of eternal life by watchful care and urgent advice and stir yourselves to bring back the wandering sheep within the walls of ecclesiastical constancy on the shoulders of good example or exhortation, lest the wolf, plotting against anyone who transgresses the canonical laws or

evades the fatherly traditions of the ecumenical councils—which God forbid!—find him and devour him. Thus they must be admonished, urged, and even forced by the great zeal of piety, to restrain themselves within the bonds of paternal sanctions with staunch faith and unrelenting constancy. Therefore, we have sent our *missi* [messengers and inspectors] who by the authority of our name are to correct along with you what should be corrected. And we append herewith certain chapters from canonical ordinances which seem to us to be particularly necessary.[1]

Among the many chapters of this document, the following shows that Charlemagne's legislation dealt with issues that in modern categories would be purely ecclesiastical matters:

And you are to see to it, O chosen and venerable pastors and rulers of the church of God, that the priests whom you send through your dioceses for ruling and preaching in the churches to the people serving God, that they rightly and justly preach; and you are not to allow any of them to invent and preach to the people new and unlawful things according to their own judgment and not according to Holy Scripture. And you too are to preach those things which are just and right and lead to eternal life, and instruct others that they are to preach these same things.[2]

During the 790s, Charlemagne's concept of a Christian empire grew, and his position as protector of the papacy was tested when Pope Leo III was driven from Rome by political rivals in 799. Charlemagne had already presented his views on the roles of temporal and spiritual authorities in a letter to the pontiff three years earlier:

For it is our task, with the aid of divine goodness, to defend the holy church of Christ everywhere from the attacks of pagans without and to strengthen it within through the knowledge of the Catholic faith. And it is your duty, O Holy Father, with your hands raised high to God, after the manner of Moses, to aid our armies so that by your intercession with God, our leader and benefactor, the Christian people may always and everywhere be victorious over the enemies of His Holy Name,

and the name of Our Lord Jesus Christ be proclaimed throughout the world.[3]

Charlemagne intervened, and the reestablishment of Leo III
on the throne of St. Peter was probably the immediate cause
of one of the most famous events of the Middle Ages—the
coronation of Charlemagne as Roman emperor (often referred
to by modern historians as the *Holy* Roman Emperor) by the
pope in St. Peter's on Christmas Day, 800. Undoubtedly there
had been discussion between the pope and the Frankish king
before that day concerning the revival of the Empire, and the
idea of empire appears frequently in the writings of Charlemagne's advisor Alcuin (c.735–804) during the decade pre-
ceding the coronation. With this in mind, the account of the
coronation written by Charlemagne's friend and biographer
Einhard is surprising:

> The truth is that the inhabitants of Rome had violently at-
> tacked Pope Leo, putting out his eyes and cutting off his
> tongue, and had forced him to flee to the King for help.
> Charlemagne really came to Rome to restore the Church,
> which was in a very bad state indeed, but in the end he spent
> the whole winter there. It was on this occasion that he received
> the title of Emperor and Augustus. At first he was far from
> wanting this. He made it clear that he would not have entered
> the cathedral that day at all, although it was the greatest of all
> the festivals of the Church, if he had known in advance what
> the Pope was planning to do.[4]

Perhaps the explanation for Charlemagne's displeasure is not
with the title but with the manner in which it was conferred.
In Roman imperial ceremony, acclamation by the people pre-
ceded the actual coronation; and it was the former that
actually conferred power. However, Leo III's coronation pre-
ceded a well-rehearsed acclamation; this is clear from another
contemporary account:

> On the most holy day of Christmas, when the king rose from
> prayer in front of the shrine of the blessed apostle Peter, to
> take part in the Mass, Pope Leo placed a crown on his head,

and he was hailed by the whole Roman people: To the august Charles, crowned by God, the great and peaceful emperor of the Romans, life and victory! After the acclamations the pope addressed him in the manner of the old emperors. The name of Patricius was now abandoned and he was called Emperor and Augustus.[5]

Charlemagne probably disliked the prominence of the pope's role in the reconstitution of the Empire, something totally absent in the Roman imperial tradition, even after Constantine. However, it was a long time before popes used this precedent as a demonstration of their right to make and unmake Roman emperors.

In 802, Charlemagne required his subjects to swear an oath of loyalty to him—even those who had done so prior to his coronation in 800—as emperor. This was the one title that he held in all the territories he ruled:

> He [Charlemagne] has given instructions that in all his kingdom all men, both clergy and laity, and each according to his vows and way of life, who before have promised fealty to him as king, should now make the same promise to him as Caesar; and those who until now have not made the promise are all to do so from 12 years old and upwards.[6]

Charlemagne had established his permanent residence in Aachen (sometimes known by its French name, Aix-la-Chapelle) in the modern state of West Germany near Cologne, where his chapel, throne, and sarcophagus survive. In the years after the coronation, Aachen was the real center of his empire rather than Rome itself; and the court was still in essence Frankish in its customs despite the classical nicknames, the Roman-inspired architecture of the chapel, and the colossal statue of the fifth-century Emperor Theodosius II. After his coronation, Charlemagne never again set foot in Rome; when he wished to bestow the imperial title on his son Louis the Pious, the ceremony took place in Aachen. Charlemagne himself crowned his son, and no ecclesiastical officials participated in the coronation.

Charlemagne had planned to divide his territories among

his sons as his Merovingian predecessors had done; but these three kingdoms were all to remain part of a single empire, with his son Louis holding the imperial title. However, all his sons but Louis predeceased him, and thus for another generation the Empire remained more or less intact.

In marked contrast to the decentralizing tendencies of the Merovingians, Charlemagne strove to bring about a high degree of uniformity to all the lands he governed. His imperial title was one key element of this unity; its importance is suggested in the text of 802 quoted above. In that same document, Charlemagne described some of the machinery he established for making a unified empire a reality:

> Our most serene and most Christian lord and emperor, Charles, has selected the most prudent and wise from among his lead-ing men, archbishops and bishops, together with venerable abbots and devout laymen, and has sent them out into all his kingdom, and bestowed through them on all his subjects the right to live in accordance with a right rule of law. . . . And the *missi* themselves, as they wish to have the favour of Al-mighty God and to preserve it through the loyalty they have promised, are to make diligent inquiry wherever a man claims that someone has done him an injustice; so everywhere, and amongst all men, in God's holy churches, among poor people, orphans and widows, and throughout the whole people they may administer law and justice in full accordance with the will and the fear of God. And if there be anything which they themselves, together with the counts of the provinces, can-not correct or bring to a just settlement, they should refer it without any hesitation to the emperor's judgment along with their reports. And in no way, whether by some man's flattery or bribery, or by the excuse of blood relationship with some-one, or through fear of someone more powerful, should anyone hinder the right and proper course of justice.[7]

Despite Charlemagne's imperial titles, his *missi*, and his charisma, the unification of the Empire was far from com-plete and indeed may not have been as extensive as the sources suggest. Moreover, the partial and fragile unity and strong government that he did create did not long outlive him both because of internal weakness and foreign invasion. Nevertheless, the idea became a part of the medieval world view.

Charlemagne's energy and genius were not limited to military and political affairs. The cultural revival and educational reform that he began and nourished are every bit as important as the other achievements of his reign. Charlemagne, a Germanic warrior chieftain, was also a man deeply committed to learning, and theology in particular:

> He spoke easily and fluently, and could express with great clarity whatever he had to say. He was not content with his own mother tongue, but took the trouble to learn foreign languages. He learnt Latin so well that he spoke it as fluently as his own tongue; but he understood Greek better than he could speak it. He was eloquent to the point of sometimes seeming almost garrulous.
>
> He paid the greatest attention to the liberal arts; and he had great respect for men who taught them, bestowing high honours upon them. When he was learning the rules of grammar he received tuition from Peter the Deacon of Pisa, who by then was an old man, but for all other subjects he was taught by Alcuin, surnamed Albinus, another Deacon, a man of the Saxon race who came from Britain and was the most learned man anywhere to be found. Under him the Emperor spent much time and effort in studying rhetoric, dialectic and especially astrology. He applied himself to mathematics and traced the course of the stars with great attention and care.[8]

This text documents Charlemagne's careful and successful search for the greatest scholars of Western Christendom to serve as tutors, teachers for his children, advisors, and ecclesiastical reformers, including men from Italy, Ireland, and Christian Spain as well as from the Frankish kingdom. By far the most important of these was Alcuin of York, the architect of the so-called Carolingian Renaissance. He expressed his enthusiasm for the revival of classical learning in somewhat exalted terms in a 799 letter to Charlemagne:

> If many people became imbued with your ideas, a new Athens would be established in Francia—nay, an Athens fairer than

the Athens of old, for it would be ennobled by the teachings of Christ, and ours would surpass all the wisdom of the ancient Academy. For this had only for its instruction the disciples of Plato; yet, moulded by the seven liberal arts, it shone with constant splendour. But ours would be endowed as well with the sevenfold fullness of the Spirit, and would surpass all secular wisdom in dignity.[9]

What precisely was this renaissance all about? Compared to the cultural revival of the twelfth century or the Italian Renaissance of the fifteenth, it was modest indeed. In order for Charlemagne to be a responsible defender and guide and in order for the Church to be a (perhaps *the*) major element of unity in his territories, it was vital that both doctrine and liturgy be uniform. That would only be possible if accurate texts of Scripture and other authoritative Christian texts were available; and that was only possible if the clergy were educated. Thus Charlemagne sought to establish schools and to make accurate copies of texts. Alcuin and others were called upon to plan a new educational system. The *Admonitio Generalis* called for the establishment of new schools:

> And let schools be established in which boys may learn to read. Correct carefully the Psalms, the signs in writing, the songs, the calendar, the grammar in each monastery or bishopric, and the catholic books; because often some desire to pray to God properly, but they pray badly because of the incorrect books. And do not permit your boys to corrupt them in reading or writing. If there is need of writing the Gospel, Psalter, and Missal, let men of mature age do the writing with all diligence.[10]

No doubt this order to establish schools for boys in every monastery and cathedral remained unfulfilled although many schools were established. Most of the cathedral schools disappeared during the ninth century, but the monastic schools provided virtually all the education in the West from the ninth to the eleventh century. And in the eleventh century, it was the re-establishment of the cathedral schools—Charlemagne's educational ideals lived on—that was largely responsible for the developments in philosophy and learning generally called the renaissance of the twelfth century.

For the curriculum of the monastic and cathedral schools, Alcuin employed the seven liberal arts, the program of study outlined by Martianus Capella in the fifth century. However, in reality grammar and rhetoric dominated the Carolingian schools. Generally the texts used to teach these subjects were from late antiquity rather than from the Augustan Age (for example the Christian historians of the fourth and fifth centuries like Eusebius and Orosius were more popular than Livy or Tacitus); however, Vergil was well known and textbooks often included selected passages from the greatest Latin writers. The study of grammar and rhetoric was to prepare clerics to study Chrisian texts and to give them the necessary tools to correct poor manuscripts, make new editions, and write intelligent commentaries. The focus of this study, in addition to the Bible, was the Latin Fathers, including many lesser known figures of the fourth and fifth centuries, but also Jerome and Augustine. Charlemagne himself had a special affection for the works of Augustine; Einhard tells us that he liked to have the *City of God* read to him at dinner.

One of the important "inventions" of the Carolingian Renaissance was a new, legible script, to replace the difficult Merovingian style, that was employed to make accurate and easily copied manuscripts of the Bible, the Fathers, and liturgical texts. This script, known today as Caroline miniscule, is the ancestor of our lower case alphabet thanks to its revival during the Italian Renaissance.

Charlemagne made important liturgical reforms, establishing the Roman liturgy throughout his empire in place of the variety of liturgical forms that had grown up in the kingdom of the Franks known as the Gallican rite. Alcuin, after receiving a copy of the Roman (i.e. Gregorian) rite, found it incomplete and inadequate; he revised it, adding a preface and a list of proper readings. In the preface, he explained the problems he encountered and what he did to solve them:

The foregoing sacramentary, although marred by many a copyist's error, could not be reckoned to be in the condition

in which it had left its author's hands, [so] it was our task
to correct and restore it, for the benefit of all. Let a careful
reader examine it, and he will promptly agree with this judgement, unless the work be again corrupted by scribes.

But since there are other materials which Holy Church
necessarily uses, and which the aforesaid Father [Gregory],
seeing that they had been already put forth by others, left
aside, we have thought it worth while to gather them like
spring flowers of the meadows, and collect them together, and
place them in this book apart, but corrected and amended and
headed with their [own] titles, so that the reader may find in
this work all things which we have thought necessary for our
times, although we had found a great many also embodied in
other sacramentaries.[11]

The Roman rite as revised by Alcuin is the direct ancestor
of the liturgy used in Roman Catholic churches today. The
Roman rite was less flexible and less dramatic than the Gallican
rite, which it replaced. Perhaps as an attempt to compensate
for what was lost in the older tradition, dramatic set pieces
were sometimes embedded in the liturgy of the Roman rite,
especially at the important feasts, as in the following example
from the introit for the Mass of Easter at the monastery of St.
Gall (c.950):

Question: Whom do you seek in the sepulchre, O followers
of Christ?
Answer: Jesus of Nazareth, who was crucified, O heaven-
dwellers. He is not here, he has risen as he had foretold; go
announce that he has risen from the sepulchre.[12]

More elaborate versions of this scene of the visitation of the
holy women to the sepulchre developed, especially in the
eleventh and twelfth centuries; scholars have seen in this
process the rebirth of drama in the West.

The purpose and goals of the Carolingian Renaissance are
summarized in a letter of Charlemagne to Baugulf, abbot of
the monastery of Fulda, written in the last decade of the eighth
century:

We, Charles, by the grace of God king of the Franks and Lombards and patrician of the Romans, to Abbot Baugulf and all your congregation and our faithful teachers entrusted to your charge, send affectionate greeting in the name of Almighty God. Be it known to your devotion, most pleasing in the sight of God, that we, along with our faithful advisors, have deemed it useful that the bishoprics and monasteries which through the favour of Christ have been entrusted to us to govern should, in addition to the way of life prescribed by their rule and their practice of holy religion, devote their efforts to the study of literature and to the teaching of it, each according to his ability, to those on whom God has bestowed the capacity to learn; that, just as the observance of a rule gives soundness to their conduct, so also an attention to teaching and learning may give order and adornment to their words, and that those who seek to please God by living aright may not fail to please him also by rightness in their speaking. For it is written: "Either by your words shall you be justified, or by your words shall you be condemned (Matthew 12:37)." For although it is better to do what is right than to know it, yet knowledge comes before action. Thus each man must first learn what he wishes to carry out, so that he will know in his heart all the more fully what he needs to do, in order that his tongue may run on without stumbling into falsehood in the praise of Almighty God. . . . We began to fear that their [the monks'] lack of knowledge of writing might be matched by a more serious lack of wisdom in the understanding of holy scripture. We all know well that, dangerous as are the errors of words, yet much more dangerous are the errors of doctrine. Wherefore we urge you, not merely to avoid the neglect of the study of literature, but with a devotion that is humble and pleasing to God to strive to learn it, so that you may be able more easily and more rightly to penetrate the mysteries of the holy scriptures. For since there are figures of speech, metaphors and the like to be found on the sacred pages, there can be no doubt that each man who reads them will understand their spiritual meaning more quickly if he is first of all given full instruction in the study of literature.[13]

Charlemagne: a Germanic chieftain who gloried in arms and enjoyed raucous drinking bouts with his men but who also enjoyed hearing Augustine read at dinner and studied Latin; a Roman emperor who kept his court in the heart of Frankish territory. These contrasts are important because they so forcefully exemplify the fusion of Germanic with Roman-Christian cultures, which is one of the great themes of early medieval history. His version of the blending of these traditions is expressed in Einhard's description of Charlemagne's educational plans for his children:

> Charlemagne was determined to give his children, his daughters just as much as his sons, a proper training in the liberal arts which had formed the subject of his own studies. As soon as they were old enough he had his sons taught to ride in the Frankish fashion, to use arms and to hunt.[14]

Charlemagne also desired to use the tools of Roman-Christian culture to preserve his people's Germanic heritage:

> At the same time he directed that the age-old narrative poems, barbarous enough, it is true, in which were celebrated the warlike deeds of the kings of ancient times, should be written out and so preserved. He also began a grammar of his native tongue.[15]

If any of this was done, it has alas been lost. However, Charlemagne's efforts to preserve the Germanic heritage did lead to the recording of several law codes.

Charlemagne's attempt to fuse the cultural traditions in the West was personal and even to some extent superficial. Learned treatises written in generations following his death did more to merge Germanic kingship with the Roman imperium than Charlemagne's words or deeds. But without Charlemagne there would have been no reason to try to do so. It is not really until the twelfth century that one can talk of a cultural and institutional fusion into the more or less consistent world view that is suggested by the term *medieval*. However, the accomplishments of Charlemagne are a necessary step toward the formation of this view.

The political and cultural achievements of Charlemagne are only a part of his legacy to the remainder of the Middle Ages; the other major part is his legend. In the years of disintegration that followed his death, he began to take on mythic proportions. How different is Einhard's biography (c.830) from that of Notker the Stammerer (mid-880s), which borrows some of its literary devices from hagiography. The following text taken from Notker shows that the Charlemagne legend was already emerging in the century of his death:

> Charlemagne, of all kings the most glorious, was standing by a window through which the sun shone with dazzling brightness. He was clad in gold and precious stones, and he glittered himself like the sun at its first rising. He rested his arm upon Heito, for that was the name of the Bishop who some time previously had been sent to Constantinople. Around the Emperor, like the host of heaven, stood his three sons, the young men who were later to share the Empire; his daughters and their mother, adorned with wisdom, beauty and ropes of pearls; his bishops, unsurpassed in their virtue and their dignified posture, and his abbots, distinguished by their sanctity and their noble demeanour; his leaders, like Joshua when he appeared in the camp of Gilgal; and his army like that which drove back the Syrians and the Assyrians out of Samaria. Had David been in their midst he would have had every reason to sing: "Kings of the earth, and all people; princes, and all judges of the earth; both young men and maidens; old men, and children: let them praise the name of the Lord."[16]

By the twelfth century, there were legends of Charlemagne going to Jerusalem and driving the Moslems out of Spain, making him the exemplar of both crusader and pilgrim. He was even canonized by a twelfth-century imperially sponsored antipope; and although the Church does not now recognize him as a saint, he was widely venerated in the Middle Ages. Statues of Charlemagne are found on churches all over Western Europe.

The most famous Charlemagne literature retells his expedition into Spain in the late 770s. Einhard presents a historical account of it, stressing the ambush of Charlemagne's rearguard by the Basques at Roncesvalles in the Pyrenees.

> [Charlemagne] marched over a pass across the Pyrenees, received the surrender of every single town and castle which he attacked and then came back with his army safe and sound, except for the fact that for a brief moment on the return journey, while he was in the Pyrenean mountain range itself, he was given a taste of Basque treachery. . . . At a moment when Charlemagne's army was stretched out in a long column of march, as the nature of the local defiles forced it to be, these Basques, who had set their ambush on the very top of one of the mountains, came rushing down on the last part of the baggage train and the troops who were marching in support of the rearguard and so protecting the army which had gone on ahead. The Basques forced them down into the valley beneath, joined battle with them and killed them to the last man. . . . In this battle died Eggihard, who was in charge of the King's table, Anshelm, the Count of the Palace and Roland, Lord of the Breton Marches, along with a great number of others. What is more, this assault could not be avenged there and then, for, once it was over, the enemy dispersed in such a way that no one knew where or among which people they could be found.[17]

By the twelfth century, this relatively unimportant incident at Roncesvalles had been transformed into an all-out apocalyptic confrontation between Christians and Moslems and given an important place in the whole scheme of salvation history. The best-known version of this story is the French *chanson de geste*, the *Song of Roland*, although versions exist in other vernacular languages and in the visual arts. In this poem Charlemagne is more than two hundred years old, with the wisdom of Solomon and the courage of David; he carries the lance that pierced Christ's side; he has the authority to absolve a sinner; and he is the conqueror of Spain, England, and Constantinople. He is presented as a man who often and effectively communes with God:

> In a green meadow he gets down from his horse,
> Kneels on the ground and prays almighty God

Tympanum from the Cathedral of Angoulême, France. 12th Century. In the lower panel (see detail) a battle scene from the *Song of Roland* is depicted. From its placement beneath the figures of St. Peter and two other apostles, we can see that the story of Roland was viewed as a story about the spread of the faith, becoming an important icon for the crusades. Although a French story, it appears in sculpture and stained glass throughout Western Europe, including Italy and Spain.

> To make the sun stop moving through the sky,
> Delay the night, and let the day remain.
> And then an angel, who often spoke with him,
> Came in great haste to give him this command:
> "Charles, speed you on! The light won't fail you now.
> God knows that you have lost the flower of France.
> You'll have your vengeance on the vile Saracen!"
> Already Charles has mounted once again.
> For Charlemagne God worked a miracle:
> The sun stops moving, and stands still in the sky.
> The pagans flee, the Franks pursue them hard.[18]

In this poem the man who described himself to be like David and Josias now also becomes like Joshua. The Charlemagne of history and the Charlemagne of legend are two of the most important figures of the Middle Ages.

The Re-emergence of Chaos in Western Europe

Louis the Pious (r.814–40), lacking his father's energy, vision, and charisma, nevertheless tried to continue some of his father's policies, especially with regard to the protection and direction of the Church. His most successful effort was in the area of monastic reform. He established a model monastery near Aachen under the leadership of Benedict of Aniane (d.821). The following text, taken from Ardo Smaragdus's life of Benedict, explains the imperially sponsored reform program, includ-the goal of monastic uniformity:

> The emperor [Louis] placed him over all the monasteries in his kingdom so that as he had instructed Aquitaine and Gothia in the ways of salvation he might also by salutary example teach Francia. There were many monasteries which had at one time been regularly instituted, but gradually, with discipline slackening, the regular routine had almost disappeared. Moreover, after he had assembled the fathers of the abbeys and many monks, he remained several days, so that just as there was one [monastic] profession for all, there might by the emperor's command be one saving rule for all the

monasteries. Accordingly, to all so placed he discussed the rule anew and elucidated obscure matters for everyone, resolved doubts, rooted out former errors, and confirmed useful customs and usages. When opinions regarding the *Rule* and all doubts were resolved, with the consent of all, he explained those usages which the *Rule* does not present clearly. He presented a capitulary on these things to the emperor for his confirmation and so that he might order it observed in all monasteries in the kingdom. To this we refer the reader desirous of more information. The emperor immediately assented to this and appointed inspectors for each monastery who were to see to it that all things which he had ordered were observed and to explain the proper procedures to those who were not informed. And so the work was carried out and speeded with the aid of divine mercy; and one established rule is universally observed by everyone and all monasteries brought to a standard of unity, as though they were instructed by one master in one place.[19]

Benedict of Aniane's interpretation of the Rule of his namesake significantly altered the development of Western monasticism. First, the liturgy was expanded so that it took up much more time than the Rule had prescribed. Manual labor was limited to housework, while tenant farmers did the agricultual labor. This was a logical change insofar as monks at this time did not come from agricultural workers but rather from landed families. However, the limitation of manual labor upset the balance between work and prayer that was central to the Rule of St. Benedict. Second, Benedict of Aniane tried to limit severely the monks' contact with the outside world, but this was really not possible so long as monasteries possessed great estates and political power.

Monasticism generally declined in the ninth century as "extra" children of nobles were sent to monasteries although they had no vocation; many monks wanted to live as much like nobles as possible within the cloister, and hunting dogs and even mistresses were not unknown within the monastic precincts. Several monastic reform movements developed in the tenth and eleventh centuries, most notably at Cluny; but these reforms began with the Rule as interpreted by Benedict of Aniane. It was not until the establishment of the Cistercian Order in the twelfth century that a significant reform of Benedictine monasticism occurred that attempted to return to a life based on the Rule stripped of all its accretions (see ch. 8).

Louis the Pious's reign was troubled by rebellious sons among whom the Empire was finally divided. One son became king of the West Franks; another, king of the East Franks; the eldest, Lothar, became king of Lotharingia, a territory containing both a corridor between the other two kingdoms and northern and central Italy. And it was the king of Lotharingia who also held the title of Roman emperor. There was still one empire, but there were three kingdoms that were in reality independent; the title of emperor counted for little. The disintegration of the Carolingian Empire did not stop here. The kings of these successor states declined in power as local magnates established virtual independence. Furthermore, when Lothar died, his kingdom was divided among his three sons; thus Lotharingia did not survive its founder. The title of Roman emperor was normally held by the ruler of one of the Italian kingdoms that developed out of the disintegration of Lotharingia, but it no longer included authority over all the territories Charlemagne once ruled. It became a political pawn of the Italian nobility; after 920, not one of them even bothered to take the imperial title.

Other developments were equally important to the Empire's history. Louis the Pious crowned Lothar as Roman emperor in 817 in Aachen, following the pattern established by his father at his own coronation. However, Louis was deeply devoted to the Roman Church and agreed to a papal coronation for Lothar in Rome in 823, renewing the close tie between the papacy and the Empire. Pope Nicholas I (r.858-67), one of the outstanding medieval popes, further sought to tie the Empire to papal policy. After the coronation of Charles the Bald as Roman emperor in Rome on Christmas Day, 875, it was no longer in doubt that the imperial coronation must be performed by the pope.

Despite the weakness of the rulers, the kingdoms of the West and East Franks remained at least theoretically intact. The stronger, that of the East Franks (Germany), had a descendant of Charlemagne on the throne until the dynasty failed to produce an heir (911). Then the monarchy became elective, with the great nobles choosing the king. The election of Otto I (the Great) in 936 was a turning point in the history of the kingdom and indeed all of Europe. His coronation is described by Widukind of Corvey:

> And when they had arrived, the dukes and the great lords with a force of the chief vassals gathered in the portico of the basilica of Charlemagne. They placed the new ruler on the throne that had been constructed there, giving him their hands and offering fealty; promising their help against all his enemies, they made him king according to their custom.
>
> . . . The king, dressed in a close-fitting tunic according to the Frankish custom, was escorted behind the altar, on which lay the royal insignia-sword with sword-belt, cloak with bracelets, staff with sceptre and diadem. . . .
>
> Going to the altar and taking from it the sword with sword-belt and turning to the king, he [Archbishop Hildibert of Mainz] said: "Accept this sword, with which you may chase out all the adversaries of Christ, barbarians, and bad Christians, by the divine authority handed down to you and by the power of all the empire of the Franks for the most lasting peace of all Christians." Then taking the bracelets and cloak, he clothed him saying, "These points [of the cloak] falling to the ground will remind you with what zeal of faith you should burn and how you ought to endure in preserving peace to the end."
>
> Then taking the sceptre and staff, he said: "With these symbols you may be reminded that you should reproach your subjects with paternal castigation, but first of all you should extend the hand of mercy to ministers of God, widows, and orphans. And never let the oil of compassion be absent from your head in order that you may be crowned with eternal reward in the present and in the future."[20]

This text shows how much the Church had become involved in the royal as well as the imperial coronations. Kingship was perceived to have a sacred character, and the annointing of a king was often considered to be one of the Church's sacraments. It was common to refer to a monarch as both king and priest; this did not mean that a king could celebrate mass or hear confession, but it did suggest a special and unique status for him.

Otto faced attacks from the East and rebellion by his nobles, but he was able to overcome both foreign and domestic enemies largely because he was supported by the Church, from whose land most of his soldiers came. In turn, it was crucial for Otto to have loyal bishops and abbots. Thus royal appointment and investiture of bishops was becoming common practice.

Otto was crowned king of the East Franks at Aachen, and he probably planned to restore the Carolingian Empire from that time on. He found his opportunity when Pope John XII was driven from Rome and called on him for help. We have observed that as far back as Pepin's reign, the papacy had come to rely on the Germanic kings north of the Alps for protection. However, during the ninth and tenth centuries, the weak successors of Charlemagne were unable to oversee and protect the papacy; and it fell victim to the Italian nobles who treated it as a political pawn. Here was Otto's chance to prove his strength. Though John XII was no model of holiness, Otto I restored him to his throne (much as Charlemagne had restored Leo III) and received the imperial crown from him. Otto spent the remaining eleven years of his life in Italy, attempting to bring northern Italy under his control. His empire was smaller than Charlemagne's, consisting of the kingdoms of the East Franks and nothern Italy. For the rest of the Middle Ages, the Empire essentially consisted of the territories of Otto rather than those of Charlemagne.

Otto arranged for his son and heir, Otto II (r.973–83), to marry the Byzantine Princess Theophano. When Otto II died, she became the regent for his infant heir Otto III (r.983–1002). Otto III grew up in Italy tutored by Greeks who had accompanied Theophano to the West. His vision of empire blended his Carolingian heritage with Byzantine imperial ideology. He even dreamed of reuniting East and West into one Roman

Empire. But his death without heirs brought about a dynastic change; although the imperial title continued, the Empire's center shifted once again to Germany.

During the reign of the Ottos, there was something of a cultural revival sometimes called the Ottonian Renaissance. Several new cathedral schools were begun, and Byzantine craftsmen influenced both sculpture and manuscript illumination. The most important element of this revival, however, was that it kept alive the achievements and goals of the Carolingian Renaissance.

The kingdom of the West Franks was much weaker and less significant than that of the East Franks. From 887 to 987, the royal title went back and forth between Carolingians and the family of the counts of Paris. In 987, Count Hugh Capet became king; the dynasty he established ruled what was soon thereafter called France until the execution of Louis XVI in 1793. Although the first Capetian kings exercised little power beyond the area around Paris, they had the support of the Church and they consistently produced male heirs, two major factors that solidified their position as hereditary monarchs.

One of the most serious problems Western Europe faced in the century and a half after Charlemagne's death was a series of invasions by non-Christians. One group of invaders, the Vikings, came from Scandinavia. The earliest Viking attacks took place in the kingdom of the Franks and England during Charlemagne's reign. Einhard described the problem and how Charlemagne dealt with it:

> Charlemagne took upon himself the task of building a fleet to ward off the attacks of the Northmen. For this purpose ships were constructed near to the rivers which flow out of Gaul and Germany into the North Sea. In view of the fact that these Northmen kept on attacking and pillaging the coast of Gaul and Germany, Charlemagne placed strongpoints and coastguard stations at all the ports and at the mouths of all rivers considered large enough for the entry of ships, so that the enemy could be bottled up by this military task force.[21]

The raids on Gaul became more serious during the reign of Louis the Pious. The following selections are from the story

Lazarus being expelled from the table of the rich man. Detail of a bronze column commissioned by Bernward of Hildesheim, Hildesheim Cathedral, 1015–1022. This is one of the masterpieces of the Ottonian Renaissance. The story is from the 16th chapter of Luke (note the dogs with the long necks licking poor Lazarus' wounds). This column, narrating a story from bottom to top, is modelled on a column in Rome commissioned by the Emperor Trajan (r. 98–117) which depicts his conquest of Dacia.

of the monks of the Monastery of St. Philibert originally located on the island of Noirmoutier:

> The frequent and unfortunate attacks of the Northmen, . . . were in no wise abating, and Abbot Hilbodus had built a castle on the island for protection against that faithless people. Together with the council of his brothers, he came to King Pepin and asked His Highness what he intended to do about this problem. Then the glorious king and the great men of the

realm—a general assembly of the kingdom was then being held —deliberated concerning the problem with gracious concern and found themselves unable to help through mounting a vigorous assault. Because of the extremely dangerous tides, the island was not always readily accessible to our forces, while all knew that it was quite accessible to the Northmen whenever the sea was peaceful. The king and the great men chose what they believed to be the more advantageous policy. With the agreement of the most serene king Pepin, almost all the bishops of the province of Aquitaine, and the abbots, counts, and other faithful men who were present, and many others besides who had learned about the situation, unanimously advised that the body of the blessed Philibert ought to be taken from the island and no longer allowed to remain there. . . .

The number of ships grew larger, and the Northmen were beyond counting. Everywhere there were massacres of Christians, raids, devastations, and burnings. For as long as the world shall last, this will remain evident by manifest signs. Whatever cities the Northmen attacked, they captured without resistance: Bordeaux, Périgueux, Saintes, Limoges, Angoulême, and Toulouse; then Angers, Tours, and Orléans were destroyed. The remains of numerous saints were carried off. What the Lord warns through the prophet came close to fulfillment: "From the north shall an evil break forth upon all the inhabitants of the land" (Jeremias I.14). We also fled to a place which is called Cunauld, in the territory of Anjou, on the banks of the Loire, which the glorious king Charles had given us for the sake of refuge, because of the imminent peril, before Angers was taken. . . .

The Northmen attacked Spain besides; they entered the Rhône River, and they devastated Italy. While everywhere so many domestic and foreign wars were raging, the year of the Incarnation of Christ 857 passed. As long as there had been in us some hope of returning to our own possessions (which, however, proved to be fruitless), the body of the blessed Philibert, as has been said, was left in his own soil. With evils surrounding us, we had not been able to obtain a definite place of security. But since a refuge was nowhere to be found, we did not permit the most holy body to be carried with us hither and yon. Now, it was more truly smuggled away from the grasp of the Northmen than carried with festive praises, and it was taken to the place we have mentioned, which is called Cunauld. This was done in such a way that, when necessity required, it might be moved elsewhere. The year of the Lord's Incarnation was 862 when the body was carried from Cunauld to Messay.[22]

This story makes clear the seriousness and the scope of Viking raids. It is a long way by boat from Scandinavia to Italy. And Louis the Pious's helplessness is equally clear, for the Vikings raided quickly and were gone long before a royal army could be summoned.

By the middle of the ninth century, some Vikings began to winter in Gaul, establishing permanent bases for their piratical operations. In 911, following some military setbacks, the Viking leader Rolf (or Rollo) agreed to become a vassal of the West Frankish king and to accept Christianity. This is the beginning of the duchy of Normandy, the name deriving from "Northmen."

England faced the same problem as Gaul, for the Vikings (usually called Danes by English historians) began to settle down in the eastern part of Britain. In fact, most of the Anglo-Saxon kingdoms were destroyed. The most western of them, Wessex, produced one of the great heros of English history, King Alfred the Great (r.871–99), who organized defenses against further Viking attacks and began the process of their conversion to Christianity. Alfred and his successors were the first kings to be recognized by all the Anglo-Saxons; in the course of the tenth century, the Danes also accepted Anglo-Saxon rule while retaining their own law. However, in the eleventh century a successful second Scandinavian attack on England brought two Danish leaders to the English throne.

In the ninth and tenth centuries Western Europe was also attacked by the Moslems. Einhard tells us that as early as Charlemagne's reign they had sacked cities on the Italian coast. These raids were essentially piratical in nature, not as serious a threat to order as those of the Vikings. Nevertheless, they disrupted traffic on the Rhone and established pirate dens on the French Riviera and even in the Alps, where they attacked merchants and kidnapped them for ransom.

Beginning in the 860s, the East Frankish kingdom came under attack from a nomadic tribe of horsemen called the Magyars (Hungarians). For almost a century they wreaked havoc in the East Frankish kingdom, also occasionally venturing into the West Frankish kingdom and even Italy. In 955, Otto the Great defeated them at the battle of Lechfeld. Soon afterwards, they settled down in the middle Danube area and accepted Christianity. Their first Christian king, Stephen, received his crown from Pope Sylvester II in the year 1000.

While the East Franks were fighting with the Magyars, they were also engaged in war with the pagan Slavs from time to time, especially the Bohemians and Poles. By 1000, both of these peoples had accepted Christianity and had begun to absorb Latin culture; in fact in the year 1000, Otto III made a pilgrimage to Poland to obtain relics of Saint Adalbert, the man most responsible for the Poles' conversion.

Taken together, these raids of Vikings, Moslems, and Magyars had disastrous short-term effects on both the continent and England. They were a main cause of the disintegration of royal authority because of royal impotence in fighting against the raiders. However, apart from the Moslems, the raiders eventually accepted Christianity and the Roman-Latin culture that went with it and became vital parts of Western Christendom. Furthermore, some Vikings settled in Iceland and Greenland and even explored America. They established Christianity in their settlements and also created an important literature, the Icelandic sagas—like so much else in medieval culture, a creative fusion of pagan and Christian. That the Vikings continued to exert a dynamic influence on European history can be seen by the fact that the Normans conquered England in 1066. The saintly Edward the Confessor, son of an Anglo-Saxon king and a Norman mother, had become king in 1042. However, he left no heir, and the throne was claimed upon his death in 1066 by both the leading Anglo-Saxon noble, Harold, and William, Duke of Normandy. Having gained the support of the pope for his claim to the throne, William invaded England, defeated and killed Harold at the battle of Hastings, and had himself crowned king on Christmas Day, 1066, at Westminster Abbey (Edward the Confessor's burial place).

The Normans Sailing to England. The Bayeux Tapestry. Late 11th Century. The Normans have all their military equipment in the boats, including horses (far right). The style of their ships reminds us of their Viking origins.

The Norman conquest was a turning point in English history. The Anglo-Saxon nobility and ecclesiastical hierarchy were replaced by Normans. William superimposed Norman institutions upon those of the Anglo-Saxons rather than starting from scratch, taking advantage of the fact that England before the conquest was the most centralized monarchy in Western Europe. Since William continued to be Duke of Normandy, England became more directly involved in continental and especially French politics. In fact, King Henry II of England (1154–89) possessed almost the entire western half of France, and England became deeply involved in his efforts to retain it. Though the English kings lost most of their continental possessions early in the thirteenth century, they desired to reconquer them. In one sense, the Hundred Years War

(1337–1453) was about English possessions in France; thus the attachment to the continent (other than with the Roman Church) that was the result of the Norman conquest was central to the history of England for the remainder of the Middle Ages.

The English language also changed; the Normans brought the French language with them into England. In the centuries after the conquest the new aristocracy spoke French, the lower classes, Anglo-Saxon. These languages began to blend, a process essentially complete by the fourteenth century. The grammatical structure of English remains essentially Germanic, but the vocabulary is divided between French and Anglo-Saxon.

Feudal Society

We have already observed the division of Charlemagne's Empire and the decline in royal authority, partly due to internal strife and partly caused by the ninth-century invasions. It is important now to ask precisely what took the place of royal authority, a question intimately related to bonds of dependence existing between free men. To begin to answer these questions, we must return to Charlemagne and even his predecessors. Both Roman and Germanic traditions included a hierarchical view of society, in part expressed by relations such as patron-client and chieftain-warrior. In the chaos of the Merovingian world, ties of dependence between freemen were common. A man who needed help protecting his property and his person would attach himself to a powerful man who would agree to aid him in return for some kind of service. And those wishing to increase their power and status could do so by acquiring the service of freemen in return for providing for their needs, usually defense. During the Carolingian period, kings encouraged all freemen to establish such relationships, and a law of 847 issued jointly by Louis the Pious's three sons tried to require it: "We wish that every free man in our kingdom select the lord whom he prefers, us or one of our faithful subjects."[23]

The term *vassal* describes the person who binds himself to another freeman and pledges loyalty and service to him; *lord* refers to the one who accepts the vassal's service, usually in exchange for protection and support. One reason that Charlemagne and his successors encouraged vassalage was to make governing easier since they required a lord to be responsible for his vassals. Charlemagne had many of his own vassals. A law dated between 801 and 813 suggests the importance of vassalage:

> If any vassal should wish to abandon his lord, he may do so only if he can prove that the lord has committed one of these crimes: first, if the lord should have unjustly sought to enslave him; second, if the lord plotted against his life; third, if the lord committed adultery with the wife of his vassal; fourth, if the lord willingly attacked him with drawn sword in order to kill him; fifth, if, after the vassal commended his hands into his, the lord failed to provide defense which he could have done. If the lord has committed any of these five offenses against his vassal, the vassal may abondon him.[24]

Often the king's vassals were men who performed military service for him. In the eighth century, the character of military service changed rapidly. Until then, footsoldiers were the basic units of the army, and all freemen bore arms. But the stirrup, an Eastern invention, changed all that by dramatically increasing the efficiency of mounted soldiers. To fight on horseback presumed a great deal of equipment, including a protective suit and several horses. Furthermore, such a soldier needed training and practice with this rather sophisticated equipment. Charlemagne sought vassals who would serve him in this capacity, and sometimes in nonmilitary capacities, but he had to provide for their support. There were several ways to do this, such as housing them in his own palace; the most common practice was to grant them a piece of land, called a *fief*, with its peasant cultivators for their lifetimes. Sometimes a fief was merely enough land to support one soldier, but other times a king granted a large fief from whose vassal he required the service of several soldiers. The men receiving such a fief usually divided it into smaller fiefs (the practice of *subinfeudation*), which were granted to men who became their vassals.

The predominantly military character of vassalage is clear from another part of the 847 law quoted above:

> And we wish that the vassal of any one of us [Charles the Bald, Louis the German, and Lothar] should accompany his lord into the army in order to fulfill his services, in no matter whose kingdom he should be. But if a general invasion of the kingdom should occur, called *Landwehr* (may it not happen!), then all the people of the realm should go together to repulse it.[25]

Land was not the only way Charlemagne provided for his vassals. To some he gave the office of count. Within a defined section of his Empire, a count held military, judicial, and financial power. To most people, the count *was* the government although Charlemagne did have his *missi* to check up on each count. These counts not only enjoyed great power but also profited from land attached to the office and a portion of the fines collected.

Because of the ineffectiveness of government after Charlemagne's death and the ineffectiveness of centralized defense in light of the Viking raids, the counts, at least de facto, became independent of those they theoretically served. They became the only source of justice and military power in their counties, relying on their vassals to perform military service for them. Vassalage was not originally inherited since it was a personal bond between two men that ceased to exist when one died. The office of count was not inheritable either; often, in fact, a king would move counts rather frequently from one county to another. By the end of the ninth century, however, the succession of both vassalage and the office of count from father to son had become common, largely because it was easier to accept a son as a vassal or a count than to dispossess him. When the Roman Emperor Charles the Bald left his Frankish possessions for a military campaign in Italy in 877, he provided for the succession to office by sons of the counts who were with him in Italy should their fathers die when they were away.

An eleventh-century edict of the Roman Emperor Conrad II illustrates the triumph of the inheritability of fiefs:

> We also command that when a vassal, great or petty, should die, his son shall receive his fief. If he has no son, but is survived by a grandson born of male issue, the grandson should in equal manner have the fief, while respecting the customs of the great *valvassores* in giving horses and arms to their lords. If he does not have a grandson born from male issue and if he should have a legitimate brother from the side of his father, and if that brother, after offending the lord, is willing to make amends and become his vassal, he should have the fief which was his father's.[26]

Since a fief was granted to provide enough income to support at least one mounted soldier, there was a conflict with the Germanic custom of a father dividing his property equally among his sons. However, the practice of primogeniture—the eldest son inheriting all the land and titles—was in general use on the continent by the eleventh century and in England by the twelfth.

The great counts treated their fiefs as their own territory. One of the characteristics of the feudal period is the treatment of political power as a private possession and its division among a large number of people.[27] Until about 1000, this trend did not normally go beneath the level of the count. However, in the eleventh century, many vassals of counts wrested political power from their lords just as the counts had done from the kings in the ninth and tenth centuries.

The developments described above did not occur at the same time or to the same degree in all parts of Latin Christendom. Vassalage and the private possession of political power existed in northern and central Italy, but the papacy and the early development of cities there limited these developments. England is particularly difficult to analyze. It was not part of the Carolingian Empire, and its history is quite different despite common problems such as Viking raids. Although there may have been some development of lordship and vassalage in preconquest England, they were essentially imposed upon England by William the Conqueror. And the Norman variety of lordship and vassalage checked the private possession of political power. Thus, England was "feudalized" as a matter of policy and not through a long period of gradual development. The same is true of southern Italy and Sicily when the Normans created a state there, and it is also true for the crusader states established in the Holy Land at the end of the eleventh century.

These developments took place most completely in the heartland of the Frankish kingdom—north of the Loire and west of the Rhine. Vassalage was not nearly as prevalent in southern Gaul, for example, and decentralization was never as complete in the kingdom of the East Franks. Furthermore, within the Frankish heartland there seems to have been almost as many variations in the relationship of lord to vassal and in the ways and degree to which the counts ruled as there are surviving documents that inform us about this period. There were some common elements, but there was nothing systematic or consistent about what is sometimes misleadingly called the "feudal system." In fact, the term *feudalism* came into use only in the seventeenth century and has lost much of its usefulness today because there are almost as many definitions as there are medieval historians. Despite regional differences, the following charter of 1110 presents clearly the most important obligations of lord and vassal. The lord in this case is the abbot of a monastery, demonstrating that the Church, as well as the laity, took part in this kind of relationship:

> In the name of the Lord, I, Bernard Atton, Viscount of Carcassonne, in the presence of my sons, Roger and Trencavel, and of Peter Roger of Barbazan, and William Hugo, and Raymond Mantellini, and Peter de Vitry, nobles, and of many other honorable men, who had come to the monastery of St. Mary of Grasse, to the honor of the festival of the august St. Mary; since lord Leo, abbot of the said monastery, has asked me, in the presence of all those above mentioned, to acknowledge to him the fealty and homage for the castles, manors, and places which the patrons, my ancestors, held from him and his predecessors and from the said monastery, as a fief, and which I ought to hold as they held, I have made to the lord abbot Leo acknowledgement and homage as I ought to do.
>
> Therefore, let all present and to come know that I the said

Bernard Atton, lord and viscount of Carcassonne, acknowledge verily to thee my lord Leo, by the grace of God, abbot of St. Mary of Grasse, and to thy successors that I hold and ought to hold as a fief, in Carcassonne, the following: [a list of manors, castles, and villages] . . . for each and all of which I make homage and fealty with hands and with mouth to thee my said lord Leo and to thy successors, and I swear upon these four gospels of God that I will always be a faithful vassal to thee and to thy successors and to St. Mary of Grasse in all things in which a vassal is required to be faithful to his lord, and I will defend thee, my lord, and all thy successors, and the monastery and the monks present and to come and the castles and manors and all your men and their possessions against all malefactors and invaders, at my request and that of my successors at my own cost; and I will give to thee power over all the castles and manors above described, in peace and in war, whenever they shall be claimed by thee or by thy successors.

Moreover I acknowledge that, as a recognition of the above fiefs, I and my successors ought to come to the said monastery, at our own expense, as often as a new abbot shall have been made, and there do homage and return to him the power over all the fiefs described above. And when the abbot shall mount his horse I and my heirs, viscounts of Carcassone, and our successors ought to hold the stirrup for the honor of the dominion of St. Mary of Grasse; and to him and all who come with him to as many as two hundred beasts, we should make the abbot's purveyance in the borough of St. Michael of Carcassone, the first time he enters Carcassone, with the best fish and meat and with eggs and cheese, honorablly according to his will, and pay the expense of the shoeing of the horses, and for straw and fodder as the season shall require.

And if I or my sons or their successors do not observe to thee or to thy successors each and all the things declared above, and should come against these things, we wish that all the aforesaid fiefs should by that very fact be handed over to thee and to the said monastery of St. Mary of Grasse and to thy successors.[28]

In a famous letter of 1020, Bishop Fulbert of Chartres describes the duties of a lord and vassal, making clear that a significant part of those duties was negative—not to do harm, not to be unfaithful.

To William, most illustrious duke of the Aquitanians, Bishop
Fulbert, the favor of his prayers:
Requested to write something regarding the character of fealty,
I have set down briefly for you, on the authority of the books,
the following things. He who takes the oath of fealty to his
lord ought always to keep in mind these six things: what is
harmless, safe, honorable, useful, easy, and practicable. Harmless, which means that he ought not to injure his lord in his
body; safe, that he should not injure him by betraying his confidence or the defenses upon which he depends for security;
honorable, that he should not injure him in his justice, or in
other matters that relate to his honor; useful, that he should not
injure him in his property; easy, that he should not make difficult that which his lord can do easily; and practicable, that he
should not make impossible for the lord that which is possible.

However, while it is proper that the faithful vassal avoid
these injuries, it is not for doing this alone that he deserves his
holding: for it is not enough to refrain from wrongdoing, unless that which is good is done also. It remains, therefore, that
in the same six things referred to above he should faithfully
advise and aid his lord, if he wishes to be regarded as worthy
of his benefice and to be safe concerning the fealty which he
has sworn. The lord also ought to act toward his faithful vassal in the same manner in all these things. And if he fails to do
this, he will be rightfully regarded as guilty of bad faith, just
as the former, if he should be found shirking, or willing to
shirk, his obligations would be perfidious and perjured. [29]

The two previous documents mention the act by which one
becomes a vassal, called fealty; normally, it was accompanied
by a sacred oath called homage. The ceremony of fealty and
homage, performed in Flanders in 1127, is described by Galbert of Bruges:

On April 7, Thursday, homages to the count were again performed; they were carried out in this order in expression of
faith and loyalty. First they did homage in this way. The count
asked each one if he wished to become wholly his man, and the
latter replied, "I so wish," and with his hands clasped and enclosed by those of the count, they were bound together by a
kiss. Secondly, he who had done homage pledged his faith to

the count's spokesman in these words: "I promise on my faith that I will henceforth be faithful to Count William and that I will maintain my homage toward him completely against everyone, in good faith and without guile." And in the third place he swore an oath to this effect on the relics of the saints. Then the count, with a wand which he held in his hand, gave investiture to all those who by this compact had promised loyalty and done homage and likewise had taken an oath.[30]

The practices described above, practical and to a great extent effective responses to the problems of the time, were formalized in the creation of ideals of lordship and vassalage. There was a desire to justify in theoretical terms power in the hands of the landed nobility and to establish a code of conduct for those who held power. The following description from Odo of Cluny's life of Saint Gerald of Aurillac (d.909), a powerful lord, clearly states the ideals of lordship:

He therefore exerted himself to repress the insolence of the violent, taking care in the first place to promise peace and most easy reconciliation to his enemies. And he did this by taking care, that either he should overcome evil by good, or if his enemies would not come to terms, he should have in God's eyes the greater right on his side. And sometimes indeed he soothed them and reduced them to peace. When insatiable malice poured scorn on peaceful men, showing severity of heart, he broke the teeth of the wicked [Ps. 57:7], that, according to the saying of Job, he might snatch the prey from their jaws [Job 29:17]. He was not incited by the desire for revenge, as is the case with many, or led on by love of praise from the multitude, but by love of the poor, who were not able to protect themselves. He acted in this way lest, if he became sluggish through indolent patience, he should seem to have neglected the precept to care for the poor. He ordered the poor man to be saved and the needy to be freed from the hand of the sinner. Rightly, therefore, he did not allow the sinner to prevail. But sometimes when the unavoidable necessity of fighting lay on him, he commanded his men in imperious tones, to fight with the backs of their swords and with their spears reversed. This would have been ridiculous to the enemy if Gerald, strengthened by divine power, had not been invincible to them.

Theophilus does fealty to the Devil. Sculpture from the Abbey Church of Souillac, France. 12th Century. The story of Theophilus making a pact with the devil was already old in the 12th Century. Here it is made relevant to a society which sees relationships in terms of lord and vassal by depicting Theophilus performing the act of fealty, thus becoming the vassal of the Devil.

And it would have seemed useless to his own men, if they had not learnt by experience that Gerald, who was carried away by his piety in the very moment of battle, had not always been invincible. When therefore they saw that he triumphed by a new kind of fighting which was mingled with piety, they changed their scorn to admiration, and sure of victory they readily fulfilled his commands. For it was a thing unheard of that he or the soldiers who fought under him were not victorious. . . . Let no one be worried because a just man sometimes made use of fighting, which seems incompatible with religion. No one who has judged his cause impartially will be able to show that the glory of Gerald is clouded by this. For some of the Fathers, and of these the most holy and most patient, when the cause of justice demanded, valiantly took up arms against their adversaries, as Abraham, who destroyed a great multitude of the enemy to rescue his nephew [Gen. 14], and King David who sent his forces even against his own son. [2 Kings 18]. Gerald did not fight invading the property of others, but defending his own, or rather his people's rights. . . . It was lawful, therefore, for a layman to carry the sword in battle that he might protect defenceless people, as the harmless flock from evening wolves according to the saying of Scripture [Acts 20:29], and that he might restrain by arms or by the law those whom ecclesiastical censure was not able to subdue.[31]

For the ideals of vassalage, the *Song of Roland* is a important source, once we remember that it reflects the time it was written (early twelfth century) rather than the time of its hero Charlemagne. Just before the battle of Roncesvalles, Roland states a vassal's obligations to his lord:

> Here we will stand, defending our great king.
> This is the service a vassal owes his lord:
> To suffer hardships, endure great heat and cold,
> And in a battle to lose both hair and hide.[32]

Ideals and historical realities are usually far apart. But the ideals of bravery and loyalty on the part of the vassal, and wisdom and justice on the part of the lord, were long-lasting measurements for those who governed and fought. Chaucer, for example, embodies them in his portrait of the knight in the *Canterbury Tales*, written shortly before 1400.

From the description of lordship and vassalage and the private possession of political power, feudalism would appear to be incompatible with strong monarchy. Yet since a powerful man like William the Conqueror consciously "feudalized" England and the clever Holy Roman Emperor Frederick Barbarossa (r.1152–90) extended lordship and vassalage as a way of increasing his power, it is necessary to re-evaluate that analysis. The political and military structure of eleventh-century France was certainly not compatible with a powerful monarchy, but a resourceful king could use some elements of it while modifying others. After all, there was really no alternative for them since they could not simply restructure society; they had to work with what existed. The historian Joseph Strayer's analysis suggests three ways that the kings adapted existing relationships and institutions to their benefit.[33]

First, they focused on the land itself, the fief, rather than on a vassal's personal service. Kings thus became willing to replace personal service with money payments. They were able to use the revenues generated by the fiefs to hire full-time soldiers and other functionaries, who were more dependable and loyal than the independent-minded vassals. Second, the kings sought to systematize the various customs and traditions that had developed over centuries. In the period when local lords operated independently of their kings, they had nevertheless continued to recognize that they were royal vassals, paying lip service to their obligations. They had ignored their kings, but they never denied the monarchy's existence or their obligations to it. As kings began to try to enforce their vassals' neglected obligations, they also claimed that any judicial powers that their vassals exercised had originated from royal grants. Although this was not necessarily true, it laid the groundwork for kings to claim appellate jurisdiction and even to revoke earlier grants. Third, kings began to develop a bureaucracy. With the money they received from their vassals (and from their other sources of income), they hired efficient and loyal administrators trained in the law. By establishing courts over which these men presided, the kings were able to convince many lesser vassals in their realms that royal justice was superior to that offered by local lords, who often relied on such primitive methods of detecting guilt as trial by battle and the ordeal. Furthermore, if a fief became vacant because of the lack of an heir or confiscation from a rebellious vassal, kings often chose not to grant it out again as a fief but rather had it administered by paid bureaucrats, who had no independent power base and whose office was not hereditary. This happened in 1206 when the king of France took away Normandy from its rebellious duke (King John of England). Although it is wrong to speak of a feudal system in the ninth, tenth, and eleventh centuries, it is proper to speak of feudal monarchies in the twelfth and thirteenth; and these are the real beginnings of the nation-states of Europe.

The ideas of lordship and vassalage came to be applied far beyond their original context, especially from the twelfth century on. For example, in the twelfth century, even though many vassals were paying their lords rather than fighting for them, writers began to apply the concept of vassalage to descriptions of relationships with women. The language of courtly literature is the language of lordship and vassalage with the man as vassal, pledging his service to a lady. Another example concerns the language and even the posture of prayer. Early Christians prayed with their arms extended to either side. The position that we associate with prayer, closed hands held together, is in fact the position of a vassal in the act of doing fealty (see the description of Galbert of Bruges above). People expressed their relationship with God the way they expressed the relationship of vassal to lord. Furthermore, hymns written to God began to use this same language, as did the hymns written to the Virgin Mary. The concept of dependent relationships that we often label "feudal" was of great importance long after the lord-vassal relationship changed radically from the time of its origins.

The Rise of Cities

One of the most important phenomena of the tenth and, even more, the eleventh century was the renewal of long-distance trade and urban life. Commerce, of course, never ceased completely in the early Middle Ages, nor did cities disappear; but the Carolingian world was essentially agrarian, and its political and cultural centers were the castles and monasteries rather than cities. In one sense, the Roman Empire of antiquity was agrarian too, since the vast majority of its inhabitants tilled the soil; this is true of all preindustrial societies. Nevertheless, the Empire's political, economic, and cultural centers were its cities. And the Church won its early converts and established its high priests, the bishops, in cities. However, during the Germanic invasions and the division of Western Europe into Germanic kingdoms, long-distance trade declined and so did the cities as centers of commerce and culture. Urban decline continued into the Carolingian period when, with a few exceptions like Venice, the city as it was known in the ancient world essentially had ceased to exist. This does not mean that cities were completely abandoned, however; they continued to be ecclesiastical centers with cathedrals, the clergy attached to them, and the laypersons they employed. Rome itself was little more than the seat of the pope, most of its great buildings deserted and crumbling.

In the tenth century, Western Europe became relatively peaceful with the defeat and conversion of the Vikings and Magyars. And for a variety of reasons, its population began to increase. However, the land could only support a certain number of people; sometimes younger sons of agricultural laborers had to leave their homes and fend for themselves, some becoming vagabonds and robbers, others obtaining a few goods, trading them wherever they were in demand. The twelfth-century *Life of St. Godric* describes such a young man. By Godric's time, some cities were already well-established, but it is likely that his activities and motivation were similar to ambitious individuals of earlier generations.

Wherefore he chose not to follow the life of a husbandman, but rather to study, learn, and exercise the rudiments of more subtle conceptions. For this reason, aspiring to the merchant's trade, he began to follow the chapman's [peddler's] way of

life, first learning how to gain in small bargains and things of
insignificant price; and thence, while yet a youth, his mind advanced little by little to buy and sell and gain from things of
greater expense. For, in his beginnings, he was wont to wander
with small wares around the villages and farmsteads of his own
neighborhood; but, in process of time, he gradually associated
himself by compact with city merchants. Hence, within a brief
space of time, the youth who had trudged for many weary
hours from village to village, from farm to farm, did so profit
by his increase of age and wisdom as to travel with associates
of his own age through towns and boroughs, fortresses and
cities, to fairs and to all the various booths of the marketplace,
in pursuit of his public chaffer [barter]. He went along the
highway, neither puffed up by the good testimony of his conscience nor downcast in the nobler part of his soul by the re-
proach of poverty. . . .

The saint . . . roamed one day over . . . stretches of fore-
shore [beach]; and, finding nothing at first, he followed on and
on to a distance of three miles, where he found three porpoises
lying high and dry, either cast upon the sands by the waves or
left there by the ebb-tide.[34]

Godric was able to sell the porpoise fat, and hard work and
great risk brought Godric success, for soon he was able to
purchase a ship. In the end, Godric gave up his hard-earned
wealth to become a hermit, but many like him continued to
increase and enjoy their fortune.

Sometimes itinerant merchants formed groups both for protection and in order to have a greater diversity of products to
sell. They went on long-distance expeditions during the good-
weather months; but in the winter they needed places where
they could collect goods, store them, and then prepare the
year's business. They looked for places convenient to the surviving Roman roads, navigable rivers, or sea coast where they
could be protected from bandits. Often merchants sought permission to settle beneath the walls of a castle or an ecclesiastical
center, in return for which they offered some of their goods.
They sometimes built permanent dwellings, and the walls of
the castles or ecclesiastical centers were sometimes extended to
incorporate them. There were problems with this type of ar-

rangement, however. The law administered by the lord of a castle or a bishop was not suited to the needs of merchants. They wanted to live by their own law, and they often paid to free themselves from the jurisdiction of ecclesiastical or "feudal" courts and other obligations they had agreed to. In other cases, the merchants simply declared themselves free from their protector's jurisdiction. To do this, they usually formed associations called *communes*. One of the best accounts of the origins of a commune is contained in the memoirs of Abbot Guibert de Nogent, describing the events in the city of Laon in the year 1112:

> The clergy and the archdeacons and the nobles, taking account of these conditions [the bishop's absence] and looking out for ways of exacting money from the people, offered them through their agents the opportunity to have authorization to create a commune, if they would offer an appropriate sum of money. Now, "commune" is a new and evil name for an arrangement for them all to pay the customary head tax, which they owe their lords as a servile due, in a lump sum once a year, and if anyone commits a crime, he shall pay a fine set by law, and all other financial exactions which are customarily imposed on serfs are completely abolished. [*Guibert's definition is too narrow and ignores the issue of judicial authority*.] Seizing on this opportunity for commuting their dues, the people gathered huge sums of money to fill the gaping purses of so many greedy men. Pleased with the shower of income poured upon them, those men established their good faith by proffering oaths that they would keep their word in this matter.[35]

When the bishop returned, he was bribed to support the commune. However, he later decided to try to keep the money and his authority too and bribed the king to release him from his oath to uphold the commune. Within a week people were in the streets shouting "Commune," and violence followed:

> While the insolent mob was attacking the bishop and howling before the walls of his palace, the bishop and the people who were aiding him fought them off as best they could by hurling stones and shooting arrows. Now, as at all times, he showed

great spirit as a fighter; but because he had wrongly and in vain taken up that other sword, he perished by the sword. Unable to resist the wreckless assaults of the people, he put on the clothes of one of his servants and fled into the warehouse of the church, where he hid himself in a container. . . . [However, the burghers found the bishop.] As he implored them piteously, ready to swear that he would cease to be their bishop, that he would give them unlimited riches, that he would leave the country, with hardened hearts they jeered at him. Then a man named Bernard of Bruyères raised his sword and brutally dashed out that sinner's brains from his holy head. Slipping between the hands of those who held him, before he died he was struck by someone else with a blow running under his eye sockets and across the middle of his nose. Brought to his end there, his legs were hacked off and many other wounds inflicted. Seeing the ring on the finger of the former bishop and not able to draw it off easily, Thiegaud cut off the dead man's finger with his sword and took the ring. Stripped naked, he was thrown into a corner in front of his chaplain's house. My God, who shall recount the mocking words that were thrown at him by passersby as he lay there, and with what clods and stones and dirt his corpse was pelted?[36]

After the violence, it took several more years before Laon's commune was finally confirmed. Although many communes were established peacefully, Guibert shows that merchants quite passionately desired to be free. This freedom that communes paid and fought for gave the cities the opportunity to develop their own institutions and eventually produced sophisticated urban governments and the great medieval trade guilds.

In Italy, cities began to emerge somewhat earlier than they did north of the Alps. This is in part because Italy was more highly urbanized in Roman times than northern Europe, in part because Italy suffered less from the ninth-century invasions than the North, but primarily because of its position in the center of the Mediterranean. Venice was engaged in trade with Constantinople and the eastern Mediterranean from its foundation at the time of the dissolution of the Roman Empire in the West. By the eleventh century, cities like Amalfi and Pisa traded in the East and carried pilgrims to the Holy Land. These

Aerial view of the Piazza del Campo, the main square of Siena, Italy. The dominant building is the city hall, constructed at the beginning of the 14th Century. Large open spaces like this were used for assemblies, preaching, festivals, and as market places.

cities too threw off the yoke of the landed nobles and eventually dominated the countryside and its inhabitants. Otto of Freising, monk and biographer of the Emperor Frederick Barbarossa, characterized the cities of northern Italy as he observed them in the 1150s:

> In the governing of their cities, also in the conduct of public affairs, they [the people of Lombardy, a region in northern Italy whose center is Milan] still imitate the wisdom of the ancient Romans. Finally, they are so desirous of liberty that, avoiding the insolence of power, they are governed by the will of consuls rather than rulers. There are known to be three orders among them: captains, vavasors, and commoners. And in order to suppress arrogance, the aforesaid consuls are chosen not from one but from each of the classes. And lest they should

exceed bounds by lust for power, they are changed every year. The consequence is that, as practically that entire land is divided among the cities, each of them required its bishops to live in the cities, and scarcely any noble or great man can be found in all the surrounding territory who does not acknowledge the authority of his city. And from this power to force all elements together they are wont to call the several lands of each [noble or magnate] their contado. Also, that they may not lack the means of subduing their neighbors, they do not disdain to give the girdle of knighthood or the grades of distinction to young men of inferior station and even some workers of the vile mechanical arts, whom other peoples bar like the pest from the more respected and honorable pursuits. From this it has resulted that they far surpass all other states of the world in riches and in power.[37]

It is clear from Otto's complete account of the Italian cities that they were reluctant to accept imperial authority, and they formed a league to oppose Frederick Barbarossa. In 1176 at Legnano, the Italian cities defeated the emperor; from that time on they were able to grow without imperial intervention although they paid lip service to the Empire, and later emperors tried several times to reimpose control over them.

The cities grew in size, wealth, and sophistication. Although the urban population of Europe in the High Middle Ages probably never exceeded 15 percent of the total population, it was a disproportionately wealthy and influential minority. The centers of education—cathedral schools and later the universities—were located in cities. The great Gothic cathedrals dominated the urban skylines. Both Dante and Chaucer were men of the cities, products of a sophisticated urban culture. Eventually even the monarchs and their increasingly complex bureaucracies established permanent seats of government in cities like Westminster (adjacent to medieval London and part of modern London) and Paris.

PART THREE

The High Middle Ages

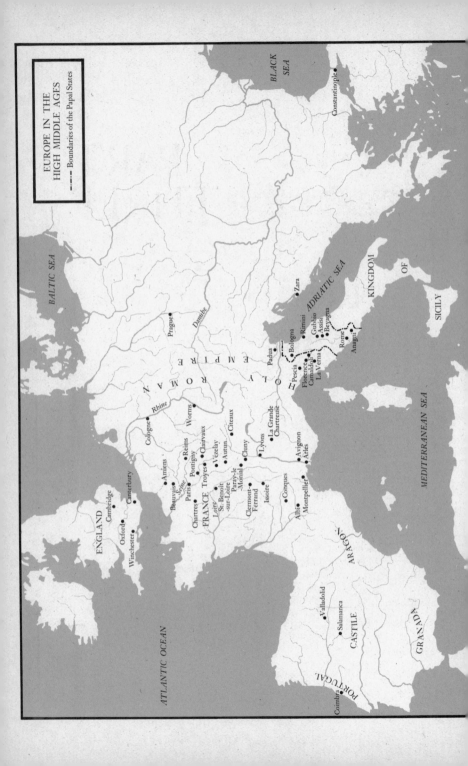

EUROPE IN THE
HIGH MIDDLE AGES

— · — · — Boundaries of the Papal States

CHAPTER EIGHT

Church, State, and Society

The Beginnings of Church Reform

Since the Church had come to control a great deal of land and since land was the chief source of wealth and warriors, lay rulers often sought and obtained control over bishoprics and even abbacies, either to bestow on trustworthy persons—usually relatives—or to sell to the highest bidder. Furthermore, parish priests were often semiliterate at best, usually serfs or peasant farmers; many were married and passed on the job to their sons. Monasteries to some extent became dumping grounds for younger sons of the landed aristocracy, many of whom were lax in their observance of the Rule of St. Benedict. These problems had their beginnings as early as the Merovingian period but intensified following the collapse of central authority after the death of Charlemagne.

In addition to all of this, the papacy suffered. It is certainly arguable that the tenth and first half of the eleventh centuries were the bleakest times in the history of the papacy. Potential for corruption came with the development of papal temporal power in central Italy, which was accelerated with the Donation of Pepin. Leo III was expelled from Rome but restored by Charlemagne. With the demise of the Holy Roman Empire, however, there was no longer a temporal power to rescue the papacy from local, essentially political squabbles. By 900, the papacy had become the plaything of Italian nobles. The depths to which the papacy had sunk can be symbolized by the example of Pope Formosus. When he died in 896, a member of the family opposed to his political policies was elected pope and convened a synod that exhumed Formosus's body, put him on trial, and convicted him of usurping the papal office. His body was stripped of the papal garments; the fingers on the right hand, used in giving the benediction, were broken; and his body was thrown into the Tiber. Clearly, the sacred and the secular, temporal and spiritual power, were thoroughly mixed and confused; from the parishes and monasteries to the great prelates and the papacy, the Church was in need of a reform.

A harbinger of a later general reform movement in the Church and the beginning of important monastic reform was the foundation of the Burgundian monastery of Cluny in 910. The most important part of its foundation charter declared that the monastery was to be completely free of lay control and even from local episcopal jurisdiction. Cluny was placed directly under papal control. In essence, this was a declaration of complete independence since the bishops of Rome at this time cared little about exercising control over a monastery far away. The monks of Cluny were not exactly like Benedict's on Monte Cassino four hundred years earlier. Their observance was based on the reforms of Benedict of Aniane in the ninth century, and included elaborate liturgical development, the use of splendid works of art, and virtually no manual labor. The Cluniacs had lay brothers or serfs to do manual labor while the monks spent as much as seven hours a day singing the monastic offices. Its independence from lay control and its way of observing the Rule of St. Benedict struck a responsive chord in monasteries throughout Western Europe. Even in the century of its foundation, Cluny established daughter houses and sent its monks to monasteries desiring the Cluniac reform. Although there really was no official Cluniac Order, the Cluniac form of monasticism spread to all parts of Latin Christendom. A key reason for the spread of Cluniac monasticism was the fact that from 948 to 1109, Cluny had only three abbots, all holy men with administrative skills. The best known of these was Hugh the Great, abbot from 1049 to 1109. It was he who oversaw perhaps a thousand monasteries that had adopted at least some of the elements of the Cluniac reform. The most trusted man in Europe, he was often called upon to try to establish peace between the papacy and the Empire; it was Hugh who began the building of the great Romanesque church at Cluny. For four hundred years the abbey church at Cluny was the largest church in Christendom; even after the building of the new St. Peter's in Rome in the sixteenth century, it remained second biggest until its destruction during the French Revolution. The buildings, habits, and works of art that existed at Cluny set it apart from the simplicity originally intended by Benedict at Monte Cassino.

In the second half of the eleventh century came the reform of the papacy and its re-emergence as an important political as well as ecclesiastical institution throughout Europe. The year 1046 was one of particular scandal in Rome. The papacy was sold by Benedict IX to a sincere reformer named Gregory VI; then Benedict reclaimed it. To add to the confusion and degradation, a rival Roman faction had its own candidate. Thus there were three claimants to the throne of Peter. The concerned Holy Roman Emperor Henry III called a synod that deposed all three, and Henry appointed a new pope. This pope and the one who succeeded him quickly died in suspicious circumstances; but Henry's third appointment, Leo IX (r.1049–54), initiated a great papal reform that is called by the general name of the Gregorian Reform, after Leo's most famous successor in the reform tradition, Gregory VII (r.1073–85). Leo recognized as the great evil of his day the encroachment of the

Restoration drawing of the Third Abbey Church of Cluny, France. 11th and 12th Centuries. The largest church in western Christendom in the Middle Ages, it was richly elaborate both in its architecture and its decoration. (Courtesy K. J. Conant)

Cistercian Abbey of Pontigny, France. 12th Century. This church best illustrates the simplicity of the style of the Cistercian Order. The many towers of Cluny contrast sharply with the unadorned lines of Pontigny, a visual comparison which is also a useful symbol of the differences between Cluniac and Cistercian monasticism.

secular on the sacred. He sought to prohibit clerical marriage, perceived as the reversal of religious and lay functions and thus a symbol of the general problem. However, the chief ill that he tried to cure was the practice of simony—the buying and selling of Church offices. The elimination of simony became the chief concern of Leo's pontificate both because of its intrinsic seriousness and because it epitomized the Church's corruption. Leo brought men to Rome to help in the reform movement and gave them the title of cardinal. These included several Cluniac monks, Hildebrand—the future Gregory VII —the irascible and coldly intellectual Humbert, and the ascetic Peter Damian. Leo was faced with the problem of enforcing his reform decrees throughout Christendom. He wrote letters, appointed legates (men given his authority in a specific geographical area or in a specific matter), held synods, and traveled with an impressive entourage to literally show Europe the reformed papacy. His activity at the dedication of the new Monastery of St. Remigius at Reims illustrates his method. After processing through the city with the relics of its patron, Saint Remigius, he demanded that all bishops take an oath in the presence of the relics that they did not buy their office. Several refused, one was deposed on the spot, and the archbishop of Reims himself was ordered to appear later in Rome. Leo meant business. His attempts to enlarge the scope of papal power also had their tragic element, however. The overzealous Cardinal Humbert placed a bull of excommunication on the altar of Santa Sophia in Constantinople in 1054. The strongwilled and politically oriented Patriarch of Constantinople, Michael Kerularios, reciprocated by excommunicating the pope. This schism proved to be permanent; only in 1965 did Pope Paul VI and the Greek Patriarch Athenogoras rescind these bulls.

A series of reformers in the tradition of Leo succeeded him on the papal throne. In 1059 Nicholas II issued a decree establishing a procedure for papal election by the cardinals; although this was altered somewhat about a hundred years later by Alexander III, it is still the basis for papal election. The purpose of this decree was to keep the election of the pope out of the

Capital, Autun Cathedral, France. 12th Century. This scene depicts
the fall of Simon the Magician, who appears in Acts 8:9–24. In
the story related there, he tried to buy the gifts of the Holy Spirit,
and was rebuked by Peter. According to popular legend, Simon
later met Peter in Rome and flew into the sky to demonstrate his
magical powers. However, when Peter prayed, Simon fell out of
the sky. The popularity of the Fall of Simon the Magician in art,
especially in Romanesque sculpture, attests to the Church's concern with the problem of simony during the period of reform.
Simon is also an important figure in later medieval literature.

hands of laypersons, including the Holy Roman Emperor; since it was a Holy Roman Emperor who appointed the first reform pope, there is a certain irony here.

The election of Cardinal Hildebrand in 1073 as Gregory VII brought to the throne of St. Peter the most experienced man in the curia. His pontificate is pivotal in understanding the subsequent history of medieval Europe. Within the curia of Leo IX, two schools of thought had developed on the relationship of spiritual to temporal authority. Peter Damian had called for real cooperation between secular and ecclesiastical leaders and was willing to be flexible in dealing with thorny matters that came to the curia; for example, he saw simony as a terrible sin but nevertheless accepted the validity of ordinations performed by simoniac bishops. Humbert on the other hand stood for ecclesiastical supremacy over the state and rejected the validity of simoniac bishops, thus coming close to the old heresy of Donatism. Gregory VII was an ardent supporter of Humbert's position.

Within two years of his accession to the papal throne, Gregory was in open conflict with the Holy Roman Emperor-elect Henry IV. The specific issue was lay investiture—the practice of a layperson, such as the Holy Roman Emperor, investiing a bishop with the *spiritual* symbols of his office. Henry knew that to control his empire in fact as well as theory he needed loyal bishops, for they controlled vast amounts of territory, the means for providing him with an army. The only way to ensure the bishops' loyalty was to have complete control over their selection and investiture. This was obviously in clear opposition to the principles of the papal reform movement to which Gregory was heir. The conflict that broke out in 1075 after Henry invested the bishop of Milan was for more than who was to hand over a ring and staff to a bishop; it was a struggle for the leadership of Latin Christendom. Gregory died in exile in 1085, but Henry faced rebellion even within his own family and died in the midst of a struggle against a major coalition of opposition in 1106.

In the year 1122, the issue of lay investiture was settled by compromise in the Concordat of Worms. Bishops were to be elected only by clergy, but an imperial representative could be present at the election. Investiture of the spiritual symbols of office was to be performed by other bishops but only after investiture of the temporal symbols was performed by the emperor or his representative. However, the larger question of the leadership of Christian society was far from being decided. The Empire was severely weakened, both in theory and practice. Bishops could no longer be selected solely by the emperor, and the bitter struggle between popes and emperors destroyed the Church's support of the Empire. Furthermore, the theory of theocratic kingship, an important buttress of the emperor's position that was developed in the Carolingian period, was swept away by the sharp distinctions between priesthood and kingship made by advocates of the papal position.

The Crusades

The era of papal reform gave birth to one of the most important and interesting phenomena of the twelfth century, the Crusades—wars to win back the Holy Land from the Moslems. The idea of a holy war against the enemies of Christendom was not new at the end of the eleventh century. Something like it existed as early as the ninth century in England during the invasion of the pagan Danes. A more clearly conceived idea of holy war developed in Spain in the eleventh century, as the surviving Christian kingdoms began the *Reconquista* to free the rest of the Iberian peninsula from the Moslems. However, the Crusades were not only the culmination of the idea of the holy war, they were also pilgrimages to the holiest shrines of Christendom, to the land where Jesus lived, to Jerusalem, the earthly model of the heavenly city.

In 1095, Pope Urban II called the First Crusade at a council held in Clermont-Ferrand. Urban sought to continue the papal reform program and to restore the papacy's dignity in the aftermath of Gregory VII's death in exile by rallying the forces of Western Europe in a great military and moral enterprise. Thus the Crusade cannot be understood apart from its context as a part of papal assertion of leadership in the West.

The plan was to send an army by land through the Byzantine Empire into the Holy Land, which the Moslems had controlled since the mid-seventh century. In fact, the emperor in Constantinople had sought papal help in forming an army to liberate Palestine, although the crusaders were by and large not willing to submit to imperial authority as he had hoped.

For those who were willing to go on the Crusade, Urban offered forgiveness of sins:

> I address those present; I proclaim it to those absent; moreover Christ commands it. For all those going thither there will be remission of sins if they come to the end of this fettered life while either marching by land or crossing by sea, or in fighting the pagans. This I grant to all who go, through the power vested in me by God.[1]

The crusaders also were given badges marking them as pilgrims, albeit special ones. The chronicler of the First Crusade, Fulcher of Chartres, describes the badge and provides an Augustinian interpretation of it:

> Oh how fitting, and how pleasing it was to us all to see those crosses made of silk, cloth-of-gold, or other beautiful material which these pilgrims whether knights, other laymen, or clerics sewed on the shoulders of their cloaks. They did this by command of Pope Urban once they had taken the oath to go. It was proper that the soldiers of God who were preparing to fight for His honor should be identified and protected by this emblem of victory. And since they thus decorated themselves with this emblem of their faith, in the end they acquired from the symbol the reality itself. They clad themselves with the outward sign in order that they might obtain the inner reality.[2]

After the crusaders arrived in Moslem territory, they found themselves ill-equipped to fight in the desert; often they were discouraged and even desperate. Fulcher gives a gruesome description of one such moment:

> Those two leaders with their men seized the two cities of Barra and Marra in an attack showing great bravery. They very

quickly captured the former, killed the citizens to a man, and confiscated everything. Then they hastened to the other city and besieged it for twenty days. Here our men suffered from excessive hunger. I shudder to say that many of our men, terribly tormented by the madness of starvation, cut pieces of flesh from the buttocks of Saracens lying there dead. These pieces they cooked and ate, savagely devouring the flesh while it was insufficiently roasted. In this way the besiegers were harmed more than the besieged.[3]

The crusaders often acted with brutality, even as they entered Jerusalem itself:

Many of the Saracens who had climbed to the top of the Temple of Solomon in their flight were shot to death with arrows and fell headlong from the roof. Nearly ten thousand were beheaded in this Temple. If you had been there your feet would have been stained to the ankles in the blood of the slain. What shall I say? None of them were left alive. Neither women nor children were spared.[4]

Even allowing for medieval exaggeration, it is clear that the crusaders often forgot that they came to reclaim the land on which the Prince of Peace had once walked. Despite the cruelties and the violence, the crusaders were hailed as heroes, especially with the capture of Jerusalem and the establishment of a Latin kingdom centered in the Holy City.

This successful Crusade was only the first of a series of papally sponsored military expeditions to the Holy Land. The Second Crusade was called in 1147, largely through the urging of Bernard of Clairvaux, because one of the cities captured by the First Crusade had fallen to the Moslems. It accomplished nothing, though it did have as its head a ruling monarch, Louis VII of France.

In 1187 the city of Jerusalem fell to the Moslems because of political problems in the kingdom and the tactics of a brilliant Moslem leader named Saladin. In response, the Third Crusade was launched, with the three most powerful monarchs in Europe—Frederick Barbarossa the Holy Roman Emperor,

Richard I (the Lion-hearted) of England, and Philip Augustus of France—participating. Again, it accomplished very little. Innocent III called the Fourth Crusade, a naval expedition that began in Venice. The crusaders did not have enough money to pay the Venetians for their transportation, so they agreed to attack the Christian city of Zara for Venice as payment. From there they proceeded to Constantinople, the largest Christian city in the world. The crusaders re-established a recently deposed emperor who promised them aid; but when he could not provide it, they captured the city and sacked it, dividing the Byzantine Empire between themselves and the Venetians. There were later Crusades to recapture the Holy Land, most notably two led by the pious King Louis IX of France (d.1270, while on Crusade). However, the digression of the Fourth Crusade, the pillaging of two Christian cities, really marked the end of the most important era of crusading history.

The effects of the Crusades were enormous. They probably reduced the level of violence in Europe, for many younger sons of nobles or small landholders greedy for more land went to the Holy Land instead of making war within Europe. Urban himself had stated that one of his reasons for calling the First Crusade was to take these violent men and turn their energy toward the Moslems both for the good of Christendom and their souls. A less fortunate effect of the First Crusade was an outbreak of anti-Semitism. Popular preachers argued that the Crusades should start at home, since Christ-killers, i.e. the Jews, were living among them. The following describes a massacre in the Holy Roman Empire:

> At the beginning of summer in the same year in which Peter and Gottschalk, after collecting an army, had set out, there assembled in like fashion a large and innumerable host of Christians from diverse kingdoms and lands; namely, from the realms of France, England, Flanders, and Lorraine. . . . I know not whether by a judgement of the Lord, or by some error of mind, they rose in a spirit of cruelty against the Jewish people scattered throughout the cities and slaughtered them without mercy, especially in the Kingdom of Lorraine, asserting it to be the beginning of their expedition and their duty against the

enemies of the Christian faith. This slaughter of Jews was done
first by citizens of Cologne. These suddenly fell upon a small
band of Jews and severely wounded and killed many; they destroyed the houses and synagogues of the Jews and divided
among themselves a very large amount of money. When the
Jews saw this cruelty, about two hundred in the silence of the
night began flight by boat to Neuss. The pilgrims and crusaders discovered them, and after taking away all of their possessions, inflicted on them similar slaughter leaving not even one
alive.[5]

A third effect was to bring the West into closer contact
with Constantinople and the Byzantine Empire. Crusaders were
awed by the size and beauty of the capital and not a little
greedy for its riches, including the luxury goods manufactured
there or brought from the East. The experience of crusaders
in the Empire created a market for Eastern goods in the West,
contributing to the development of international commerce and
the rise of cities. The Crusades stimulated trade in other ways
as well. There was a constant flow of pilgrims and soldiers
from West to East. Furthermore, the crusading states established in the Holy Land needed goods from the West, weapons
and supplies for example. For both men and material, the sea
was the easiest and safest route, thus contributing especially to
the growth of Italian cities.

The idea of the Crusade came to be applied in the thirteenth
century to wars within Europe itself. Innocent III (r.1198–
1216) launched a Crusade against Albigensian heretics in southern France; Innocent IV (r.1245–54) organized a Crusade
against the Holy Roman Emperor and his family, applying the
idea of a holy war to heretics or even political enemies of the
papacy. This kind of "crusade" continued into the sixteenth
century.

Finally, the Crusades had a significant impact on the literature and art of the twelfth century. The *Song of Roland*,
composed between the First and Second Crusades, is replete
with the language and ideals of the Crusades. The tympanum
of the Church of St. Mary Magdalen in Vézelay, under which
Bernard preached the Second Crusade, embodies a Crusade

motif. Both works place the Crusades in the scriptural context of completing the task given to the Church by Christ as
a precondition to his return—the preaching of the Gospel to
the ends of the earth. The zeal of the crusading spirit, the goals
of crusading for both the Church and individual crusaders, and
the theology of the Crusades are well summed up in a letter
of Bernard of Clairvaux to England to recruit men for the
Second Crusade:

Now is the acceptable time, now is the day of abundant salvation. The earth is shaken because the Lord of heaven is losing
his land, the land in which he appeared to men, in which he
lived amongst men for more than thirty years; the land made
glorious by his miracles, holy by his blood; the land in which
the flowers of his resurrection first blossomed. And now, for
our sins, the enemy of the Cross has begun to lift his sacrilegious head there, and to devastate with the sword that blessed
land, that land of promise. Alas, if there should be none to
withstand him, he will soon invade the very city of the living
God, overturn the arsenal of our redemption, and defile the
holy places which have been adorned by the blood of the
immaculate lamb. They have cast their greedy eyes especially
on the holy sanctuaries of our Christian Religion, and they long
particularly to violate that couch on which, for our sakes, the
Lord of our life fell asleep in death. . . .

Your land is well known to be rich in young and vigorous
men. The world is full of their praises, and the renown of their
courage is on the lips of all. Gird yourselves therefore like men
and take up arms with joy and with zeal for your Christian
name, in order to "take vengeance on the heathen, and curb
the nations." For how long will your men continue to shed
Christian blood; for how long will they continue to fight
amongst themselves? You attack each other, you slay each
other and by each other you are slain. What is this savage
craving of yours? Put a stop to it now, for it is not fighting
but foolery. Thus to risk both soul and body is not brave but
shocking, is not strength but folly. But now, O mighty soldiers,
O men of war, you have a cause for which you can fight without danger to your souls; a cause in which to conquer is glorious and for which to die is gain.[6]

The New Monastic Orders

The period of papal reform and conflict with the Empire was
also important for the development of monasticism. The
Cluniac reform did not satisfy those who longed for the simplicity and rigor of early monasticism and who believed that
the Cluniacs had not "retreated" far enough from secular involvement. In the eleventh century several new orders of hermits emerged, including the Camaldolese in Italy and, more
important, the Carthusians in France. The Cistercian Order was
founded in 1098 as a reform of Cluniac monasticism, returning
to the practice of the Rule as Benedict had intended it to be
lived.

Bruno of Cologne founded a hermit order of monks with the
establishment of La Grande Chartreuse in the wilderness near
Grenoble in 1084. The ideal to which Bruno looked was that
of the desert fathers such as Saint Antony. Although Bruno
soon was called to Italy and died there, the monastery grew
and soon daughter houses (charterhouses) sprang up. By the
middle of the twelfth century, the *Consuetudines*, a Carthusian
Rule, had been established. The order remained small and few
Carthusians played important roles in church politics, but
Carthusian monks were highly respected. In the fourteenth
century, cities all over Europe encouraged the Carthusians to
make a foundation in their city in order to ward off the plague.
Noble families in Burgundy and Lombardy endowed huge
Carthusian houses, which were also the family's burial grounds.
The Carthusians' reputation was that they retained the purity
of the founders: "Never reformed because never deformed."
Their desire to return to the spirituality of the early monks of
the desert and to find God in solitude is carefully explained in
the *Golden Epistle*, a work written by a Cistercian monk,
William of St. Thierry, to a fledgling Carthusian house:

> The man who has God with him is never less alone than when
> he is alone. It is then he has undisturbed fruition of his joy,
> it is then he is his own master and is free to enjoy God in

himself and himself in God. It is then that in the light of truth
and a serenity of a clean heart a pure soul stands revealed to
itself without effort, and the memory enlivened by God freely
pours itself out in itself. Then either the mind is enlightened
and the will enjoys its good or human fraility freely weeps
over its shortcomings.[7]

The essence of Carthusian spirituality is embodied in a letter
written by Guigo, fifth prior of La Grande Chartreuse:

> But the poor and lonely life, hard in its beginning, easy in its
> progress, becomes, in its end, heavenly. It is constant in adver-
> sity, trusty in hours of doubt, modest in those of good fortune.
> Sober fare, simple garments, laconic speech, chaste manners.
> The highest ambition, because without ambition. Often
> wounded with sorrow at the thought of past wrong done, it
> avoids present, is wary of future evil. Resting on the hope of
> mercy, without trust in its own merit, it thirsts after heaven,
> is sick of earth, earnestly strives for right conduct, which it
> retains in constancy and holds firmly for ever. It fasts with
> determined constancy in love of the cross, yet consents to eat
> for the body's need. In both it observes the greatest modera-
> tion, for when it dines it restrains greed and when it fasts, van-
> ity. It is devoted to reading, but mostly in the scripture canon
> and in holy books, where it is more intent upon the inner ar-
> row of meaning than on the spume of words. But you may
> praise or wonder more at this: that such a life is continually
> idle yet never lazy. For it finds many things indeed to do, so
> that time is more often lacking to it than this or that occupa-
> tion. It more often laments that its time has slipped away than
> that its business is tedious.[8]

The Cistercian Order was founded at Cîteaux (Cistercium in
Latin) in 1098 by Robert of Molesmes. Like Bruno, he soon
left but the foundation remained; within a century over a
thousand Cistercian foundations for men and women were
established in Europe. The Cistercian ideal was a strict return
of the simplicity of Benedict's Rule. There was to be no fancy
sculpture or paintings, no elaborate liturgy, no rich vestments,
and all monks were to perform manual labor. However, there

were elements of Cistercian monasticism that had no precedent in the Rule. First, monks were divided into two classes—choir monks, who sang the entire Divine Office prescribed by the Rule and did only light physical work, and lay brothers, who sang an abbreviated Divine Office and did most of the manual labor. These two groups of monks within a monastery had separate living quarters and even separate sets of choir stalls in church. The second departure from the Rule was that the Cistercians had a constitution and governing structure of the order, described in the *Charter of Charity*:

> It seems proper to us, that all our monasteries should have the same usages in chanting, and the same books for the divine office day and night and the celebration of the holy sacrifice of the Mass, as we have in the New Monastery; that there may be no discord in our daily actions, but that we may all live to- gether in the bond of charity under one rule, and in the prac- tice of the same observances. . . .
>
> The Abbot of a mother-house shall visit annually, either in person or by one of his co-abbots, all the filiations of his own monastery. And if he should visit the brethren more frequently than this, let it be to them a subject of joy. The four abbots of La Ferte, Pontigny, Clairvaux and Morimond, shall visit in per- son, unless prevented by sickness, once in the year, and on the day which they shall appoint, the monastery of Citeaux, besides their attendance at the General Chapter, unless one of them is prevented by grave illness. . . .
>
> But all the abbots of our Order shall meet each year in Gen- eral Chapter, without excuse, except they are prevented by grievous sickness; and then they shall depute a proper repre- sentative. An exception is made also in the case of those who live in too distant countries, which shall be decided by the Chapter.[9]

Clearly there was a uniformity in the Cistercian Order foreign to Benedict or the network of monasteries affiliated with Cluny.

The order's popularity in the twelfth century was largely due to the genius and energy of one man—Bernard, abbot of Clairvaux (d.1153). He was an advisor to popes and kings, mystic, theologian, and poet, one of the great literary figures and saints of the Middle Ages. He was also the relentless foe of the philosopher Peter Abelard, the moving force behind the Second Crusade, and a showman of some ability. An example of the last occurred when he preached the Second Crusade at Vézelay in 1147. He worked up such fervor for the Crusade that men began to cut crusaders' badges out of available cloth to pin on themselves; when the cloth ran out, Bernard took off his habit so that more badges could be made.

Bernard has been called "the last of the Fathers." Although well versed in classical rhetoric, he displayed little interest in the development of Scholastic methodology, which was the preoccupation of some of his contemporaries like Peter Abelard; and he doubted the value of Aristotle as a way to illuminate the faith. His concern—deeply rooted in the mystical tradition—was with the direct experience of God, rather than with what dialectic could say *about* God. The Cistercian quest for experiential knowledge of God is embodied in one of Bernard's most important works, the eighty-six sermons on the Song of Songs. The following passage from sermon three exemplifies Bernard's method:

Today the text we are to study is the book of our own experience. You must therefore turn your attention inwards, each one must take note of his own particular awareness of the things I am about to discuss. I am attempting to discover if any of you has been privileged to say from his heart: "Let him kiss me with the kiss of his mouth." [Song 1:1] Those to whom it is given to utter those words sincerely are comparatively few, but anyone who has received this mystical kiss from the mouth of Christ at least once, seeks again that intimate experience, and eagerly looks for its frequent renewal. I think that nobody can grasp what it is except the one who receives it. For it is "a hidden manna" [Rev 2:17] and only he who eats it still hungers for more. [Sir. 24:29] It is "a sealed fountain" [Song 4:12] to which no stranger has access; only he who drinks still thirsts for more. [Sir 24:29] Listen to one who has had the experience, how urgently he demands: "Be my saviour again, renew my joy." [Ps 50:14] But a soul like mine, burdened with sins, still subject to carnal passions [II Tim 3:6], devoid of any knowledge of spiritual delights, may not presume to make such a request, almost totally unacquainted as it is with the joys of the supernatural life.

I should like however to point out to persons like this that there is an appropriate place for them on the way of salvation. They may not rashly aspire to the lips of the most benign Bridegroom, but let them prostrate with me in fear at the feet of a most severe Lord. Like the publican full of misgiving, [Lk 18:13] they must turn their eyes to the earth rather than up to heaven. Eyes that are accustomed only to darkness will be dazzled by the brightness of the spiritual world, [Prov. 25:27] overpowered by its splendor, repulsed by its peerless radiance and whelmed again in a gloom more dense than before. All you who are conscious of sin, do not regard as unworthy and despicable that position where the holy sinner laid down her sins, and put on the garment of holiness. There the Ethiopian changed her skin, [Jer 13:23] and, cleansed to a new brightness, could confidently and legitimately respond to those who insulted her: [Ps 118:42] "I am black but lovely, daughters of Jerusalem." [Song 1:4] You may ask what skill enabled her to accomplish this change, or on what grounds did she merit it? I can tell you in a few words. She wept bitterly, [Lk 22:62] she sighed deeply from her heart, she sobbed with a repentance that shook her very being, till the evil that inflamed her passions was cleansed away. The heavenly physician came with speed to her aid, because "his word runs swiftly." [Ps 147:15] Perhaps you think the Word of God is not medicine? Surely it is, a medicine strong and pungent, testing the mind and the heart. [Ps 7:10] "The Word of God is something alive and active. It cuts like any double-edged sword but more finely. It can slip through the place where the soul is divided from the spirit, or the joints from the marrow: it can judge the secret thoughts." [Heb 4:12] It is up to you, wretched sinner, to humble yourself as this happy penitent did so that you may be rid of your wretchedness.[Lk 7:37ff] Prostrate yourself on the ground, take hold of his feet, soothe them with kisses, sprinkle them with your tears and so wash not them but yourself. Thus you will become one of the "Flock of shorn ewes as they come up from the washing." [Song 4:2] But even then you may not dare to lift up a face suffused with shame and grief, until you hear the sentence: "Your sins are forgiven," [Lk 7:48] to be followed by the summons: "Awake, awake, captive daughter of Sion, awake, shake off the dust." [Is 52:1-2][10]

Much can be said about this sermon. In Bernard's allegorical reading, the kiss of the lips of the Song of Songs becomes union between the soul and Christ, the direct experience with God himself. Bernard suggests that the movement toward this ecstatic experience with God is an inward and thus intensely personal one. One finds God within oneself since humans are made in God's image. However, in order to discover this true self, one must strip away the sin that separates one from God and keeps one from God's image within oneself. The sermon starts with what Bernard calls the book of experience, which is essentially this experience of self. From there, the movement toward ultimate union is in three stages, called by Bernard the three kisses. The first stage, the kiss of the feet, is repentance; the kiss of the hand is perseverance; the kiss of the lips is the union itself. In describing this process, Bernard brings together over fifty scriptural references, which by no means come exclusively from the Song of Songs. Bernard, proceeding almost associatively, brings in Scripture wherever he thinks it will fit. A reading of this passage in fact shows that all of Scripture is such an immediate part of Bernard's own experience that he sees it as a unity; he draws on his immense, almost spontaneous knowledge of it to give meaning to the most diverse attitudes. Bernard thinks scripturally and thus is able to draw freely from all parts of Scripture. However, his primary interest is not in giving a systematic exegesis of each verse of the Song of Songs; in fact, there are sermons in this collection that are not really commentaries on any passage of the Song but instead are insights Bernard has had while reading the book.

Bernard maintained a lively correspondence with Peter the Venerable, abbot of Cluny from 1122 to 1156. Bernard criticized elements of the Cluniac observance, and Peter's reforms were clearly influenced by Bernard although he defended many of Cluny's practices against Bernard's invectives. Bernard was even stronger in his condemnation of laxity in the monastery. In a diatribe against the Cluniacs, but in reality intended to reach anyone living under the Benedictine rule, Bernard brings together considerable gifts for satire and invective with his burning desire for reform. Perhaps Bernard's most quoted passages deal with the artistic splendor of Cluny and its dependencies:

> What excuse can there be for these ridiculous monstrosities in the cloisters where the monks do their reading, extraordinary things at once beautiful and ugly? Here we find filthy monkeys and fierce lions, fearful centaurs, harpies, and striped tigers, soldiers at war, and hunters blowing their horns. Here is one head with many bodies, there is one body with many heads. Over there is a beast with a serpent for its tail, a fish with an animal's head, and a creature that is horse in front and goat behind, and a second beast with horns and the rear of a horse. All round there is such an amazing variety of shapes that one could easily prefer to take one's reading from the walls instead of from a book. One could spend the whole day gazing fascinated at these things, one by one, instead of meditating on the law of God. Good Lord, even if the foolishness of it all occasion no shame, at least one might balk at the expense. I shall say nothing about the soaring heights and extravagant lengths and unnecessary widths of the churches, nothing about their expensive decorations and their novel images, which catch the attention of those who go in to pray, and dry up their devotion. To me they seem like something out of the Old Testament; but let them be since it is all to the glory of God.[11]

Bernard's literary gifts are here apparent. As in so much of medieval humor, the comic aspects of the passage are intended to forcefully heighten the reader's awareness of deviation from an ideal, in this case the ideal of Benedictine austerity. This same combination of zeal and literary talent characterizes much of Bernard's writing, which accounts for his subsequent influence on such advocates of reform as Dante and even Martin Luther.

Some have seen in this passage evidence that Bernard was an iconoclast without aesthetic sensibility. This is to seriously misread the text. Bernard, firmly in the tradition of Augustine, carefully distinguishes between means and ends, inveighing against an art that comes dangerously close to becoming an end in itself. For Bernard, no less than for Augustine, the purpose of art is to lead viewers from the visible to the invisible. The excessively decorative art that Bernard decries here is dangerous because its details can easily command attention in and for themselves, waylaying the viewers and keeping them from moving to the deeper realities that art should point toward. This is seen as an especial danger in a monastery, where the Rule demands a unique kind of austerity and where deviation from this austerity could destroy monastic harmony.

Throughout his writings Bernard recognizes that different demands are made by different vocations; what is totally out of place in the austerity of a monastery may well have its place in other vocations. He recognizes, as did Gregory the Great before him, that art works can be books for the layperson; but for monks, who can read, it should not be necessary. The kind of piety that art can excite ought to be in a monk to begin with:

> It is not the same for monks and bishops. Bishops have a duty toward both wise and foolish. They have to make use of material ornamentation to rouse devotion in a carnal people, incapable of spiritual things. But we no longer belong to such people. For the sake of Christ we have abandoned all the world holds valuable and attractive. All that is beautiful in sight and sound and scent we have left behind, all that is pleasant to taste and touch. To win Christ we have reckoned bodily enjoyments as dung. (Phil 3:8)[12]

Despite the differences between the Cluniacs and the Cistercians in the twelfth century, it is important to remember that they shared the common inheritance of the Rule, the Fathers, and a long tradition of monastic spirituality. When one compares both forms of Benedictine monastericism with anything nonmonastic—for example the revival of Aristotle in the cathedral schools—the essential unity of monastic culture becomes clear. There are important analogies to be made between monastic writers such as Bernard and the great monastic art and architecture of the period called Romanesque, nothwith-

Interior of the Church of Mary Magdalen, Vézelay, France. 12th Century. This is the best surviving example of an interior of a Cluniac church. (Archives Photographiques, Paris)

standing Bernard's objections to some of its excesses. As the great monastic scholar Jean Leclercq writes in his seminal work *The Love of Learning and the Desire for God*: "Just as the cathedrals of the thirteenth century have been compared to theological *summas*, monastic writings of the Romanesque period may be likened to the abbey churches of the period: the same simplicity, the same solidity, the same vivacity of biblical imagination."[13]

Secular and Ecclesiastical Authority

By the middle of the twelfth century, the papacy had found that canon law was the best means by which to exert the Church's authority throughout Latin Christendom. Gratian's collection of canons and the study of church law at the emerging University of Bologna (see ch. 9) provided both a body of law and able practitioners and interpreters of it. From the middle of the century, canon lawyers usually occupied the papal office. Increasingly, the pope perceived himself as the head of a system of ecclesiastical courts; and many of the cases adjudicated in these courts involved property settlements rather than moral judgments. One of those most concerned with this new orientation of the papacy was Bernard of Clairvaux. When one of his former novices at Clairvaux was elected pope as Eugenius III in 1145, he wrote to tell his former charge exactly what he thought of the turn the papacy had taken:

> I ask you, what is the point of wrangling and listening to litigants from morning to night? And would that the evil of the day were sufficient for it, but the nights are not even free! Your poor body scarcely gets the time which nature requires for rest before it must rise for further disputing. . . . What is more servile and more unworthy, especially for the Supreme Pontiff, than every day, or rather every hour, to sweat over such affairs for the likes of these. Tell me this, when are we to pray or to teach the people? When are we to build up the Church or meditate on the law? Oh yes, every day laws re-

sound through the palace, but these are the laws of Justinian, not of the Lord.[14]

However, Bernard, clearly distinguising between the person and the office, spoke of the power of the pope in the most exalted terms.

The use of canon law to enforce and advance papal policy led to conflicts with secular authorities. The powerful Holy Roman Emperor Frederick Barbarossa (r.1152–90) created a schism by renouncing his allegiance to Alexander III and choosing his own pope. The issue between pope and Empire was the legal relationship of pope to emperor and the question of the pope's right to intervene in the Empire's affairs. Although Frederick ultimately submitted to Alexander's authority, the issue was by no means settled.

Another conflict between the Church and a secular ruler took place in England over the right of the king to try clerics in royal courts. The protagonists were the Archbishop of Canterbury Thomas à Becket (d.1170) and King Henry II (r.1154–89). The most dramatic event in this conflict, of course, was Becket's murder. But the issue at stake was settled in a compromise that preserved the Church's demand that clergy be tried in ecclesiastical courts.

In the last part of the twelfth century, the papal curia moved somewhat cautiously with regard to the monarchies, on the heels of the dramatic conflicts with Frederick Barbarossa and Henry II. Furthermore, the popes toward the end of the cen-

Entrance into Heaven and Entrance into Hell. Details of the tympanum of the Church of Saint Foi, Conques, France. 12th Century. Part of a depiction of the Last Judgment, they show the stark contrast between reward and punishment which is the essence of the theme of judgment. The serenity of the saved souls being ushered through the gate of paradise by Saint Peter contrasts with the anguish of the damned about to be pushed through the gaping jaws of hellmouth by a devil. Note the legs of one sinner in the mouth.

tury, generally old, sought to consolidate the achievements of their predecessors like Alexander III (r.1159–81) rather than seek confrontation or assert new claims. However, in 1198 the thirty-seven-year-old Cardinal Lothario dei Segni was elected, taking the name Innocent III. With him came the apex of papal political power and influence, the development of a theory of papal supremacy, and an attempt to reform the Church and define doctrine.

Innocent III held the position that the pope received both spiritual and temporal authority from God. His exalted notion of papal power can be seen in some of his early statements after assuming the throne of Peter:

> You see then who is this servant set over the household, truly the vicar of Jesus Christ, successor of Peter, annointed of the Lord, a God of Pharaoh, set between God and man, lower than God but higher than man, who judges all and is judged by no one. . . .

> Just as the founder of the universe established two great lights in the firmament of heaven, a greater one to preside over the day and a lesser to preside over the night, so too in the firmament of the universal church, which is signified by the word heaven, he instituted two great dignities, a greater one to preside over souls as if over day and a lesser one to preside over bodies as if over night. These are the pontifical authority and the royal power. Now just as the moon derives its light from the sun and is indeed lower than it in quantity and quality, in position and in power, so too the royal power derives the splendor of its dignity from the pontifical authority. . . .[15]

Innocent was a brilliant statesman more interested in shaping the development of Christian Europe than in winning theoretical battles. When he dealt with matters in which there was some question of his right to intervene, he used whatever argument would meet least resistance. From Innocent, therefore, we get no fully developed, carefully argued theory of papal supremacy but rather a patchwork of statements and actions. In one case he would claim the right to intervene because an oath was involved (and the Church was the guardian of oaths); in another he would claim the right because sin was involved. Innocent found grounds upon which to intervene in the affairs of Europe whenever he wanted, though he never claimed the right to do so simply because he was lord of the world.

During Innocent's rule he faced a major outbreak of heresy in southern France. In 1174, a merchant of Lyons named Valdes (sometimes written Waldo or even Peter Waldo) sold all that he had and dedicated himself to a life of poverty. He and his followers attacked the wealth of the Church and the clergy's abandonment of their pastoral role. He wished to preach but could not get a license from his bishop. Valdes and his followers were condemned by a synod in 1184; after this, they became more radical, attacking the priesthood in more fundamental ways. At about the same time there occurred a widespread heretical movement centered in Albi, in southern France, called the Albigensian or Cathar heresy, a dualist heresy similar to that of the earlier Gnostics and Manichees. The Albigensians attracted many followers, the ascetic lives of their leaders contrasting favorably with the clergy of the area. By the time of Innocent III, these movements posed a serious threat to Catholicism. Innocent sought to put an end to these heresies peacefully. He sent preachers into the strongholds of the Albingensian movement to try to win them back to the Roman fold. He approved the founding of the Franciscan and Dominican orders, preaching orders that combined poverty and simplicity with loyalty to the pope and the Church (see ch. 10). He welcomed back groups of heretics who were willing to submit to the papacy. However, after preaching failed to win back sufficient numbers to Rome, and after a papal legate was murdered, he launched a Crusade against the Albingensians, a Crusade that eventually eliminated them as a threat to the unity of Latin Christendom.

Nonetheless, Innocent was genuinely interested in reform. In addition to approving the Franciscan and Dominican orders, he called the Fourth Lateran Council, which met in Rome in 1215. It limited the number of new orders, tried again to eliminate simony, and defined dogma more carefully in response to heretical movements and differences of opinion among theologians. Three actions by the Fourth Lateran Council were particularly important. First, the number of sacraments was defined. In the early Middle Ages, the Church had not spoken authoritatively about the number of sacraments. Before and during the investiture contest many felt that the anointing of a king was a sacrament, a notion discredited after the Concordat of Worms. The theology that was developing with the rediscovery of Aristotle emphasized order and classification. Theologians now wanted to define precisely what a sacrament was and how many there were. The definition of a sacrament as "an outward and physical sign of an inward and spiritual grace" became standard. The Fourth Lateran Council decreed seven sacraments: baptism, confirmation, penance, Eucharist, extereme unction (now called sacrament of the sick), holy orders (ordination), and marriage. Second, Innocent's council defined a doctrine concerning the Eucharist, the doctrine of transubstantiation. Following Aristotle, the council spoke of the bread and wine as consisting of substance (what they are by nature) and accidents (their appearance). The accidents of bread include its texture, color, shape, size; these could change without bread ceasing to exist. According to the Council, when the bread and wine are consecrated, the substance of the bread and wine is changed into the substance of the body and blood of Christ; only the accidents of the bread remain. Thus the sacrament is in its nature—substance—Christ's body and blood.

Finally, the council decreed that only the clergy could receive wine at communion (i.e. transubstantiated wine). Laypeople were to receive the Eucharist only under one kind or species (i.e. transubstantiated bread). This decree, modified only by the Second Vatican Council in the mid-twentieth century, symbolizes a development in the Church beginning with the investiture contest. The clergy, in stressing their rights and their differences from the laity, had come to treat the laity as almost peripheral to the Church. Several developments in the twelfth century embody this: masses were celebrated without the presence of the laity despite the fact that this had once been considered essential. Altars were often moved against the east walls of churches, and thus priests consecrated the sacrament with their backs to people. Sometimes screens were built between the nave, where the laity stood, and the choir so that the consecration could not even be seen. They were not encouraged to take communion frequently; often they received only once a year at Easter. Laypeople were being excluded from an integral place in the Church. The Waldensian and Albigensian movements appealed to the laity in part because of this exclusion by the ecclesiastical hierarchy. As a way of increasing lay participation, veneration of the Eucharist increased. The feast of *Corpus Christi* (Latin for "the body of Christ") was instituted in the thirteenth century. This feast usually consisted of a procession through the street with the local bishop carrying the consecrated host for the veneration of the people. This feast became an important motif in late medieval art, as well as an important source in the development of vernacular drama, called *Corpus Christi* cycles in England.

After the death of Innocent III in 1216, the papacy gradually began a long period of decline and decay. In part this was due to the all-out struggle that developed between the papacy and the Holy Roman Emperor Frederick II. Frederick was also king of Sicily—including southern Italy as well as the island of Sicily. Thus he was lord of both northern and southern Italy, leaving the pope pinched in the papal states between Frederick's holdings. Furthermore, Frederick was a brilliant politician who desired and enjoyed the use of power; caring little about Christianity, his court at Palermo was a mixture of Roman Catholics, Eastern Orthodox, Moslems, and Jews. When open war came between the pope and the emperor, more and more of the Church's money was diverted to hire mercenaries to defend the pope's temporal possessions. The Church suffered in its reputation as the popes preoccupied themselves with eliminating Frederick and his family, the Hohenstaufens. They were successful thanks to the timely death of Frederick II in 1250 and the efforts of French mercenaries commanded by Charles of Anjou. Charles became king of Sicily while the emasculated office of Holy Roman Emperor remained vacant for twenty-three years. However, this papal victory was short-lived. In 1282 a revolt in Palermo led to the expulsion of the French from the island of Sicily, although Charles continued to rule southern Italy from his court in Naples. The Holy Roman Empire was revived beginning in 1273 with the election of Rudolf of Habsburg. By the beginning of the fourteenth century, the emperor was looking for a way of re-establishing de facto as well as de jure control over northern Italy, which had become a series of independent city-states after a league of Italian cities defeated Frederick Barbarossa at the battle of Legnano in 1176.

Political activities were only one cause of the demise of the papacy. The popes sought, often high-handedly, to centralize power in Rome. This involved taking cases out of the hands of bishops and either conducting trials directly in Rome or sending papal legates to conduct them. Furthermore, the new mendicant orders, the Franciscans and Dominicans, were directly under the authority of the pope and thus in some ways free from episcopal control. In the thirteenth century these mendicants began to carry out some of the traditional functions of the secular clergy. They built huge churches in cities and preached to large crowds there, luring many laypeople away from their parishes; they heard confessions and buried the dead. Most important they collected money in their churches that was split between the orders and Rome; the bishops and secular clergy got none. Thus, there was a great struggle within the Church between the secular clergy on one side and the pope and mendicants on the other. Some bishops began to turn to their secular lords to form a united front against papal centralization.

Another strong element in the decline of the papacy in European society stems from the development of nation-states. The revival of Roman law was beneficial to secular rulers because with it they could provide better justice, weakening the control over justice that the nobility had acquired in the decline of the Carolingian Empire. Kings such as Henry II (r.1154–89) and Edward I (r.1272–1307) in England and Louis VII (r.1137–80), Philip Augustus (r.1180–1223), Louis IX (r.1226–70), and Philip IV (r.1285–1314) in France molded their monarchies into strong, politically viable entities. Both monarchies established royal courts as courts of last appeal; both hired Roman lawyers, men loyal to their paymasters, to function both as judges and as bureaucrats throughout the kingdoms. England's common law developed from the reign of Henry II; and Edward I, who strove for greater royal power through the use of law, is sometimes referred to as the English Justinian. The French kings had to limit the power of independent vassals. The most significant victory for the French came when most of the land in France controlled by the English kings (virtually the entire west of France) was regained by Philip Augustus at the expense of the unstable King John (r.1199–1216). These lands were not granted to other nobles as fiefs but governed directly by the crown through his bureaucrats.

With the rediscovery of Aristotle in the thirteenth century, monarchs were able to construct theoretical arguments for their existence independent of the ecclesiastical hierarchy. As we have seen, Augustine viewed the state as a necessary result of sin; thus the state's main function is to police. This concept dominated the early Middle Ages, and the popes of the Gregorian era based their argument for papal supremacy on the inherent superiority of Church over state. However, Aristotle's idea of the state was different. To him the state is a positive and creative force; people are by nature, says Aristotle, political animals. Although Thomas Aquinas (d.1274) was by no means a royal propagandist, a few short selections from his writings show how the Aristotelian view of the state became incorporated into medieval political thought:

The ultimate end of the whole universe is considered in theology which is most important without qualification. He [Aristotle] says that it belongs to political science to treat the ultimate end of human life.

And, since the things that come to man's use are ordained to man as to their end, and the end takes precedence over the things that are for the end, it is therefore necessary that this whole, which is the state, take precedence over all wholes that may be known and constituted by human reason.

A free man may be ruled by another when the latter directs him to his own good or to the common good. And such govern-

ment over man by man would have existed, for two reasons, in
the state of innocence. First, because man is a naturally social
animal; man even in the state of innocence would have lived
in society. Social life among many could not exist, however,
unless someone took the position of authority to direct them
to the common good.[16]

This last statement shows the contrast between Thomas and
Augustine. And one can see that there is nothing in Thomas
to imply that secular power is derived from or commanded
by the ecclesiastical authorities.

The revival of Roman law coupled with the revival of
Aristotle combined to provide the theoretical underpinning for
the emerging states in their struggle with the ecclesiastical
hierarchy. This development of the "lay thesis" combined with
the politicization and centralization of the Church resulted in
still another major church-state controversy, one that ended
in a crushing defeat for the pope.

A struggle between Pope Boniface VIII and the wily Philip
IV of France broke out at the end of the thirteenth century
over the right of royal taxation of the French clergy. Philip
began to tax the clergy because he was involved in war and
in need of money; Boniface demanded that he stop. Philip responded by saying that if he were not allowed to tax the
clergy, he would not allow any money to leave France, including all the money collected by ecclesiastical powers for the
pope. Boniface backed down by conceding that Philip could
tax the clergy without his permission in an emergency and by
further conceding that Philip could define an emergency. It
seemed that Philip, who clearly had won, then picked a fight
with Boniface almost for the sake of further weakening him.
After several threats and counterthreats, Boniface published the
bull *Unam Sanctam* in 1302, which said little that popes had
not said before, but made clear his belief in papal control of
all facets of society:

> Certainly anyone who denies that the temporal sword is in
> the power of Peter has not paid heed to the words of the Lord
> when he said, "Put up thy sword into its sheath" (Mt 26:52).

Both then are in the power of the church, the material sword and the spritual. But the one is exercised for the church, the other by the church, the one by the hand of the priest, the other by the hand of kings and soldiers, though at the will and suffrance of the priest. One sword ought to be under the other and the temporal authority subject to the spiritual power. . . .

Therefore, if the earthly powers errs, it shall be judged by the spiritual power, if a lesser spiritual power errs it shall be judged by its superior, but if the supreme spiritual power errs it can be judged only by God not by man, as the apostle witnesses, "The spiritual man judgeth all things and he himself is judged by no man" (1 Cor 2:15). Although this authority was given to a man and is exercised by a man it is not human but rather divine, being given to Peter at God's mouth, and confirmed to him and to his successors in him, the rock whom the Lord acknowledged when he said to Peter himself "Whatsoever thou shalt bind" etc. (Mt 16:19). Whoever therefore resists this power so ordained by God resists the ordinance of God unless, like the Manicheans, he imagines that there are two beginnings, which we judge to be false and heretical, as Moses witnesses, for not "in the beginnings" but "in the beginning" God created heaven and earth (Gen 1:1). Therefore we declare, state, define and pronounce that it is altogether necessary to salvation for every human creature to be subject to the Roman Pontiff.[17]

Philip did not lay down and play dead with the publication of *Unam Sanctam*. He waged a propaganda campaign accusing Boniface of every crime from heresy to sodomy. Philip sent a mission to Boniface's residence at Anagni; and although accounts vary, there is reason to think that Philip's men assaulted him physically as well as verbally. At any rate, Boniface died soon afterwards. His successor (following the brief pontificate of Benedict XI) was a Frenchman, Clement V (r.1305–14), who sought to placate the French monarchy by trying to explain away some of Boniface's stronger statements. In spite of this, the king prevented Clement from going to Rome, keeping him on the other side of the Alps. Clement settled down in a piece of land in the southeastern corner of France, which belonged at the time to the king of Naples, in the city of

Avignon. By the 1330s it became clear that the popes would remain in Avignon indefinitely, and a magnificent papal palace, which still stands today, was built there. The papacy lost in its struggle to control European society, sometimes appearing to be little more than a plaything of the French monarchy. It was not until 1377 that the papacy returned to Rome, ending a period of papal history often called the Babylonian captivity.

About the time of the conflict between Boniface VIII and Philip IV, an important political treatise was written by the Dominican John of Paris, who argued that God gave some power directly to kings and some power directly to the pope. It was obvious to John that the papacy could not have instituted royal power because there were monarchies before the bishopric of Rome was established. John recognized that the popes could control property and have political authority, but only insofar as they had been granted it. Even then the pope was viewed primarily as an administrator. In essence the pope governed souls and had no jurisdiction over bodies; kings on the other hand ruled bodies but could not bind and loose souls. This concept of the separation of powers, which had existed in germ since the time of the investiture contest, became more widely accepted in Europe; this was in part because of the powerful arguments of its advocates but primarily because it was the theory that was closest to the de facto relationship between temporal and ecclesiastical powers, appealing to thinkers sympathetic to the Aristotelian reliance on empirical reality as a starting point.

However, although the Holy Roman Emperor was no longer the de jure or de facto secular head of Western Christendom by 1300, there were those who clung to the notion that only a universal rule on earth by the Roman Emperor would defeat papal claims to supremacy in secular matters and bring peace to Europe. The most important writer to hold this view was Dante (1265–1321) in his *On World Government*:

> Since it appears that the whole of mankind is ordained to one end, as we proved above, it should therefore have a single rule and government, and this power should be called the Monarch

or Emperor. And thus it is plain that for the well-being of the world there must be a single world-rule or empire. . . .

Therefore mankind in submitting to a single government most resembles God and most nearly exists according to the divine intention, which is the same as enjoying well-being, as was proved at the beginning of this chapter. . . .

And so I maintain that though Peter's successor may loose or bind in performing the duties of the office entrusted to Peter, it does not follow that he can therefore loose or bind imperial laws or decrees, as they maintain, unless it can be proved that this is related to the power of the keys; and it is the contrary of this which I shall prove.[18]

We have already seen that kings were anxious to hire lawyers to enhance their authority. Since a king's vassals originally owed the king obligations of service only, one must ask where he got money to pay these lawyers. One source of revenue was from the newly developing cities, which were willing to pay for the right to govern themselves in certain matters. The other source was from the vassals themselves; it became common for the king to commute their obligations from fighting and hospitality to money. This way the king could hire soldiers as well as lawyers, who would fight for him not just for forty days but all year, and who were loyal to him as long as they were being paid. Commutation of services was usually for a fixed sum in perpetuity; however, inflation meant that the amounts paid did not long suffice. The kings of Europe could not "live on their own." A king could ask his vassals for more money, but the vassals had to approve of extra payment. The need for more money came about the time that Roman law was revived in Western Europe. The Justinian Code contained a significant amount of corporation law, which came to be applied to monasteries, cathedral chapters, the Church as a whole, cities, guilds, and even nations. In other words, it created ficticious personalities, corporations as legal entities that were treated like persons. Corporations such as guilds and monasteries increasingly found themselves parties in adjudication. Using a Roman legal formula, many of these corporations came to appoint permanent officials called procurators who would be given *plena potestas* (full power) to speak for the entire corporation.

Soon kings found that it was sometimes valuable to negotiate, not with individual cities, but rather with their representatives, who would have *plena potestas* to speak for and bind those whom they represented. Furthermore, kings could ask these representatives to come together to talk about affairs of the entire nation (including but not limited to money) and to give their consent. In asking, they often cited another piece of Roman law that originally applied to corporations: "What touches all must be approved by all." In the late twelfth and thirteenth centuries rulers, honoring this principle, began to call assemblies of representatives with *plena potestas*; these are what we call representative institutions or parliaments. The latter name immediately calls to mind the English Parliament, which had developed into the most powerful representative institution by the end of Middle Ages, though neither was it the first nor was it necessarily clear in the thirteenth century that it was to be the strongest representative institution in Europe. The Cortes of the Spanish kingdom of Aragón was meeting before the end of the twelfth century; and Pope Innocent III, as temporal ruler of the papal states, called a representative assembly at the beginning of the thirteenth century. Even the Fourth Lateran Council's summons sounded much like those of rulers calling together representatives. By the end of the thirteenth century there were representative assemblies in the kingdoms of Sicily, England, and the Holy Roman Empire; and Philip IV called the first Estates General during his quarrel with Boniface VIII. In this brief and schematic discussion of the origin of representative institutions, it is important to remember that they evolved slowly from the lord-vassal relationship, the rise of cities, the centralization of authority, and the revival of Roman law.

The controversy concerning the right relationship between secular and spiritual authorities—or church and state—reached a new level of intensity in the eleventh through thirteenth centuries. This tension was at times destructive, as the struggles we have just described indicate; but at other times it was responsible for much that was creative and vital during the period. Neither the pagan classics nor the Bible dealt with the conflict, which was a unique product of medieval society. Thus although thinkers continued to look to those old texts, they had to use them in creative new ways, since it was impossible simply to copy past arguments or practices.

CHAPTER NINE

The Renaissance
of the Twelfth Century

During the Carolingian period, there was a cultural revival, a renaissance, which quite consciously looked to antiquity for models and inspiration. Much of this classical revival, however, was dependent on late Latin writers and collections of passages anthologized from the older Latin writers. Furthermore, most of the great figures of the Carolingian Renaissance were educated in a monastic context, where the study of the classics was clearly subordinate to the goals of the Christian and more specifically the monastic life. Nevertheless, the achievements of the Carolingian Renaissance were significant; and they were not forgotten or completely abandoned even during the years of political disintegration, monastic corruption, and invasion that followed.

Scholars today generally regard the cultural and intellectual revival of the twelfth century (more accurately c.1050–c.1250) as *the* medieval renaissance, referring to it as the renaissance of the twelfth century. During this time, there was an intense interest in Latin and Greek authors who had been either unknown or ignored in the West for centuries. Beginning in schools established in Carolingian times, scholars building on the Carolingian heritage discovered new sources, tools, and methods for the study of theology, using, but significantly altering, the dominant Augustinianism of early medieval Europe. Achievements sparked by discoveries from classical antiquity also occurred in law, science, and medicine, achievements that had an impact on every facet of intellectual activity, as well as on the development of papal power and the building of nation-states. And to transmit this new knowledge, the institution known as the university emerged.

In the millenial year, 1000, Sylvester II (Gerbert of Aurillac) was pope. That he was pope at the beginning of the second millenium is symbolic of the intellectual changes that were to sweep Europe since Gerbert himself was one of the first persons of his time to initiate those changes. He was well versed in the first part of the trivium—grammar—and was one of the first since the Carolingian age to seriously study the other parts—rhetoric and logic. In a letter dated 985, he explained the relationship between good living and good speaking:

> Since philosophy does not separate ways of conduct and ways of speaking, I have always added the fondness for speaking well to the fondness for living well, although by itself it may be more excellent to live well than to speak well, and if one be freed from the cares of governing, the former is enough without the latter. But to us, busied in affairs of state, both are necessary. For speaking effectively to persuade and restrain the minds of angry persons from violence by smooth speech are both of the greatest usefulness. For this activity, which must be prepared beforehand, I am diligently forming a library.[1]

Gerbert was also interested in the quadrivium and constantly sought out manuscripts of classical works on all the liberal arts. He also either invented or spread the knowledge of several mathematical and scientific devices, such as the abacus.

The consequences of Gerbert's intellectual activities were greater than he could possibly have realized. To pursue the study of rhetoric required the close study of Latin writers like Cicero. To learn logic meant the careful examination of that small portion of the writings of Aristotle that had been translated into Latin by Boethius, as well as other works by Greek philosophers. Thus, the writings of the ancient Greeks soon became indispensible to medieval students.

One of the most influential texts on the philosophical upsurge in the generations following Gerbert was written by the Greek Neoplatonist Porphyry (c.232–303) and existed in a Latin translation. The following excerpt raised a question which engaged philosophers for the rest of the Middle Ages:

> Next, concerning genera and species, the question indeed whether they have a substantial existence, or whether they consist in bare intellectual concepts only, or whether if they have a substantial existence they are corporeal or incorporeal, and whether they are separable from the sensible properties of the things (or particulars of sense), or are only in those properties and subsisting about them, I shall forbear to determine. For a question of this kind is a very deep one and one that requires a long investigation.[2]

This text, which authors like Boethius had already commented on, stimulated debate and aroused passions from the eleventh century on. Porphyry has outlined three possible positions on the question of universals. One, following Plato, is that universals (genera) have a real existence independent of any individual examples (species) of them. For those who hold this position, individuals are real to the degree that they partake of the universal. For example, an individual person exists because he or she is a part of humanity, the universal. This position is usually called extreme realism. When this concept was applied to Christian theology, problems arose. Universals were thought to have their existence in God and since individuals were real only in as much as they were part of the universal, extreme realists were open to the charge of pantheism, a belief destructive of the basic Judaeo-Christian distinction between creator and creature. In the eleventh century, William of Champeaux and others came very close to a pantheistic view of the universe. Extreme realism continued to have its adherents for the rest of the Middle Ages, most notably the English theologian John Wyclif (d.1384).

The opposite of extreme realism is nominalism. Adherents of this position argue that universals have no real existence but are only names we use to categorize individuals. Humanity, for a nominalist, exists only as a name, as a sound, or as a series of marks on a piece of paper to represent a group of individuals, which are the only real things. This position also caused trouble for its adherents when applied to Christian teachings, for it seemed to force them to deny either the plurality or the unity of the Trinity. In 1093, a regional synod forced Roscelin to repudiate his nominalist teachings on the Trinity. Nevertheless, nominalism survived and had many notable adherents in the late Middle Ages, including William of Ockham (c.1300–c.1349) and John Gerson (1363–1429).

Between these two extremes falls a position, essentially Aristotle's, called moderate realism or conceptualism. Its followers assert that universals are real but not independent of individual examples. Thus "humanity" is real, referring to those qualities shared by all individual persons and discovered through the observation of individuals. This middle-of-the-road position was accepted by many medieval philosophers, including Thomas Aquinas.

Some of the eleventh-century scholars who tried to apply these pagan philosophical categories to Christian theology got themselves in trouble with the ecclesiastical authorities, and many pious people doubted the value of trying to use pagan philosophy for the purpose of illuminating Christianity. The man who did the most to make respectable the application of ancient philosophy to Christian revelation was a monk, later archbishop of Canterbury, named Anselm (c.1033–1109). No rationalist, he was steeped in Augustinian theology and monastic spirituality. However, as Anselm explains at the beginning of his famous treatise *Why God Became Man*, reason has a role to play in understanding and explaining faith:

Both by word of mouth and by letter I have received many
earnest requests that I should commit to writing the proofs of
a particular doctrine of our faith, as I usually present them to
inquirers. I am told that these proofs are thought to be both
pleasing and adequate. Those who make this request do not
expect to come to faith through reason, but they hope to be
gladdened by the understanding and contemplation of the
things they believe, and as far as possible to be "ready always
to satisfy everyone that asketh" them "a reason of that hope
which is in" them. . . . And since investigations that are carried
on by means of question and answer are clearer to many (especially to slower) minds, and so are more acceptable, I shall
take one of those who discuss this subject . . . to debate with
me, so that in this way Boso may ask and Anselm answer.[3]

Anselm also developed a proof for the existence of God, the
so-called ontological proof:

And it [God] assuredly exists so truly that it cannot be conceived not to exist. For, it is possible to conceive of a being
which cannot be conceived not to exist; and this is greater than
one which can be conceived not to exist. Hence, if that, than
which nothing greater can be conceived, can be conceived not
to exist, it is not that, than which nothing greater can be conceived. But this is an irreconcilable contradiction. There is,
then, so truly a being than which nothing greater can be conceived not to exist; and this being thou art, O Lord, our God.
   So truly, therefore, dost thou exist, O Lord, my God, that
thou canst not be conceived not to exist; and rightly. For, if
a mind could conceive of a being better than thee, the creature
would rise above the Creator; and this is most absurd. And,
indeed, whatever else there is, except thee alone, can be conceived not to exist. To thee alone, therefore, it belongs to exist
more truly than all other beings, and hence in a higher degree
than all others. For, whatever else exists does not exist so truly,
and hence in a less degree it belongs to it to exist. Why, then,
has the fool said in his heart, there is no God (Ps 14:1), since
it is so evident, to a rational mind, that thou dost exist in the
highest degree of all? Why, except that he is dull and a fool?[4]

The text of Anselm's argument has been commented upon
more than any other philosophical text of comparable size from

the Middle Ages. Even without attempting to engage the numerous philosophical problems this argument presents, one can see from the text how Anselm proceeds by means of a number of clearly articulated logical steps.

Anselm was a monk trained in monastic schools. However, by the time of his death, there had developed in France several important cathedral schools with teachers who were clerics but not monks. Some of the greatest teachers and students went from school to school. The rapidity of this important change in medieval education is testified to in the memoirs of Guibert de Nogent, written about 1115:

> There was a little before that time, and in a measure there was still in my youth, such a scarcity of teachers that hardly any could be found in the towns, and in the cities there were very few, and those who by good chance could be discovered had but slight knowledge and could not be compared with the wandering scholars of these days.[5]

The most famous pupil and teacher to emerge from the French cathedral schools of the early twelfth century was Peter Abelard (1079–1142). Although he is chiefly known in modern times because of his adventures and misadventures with Heloise, strikingly told in his autobiographical *History of My Misfortunes*, his role in the intellectual development of the twelfth century is extraordinarily important. His most famous work was the *Sic et Non (Yes and No)*. In the preface, strongly influenced by the biblical scholarship of Jerome as well as by pagan philosophy, he explains the need for a scholarly, logical examination of the writings of the Christian Church, including Scripture itself:

> Why should it seem surprising if we, lacking the guidance of the Holy Spirit through whom those things were written and spoken, the Spirit impressing them on the writers, fail to understand them? Our achievement of full understanding is impeded especially by unusual modes of expression and by the different significances that can be attached to one and the same word, as a word is used now in one sense, now in another. Just as there are many meanings so there are many words. Tully

[Cicero] says that sameness is the mother of satiety in all things, that is to say it gives rise to fastidious distaste, and so it is appropriate to use a variety of words in discussing the same thing and not to express everything in common and vulgar words. . . .

We must also take special care that we are not deceived by corruptions of the text or by false attributions when sayings of the Fathers are quoted that seem to differ from the truth or to be contrary to it; for many apocryphal writings are set down under names of saints to enhance their authority, and even the texts of divine Scripture are corrupted by the errors of scribes. That most faithful writer and true interpreter, Jerome, accordingly warned us, "Beware of apocryphal writings . . ."

In view of these considerations we have undertaken to collect various sayings of the Fathers that give rise to questioning because of their apparent contradictions as they occur to our memory. This questioning excites young readers to the maximum of effort in inquiring into the truth, and such inquiry sharpens their minds. Assiduous and frequent questioning is indeed the first key to wisdom. Aristotle, that most perspicacious of all philosophers, exhorted the studious to practice it eagerly, saying, "Perhaps it is difficult to express oneself with confidence on such matters if they have not been much discussed. To entertain doubts on particular points will not be unprofitable." For by doubting we come to inquiry; through inquiring we perceive the truth, according to the Truth Himself. "Seek and you shall find," He says, "Knock and it shall be opened to you."[6]

The body of this work consists of one hundred fifty-eight questions, such as, "Is God all powerful, or no?" and "Is God the author of evil, or no?" For each, Abelard assembled texts from Scripture and the Fathers for both sides of the question. He did not give the correct answer himself but suggested rather that it is to be attained by applying reason to the assembled texts.

Abelard, stressing the role of human reason in attaining Christian truth, came into conflict with Bernard of Clairvaux, whose approach to God was quite different. Bernard pursued Abelard (who ultimately found refuge at Cluny) with a fevor almost resembling that of later inquisitors. At his instigation, some of Abelard's writings were condemned by a French synod. Despite Bernard's attack, the use of the principles of Aristotelian logic to deal with theological questions continued. Peter Lombard (c.1100–60) wrote the *Four Books of Sentences* in dialectical style, and this work became the basic textbook for the study of theology for the rest of the Middle Ages. Almost all the great theologians, including Thomas Aquinas, wrote commentaries on this important book.

The cathedral schools excelled not only in the study of logic but also in the other liberal arts. The importance of grammar and rhetoric in the educational programs of the cathedral schools is best seen in the description of Bernard of Chartres, a famous teacher of that city's cathedral school, by his pupil John of Salisbury (c.1115–80):

Bernard of Chartres, the greatest font of literary learning in Gaul in recent times, used to teach grammar in the following way. He would point out, in reading the authors, what was simple and according to rule. On the other hand, he would explain grammatical figures, rhetorical embellishment, and sophistical quibbling, as well as the relation of given passages to other studies. He would do so, however, without trying to teach everything at one time. On the contrary, he would dispense his instruction to his hearers gradually, in a manner commensurate with their powers of assimiliation. And since diction is lustrous either because the words are well chosen, and the adjectives and verbs admirably suited to the nouns with which they are used, or because of the employment of metaphors, whereby speech is transferred to some beyond-the-ordinary meaning for sufficient reason, Bernard used to inculcate this in the minds of his hearers whenever he had the opportunity. In view of the fact that exercise both strengthens and sharpens our mind, Bernard would bend every effort to bring his students to imitate what they were hearing. In some cases he would rely on exhortation, in others he would resort to punishments, such as flogging. Each student was daily required to recite part of what he had heard on the previous day. . . . He [Bernard] would also explain the poets and orators who were to serve as models for the boys in their introductory exercises in imitating prose and poetry. Pointing out how the diction of the authors was so skillfully connected, and what they had to say was so elegantly concluded, he would admonish his students to follow their example. And if, to embellish his work, someone had sewed on a patch of cloth filched from an external source, Bernard, on discovering this, would rebuke him for his plagiary, but would generally refrain from punishing him. After he had reproved the student, if an unsuitable theme had invited this, he would, with modest indulgence, bid the boy to rise to real imitation of the [classical authors], and would bring about that he who had imitated his predecessors would come to be deserving of imitation by his successors. He would also inculcate as fundamental, and impress on the minds of his listeners, what virtue exists in economy; what things are to be commended by facts and what one's choice of words, where concise and, so to speak, frugal speech is in order, and where fuller, more copious expression is appropriate; as well as where speech is excessive, and wherein consists just measure in all cases. Bernard used also to admonish his students that stories and poems should be read thoroughly, and not as though the reader were being precipitated to flight by spurs. Wherefor he diligently and insistently demanded from each, as a daily debt, something committed to memory. At the same time, he said that we should shun what is superfluous. According to him, the works of distinguished authors suffice. . . .

A further feature of Bernard's method was to have his disciples compose prose and poetry every day, and exercise their faculties in mutual conferences, for nothing is more useful in introductory training than actually to accustom one's students to practice the art they are studying. Nothing serves better to foster the acquisition of eloquence and the attainment of knowledge than such conferences, which also have a salutary influence on practical conduct, provided that charity moderates enthusiasm, and that humility is not lost during progress in learning.[7]

The emphasis on the study of the writings of classical antiquity, the Bible, and the Fathers that is so clear in the works of Abelard and John of Salisbury is explained in a famous metaphor of Bernard of Chartres:

Bernard of Chartres used to compare us to dwarfs perched on the shoulders of giants. He pointed out that we see more and farther than our predecessors, not because we have keener vision or greater height, but because we are lifted up and borne aloft on their gigantic stature.[8]

All of the writers examined so far had only small portions of the writings of Aristotle at their disposal, those translated by Boethius. In the second half of the twelfth century and the beginning of the thirteenth, translations were made of virtually all the extant writings of Aristotle. Generally the translations came not from Greek manuscripts available in Constantinople but rather from Arabic translations in Islamic Spain. Along with the works of Aristotle came commentaries from Jewish and especially Islamic philosophers on Aristotle's works that were to be crucially important guides to "The Philosopher"— as Aristotle came to be known to the Middle Ages—for theologians such as Thomas Aquinas. Islamic philosophers such as Avicenna and Averroës not only exerted a great deal of influence as guides to Aristotle, they also were used by groups later declared heretical, such as the thirteenth-century Latin Averroists in Paris.

Which one thinks of the variety of subject matter about which Aristotle wrote (logic, metaphysics, physics, ethics, political theory, biology, etc.), one can begin to imagine the impact of the return of the Aristotelian corpus to Western Europe. In addition, many scientific works from Greek antiquity, such as the writings of Ptolemy, Galen, and Euclid, were translated along with Arabic commentaries and additions. These writings gave to Europe a philosophy that argued that knowledge comes from sense perception plus a great deal of scientific writing to complement that philosophy. As this material came to be absorbed into Western Europe, philosophers began to conceive of ways to arrange it comprehensively. They began to organize well-ordered series of questions according to the rules of logic that attempted to deal with all human knowledge in a systematic way. This type of work is called a *summa*; and in the thirteenth century several were written, most importantly the *Summa Theologiae* of Thomas Aquinas.

The towering figure of Thomas Aquinas (c.1224–74) most

often comes to mind when a modern student thinks of philosophy in the Middle Ages. And without doubt, there is justice to this association. Thomas's works, and in particular his *Summa Theologiae*, stand among the most impressive achievements of the Middle Ages, alongside the *Divine Comedy* and Chartres Cathedral, works to which they are very often compared. Yet seeing Thomas in this exalted position can lead to a distortion, obscuring the real similarities in thought that he shares with other thinkers of the Middle Ages. Thomas's greatness has much to do with the long tradition of which he is a part. Like so much else that is best in medieval culture, his very originality lies in his ability to assimilate the available resources of his milieu. In his absolutely thorough familiarity with Scripture, he is one with every important writer, thinker, or artist of the Middle Ages. Next to Scripture, Augustine, the very theologian to whom his system is usually contrasted, is his most quoted source. In addition, Thomas's thought is also heavily dependent on many other Fathers of the Church, particularly Pseudo-Dionysius, Boethius, and Gregory the Great.

Many of Thomas's works are themselves commentaries on the writings of others. The writing of commentaries was an essential part of the philosophical training in the medieval schools; Thomas differs from the other scholars who learned according to this method only in that several of his commentaries are acknowledged masterpieces, among which are those on Peter Lombard, Boethius, Pseudo-Dionysius, and, most important, Aristotle. The rediscovery of Aristotle in the West was a sensational event because of its implications in almost every field of knowledge. And it was a sensational event in another sense as well—because of the controversy it aroused. In many important areas, such as the origin and creation of the world, there is an incompatibility between Aristotelian and Christian thought. From the twelfth century on, there was continual, strong objection to the study of Aristotle. Even though the entire Aristotelian corpus was placed on the curriculum at the University of Paris in 1255, the fight for legitimacy was by no means over. In one sense, Thomas's use of Aristotle brings to fruition a revolution in thought that began with twelfth-century thinkers. In another sense, Thomas must be seen as a revolutionary because he took upon himself the task not simply of using this Aristotelianism in an uneasy peace with Christian thought but of having Christian thought assimilate Aristotelianism. Thomas's achievement is to have assimilated Aristotle into a larger tradition, a vaster framework, and to have shown that there is no essential conflict between the approach through faith and the approach through reason. His ability to bring together so many seemingly disparate sources into a harmonious balance is perhaps unmatched in any thinker.

For a philosopher, one test of greatness is a concern with large questions rather than small ones. By this criterion, Thomas is a great philosopher because he writes about the most important questions—about God, humanity's place in the universe, and the relation between all the different parts of the universe—with a tenacious thoroughness. What gives Thomas his particular importance, however, is not only that he deals with the large questions but that he sees them in a certain order, in a relationship to each other. His synthesis is an achievement in ordering both the large questions and the intellectual traditions that have dealt with them. What the Scholastics developed, and what Thomas as the greatest of the Scholastics perfected, was a method, a means of examining and commenting on reality as they saw it, through logic and discipline and organization. The form of Scholasticism, as much as its content, was one of the significant intellectual achievements of the Middle Ages.

The basic building block in Thomas's system is the *article*. In principle its form is very simple. In the tradition of dialectic, which was given such impetus by Abelard, Thomas divides the arguments concerning any proposition into *sic et non* (yes and no) and then lists the arguments on each side. When these arguments have been given, he presents a conclusion, a synthesis. One result of this technique is that it allows him to find a logical way of bringing together all the various opinions on a given issue. Here, for example, is one of the articles in which Thomas deals with whether we can know God by our natural reason in this life:

1. It seems that we cannot in this life know God by natural reason. For Boethius says, "The reason cannot grasp simple forms." Now God, as has been shown, is supremely a simple form. Therefore natural reason cannot attain a knowledge of him.

2. According to Aristotle the soul understands nothing by natural reason without images. But since God is incorporeal there can be no image of him in our imagination. So then he cannot be known to us by natural reason.

3. Natural reason is common to the good and the bad, for human nature is common to both. Knowledge of God, however, belongs only to the good, for Augustine says, "The weak eye of the human mind is not fixed on that excellent light unless purified by the justice of faith." Therefore God cannot be known by natural reason.

On The Other Hand we read in Romans, "What may be known about God is manifest to them," i.e. what can be known about him by natural reason.

Reply: The knowledge that is natural to us has its source in the senses and extends just so far as it can be led by sensible things; from these, however, our understanding cannot reach to the divine essence. Sensible creatures are effects of God which are less than typical of the power of their cause, so knowing them does not lead us to understand the whole power of God and thus we do not see his essence. They are nevertheless effects depending from a cause, and so we can at least be led from them to know of God that he exists and that he has whatever must belong to the first cause of all things which is beyond all that is caused.

Thus we know about his relation to creatures—that he is the cause of them all; all the difference between him and them—that nothing created is in him; and his lack of such things is not a deficiency in him but due to his transcendence.

Hence: 1. The reason can know *that* a simple form is, even though it cannot attain to understanding of *what* it is.

2. God is known to the natural reason through the images of his effects.

3. Knowledge of God in his essence is a gift of grace and belongs only to the good, yet the knowledge we have by natural reason belongs to both good and bad. Augustine says, "I do not now approve what I said in a certain prayer, 'O God who hast wished only the clean of heart to know truth . . .' for it could be answered that many who are unclean know many truths," i.e., by natural reason.[9]

The schematic form apparent in the method makes clear that a primary aim of the procedure is to reduce all the work that was required to raise, discuss, and solve this question to simple elements. Nevertheless, the method is much more subtle than a first glance at the procedure might suggest. First of all, even though articles in the *Summa* invariably begin with statements *sic* and *non*, for and against the question that is being argued, they are not brought together simply to find an immediate answer to the question; nor are they brought together to set up straw men to be knocked down in the synthesis that follows; nor are these arguments simply opposed to one another. They are brought together rather so that the mind can begin to consider all the possibilities inherent in the question. They represent different possibilities that need to be tried out in order to fully explore the question, to push the possibilities for research to their limit. The entire process of inquiry, starting from the beginning of a question and working through to the end, becomes a dialectical process whose intention is to enable the mind to work at its highest level. The third part of the article, the synthesis, either attempts to solve the problem (as in this example) or attempts at least to give the principles by means of which the problem might be solved. The solution proposed will clearly agree more with one side of the argument presented in the *sic* and *non* than in the other. However, the arguments that Thomas does not agree with are not simply rejected. Instead he analyzes these arguments in order to show how their position is founded on partial truth and then attempts to embody this truth within a wider framework. In this example, the *non* arguments are true as far as they go, but as the synthesis shows they do not go far enough.[10]

One sees in every step of the argument a strict logical development, each point following from another. And if one steps back to view the development, not of a single argument, but of the *Summa* as a whole, the same logic is evident. There is a movement from the large, comprehensive outline of the work as a whole, to the major divisions of this outline, to smaller subdivisions within the major divisions, down to individual articles. One could reasonably argue that every writer carefully organizes the relationship between the parts and the whole. In Augustine's *Confessions*, for example, the individual incidents are all related to the major thematic consideration—the story of Augustine's own conversion as an exemplar. What differentiates Scholasticism, as perfected by Thomas, is that the organization is made explicit. There is no attempt made to hide the outline; in fact, the outline and structure, almost independent of content, are themselves embodiments of order. A century after Thomas, concern for form would all but overwhelm concern for significant content; and the great medieval synthesis would break up, as more and more was said about less and less. But during the thirteenth century, Thomas exemplified a method of thinking and writing that was a very powerful tool for assimilating and describing reality.

Scholasticism was a way of thinking that had resonances in many other areas. Erwin Panofsky, in his book *Gothic Architecture and Scholasticism*, suggests that the characteristic features of Scholasticism are embodied in another *summa* of medieval thought, the Gothic cathedral.[11] One of the distinguishing features of Gothic that sets it apart from the earlier Romanesque is that it aims to be complete and comprehensive in its sculptural programs and its stained glass windows. All the truths of Christianity are embodied in stone and glass in each cathedral: creation; Old Testament history and prophecy; the mysteries of the Incarnation, Passion, and Resurrection; the story of the Church; and especially the Last Judgment. To achieve this comprehensive vision, it is necessary, no less than in a Scholastic treatise, to establish very clearly the relationship between the parts and the whole. In Gothic, clear principles of subordination are always present, so that each figure, statue, or

story must not be seen simply in itself, but in terms of its placement, and thence as it is related to the comprehensive sculptural
arrangement in the cathedral as a whole. Specifically, a statue
sculpted near one of the portals of a Gothic cathedral is invariably part of a larger group. If this group is a depiction of
Old Testament figures, it will be balanced by a grouping of
New Testament figures. Both groupings will be related to the
sculptural programs in the arch over the doorway, called a
tympanum. And this entire grouping will have its place in the
totality, as part of a clearly articulated design. Moreover, as in
Scholastic writings, the Gothic cathedral makes no attempt to
conceal the outlines of its structure. Just as the Scholastic
document is put together by means of a logical method that
at all points is evident to the reader, so also are the "outlines"—
the structure—of the cathedral evident: that typically Gothic
structural device, the flying buttress, is on the outside of the
cathedral, and hence clearly evident. The pillars, supporting the
vaulting on the inside, are similarly evident. Thus the form of
the cathedral, how it is put together, stands out independently
of the content, what it is expressing, in a way that is analogous
to the relationship between form and content in Scholasticism.

It would be wrong to suggest that the builders of the Gothic
cathedral had the *Summa* in one hand and their blueprints in the
other. Indeed, the closer one looks, the more one sees that there
are diffierences as well as similarities; there are always inherent
dangers in suggesting analogies. But the analogy between
Gothic architecture and Scholasticism helps establish the
shared point of view of the age; in the thirteenth century
this includes a tendency toward order and comprehensiveness,
and the explicit organization of form.

Another significant point of contact between Scholasticism
and the Gothic cathedral is the Aristotelian reliance on the
senses. For Thomas, following Aristotle, philosophy begins
with sense experience. In the Gothic, this can be seen in the
more realistic representation of figures in sculpture. This is not
to say that these works lost their iconographic significance;
rather, this significance was now expressed in figures that
looked more like real people or animals or plants than was true

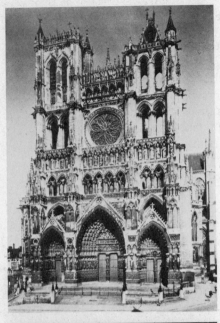

Amiens Cathedral, France. 13th Century. The front view gives a sense of its size and beauty.

A detail from the façade, the sign of Scorpio and a man crushing grapes. Around one of the portals of the cathedral are the twelve signs of the zodiac and the agricultural labors appropriate for each month of the year. Scorpio, a sign in autumn, was the time for making wine in France. The cycle of the year is seen in relation to events outside of time such as the Last Judgment, which is depicted on the adjacent portal.

The nave, which soars to a height of 142 feet.

These elegant flying buttresses were also the supports which allowed the gothic cathedrals to soar to great heights and to let in great amounts of light. Thus the gothic cathedral could be seen as an earthly model which approximated the heavenly city.

Above, capital, Monastery of
St. Benoit-sur-Loire, France.
11th Century.
Right, façade sculpture, Reims
cathedral, 13th Century. These
two depictions of the visitation
of Mary and Elizabeth (*Luke*
1) show the movement toward
an increased realism from Romanesque to Gothic. (Lauros/
Giraudon)

of Romanesque. These Scholastic elements can also be found in the literature that was written during and after this time. Dante's *Divine Comedy*, written at the beginning of the fourteenth century, is often called a literary *summa*. Some useful sense of that work can be gained by this rough analogy: It is a work of comprehensive scope, taking for its subject matter an account of nothing less than the states of souls after death, and the relationship of God to all creation, living and dead; it is a work that depends on a great many other sources from classical antiquity through the Middle Ages—as Aristotle is to Aquinas, so is Vergil to Dante. Like Thomas, Dante is a supreme master of assimilation. And the *Comedy*, too, is clear and explicit in its outline, and in articulating the relationship between the parts and the whole. In addition, Dante draws heavily on the actual philosophy of Thomas for many of the underpinnings of the *Comedy*. Some of these elements are also present in works that are not so obviously dependent on a scholastic milieu. In Chaucer's *Troilus and Criseyde*, for example, the way in which the action of the story is outlined in advance by the narrator can be related to the concern with an explicit rendering of the relationship between the parts and the whole that is one of the heritages of Scholasticism. Moreover, at this time, characters in literary works achieve a greater degree of verisimilitude, becoming much more recognizably lifelike than in previous literature.

The revival of philosophy in the twelfth and thirteenth centuries was paralleled in the field of law. One of the most important rediscoveries from the past was the Code of Justinian, the corpus of Roman law compiled during the reign of the sixth-century Byzantine Emperor Justinian. The exact means of discovery is disputed among historians, but by the early twelfth century it was known and being studied in Italy, especially Bologna. The code, containing the law of the Roman Empire, was created for a society quite different from twelfth-century Europe; much of the municipal, corporate, and trade law would appear on the surface to be largely irrelevant to medieval society. Nevertheless, Italian communes and medieval kings began to make use of certain relevant parts of the code, although they "medievalized" it, just as a medieval artist portrayed the Roman soldiers at Christ's tomb as medieval knights. Passages that had one meaning in the ancient world took on a very different significance in feudal Europe. Perhaps as much as its specific sections, monarchs were interested in the idea of a unified code of law for their kingdoms that recognized the authority of the ruler as the origin of the law. King Philip Augustus of France (r.1180–1223) used Roman law and lawyers to try to consolidate his authority over his independent-minded vassals, and the Holy Roman Emperor Frederick Barbarossa (r.1152–90) used certain texts from the Justinian Code to try to justify his claim of independence from the pope. Even the development of English common law under King Henry II (r.1154–89) was affected by the renewed interest in the law of the Roman Empire.

Not only did kings realize the value of Roman law and an organized body of legal material, but the Church did too. One thing that kept the Gregorian reform from achieving greater success in its attempt to centralize ecclesiastical authority was the lack of an authoritative and organized body of canons (laws of the Church). At the beginning of the twelfth century, canon law was a confused and often contradictory mixture of Scripture, patristic writings, papal letters and bulls, and conciliar and synodal decrees. Several attempts had been made at collecting canons, but none was complete enough or widely enough accepted to be authoritative. Thus the law of the Church was in fact quite different in one part of Europe than in another.

At Bologna between 1140 and 1150 a Camaldolese monk named Gratian published a book entitled *A Concord of Discordant Canons*, usually known as the *Decretum*. It was a collection of canons in dialectical form—influenced by the revival of Aristotle. Much of the material was organized around a series of hypothetical situations. For example, one can see how many legal principles Gratian could explore from the following:

Gratian: A certain noblewoman was informed that she was sought in marriage by the son of a certain noble. She gave her consent. But one who was not a noble and who was of slave condition offered himself in the name of the first man and took

her as a wife. The one who had first pleased her finally came
and sought her in marriage. She complained that she was deceived and wanted to be joined to the first man. It was first
asked here: was there marriage between them? Secondly, if she
first thought that he was a free man and afterwards learned
that he was a slave, is it lawful for her to withdraw at once
from him?[12]

The superiority of the *Decretum* over other collections of
canons was quickly recognized. Thus the *Decretum* and later
collections of decrees made after its publication came into
widespread use throughout Europe in ecclesiastical courts and
became the basic textbooks of canon law, much as the Code
of Justinian was to civil law and Peter Lombard's *Sentences*
was to theology. Many commentaries were written on the
Decretum, often making use of new hypothetical questions
such as "what if the pope invents a new heresy?" or even
"what is to be done if the pope fornicates on the altar of St.
Peter's?" One question discussed in many commentaries was the
familiar one of the relationship between spiritual and temporal
authorities. The twelfth-century canonist Alanus writes:

> But in truth, and according to the Catholic faith, he [the Em-
> peror, meaning secular rulers in general] is subject to the pope
> in spiritual matters and also receives his sword from him, for
> the right of both swords belongs to the pope. This is proved
> by the fact that the Lord had both swords on earth and used
> both as is mentioned here, and he established Peter as his vicar
> on earth and all Peter's successors. Therefore today Innocent
> [II] has by right the material sword. If you deny this you are
> saying that Christ established a secular prince as his vicar in this
> regard. Again Peter said to the Lord, "Behold, here are two
> swords" [Lk. 22:38], so the material sword too was with Peter.
> Again if the emperor was not subject to the pope in temporali-
> ties he could not sin against the church in temporalities. Again
> the church is one body and so it shall have only one head or
> it will be a monster.[13]

This text is a good example of how lawyers no less than
theologians used Scripture and its exegesis as their fundamental

authority. The Luke text involving the two swords was universally believed to refer to the secular and ecclesiastical powers. However, the text was subject to more than one interpretation. Here is the analysis of another twelfth-century canonist, Huguccio of Pisa:

> Here it can clearly be gathered that each power, the apostolic and imperial, was instituted by God and that neither is derived from the other and that the emperor does not have the sword from the apostle. . . . Again the words, "Behold, here are two swords" [Lk. 22:38] were spoken to symbolize the fact that the two powers, namely the apostolic and imperial, are distinct and separate.[14]

Some of the commentaries written on the *Decretum* became important authorities, cited in legal disputes for centuries. Furthermore, almost all the popes from the mid-twelfth century on were canon lawyers who had studied and written commentaries on the *Decretum*. For example, Pope Innocent IV (r.1245–54) was probably the most significant legal commentator of his generation.

The renewed interest in philosophy and law that was such an integral part of the twelfth-century renaissance led to the development of new educational institutions. The monastic schools were not concerned with these subjects, and the cathedral schools generally remained wedded to the seven liberal arts, emphasizing grammar and rhetoric as described in the writings of John of Salisbury. By the end of the twelfth century, a university had been established at Bologna; it was the center for the study of law, both civil and canon. Its students and later its faculty formed corporations (the word "universitas" means "corporation or guild") for protection and were granted monopolies by the city government. The faculty set the curriculum and gave certificates of membership in the guild of teachers to students who completed their study—the origin of the degree system. In Paris, a university was in existence by 1200; its specialties were the undergraduate arts curriculum (mostly Aristotle) and theology; for hundreds of years the faculty of theology at Paris was an important voice in the Church. From these two universities came most of the other medieval universities. Following the Paris model were Oxford, Cambridge, Prague, and others in northern Europe while Bologna served as a model for Montpellier, Salamanca, Valladolid, Coimbra, Padua, and others in the Mediterranean region. For the rest of the Middle Ages, the most important theologians and members of the church hierarchy came from the universities. As mentioned previously, most popes of the High Middle Ages were Bologna-trained canon lawyers; and many of the great theologians, including Thomas Aquinas and Bonaventure, taught at the University of Paris. On the other hand, much of the subject matter of the seven liberal arts, with the exception of dialectic, was not taught in the universities and thus was reduced to being the preliminaries to the university curricula.

The renaissance of the twelfth century changed the course of the intellectual history of the West. In addition to the new institution for the transmission and generation of knowledge, there was a shift in the intellectual centers from the monasteries to the cities. There was also a shift from the experiential theology of the cloister to something much more like a modern academic subject: Scholastic theology emphasized organization, definition, and description rather than experience and exhortation to the good life. The literary quality of monastic writing gave way to the precise repetitive structure and technical well-defined vocabulary of the *Summa*. Some saw this as progress while others like Saint Bernard deplored the change. But none denied the importance of the shift.

The cultural changes of the twelfth century were not limited to philosophy and law. Literature too was transformed during this period, although the major centers of literary activity were the courts, not the universities, and the literature was written in the vernacular languages, not Latin. Latin literature, however, continued to flourish in the schools and the monastic centers: lyric poetry, a product of the schools, was an important genre in the twelfth century. Alan of Lille (c.1116–1203), whose major works, the *Complaint of Nature* and the *Anti-claudianus*, creatively fuse Platonism with Christianity, was an important narrative poet who greatly influenced subsequent literature. Latin Church drama, elaborately staged sung dramatic pieces, usually presented in connection with the liturgical cycle, flourished under the direct auspices of school and monastery. But it is the vernacular literature of the courts of France, which establishes themes and patterns that have continued to influence European storytellers until the present. From the end of the twelfth century until the close of the Middle Ages, some of the most important literary monuments of European culture were written in vernacular language: including the Arthurian romances of Chrétien de Troyes and the *Romance of the Rose* of Guillaume de Lorris and Jean de Meun in French; Wolfram von Eschenbach's *Parzival* in German; Dante's *Divine Comedy* in Italian; and Chaucer's *Canterbury Tales* in English.

The late twelfth century saw an important change in subject matter in narrative poetry. (Stories were generally told in verse rather than prose in classical antiquity, in the Middle Ages, and beyond until the rise of the novel in the eighteenth century.) When Europe had been under constant siege from Moslems and Norsemen, its literature understandably reflected a militant spirit. The kind of story that the people of the early Middle Ages most enjoyed hearing—in addition to how a saint reached heaven—was an idealized story of a brave warrior fighting against overwhelming odds, finally meeting a glorious death in battle. *Beowulf* and the *Song of Roland* are two illustrative examples. Toward the end of the twelfth century, the emphasis shifts to stories of courtly quests and adventures that a knight undertakes, often to win the love of a lady.

One way of viewing this extremely significant shift, usually described as the change from epic to romance, is to see how the new leisure of a society no longer primarily concerned with self-preservation was reflected in its literature: tournaments, feasts, and entertainments at court, all presented with great color and splendor, idealize society's new self-awareness. A second way is by noting the changed role of women. The most striking thing about women in the *Song of Roland* is their absence. They fare somewhat better in *Beowulf*, but because the heroic ideal is bravery in battle, they are nonetheless second-class citizens. In the romance, by contrast, women often are the focal point for the action. The hero, often motivated in his actions by the powerful and sometimes all-consuming emotion of romantic love, must now be courteous as well as brave; and a new literary language develops to describe the ideal of courtesy. The relationship between love, courtesy, and adventure is embodied in the following passage from Chrétien de Troyes's (fl.1160–1190) *Erec and Enide*:

> Now that Enide was very happy and had everything she de-sired, her great beauty returned to her; for her great distress had affected her so much that she was very pale and wan. Now she was embraced and kissed, now she was blessed with all good things, now she had her joy and pleasures; for unadorned they lie in bed and each enfolds and kisses the other; nothing gives them so much joy. They have had so much pain and sorrow, he for her, and she for him, that now they have their satisfac-tion. . . . But now they must go on their way; so they asked his leave to depart from Guivret, in whom they had found a friend indeed.[15]

In this passage the love between Erec and Enide is both a re-ward for past deeds and a spur to the deeds he is about to perform.

A corresponding change in style accompanies the change in subject matter from epic to romance, for which the change from Romanesque to Gothic style in the visual arts provides a useful analogy. The monsters of Romanesque art allow easy identification between good and evil. In Gothic, however, the style achieves a uniformity of elegance that precludes such easy identification. For example, on the facades of several Gothic cathedrals—Strasbourg and Paris to name two—are allegorical figures who represent the Old and New Testament. However, these figures cannot be identified on the basis of style, one being almost identical with the other to the viewer following the elegantly flowing rhythms of each body. It is only by a consideration of the iconographic attributes of each figure that the viewer can identify them: the Old, blindfolded, carries the tables of the Synagogue with her; the New carries the chalice of the New Covenant. A similar example on the facade of the Cathedral of Amiens shows the kings who were prefigurations of Christ in the Old Testament sharing a stylistic identity with Herod, his persecutor in the New.

In the romance, as in Gothic art, stylistic elegance does not imply moral approval, as the following passage from *Erec and Enide* illustrates. An evil count, wishing to kill Erec and seduce Enide, speaks as follows:

> I ask a favor of you, and may it not displease you. As an act of courtesy and as a pleasure, I would fain sit by yonder lady's side. With good intent I came to see you both, and you should see no harm in that. I wish to present to the lady my service in all respects. Know well that for love of you I would do whatever may please her.[16]

The immediate context of his speech makes the count's treacherous intentions clear to the reader, if not to Erec, contradicting the eloquence with which it is presented. To engage the moral concerns that are often central to the romance, the reader must be aware of both the context and the possible iconographic significance of an action. The increased knowledge of classical antiquity that was the catalyst for the achievements in philosophy and law during the twelfth-century renaissance played a significant part in its literary achievement as well. Learned clerks looked to the past to give distance and dignity to the romance, and at the same time to serve as a model for the present. They saw themselves as the heirs of a storytelling art that had passed from Greece to Rome to France. This *translatio* —translation in the literal sense of being moved from one place to another—is illustrated by a passage from the beginning of Chrétien's *Cligès*:

> Our books have informed us that pre-eminence in chivalry and learning once belonged to Greece. Then chivalry passed

to Rome, together with that highest learning which now has come to France. God grant that it may be cherished here, and that it may be made so welcome here that the honor which has taken refuge with us may never depart from France: God had awarded it as another's share, but of Greeks and Romans no more is heard, their fame is passed, and their glowing ash is dead.[17]

Not surprisingly, many romances retell stories and legends of antiquity, most often stories set in Troy or Thebes (generically though somewhat misleadingly called the "Matter of Rome" by some modern scholars). Many go back to another "past" for their setting. For example, the adventures of King Arthur and his knights of the round table were: the material for folklore and legend in the early Middle Ages; incorporated into a historical work, Geoffrey of Monmouth's *History of the Kings of Britain*, in 1147; and turned to specifically literary use in five romances by Chrétien de Troyes in the 1170s (*Erec and Enide*, *Cligès*, *Yvain*, *Lancelot*, and *Percival*). From the time of Chrétien until Edmund Spenser at the end of the sixteenth century, Arthurian romance was a central focus for European narrative literature; and it continues as a subject matter for contemporary writers. Whether the setting be Troy or Britain (Arthurian material is often called the "Matter of Britain"), writers of romance make extensive use of the Latin poets, especially Ovid, in their works, often achieving a sophistication that supports their claims for the translation of knowledge from Rome to France.

One of the most significant changes from epic to romance is in the emphasis on interior description—debates and monologues that take place within the mind of the speaker. The epic emphasizes forceful action and descriptions of changeless, static values: life is a battle between good and evil. In the romance the image of life as a journey comes to dominate; and the battlefield is now more explicitly in the mind of each character, whose inner movement, change, and growth the reader is allowed to observe. In the following extracts, the description of Charlemagne from the *Song of Roland* and the description of the hero of Chrétien's *Lancelot* are juxtaposed to exemplify this change:

> The Emperor Charles is jubilant and gay;
> The lofty walls of Cordres are torn down,
> His catapults have laid its towers low;
> His knights rejoice, for great is their reward—
> Silver and gold, and costly gear for war. . . .
> A throne is placed—it's made of purest gold.
> There sits the king, the ruler of sweet France;
> White is his beard, and silver streaks his hair,
> Handsome his form, his bearing very proud:
> No stranger needs to have him pointed out.
> The Saracens dismount and come on foot
> To greet the king, as friendly envoys would.[18]

It was unlucky for him that he shrank from the disgrace and did not jump in at once, for he later regretted the delay. Reason, which is inconsistent with the dictates of love, bids him refrain from getting in, warning him and counselling him not to do or undertake anything for which he may reap shame and dishonor. Yet reason which dares thus to speak to him reaches only his lips, not his heart; for love is enclosed within his heart, urging him to mount at once into the cart. So he jumps in, since love will have it so, feeling no concern about the shame; he is prompted by love's commands.[19]

In *Roland*, action and description are simple and straightforward, expressing the differences between Christian and pagan as forcefully as possible; that struggle, as embodied in the attitude of the militant Christian, is what the poem is most fundamentally about. In Chrétien's work there is a struggle too, but it is experienced inside the hero's mind. The conflict between reason and love described in the passage is presented by suspending the external action of the poem to present an idealized account of an internal debate. This inward turning quite probably reflects the influence of monastic spirituality. Bernard of Clairvaux begins his Third Sermon on the Song of Songs by exhorting his audience to turn inward, to examine their own spirituality, a spiritual self-analysis that characterizes the essence of the Cistercian monastic search (see ch. 8). The habit of examining spiritual states, which developed in the monasteries, spread beyond the cloister and became part of the storytelling art that flourished in the courts.

Throughout the Middle Ages, the short poem or lyric was an important genre in Latin literature. The twelfth century saw the rise of the lyric in the vernacular languages as well, an important development that began in the south of France, the result of a group of professional poets known as troubadors, writing in a Romance language called Provençal. The lyrics—which were written to be sung, sometimes by the troubadors themselves and sometimes by traveling entertainers called jongleurs—are intensely emotional; and by far the most important emotion they express is love. The speaker of the poem is usually a knight-errant expressing his feelings toward his lady and, perhaps more important, the results of her actions on his feelings. The love is usually unfulfilled: longing, separation, and departure are all standard themes. The poems are also very skillfully wrought, as if the ideas of love were taken for granted by the poet, who must then decide the most ingenious and skillful way to express them. Thus many elaborate formal patterns were developed, with very complicated stanzaic structures and rhyming patterns, as well as elaborate plays on words. The following stanza, the beginning of a poem by Bernart de Ventadorn (fl.1140–80), shows how love becomes the source of poetic inspiration:

> A song cannot in any way have value
> If the singing doesn't spring from the heart,
> And the singing cannot well from the breast
> Unless its source is fine, true love.
> And so my verse looms high,
> For I have joy from love, devoting there
> My mouth and eyes, my heart and mind.[20]

Many of the important lyric forms in the subsequent history of European poetry grow out of forms originally developed by the troubadors. The sonnet, for example, is a variation that was developed in Sicily, one of the places where troubador songs flourished. This influence was felt in the flowering of the lyric all over Europe, in Italy, in France, and in Germany. Indirectly, and much later, they influenced English poetry as well, through translations from Italian in the Renaissance.

CHAPTER TEN

Francis of Assisi and the Mendicants

In 1182 in Assisi a man was born who transformed medieval spirituality. His name was Francesco Bernardone, Francis of Assisi. From several accounts of his life written shortly after his death (1226) by those who knew him or had access to people who knew him, a picture of Francis as a figure unique in the history of the Church emerges. Like the Gospels themselves, which present the meaning of Jesus' life and teaching rather than biographies of Jesus in any modern sense, these accounts display the variety of meaning that Francis had for his own time, using the conventions of hagiography to dramatize his significance. Of these lives the one by Bonaventure (published in 1263) is most important because upon its appearance earlier lives were ordered destroyed. Today these early lives survive in a small number of manuscripts, providing us

Fresco, Church of San Francesco, Assisi. 13th Century, Cimabue.
This fresco, one of the early depictions of Francis, captures his
spirit of poverty and humility.

with valuable information and insight. This is especially true of the two early semiofficial lives by the Franciscan Thomas of Celano. However, they were of little direct influence after the appearance of Bonaventure's life although they were the most important sources for it. Bonaventure's life of Francis existed in thousands of manuscripts by the end of the Middle Ages and was well known to virtually every friar. Furthermore, copies of the life circulated outside the order, and stories from it were painted in countless Franciscan churches to be seen by all who entered them. It was from Bonaventure that people of the late Middle Ages, learned and unlearned, knew the events and meaning of the life of Saint Francis of Assisi; and it is the account upon which this chapter is primarily based.

Until he was almost twenty-five Francis lived the typical life of a merchant's son, helping in the family business, frolicking with his friends, and dreaming of being skilled and brave at arms. After an illness, however, he began to experience deep religious feelings. He would wear ragged garb and give away money from the family business to the poor, understandably irritating his father, who summoned Francis before the court of the bishop of Assisi to get back all his possessions. Francis stood before his father and the bishop, stripped himself naked, and returned his clothes to his father, declaring that he would now speak only of his Father in heaven. Bonaventure's account of this extraordinary event is prefaced by a description and interpretation of several visions Francis had had. The first occurred shortly after he had given his cloak to a poverty-stricken knight:

> The following night, when he had fallen asleep, God in his goodness showed him a large and splendid palace full of military weapons emblazoned with the insignia of Christ's cross. Thus God vividly indicated that the compassion he had exhibited toward the poor knight for love of the supreme King would be repaid with an incomparable reward. And so when Francis asked to whom these belonged, he received an answer from heaven that all these things were for him and his knights. When he awoke in the morning, he judged the strange vision to be an indication that he would have great prosperity; for

he had no experience in interpreting divine mysteries nor did he know how to pass through visible images to grasp the invisible truth beyond. Therefore, still ignorant of God's plan, he decided to join a certain count in Apulia, hoping in his service to obtain the glory of knighthood, as his vision seemed to foretell.[1]

As Bonaventure explains, Francis fails to understand this first divine summons. He takes the vision quite literally, immediately wanting to go and become a soldier; Bonaventure tells the reader that what Christ intended rather was to show Francis how to become a spiritual soldier—a soldier of Christ. In a subsequent vision he again receives a command from Christ, this time to repair his Church:

> One day when Francis went out to meditate in the fields (Gen. 24:63), he walked beside the church of San Damiano which was threatening to collapse because of extreme age. Inspired by the Spirit, he went inside to pray. Prostrate before an image of the Crucified, he was filled with no little consolation as he prayed. While his tear-filled eyes were gazing at the Lord's cross, he heard with his bodily ears a voice coming from the cross, telling him three times: "Francis, go and repair my house which, as you see, is falling completely into ruin."
>
> Trembling with fear, Francis was amazed at the sound of this astonishing voice, since he was alone in the church; and as he received in his heart the power of the divine words, he fell into a state of ecstasy. Returning finally to his senses, he prepared to obey, gathering himself together to carry out the command of repairing the church materially, although the principal intention of the words referred to that Church which Christ purchased with his own blood (Acts 20:28), as the Holy Spirit taught him and as he himself later disclosed to the friars.[2]

Once again, Francis understands and acts upon the letter of the command but not its spirit. Only later does he come to understand its full meaning. Francis's whole life, as recorded by Bonaventure, follows this movement to deeper and deeper levels of spiritual understanding.

After Francis rejected his earthly father and accepted his

Father in heaven—the first event in his life showing that he has learned to move from the letter to the spirit—he settled at a small church dedicated to Mary called the Porziuncula. A few men from Assisi and the vicinity sold all their earthly possessions and came to live with him, doing good deeds and menial work, living in poverty, and even ministering in Christ-like fashion to lepers. When the number of followers grew to be about twelve, Francis went to Pope Innocent III and asked permission to found an order (1209). According to legend, Innocent dreamt that the Lateran Basilica (the cathedral of Rome) was falling until a man dressed in a coarse tunic with a cord for a belt propped it up. He saw Francis, recognized him as the man in the dream, and approved a simple rule for his new order, the Friars Minor, made up largely of biblical quotations. When one thinks of the splendor and high politics of Innocent's pontificate, it seems remarkable that he would agree even to see Francis, let alone give him, a layperson, permission to found an order dedicated to absolute poverty and the preaching of repentance. Perhaps Innocent saw that this kind of order could show Christendom that the Church still held to the ideals of the Gospel and that one did not have to join a heretical sect to practice them. Perhaps Innocent was genuinely moved by Francis and the poor men from Assisi. In any case, it is impressive both that Innocent in his splendor recognized the validity of the ideal of Francis and that the poor Francis recognized the validity of the authority of Innocent, Christ's vicar and Peter's successor. In a sense these two great men complemented each other. In Innocent III men saw an imitation of Christ in all his splendor and glory and power, in Francis an imitation of Christ in his humanity—poor and humble.

After Innocent's approval of the order, it grew rapidly. Soon there were Franciscans everywhere. A governing structure was established, the center of which was an annual chapter held at the Porziuncula. Francis also established a female branch of the movement called the Poor Clares, named after Clare of Assisi, the first woman converted to Francis's way of life. A "third order" was also established for those in secular life who could not fully practice Franciscan poverty but who held

Franciscan ideals and practiced certain elements of that ideal. One way of understanding the ideals of the early Franciscans is to see them as a kind of offshoot of Benedictine monasticism, another attempt to return to monastic simplicity. The interweaving of prayer and works practiced by the early followers of Francis was very similar to that prescribed by Benedict. However, the significant difference is that for Francis and his followers their monastery became the world all around them, and their work was ministering to the world's needy, primarily in the cities.

Francis himself continued to live a life of utmost poverty and simplicity. He traveled a great deal, working and begging for what he needed. He spent periods of time alone in caves or hermitages for prayer. He desired to try to convert Moslems to Christianity and sought martyrdom in this venture. He did go to Syria but made no significant conversions.

As the order increased in size, some of the brothers desired to study, but Francis discouraged this. Once the friars asked him whether he was pleased that the learned men, who had by that time been received into the order, should devote themselves to the study of sacred Scripture. He replied: "I am indeed pleased, as long as they do not neglect application to prayer, after the example of Christ, of whom we read that he prayed more than he read, and as long as they study not only in order to know what they should say but in order to practice what they have heard and when they have put it into practice themselves to propose it to others likewise."[3] Clearly, Francis envisioned the Friars Minor as men of simplicity, humility, and, most of all, poverty, for poverty was at the very center of this movement, as it was the center of Francis's life:

> One day when he was devoutly hearing a Mass of the Apostles, the Gospel was read in which Christ sends forth his disciples to preach and explains to them the way of life according to the Gospel: that they should not keep gold or silver or money in their belts, nor have a wallet for their journey, nor two tunics, nor shoes, nor staff (Matt. 10:9). When he heard this, he grasped its meaning and committed it to memory. This lover of apostolic poverty was then filled with an indescribable joy

and said: "This is what I want; this is what I long for with all
my heart." He immediately took off his shoes from his feet,
put aside his staff, cast away his wallet and money as if ac-
cursed, was content with one tunic and exchanged his leather
belt for a piece of rope. He directed all his heart's desire to
carry out what he had heard and to conform in every way to
the rule of right living given to the apostles. . . .

Among the gifts of grace which Francis received from God
the generous Giver, he merited as a special privilege to grow
in the riches of simplicity through his love of the highest poverty. The holy man saw that poverty was the close companion of the Son of God, and now that it was rejected by
the whole world, he was eager to espouse it in everlasting love.
For the sake of poverty he not only left his father and mother,
but also gave away everything he had. No one was so greedy
for gold as he was for poverty; nor was anyone so anxious to
guard his treasure as he was in guarding this pearl of the Gospel. In this especially would his sight be offended if he saw
in the friars anything which did not accord completely with
poverty. Indeed, from the beginning of his religious life until
his death, his only riches were a tunic, a cord and underclothes;
and with this much he was content. He used to frequently call
to mind with tears the poverty of Jesus Christ and his mother,
claiming that it was the queen of the virtues because it shone
forth so preeminently in the King of Kings and in the Queen,
his mother.

When the friars asked him at a gathering what virtue does
more to make one a friend of Christ, he replied as if opening up
the hidden depths of his heart: "Know, brothers, that poverty
is the special way to salvation, as the stimulus of humility and the
root of perfection, whose fruit is manifold but hidden. This is
the Gospel's treasure hidden in a field (Matt. 13:44); to buy
this we should sell everything, and in comparison to this we
should spurn everything we cannot sell.[4]

Poverty for Francis and his followers, as this passage indicates,
was not an end in itself so much as the means of aligning themselves by direct imitation with the Christ of the Gospels. Here,
as in so much of Franciscan writing, the language of Scripture
provides the basic iconography. Francis not only insisted that
each friar give up all his property, he also wanted the order to

have no money or property collectively. According to Franciscan imagery, Francis was said to have married Lady Poverty. A story from a thirteenth-century work called the *Mirror of Perfection* perhaps best sums up Francis's attitude toward money:

> As a true friend and imitator of Christ, Francis, despising perfectly all things which are of this world, did above all things execrate money; and by word and example urged his brethren to flee it as if it were the devil. For this maxim had been given by him to the friars, that they should measure with one price of love, dung and money. Now it happened on a day that a certain layman entered the church of St. Mary of the Porziuncula to pray, and put some money for an offering near the cross, which when he had departed, a certain friar taking innocently in his hand, threw into the window. But when this was told to blessed Francis, that friar seeing himself taken in a fault, sought pardon, and throwing himself on the ground, offered himself to punishment. The holy Father reproved him, and very severely blamed him for moving the money, and bade him lift the money from the window with his mouth and convey it without the hedge of the dwelling, and put it with his own mouth on the dung of an ass. And all they that did see and hear were filled with very great fear, and from that time forth did despise money more than the dung of an ass, and daily were they animated with new examples to contemn it altogether.[5]

As the order grew, it became necessary to have a more carefully drawn up and comprehensive rule than that earliest set of principles that Innocent III agreed to in 1209. Thus in 1221 the First Rule was published; it is clearly Francis's in spirit though no doubt he had help in the precise language. However, even this rule was soon seen as inadequate because of its lack of legal terminology, and another rule was promulgated in 1223. Francis, helped and perhaps at times cajoled by the order's official protector, Cardinal Hugolino (the future Pope Gregory IX), made some concessions in this rule. Two main emphases of this 1223 rule were the order's obedience to the pope—there was going to be no straying of these friars into heresy—and the friars' restraint from condemning those who do not live in poverty. There were concessions to those friars who were priests with regard to possessing books. Furthermore, the increasingly elaborate hierarchy of the order was spelled out. Despite these concessions, which Francis probably agreed to reluctantly, there was still a strong statement with regard to money:

> I strictly forbid all the friars to accept money in any form, either personally or through an intermediary. The ministers and superiors, however, are bound to provide carefully for the needs of the sick and the clothing of the other friars, by having recourse to spiritual friends, while taking into account differences of place, season, or severe climate, as seems best to them in the circumstances. This does not dispense them from the prohibition of receiving money in any form.[6]

In Francis's last years, he saw friars begin to relax the original rigor of the order. Reacting against what he saw as an excessive reliance on property, he ordered a house of studies that had been erected for the friars in Bologna to be torn down. On his deathbed, he dictated a last testament, recalling his first years in the religious life and imploring the friars to preserve the simplicity and poverty of those happy times:

> [In the beginning] those who embraced this life gave everything they had to the poor. They were satisfied with one habit which was patched inside and outside, and a cord, and trousers. We refused to have anything more. Those of us who were clerics said the Office like other clerics, while the lay brothers said the Our Father, and we were only too glad to find shelter in abandoned churches. We made no claim to learning and we were submissive to everyone. I worked with my own hands and I am still determined to work; and with all my heart I want all the other friars to be busy with some kind of work that can be carried on without scandal. Those who do not know how to work should learn, not because they want to get something for their efforts, but to give good example and to avoid idleness. When we receive no recompense for our work, we can turn to God's table and beg for alms from door to door.

God revealed a form of greeting to me, telling me that we should say, "God give you peace."

The friars must be very careful not to accept churches or poor dwellings for themselves, or anything else built for them, unless they are in harmony with the poverty which we have promised in the Rule; and they should occupy those places only as strangers and pilgrims. In virtue of obedience, I strictly forbid the friars, wherever they may be, to petition the Roman Curia, either personally or through an intermediary, for a papal brief, whether it concerns a church or any other place, or even in order to preach, or because they are being persecuted. If they are not welcome somewhere, they should flee to another country where they can lead a life of penance, with God's blessing. . . .

In virtue of obedience, I strictly forbid any of my friars, clerics or lay brothers, to interpret the Rule or these words, saying, "This is what they mean." God inspired me to write the Rule and these words plainly and simply, and so you too must understand them plainly and simply, and live by them, doing good to the last.[7]

Francis grew deeper in contemplation with special devotion to the Christ Crucified, the Christ who spoke to him from the Cross in San Damiano, whom he finally was able to accept with full spiritual understanding. This devotion culminated, according to tradition, in Francis's receiving the very wounds of Christ (the stigmata) while in contemplation on the mountain of La Verna in 1224. Bonaventure describes this taking on of the wounds of Christ:

By the Seraphic ardor of his desires, he was being borne aloft into God; and by his sweet compassion he was being transformed into him who chose to be crucified because of the excess of his love (Eph. 2:4). On a certain morning about the feast of the Exaltation of the Cross, while Francis was praying on the mountainside, he saw a Seraph with six fiery and shining wings descend from the height of heaven. And when in swift flight the Seraph had reached a spot in the air near the man of God, there appeared between the wings the figure of a man crucified, with his hands and feet extended in the form of a cross and fastened to a cross. Two of the wings were lifted above his head, two were extended for flight and two covered his whole body. When Francis saw this, he was overwhelmed and his heart was flooded with a mixture of joy and sorrow. He rejoiced because of the gracious way Christ looked upon him under the appearance of the Seraph, but the fact that he was fastened to a cross pierced his soul with a sword of compassionate sorrow (Luke 2:35).

He wondered exceedingly at the sight of so unfathomable a vision, realizing that the weakness of Christ's passion was in no way compatible with the immortality of the Seraph's spiritual nature. Eventually he understood by a revelation from the Lord that divine providence had shown him this vision so that, as Christ's lover, he might learn in advance that he was to be totally transformed into the likeness of Christ crucified, not by the martyrdom of his flesh, but by the fire of his love consuming his soul.

As the vision disappeared, it left in his heart a marvelous ardor and imprinted on his body markings that were no less marvelous. Immediately the marks of nails began to appear in his hands and feet just as he had seen a little before in the figure of the man crucified. His hands and feet seemed to be pierced through the center by nails, with the heads of the nails appearing on the inner side of the hands and the upper side of the feet and their points on the opposite sides. The heads of the nails in his hands and his feet were round and black; their points were oblong and bent as if driven back with a hammer, and they emerged from the flesh and stuck out beyond it. Also his right side, as if pierced with a lance, was marked with a red wound from which his sacred blood often flowed, moistening his tunic and underwear.[8]

The story of the stigmata vividly embodies two themes central to Francis's life—the imitation of Christ and the devotion to Christ Crucified.

One of the most striking qualities of Francis was his great joy. Throughout all his privation and tears he could and did continue to sing praises to God and rejoice in all creation. Francis loved nature, seeing all things, whether human, animal, or inert, as his brothers and sisters, all created by the same

Panel Painting by Bonaventura Berlinghieri of Lucca. Church of
San Francesco, Pescia, Italy. A.D. 1235. This is the earliest depiction
of Francis receiving the stigmata (the wounds of Christ).

loving God. Many of the stories of the life and miracles of Francis involve animals:

> When he was approaching Bevagna, he came to a spot where a large flock of birds of various kinds had come together. When God's saint saw them, he quickly ran to the spot and greeted them as if they were endowed with reason. They all became alert and turned toward him, and those perched in the trees bent their heads as he approached them and in an uncommon way directed their attention to him. He went right up to them and solicitously urged them to listen to the word of God, saying: "Oh birds, my brothers, you have a great obligation to praise your Creator, who clothed you in feathers and gave you wings to fly with, provided you with the pure air and cares for you without any worry on your part." While he was saying this and similar things to them, the birds showed their joy in a remarkable fashion: They began to stretch their necks, extend their wings, open their beaks and gaze at him attentively. He went through their midst with amazing fervor of spirit, brushing against them with his tunic. Yet none of them moved from the spot until the man of God made the sign of the cross and gave them his blessing and permission to leave; then they all flew away together.[9]

The following story is taken from a popular collection of Franciscan stories compiled at the beginning of the fourteenth century called *The Little Flowers*:

> In the days when St. Francis abode in the city of Gubbio, a huge wolf, terrible and fierce, appeared in the neighborhood, and not only devoured animals but men also; in such wise that all the citizens went in great fear of their lives, because ofttimes the wolf came close to the city. And when they went abroad, all men armed themselves as were they going forth to battle; and even so none who chanced on the wolf alone could defend himself; and at last it came to such a pass that for fear of this wolf no man durst leave the city walls. Wherefore St. Francis had great compassion for the men of that city, and purposed to issue forth against that wolf, albeit the citizens, with one accord, counselled him not to go. But he, making the sign of the holy cross, and putting all his trust in God, set forth from

Panel Painting by Bonaventura Berlinghieri of Lucca. Church of San Francesco, Pescia, Italy. A.D. 1235. Francis, accompanied by two other friars, preaches his famous sermon to the birds.

the city with his companions; but they, fearing to go farther, St. Francis went his way alone towards the place where the wolf was. And lo! the said wolf, in the sight of much folk that had come to behold the miracle, leapt towards St. Francis with gaping jaws; and St. Francis, drawing nigh, made to him the sign of the most holy cross and called him, speaking thus, "Come hither, friar wolf; I command thee in the name of Christ that thou do hurt neither to me nor to any man." Marvellous to tell! no sooner had St. Francis made the sign of holy cross than the terrible wolf closed his jaws and stayed his course; no sooner was the command uttered than he came, gentle as a lamb, and laid himself at the feet of St. Francis. . . . And when all the people were gathered together there, St. Francis stood forth and preached to them, saying, among other things, how

that for their sins God had suffered such calamaties to befall
them, and how much more perilous were the flames of hell
which the damned must endure everlastingly than was the
ravening of a wolf that could only slay the body; and how
much more to be feared were the jaws of hell, since that for
fear of the mouth of a small beast such multitudes went in fear
and trembling. "Turn ye, then, dearest children, to God, and
do fitting penance for your sins, and so shall God free you
from the wolf in this world and from eternal fire in the world
to come."[10]

Francis's love for nature and God's creatures was never an
end in itself. As this story demonstrates, Francis's taming of the
wolf becomes an opportunity for him to preach repentance to
people more concerned with the bodily harm a wolf can cause
than the spiritual harm caused by their own sin. Also, because
all creatures reflect the glory of the creator, Francis here uses
the wolf to let others see this same glory. His love for nature
becomes a sermon to be read by the people so that they too
can see in nature a sign that will help them move from visible
creation to the creator himself, even as Francis embodies this
same movement in his own life. Thus his life can be seen as
a sequence of dramatic gestures that vividly recreated the essence of the Gospel message for the people of his own time.

Bonaventure takes Francis's great love of God's creatures
and portrays it in a language probably foreign to Francis but
intelligible to the learned friars of his day:

> Aroused by all things to the love of God, he rejoiced in all the
> works of the Lord's hands and from these joy-producing mani-
> festations he rose to their life-giving principle and cause. In
> beautiful things he saw Beauty itself and through his vestiges
> imprinted on creation he followed his Beloved everywhere,
> making all things a ladder by which he could climb up and
> embrace him who is utterly desirable. With a feeling of un-
> precedented devotion he savored in each and every creature—
> as in so many rivulets—that Goodness which is their fountain-
> source. And he perceived a heavenly harmony in the conso-
> nance of powers and activities God has given them, and like the
> prophet David sweetly exhorted them to praise the Lord.[11]

The last line of the text probably refers to the fact that shortly before his death, Francis wrote a poem in Italian—the earliest surviving piece of Italian literature—usually called the "Canticle of the Creatures." In it, Francis the poet shows that his love for all creatures, even "Sister Bodily Death," comes from his understanding of the relation between God and all of his creation:

> Most High Almighty Good Lord,
> Yours are the praises, the glory, the honor, and all
>   blessings!
> To You alone, Most High, do they belong,
> And no man is worthy to mention You.
>
> Be praised, my Lord, with all Your creatures,
> Especially Sir Brother Sun,
> By whom You give us the light of day!
> And he is beautiful and radiant with great splendor.
> Of You, Most High, he is a symbol!
>
> Be praised, my Lord, for Sister Moon and the Stars!
> In the sky You formed them bright and lovely and fair.
>
> Be praised, My Lord, for Brother Wind
> And for the Air and cloudy and clear and all Weather,
> By which You give sustenance to Your creatures!
>
> Be praised, My Lord, for Sister Water,
> Who is very useful and humble and lovely and chaste!
>
> Be praised, my Lord, for Brother Fire,
> By whom You give us light at night,
> And he is beautiful and merry and mighty and strong!
>
> Be praised, my Lord, for our Sister Mother Earth,
> Who sustains and governs us,
> And produces fruits with colorful flowers and leaves!
>
> Be praised, my Lord, for those who forgive for love of You
> And endure infirmities and tribulations.

Blessed are those who shall endure them in peace,
For by You, Most High, they will be crowned!

Be praised, my Lord, for our Sister Bodily Death,
From whom no living man can escape!
Woe to those who shall die in mortal sin!
Blessed are those whom she will find in Your most
    holy will,
For the Second Death will not harm them.

Praise and bless my Lord and thank Him
And serve Him with great humility![12]

    Francis died in his beloved Porziuncula in 1226; he was per-haps the best-loved man in Europe at the time. It was only two years later that he was canonized by his friend Pope Gregory IX; in 1230 his relics were placed in the newly begun Basilica of St. Francis, soon to be adorned by frescoes by Cimabue and an artist traditionally thought to be Giotto. On Francis's last journey, the vicar of the order sent bodyguards with Francis so that if he died, his body could be returned to Assisi, which would then become a center of pilgrimage. The fight for Fran-cis's body and the splendor of his final resting place hardly seem characteristic of the ideals of Francis himself. There was a paradox inherent in his popularity, for in the very act of preserving his legacy for future generations, his followers did violence to the spirit of his teaching. Soon after his death there was a turning away from a strict interpretation of the rule of 1223, a turning that Francis himself saw the genesis of and strongly opposed. Once again, his very popularity was in some sense responsible. Many were those who were led to follow him; but Francis was surely a unique individual, and there were few who could follow his teaching in all its uncompromising rigor.

    The problem of how Francis's followers were to preserve his message remained a burning issue in the subsequent generations of Franciscan history, and forms an important chapter in the history of medieval spirituality. The early legends and biogra-phies of Francis made his ideals of poverty and humility clear to all of Europe; yet how these ideals were to be carried out by his followers was not so clear. The brotherhood that grew up almost spontaneously around Francis had few outward signs of community organization in the beginning. But its growth from a spontaneous brotherhood to a large order was accompanied by a process of institutionalization that changed its outward look in many ways. The absolute poverty that Francis demanded of his followers was to be realized by begging alms from day to day. But this was simply not as practical for thousands as it had been for one man and his few followers. The ideal of absolute poverty had to be balanced against the need for a certain amount of security. In order to further the ideal of humility, Francis insisted that no distinction be made within the order between those who were priests and those who were not. Yet as more and more priests entered the order, it was simply not possible to treat them in exactly the same way as laymen. They needed altars on which to say Mass, liturgical books with which to say the Divine Office. Francis insisted that his followers avoid contact with learning, believing that it interfered with both poverty and humility. Yet more and more learned men joined the order. And when Franciscan preaching began to include the correction and conversion of heresy, it became increasingly evident that some accommodation to learning was necessary. Were these changes the necessary condition for an organic continuation of the spirit of Francis, or were they a repudiation of his ideals, a total break with the past?

In the thirteenth century, the majority of Franciscans accepted modifications of the absolute poverty, the simplicity, and the nonacademic tone of early Franciscanism; they eventually came to be called Conventional Franciscans. However, a group later called the Spirituals fought all modifications of the original simplicity and absolute poverty that Francis himself had prescribed in the Rule of 1223 and the Testament.

As early as about 1250, some friars of the strict party made use of the writings of the twelfth-century Cistercian abbot and prophet Joachim of Fiore. Joachim had divided history into three ages, each corresponding to a person of the Trinity;

and he declared that the third and final age, the Age of the Holy Spirit, was to be ushered in by "new spiritual men." A friar named Gerard of Borgo San Donnino took over this Joachite scheme, identifying the new spiritual men with Francis and his followers (that is, with themselves). One of those who became a follower of Gerard was John of Parma, minister general of the order. Like Joachim, they believed that in this Age of the Holy Spirit the institutional Church, which from the beginning had supported modifications of Francis's ideals, would be unnecessary. They believed that the Antichrist was already alive, identifying him first with the Holy Roman Emperor Frederick II and then with several popes who strongly supported the Conventual position. When Bonaventure was elected minister general to replace John of Parma in 1257, one of his chief tasks was to suppress the extreme followers of Joachim within the Franciscan order.

One of the greatest thinkers and writers of the Middle Ages, Bonaventure used his extraordinary talents as a philosopher and theologian to translate the ideals of Francis into a more permanent form. In addition to his *Life of St. Francis*, he wrote such quintessentially Franciscan works as the *Defense of the Mendicants* (his examination of the poverty question), and the *Soul's Journey into God* (inspired by Francis's reception of the stigmata), works that earned him the not inappropriate title of "second founder" of the order.

Bonaventure himself was certainly sympathetic with the less extravagant claims of the Spirituals, that is, he too saw Francis as a figure unique in history and somehow to be identified with apocalyptic expectations (see ch. 4), identifying him specifically with the Angel of the Sixth Seal from the Book of Revelation. Bonaventure died in 1274, but the struggle between the Spirituals and the Conventuals continued. In the fourteenth century, the Spirituals were condemned by the papacy and several prominent adherents were imprisoned. Three Spiritual writers, Peter John Olivi (c.1248–98), Angelo Clareno (d.c.1323), and Ubertino da Casale (1259–c.1338), were among the most important apocalyptic writers of the late Middle Ages.

The Franciscan movement influenced all forms of expression. In their attempt to preach the Gospel to the widest possible audience, the Franciscans greatly extended the techniques of medieval preaching and transformed popular piety, influencing such literary forms as vernacular lyric poetry and drama in the process. Their influence on art was equally significant. Cycles of the life of Francis portrayed on walls and panels what the early lives and legends had described in words. Francis's devotion to Christ Crucified and to the humanity of Christ provided a new focus for art; an increased realism in depicting the Crucified Christ developed in the wake of the movement. The Franciscan emphasis on the created universe in all its variety as a road leading the soul to God greatly affected the visual arts and paralleled the revival of Aristotle, whose medieval adherents began with sense perception and argued toward God as the cause of creation. Together, these two beliefs explain the new realism that is one of the marks of the Gothic style.

The Franciscans were not the only new order to be established at this time. A contemporary of Francis's from Spain named Dominic de Guzman established the other important mendicant (begging) order, the Dominicans. Dominic, concerned with the Albigensian heresy that was raging in southern France, went there to attempt to win people back to Roman Catholic orthodoxy. He came to realize that one reason heresy had infected the area was that ignorant clergy were not preaching the word of God to the people. He desired to found an order of preachers loyal to Rome that would be able to win people back from heresy. At the Fourth Lateran Council (1215), it had been decreed that there would be no more new orders. However, in 1216 Dominic finally incorporated his preaching order by using a rule already in existence. Dominic, inspired by the ideals of Francis, also wished his friars to practice individual and collective poverty. Like the Franciscans, the Dominicans grew rapidly. In addition to the preaching for which they were founded (their official name is the Order of Preachers), they later often held positions in the Inquisition.

Unlike the Franciscans, the Dominicans had a need for education from the start because of their function as preachers of doctrine. They desired to study theology at the emerging universities; however, theology was a graduate course to which students were admitted only after completing the arts course, usually about six years. The Dominicans wanted to enter theology directly, without taking the arts course, causing tremendous struggles within the universities, especially in Paris, between themselves and the secular clergy. Generally, the Dominicans won and established their own schools in university cities to prepare members of the order for the study of theology. It is no accident that many of the greatest theologians of the thirteenth century were Dominicans, including Albertus Magnus and most importantly Thomas Aquinas. The Franciscans soon desired similar theological training for themselves; thus at the universities of Europe in the thirteenth century, one also finds Franciscans like Roger Bacon and Bonaventure.

While the Dominican zeal was involved in the elimination of heresy in Western Europe, the Franciscan missionary spirit (recalling that Francis had gone to convert Moslems) took friars into North Africa and all the way to China. Franciscans carried out missions to the Mongols, and a Christian community was established in Peking under a Franciscan archbishop.

Both mendicant orders operated primarily in cities, where they preached, taught, and often operated hospitals, homes for reformed prostitutes, schools, and other charitable enterprises. Because of their popularity, the orders received many gifts from pious donors and soon became wealthy, which often seemed to make them desirous of still more wealth. As the mendicant orders continued to change and to grow away from the ideals of Francis and Dominic, the orders came under severe attack from several quarters. Stories from Franciscan and Dominican lore, which had very quickly become part of the iconography depicting the ideals of Christianity for the late Middle Ages, were now seen in a new context. The veneration paid to Francis and Dominic, to Franciscans such as Anthony of Padua, Bonaventure, and Louis of Toulouse, and to Dominicans such as Peter Martyr and Thomas Aquinas, was contrasted with the degeneration of later times. Poets of the stature of

Dante and Chaucer portray the decline from original purity to the corruption of their own times. In the *Paradiso*, Dante shows the great mendicant saints lamenting the degeneracy of their orders. Chaucer, likewise, paints a lurid picture of the mendicants of his day in the *Friar's Tale* and the *Summoner's Tale*.

Conclusion

Certain concerns have clearly dominated our depiction of the Middle Ages: the centrality of the Bible, not only as a spiritual guide, but as a guide to subjects far removed from religion; the substantial continuity with the ancient world; the fusion of Christian and classical cultures, and their interaction with that of the Germans; the importance of the Church in its institutional and spiritual roles under the leadership of the papacy. In all the developments between the time of the ancient world and 1300 that we have charted in the course of the book, these elements remain constant, supporting the presupposition argued in the introduction that it is not wrong to speak of a medieval world view. But what happens next? Certainly events occurred in the fourteenth century that significantly altered the course of European history: the Avignon papacy, followed by a forty-year papal schism; the arrival of the bubonic plague, which probably reduced the population of Europe by a third; the Hundred Years War. Without in any way denying the importance of these events and their permanent impact on the course of Western civilization, it is nonetheless important to point out that they did not change the institutions and values that we have described as the medieval world view. For example, the Hundred Years War was fought in large part because of the English kings' involvement in French politics, an involvement that dates back to 1066. And although the methods of warfare were considerably different from earlier centuries, the ideals of warfare were those established in the eleventh and twelfth centuries. The fourteenth century also produced figures of permanent genius—Dante, Chaucer, Giotto, and William of Ockham, to name four obvious examples. Dante and Chaucer, at the beginning and the end of the century respectively, were both artists deeply engaged in the political and intellectual currents of their time, but they were also artists with an extraordinary ability to harness the intellectual energy of previous centuries and make it their own. Giotto, justifiably called the founder of Renaissance realism in painting, is with equal justification seen as the epitome of an iconographic tradition whose lines of development we have tried to trace. William of Ockham, whose nominalism presented the most serious challenge to the Thomistic synthesis of faith and reason, launched his challenge from within the philosophical categories, already defined in the eleventh and twelfth centuries, that ultimately go back to concepts discussed by Plato and Aristotle.

Everyone agrees however that the Middle Ages is over. And if it did not end in the fourteenth century, it had to have ended sometime. A case can be made that what changed in the fourteenth century was the rate of change and this might be a contributing factor to the end of the Middle Ages. In the fifteenth century, one begins to find writers who consciously reject the culture that had been developing since the fall of the Roman Empire, and who consequently attempted to recreate the culture of the ancient world freed from "barbarian accretions." The Protestant reformers of the sixteenth century sought out the "true Christianity" that existed before the development of medieval institutions and distortions. The sixteenth century saw the discovery and exploration of the New World and Asia. The danger in looking toward all this change and its implied rejection of certain elements of the medieval world view is that it encourages us to forget how much continuity still existed with the medieval tradition. Neither Petrarch (1304–74) nor Luther (1483–1546) is understandable outside the Augustinian tradition; there were English Protestant Thomists in the sixteenth century; many of the missionaries to the New World took their inspiration from Francis of Assisi and their theory of conversion from Gregory the Great.

More significant than the break with the medieval past during the Renaissance is the one caused by the scientific revolution beginning with Copernicus (1473–1543), for it is the scientific world view and its attendant technological progress which most decisively separates us from the Middle Ages. Nevertheless, it is important to remind ourselves that although the world view of the Middle Ages did indeed break down, many of its individual elements have been integrated into our own civilization. Bernard of Chartres was surely correct in describing the sages of his time as dwarfs perched on the shoulders of giants. This image can perhaps also be applied in our time as well: we are continuing to learn the extent to which our civilization is perched on the shoulders of the Middle Ages.

Notes

ONE: The Bible

1. All quotations from the Psalms are from the version for singing of Joseph Gelineau (New York: Paulist Press, 1966). All other biblical quotations are from the Knox translation (New York: Sheed and Ward, 1956). We have used the Gelineau version of the Psalms because it most clearly recreates the poetic spirit of the original; we have used the Knox translation because it is a translation made primarily from the Latin Vulgate.

TWO: The Classical Heritage

1. David Knowles, *The Evolution of Medieval Thought* (New York: Random House, 1962), pp. 3–4.
2. Ibid., p. 11.
3. Ibid., p. 13.
4. Ed. Moses Hadas, *Basic Works of Cicero* (New York: Random House, 1951), p. 162.

5. Ibid., p. 168.
6. Vergil, *Aeneid*, trans. W. F. Jackson Knight (Baltimore: Penguin, 1956), pp. 160–61.
7. Trans. J. W. Mackail, *Virgil's Works* (New York: Random House, 1950), p. 274.
8. Ovid, *Metamorphoses*, trans. Mary M. Innes (Baltimore: Penguin, 1955), pp. 231–32.
9. *Aeneid*, pp. 172–73.

THREE: Early Christianity

1. Trans. Maxwell Staniforth in *Early Christian Writings* (Baltimore: Penguin, 1968), pp. 89–90.
2. From "The Epistle to the Trallians" in ibid., p. 95.
3. From "Against Heresies," trans. and ed. Cyril C. Richardson, *Early Christian Fathers* (New York: Macmillan, 1970), p. 372.
4. Leo the Great, *Letters and Sermons* in *Library of Nicene and Post-Nicene Fathers* XII, 2nd series, trans. Charles Lett Feltoe (Grand Rapids: William B. Eerdmans, rpt. 1952), p. 117.
5. See "The First Apology" of Justin Martyr in Richardson, esp. p. 272.
6. David Ayerst and A. S. T. Fisher, eds., *The Records of Christianity* v. 1 (Oxford: Basil Blackwell, 1971), p. 113.
7. From "On First Principles," in Maurice Wiles and Mark Santer, eds., *Documents in Early Christian Thought* (Cambridge: Cambridge University Press, 1975), pp. 144–45.
8. From "On the Objections of the Heretics," in Ayerst and Fisher, pp. 95–96.
9. See Henry Chadwick, *The Early Church* (Baltimore: Penguin, 1967), pp. 90–93.
10. Ayerst and Fisher, p. 16.
11. From "The epistle to the Romans," in Staniforth, pp. 104–5.
12. From "The Martyrdom of Polycarp," in Staniforth, p. 162.
13. Jacobus de Voragine, *The Golden Legend*, trans. Granger Ryan and Helmut Ripperger (New York: Arno Press, 1941), pp. 441–42.
14. From "The Martyrdom of Felix the Bishop," in Herbert Musurillo, ed. and trans., *The Acts of the Christian Martyrs* (Oxford: Clarendon Press, 1972), pp. 267–69.
15. Trans. International Committee on English in the Liturgy, *Latin Mass Booklet* (Alcester: C. Goodliffe Neale, 1975), pp. 3–4.

16. Trans. Lewis Thorpe, *The History of the Franks* (Baltimore: Penguin, 1974), pp. 107–8.

17. From "Life of St. Ambrose," in Roy J. Defarrari, ed., *Early Christian Biographies* in *The Fathers of the Church* v. 15 (Washington: Catholic University of America Press, 1952), pp. 46–47.

18. In J. Stevenson, ed., *Creeds, Councils, and Controversies: Documents Illustrative of the History of the Church A.D. 337–461* (London: SPCK, 1966), p. 161.

19. Dante, *Inferno*, trans. John D. Sinclair (Oxford: Oxford University Press, 1939), p. 243.

20. From "On Simony," in Matthew Spinka, ed., *Advocates of Reform* in *Library of Christian Classics* (London: SCM, 1953), p. 224.

FOUR: The Latin Fathers: Jerome and Augustine

1. St. Jerome, *Letters* in *Library of Nicene and Post-Nicene Fathers*, VI, 2nd series, trans. W. H. Fremantle (Grand Rapids: William B. Eerdmans, rpt., 1952), p. 35. This and the following quotation from Jerome can be found in Brian Tierney, ed., *The Middle Ages: Sources of Medieval History* (New York: Alfred A. Knopf, 1970), pp. 31–33.

2. Fremantle, p. 149.

3. Emile Mâle, *The Gothic Image: Religious Art in France of the Thirteenth Century* (New York: Harper and Row, 1958).

4. Augustine, *On Christian Doctrine*, trans. D. W. Robertson, Jr. (Indianapolis: Bobbs-Merrill, 1958), pp. 9–10.

5. Ibid., p. 43.

6. Ibid., pp. 94–95.

7. Ibid., pp. 37–38.

8. Ibid., p. xv.

9. Ibid., p. 30.

10. Ibid., p. 75.

11. Augustine, *Confessions*, trans. R. S. Pine-Coffin (Baltimore: Penguin, 1961), p. 168.

12. Eric Auerbach, *Mimesis* (Princeton: Princeton University Press, 1953), pp. 58–65.

13. *Confessions*, pp. 121–23.

14. Ibid., p. 21.

15. Jacobus de Voragine, *The Golden Legend*, trans. Granger

Ryan and Helmut Ripperger (New York: Arno Press, 1941), pp. 610–12.

16. *Confessions*, pp. 177–78.
17. Dante, *Inferno*, trans. John D. Sinclair (Oxford: Oxford University Press, 1939), p. 79.
18. *Confessions*, pp. 107–8.
19. Augustine, *Concerning the City of God Against the Pagans*, trans. Henry Bettenson (Baltimore: Penguin, 1972), p. 1091.
20. Ibid., p. 652.
21. Ibid., p. 859.
22. Ibid., pp. 547–48.
23. Ibid., pp. 549–50.
24. Ibid., p. 553.
25. Ibid., p. 596.
26. Ibid., p. 875.
27. Ibid., p. 213.

FIVE: The Transition from Ancient to Medieval

1. Trans. Alfred John Church and William Jackson Brodribb, *Complete Works of Tacitus*, ed. Moses Hadas (New York: Random House, 1942), p. 712.
2. Ibid., p. 715.
3. Ibid., pp. 715–16.
4. Trans. and ed. Katherine Fischer Drew, *The Lombard Laws* (Philadelphia: University of Pennsylvania Press, 1973), p. 62.
5. Trans. and ed. Katherine Fischer Drew, *The Burgundian Code* (Philadelphia: University of Pennsylvania Press, 1949), p. 23.
6. Trans. W. B. Anderson, *Sidonius: Poems and Letters* II, *Loeb Classical Library* (Cambridge: Harvard University Press, 1965), p. 287.
7. Gregory of Tours, *The History of the Franks*, trans. Lewis Thorpe (Baltimore: Penguin, 1974), p. 63.
8. Ibid., pp. 167–68.
9. Ibid., p. 154.
10. "Anonymous Vatesianus," trans. John C. Rolfe, in *Ammianus Marcellinus* III, *Loeb Classical Library* (Cambridge: Harvard University Press, 1939), pp. 545, 547.
11. Gregory of Tours, pp. 143–44.
12. Ibid., p. 144.
13. Bede, *A History of the English Church and People*, trans. Leo Sherley-Price (Baltimore: Penguin, 1955), pp. 86–87.

14. Ibid., p. 76.
15. Ibid., p. 77.
16. Ibid., p. 69.
17. Ibid., p. 85.
18. Ibid., pp. 236-37.
19. Ibid., p. 206.
20. Trans. William C. McDermott in *Monks, Bishops and Pagans: Christian Culture in Gaul and Italy, 500–700*, ed. Edward Peters (Philadelphia: University of Pennsylvania Press, 1975), pp. 79–80.
21. Trans. and ed. Ludwig Bieler, *The Irish Penitentials* (Dublin: The Dublin Institute for Advanced Studies, rpt., 1975), pp. 113, 115.
22. Ibid., pp. 131, 133.
23. Ibid., p. 131.
24. Trans. and ed. Ephraim Emerton, *The Letters of Saint Boniface* (New York: W. W. Norton, rpt., 1976), pp. 48–49. (Originally in the *Columbia University Records of Civilization*.)
25. Ibid., pp. 115–16.
26. Ibid., p. 92.
27. Gregory the Great, *The Book of Pastoral Rule and Selected Epistles* in *Library of Nicene and Post-Nicene Fathers* XII, 2nd series, trans. and ed. James Barmby (Grand Rapids: William B. Eerdmans, rpt., 1952), pp. 228–29.
28. Gregory the Great, *Selected Epistles* in *Library of Nicene and Post-Nicene Fathers* XIII, 2nd series, trans. and ed. James Barmby (Grand Rapids: William B. Eerdmans, rpt., 1952), p. 53.
29. Gregory the Great, *Pastoral Care* in *Ancient Christian Writers*, trans. Henry Davis (New York: Newman Press, rpt., 1978), pp. 23–24, 51–52.
30. Gregory the Great, *Morals on the Book of Job* in *Library of Fathers of the Holy Catholic Church*, trans. John Henry Parker (Oxford, 1847), pt. 5, book 23, pp. 1–2. An excerpt is available in Robert Brentano, ed., *The Early Middle Ages, 500–1000* (New York: The Free Press of Glencoe, 1964), pp. 104–6.
31. Boethius, *The Consolation of Philosophy*, trans. Richard Green (Indianapolis: Bobbs-Merrill, 1962), pp. 21–22.
32. Ibid., p. 43.
33. Ibid., p. 104.
34. Ibid., p. 109.

35. Ibid., pp. 91, 92.
36. Ibid., p. 9.
37. Adapted from M. L. W. Laistner, *Thought and Letters in Western Europe A.D. 500 to 900* (Ithaca: Cornell University Press, 1931), p. 123.
38. Jacobus de Voragine, *The Golden Legend*, trans. Granger Ryan and Helmut Ripperger (New York: Arno Press, 1941), p. 177.
39. Ibid., p. 619.
40. Pseudo-Dionysius, *The Divine Names and the Mystical Theology*, trans. C. E. Rolt (London: SPCK, 1940), pp. 56–59.
41. Otto von Simson, *The Gothic Cathedral* (New York: Harper and Row, 1962), p. 50.
42. Ibid., p. 50.
43. Dante, *Paradiso*, trans. John D. Sinclair (New York: Oxford University Press, 1939), p. 19.
44. *The Golden Legend*, p. 621.

SIX: Monasticism

1. Trans. and ed. Robert C. Gregg, *Athanasius: The Life of Antony and the Letter to Marcellinus* in *The Classics of Western Spirituality* (New York: Paulist Press, 1980), p. 31.
2. Ibid., pp. 66–67.
3. Ibid., p. 46.
4. Saint Antony, *The Wisdom of the Desert*, trans. Thomas Merton (New York: New Directions, 1960), p. 29.
5. Ibid., p. 62.
6. *Athanasius*, pp. 83–84.
7. Trans. Edgar C. S. Gibson, *The Works of John Cassian* in *Library of Nicene and Post-Nicene Fathers* XI, 2nd series (Grand Rapids: William B. Eerdmans, rpt., 1952), pp. 280–81.
8. *Conferences*, in ibid., p. 298.
9. Gregory the Great, *Dialogues*, trans. Myra L. Uhlfelder (Indianapolis: Bobbs-Merrill, 1967), pp. 6–7.
10. Trans. Leonard J. Doyle, *Saint Benedict's Rule for Monasteries* (Collegeville, Minn.: The Liturgical Press, 1948), pp. 5–6.
11. Ibid., pp. 12–13.
12. Ibid., pp. 67–68.
13. Ibid., pp. 20–21.
14. Ibid., pp. 57–59, 76–77.

SEVEN: The Carolingian World and Its Aftermath

1. Charlemagne, "Admonitio generalis" in *Christianity Through the Thirteenth Century*, trans. and ed. Marshall W. Baldwin (New York: Harper & Row, 1970), pp. 115–16.
2. Ibid., pp. 117–18, 119.
3. Ibid., pp. 119–20.
4. Einhard, *The Life of Charlemagne* in *Two Lives of Charlemagne*, trans. Lewis Thorpe (Baltimore: Penguin, 1969), p. 81.
5. Trans. Bernhard Walter Scholz, *Royal Frankish Annals* in *Carolingian Chronicles* (Ann Arbor: University of Michigan Press, 1970), p. 81.
6. "General Capitulary for the *missi*," trans. H. R. Loyn and J. Percival, *The Reign of Charlemagne* (London: Edward Arnold, 1975), pp. 74–75.
7. Ibid., p. 74.
8. *Two Lives of Charlemagne*, p. 79.
9. Trans. Robert Folz, *The Coronation of Charlemagne* (London: Routledge and Kegan Paul, 1974), p. 68.
10. *Christianity Through the Thirteenth Century*, p. 117.
11. Ibid., p. 146.
12. Ed. David Bevington, *Medieval Drama* (Boston: Houghton Mifflin, 1975), p. 26.
13. *The Reign of Charlemagne*, pp. 63–64.
14. *Two Lives of Charlemagne*, p. 74.
15. Ibid., p. 82.
16. Ibid., pp. 141–42.
17. Ibid., pp. 64–65.
18. Trans. Patricia Terry, *The Song of Roland* (Indianapolis: Bobbs-Merrill, 1965), ll. 2448–60.
19. *Christianity Through the Thirteenth Century*, p. 132.
20. Trans. and ed. Boyd H. Hill, *Medieval Monarchy in Action: The German Empire from Henry I to Henry IV* (New York: Barnes & Noble, 1972), pp. 113–15.
21. *Two Lives of Charlemagne*, pp. 71–72.
22. Trans. and ed. David Herlihy, *The History of Feudalism* (New York: Walker, 1970), pp. 10, 11–13.
23. Ibid., p. 87.
24. Ibid.
25. Ibid., pp. 87–88.
26. Ibid., pp. 108–9.
27. Joseph R. Strayer, "The Two Levels of Feudalism," in *Life and*

Thought in the Early Middle Ages, ed. Robert S. Hoyt (Minneapolis: University of Minnesota Press, 1967), p. 51.

28. Trans. in *Pennsylvania Translations and Reprints Series*, vol. 4, no. 3, and reprinted in *Medieval History: A Sourcebook*, ed. Donald A. White (Homewood, Illinois: Dorsey Press, 1965), pp. 268–70.

29. Trans. and ed. F. A. Ogg, *A Sourcebook of Medieval History* (New York: American Book Company, 1907), pp. 220–21 and reprinted in *The History of Feudalism*, p. 97.

30. Galbert of Bruges, *The Murder of Charles the Good, Count of Flanders*, trans. James Bruce Ross (New York: Harper & Row, 1967), pp. 206–7.

31. Gerald of Aurillac, *St. Odo of Cluny*, trans. Dom Gerard Sitwell (New York: Sheed & Ward, 1958), pp. 99–101.

32. *The Song of Roland*, ll, 1009–12.

33. Strayer, "The Development of Feudal Institutions" in *Twelfth-Century Europe and the Foundations of Modern Society*, eds. Marshall Clagett et al. (Madison: University of Wisconsin Press, 1965), pp. 76–88. This essay and the other Strayer essay cited above are both reprinted in *Medieval Statecraft and the Perspectives of History: Essays by Joseph R. Strayer* (Princeton: Princeton University Press, 1971).

34. Trans. and ed. G. G. Coulton, *Social Life in Britain from the Conquest to the Reformation* (Cambridge: Cambridge University Press, 1918), pp. 415ff and reprinted in *Medieval Europe*, eds. William H. McNeill and Schuyler O. Houser (New York: Oxford University Press, 1971), pp. 91–92.

35. Trans. John F. Benton, *Self and Society in Medieval France: The Memoirs of Abbot Guibert of Nogent* (New York: Harper & Row, 1970), p. 167.

36. Ibid., pp. 175–76.

37. Otto of Freising, *The Deeds of Frederick Barbarossa*, trans. Charles C. Mierow (New York: W. W. Norton, rpt., 1966), pp. 127–28. (Originally in the *Columbia University Records of Civilization*.)

EIGHT: Church, State, and Society

1. Fulcher of Chartres, *A History of the Expedition to Jerusalem, 1095–1127*, trans. Frances Rita Ryan (New York: W. W. Norton, rpt., 1973), p. 66.

2. Ibid., p. 68.
3. Ibid., p. 117.
4. Ibid., pp. 121–22.
5. Albert of Aix, *Chronicle* in *The First Crusade: The Accounts of Eye-Witnesses and Participants*, trans. A. C. Krey (Princeton: Prineton University Press, 1921) and reprinted in Edward Peters, ed., *The First Crusade* (Philadelphia: University of Pennsylvania Press, 1971), p. 102.
6. Trans. and ed. Bruno Scott James, *The Letters of St. Bernard of Clairvaux* (Chicago: Henry Regnery, 1953), pp. 461–62.
7. William of St. Thierry, *The Golden Epistle: A Letter to the Brethren at Mont Dieu* in *Cistercian Fathers Series* v. 12, trans. Theodore Berkeley, OCSO (Kalamazoo: Cistercian Publications, 1971), pp. 19–20.
8. Trans. Thomas Merton, *The Solitary Life: A Letter of Guigo* (Worcester: privately printed, 1963), pp. 7–9.
9. Trans. A Monk of Gethsemani, *Compendium of the History of the Cistercian Order* (Gethsemani, Kentucky: Order of Cistercians of the Strict Observance, 1944), pp. 356, 357.
10. *On the Song of Songs I* in *Cistercian Fathers Series* v. 4, trans. Kilian Walsh, OCSO (Kalamazoo: Cistercian Publications, 1971), pp. 16–17.
11. In Bernard of Clairvaux, *Treatises I* in *Cistercian Fathers Series* v. 1, trans. Michael Casey, OCSO (Kalamazoo: Cistercian Publications, 1970), pp. 63–64, 66.
12. Ibid., p. 64.
13. Jean Leclercq, *The Love of Learning and the Desire for God* (New York: Fordham University Press, 1974), p. 306.
14. Bernard of Clairvaux, *Five Books on Consideration: Advice to a Pope* in *Cistercian Fathers* v. 13, trans. John D. Anderson and Elizabeth T. Kennan (Kalamazoo: Cistercian Publications, 1976), pp. 29, 31–32.
15. Pope Innocent III, "Sermon on the consecration of a pope," and "Letter to the prefect Acerbus and the nobles of Tuscany" in *The Crisis of Church and State 1050–1300*, trans. Brian Tierney (Englewood Cliffs: Prentice-Hall, 1964), pp. 132–33.
16. Trans. and ed. Mary Clark, *An Aquinas Reader* (New York: Doubleday, 1972), pp. 363, 364–65, 367.
17. Pope Boniface VIII, "Unam Sanctam" in Tierney, pp. 188–89.
18. Dante, *On World Government*, trans. Herbert W. Schneider (Indianapolis: Bobbs-Merrill, 1957), pp. 9, 11, 64.

NINE: Twelfth-Century Renaissance

1. Trans. and ed. Harriet Pratt Lattin, *The Letters of Gerbert* in *Columbia University Records of Civilization* (New York: Columbia University Press, 1961), p. 90.
2. Quoted in Nathan Schachner, *The Medieval Universities* (New York: A. S. Barnes and Company, 1962), p. 19.
3. Trans. and ed. Eugene R. Fairweather, *Why God Became Man* in *A Scholastic Miscellany: Anselm to Ockham* in *Library of Christian Classics* X (New York: The Macmillan Company, rpt., 1970), pp. 101–2.
4. Trans. S. W. Deane, *Proslogium* in *St. Anselm, Basic Writings* (LaSalle, Illinois: Open Court Publishing Company, 1962), pp. 8–9.
5. Trans. John F. Benton, *Self and Society in Medieval France: The Memoirs of Abbot Guibert of Nogent* (New York: Harper & Row, 1970), p. 45.
6. Trans. and ed. Brian Tierney, *The Middle Ages: Sources of Medieval History*, 3rd ed. (New York: Alfred A. Knopf, 1978), pp. 168–69.
7. Trans. Daniel D. McGarry, *The Metalogicon of John of Salisbury* (Gloucester, Massachusetts: Peter Smith, 1971), pp. 67–70.
8. Ibid., p. 167.
9. Thomas Aquinas, *Summa Theologiae* v. 1, trans. Thomas Gilby (Garden City: Doubleday, 1969), pp. 191–92.
10. M.-D. Chénu, *Toward Understanding St. Thomas* (Chicago: Henry Regnery & Company, 1964), esp. chs. 4 and 5, gives a cogent analysis of Thomas's method.
11. Erwin Panofsky, *Gothic Architecture and Scholasticism* (New York: World Publishing Company, 1957).
12. Gratian, *Decretum*, trans. John T. Noonan in *The Records of Medieval Europe*, ed. Carolly Erikson (Garden City: Doubleday, 1971), p. 206.
13. Alanus, "Commentary on DIST 96 c.6" in *The Crisis of Church and State 1050–1300*, trans. Brian Tierney (Englewood Cliffs: Prentice-Hall, 1964), p. 123.
14. Ibid., p. 122.
15. Chrétien de Troyes, *Erec and Enide* in *Arthurian Romances*, trans. W. W. Comfort (New York: Dutton, 1914), p. 68.
16. *Arthurian Romances*, p. 93.
17. Ibid., p. 91.

18. Trans. Patricia Terry, *The Song of Roland* (Indianapolis: Bobbs-Merrill, 1965), ll. 96–100, 115–21.
19. *Arthurian Romances*, p. 203.
20. Trans. and ed. James J. Wilhelm, *Medieval Song* (New York: Dutton, 1971), pp. 141–42.

TEN: Francis of Assisi and the Mendicants

1. Trans. and ed. Ewert Cousins, *Bonaventure: The Soul's Journey into God: The Tree of Life, The Life of Francis* in *The Classics of Western Spirituality* (New York: Paulist Press, 1978), pp. 187–88.
2. Ibid., pp. 191–92.
3. Ibid., pp. 280–81.
4. Ibid., pp. 199–200, 239–40.
5. Ed. Father Hugh McKay, *The Little Flowers of St. Francis, The Mirror of Perfection, St. Bonaventure's Life of St. Francis* (New York: Dutton, 1910), p. 196.
6. Ed. Marion A. Habig, *St. Francis of Assisi: Writings and Early Biographies* (Chicago: Franciscan Herald Press, 1972), pp. 60–61.
7. Ibid., pp. 68–69.
8. *Bonaventure*, pp. 305–6.
9. Ibid., pp. 294–95.
10. *The Little Flowers of St. Francis*, pp. 38–41.
11. *Bonaventure*, pp. 262–63.
12. Ed. Raphael Brown, *The Little Flowers of St. Francis* (Garden City: Doubleday, 1958), pp. 317–18.

Bibliography

This bibliography is designed to make primary sources, standard references, and important secondary works more readily accessible. We have attempted to be representative, but by no means comprehensive, not simply because a comprehensive bibliography would itself take up more space than the entire present volume but also because such a biliography would include many items useful exclusively to the specialist. Many if not most of the secondary works included are themselves valuable bibliographical tools, both in the formal bibliographies they contain and in their notes.

I. PRIMARY SOURCES

Multiple translations exist of all the classical writers mentioned in the text, and of most of the medieval writers as well. In general, it is a good idea to use recent translations, which tend to be more accessible on first reading. Since we have tried to follow this principle in our own quotations within the text, the editions we use are themselves a good guide for suggested reading in primary sources. A student wishing to learn more about Augustine should go to Augustine and read the *Confessions* or the *City of God*. As a supplement to these editions, we list some of the more useful single-volume collections and anthologies, and some of the most important series. Three important guides to primary sources are:

Farrar, Clarissa P. and Evans, Austin P. *Bibliography of English Translations from Medieval Sources.* New York: Columbia University Press, 1946.

Ferguson, Mary Ann. *Bibliography of English Translations from Medieval Sources 1943–1967.* New York: Columbia University Press, 1974.

Pullan, Brian. *Souces for the History of Medieval Europe.* New York: Barnes and Noble, 1966.

A. Single-Volume Collections of Sources

Baldwin, Marshall W., Ed. *Christianity Through the Thirteenth Century.* New York: Harper and Row, 1970.

Bevington, David, Ed. *Medieval Drama.* Boston: Houghton Mifflin, 1975.

Brentano, Robert, Ed. *The Early Middle Ages, 500–1000.* New York: The Free Press of Glencoe, 1964.

Brooke, Rosalind. *The Coming of the Friars.* New York: Barnes and Noble, 1975.

Brundage, James A., Ed. *The Crusades: A Documentary Survey.* Milwaukee: Marquette University Press, 1962.

Dawson, Christopher, Ed. *Mission to Asia.* New York: Harper and Row, 1966.

Erickson, Carolly, Ed. *The Records of Medieval Europe.* Garden City: Doubleday, 1971.

Habig, Marion A., Ed. *St. Francis of Assisi: Writings and Early Biographies.* Chicago: Franciscan Herald Press, 1972.

Herlihy, David, Ed. *Medieval Culture and Society.* New York: Harper and Row, 1968.

———, Ed. *The History of Feudalism.* New York: Walker and Company, 1970.

Hennecke, E. and Scheemelcher, W., Eds. *New Testament Apocrypha,* 2 vols. Philadelphia: Westminster Press, 1963.

Hill, Boyd H., Ed. *Medieval Monarchy in Action: The German Empire from Henry I to Henry IV.* New York: Barnes and Noble, 1972.

Hyman, Arthur and Walsh, James J., Eds. *Philosophy in the Middle Ages.* Indianapolis: Hackett, 1973.

Lerner, Ralph and Mahdi, Mushin, Eds. *Medieval Political Philosophy.* Ithaca: Cornell University Press, 1963.

McNeill, William H. and Houser, Schuyler, Eds. *Medieval Europe.* New York: Oxford University Press, 1971.

Miller, Joseph M. et al., Eds. *Readings in Medieval Rhetoric.* Bloomington: Indiana University Press, 1973.

Peters, Edward, Ed. *Monks, Bishops and Pagans: Christian Culture in Gaul and Italy, 500–700.* Philadelphia: University of Pennsylvania Press, 1975.

———, Ed. *Heresy and Authority in Medieval Europe.* Philadelphia: University of Pennsylvania Press, 1980.

Robertson, D. W., Jr., Ed. *The Literature of Medieval England.* New York: McGraw-Hill, 1970.

Shapiro, Herman, Ed. *Medieval Philosophy.* New York: Modern Library, 1964.

Strunk, Oliver, Ed. *Source Readings in Music History: Antiquity and the Middle Ages.* New York: W. W. Norton, 1965.

Tierney, Brian, Ed. *The Middle Ages: Sources of Medieval History*, 3rd ed. New York: Alfred A. Knopf, 1978.

White, Donald A., Ed. *Medieval History: A Sourcebook.* Homewood, Illinois: Dorsey Press, 1965.

B. Series

Ancient Christian Writers. Now published by Paulist Press. Volumes include works by such authors as Augustine, Gregory the Great, and Ambrose.

Cistercian Fathers Series. Kalamazoo: Cistercian Publications. These are recent translations (the series is not yet complete), of one of the most important sources of medieval spirtuality, including the best translations of Bernard of Clairvaux.

Classics of Western Spirituality. Ramsey, N.J.: Paulist Press. More than half of the volumes published thus far in these excellent paperback translations contain the works of authors covered in this volume. Sample volumes include Philo of Alexandria, Gregory of Nyssa, Origen, Athanasius, Bonaventure, Richard of St. Victor, and a volume on medieval apocalypticism that includes writings of Joachim of Fiore.

Columbia University Records of Civilization. New York: Columbia University Press.

Documentary History of Western Civilization. New York: Harper and Row.

Documents of Medieval History. London: Edward Arnold.

English Historical Documents. New York: Eyre and Spottiswoode.

Everyman Library. New York: Dutton. Several volumes in this series contain medieval selections, including one on Francis of Assisi, one on Chrétien de Troyes, and one on Marie de France.

Fathers of the Church. Reprinted by Catholic University of America Press.

Library of Christian Classics. Philadelphia: Westminster Press.

The Library of Liberal Arts. Indianapolis: Bobbs-Merrill.

Loeb Classical Library. Cambridge: Harvard University Press. A standard, comprehensive source for classical and early Christian writers, these volumes consist of the original Latin or Greek with facing-page English translation.

Norton Critical Editions. New York: Norton. These are texts of primary sources (sample medieval titles: Boccaccio's *Decameron*, *Middle English Lyrics*) accompanied by relevant criticism. In addition, Norton has reprinted in paperback editions many of the *Columbia University Records of Civilization*, including such works as Andreas Capellanus's *Art of Courtly Love*, and Gregory of Tours's *History of the Franks*.

Penguin Classics. New York: Penguin. An invaluable collection. More works of medieval literature, history, and spirituality in English translation appear in Penguin editions than in any other source.

The Pontifical Institute of Medieval Studies Sources in Translation. Toronto: Pontifical Institute of Medieval Studies.

A Select Library of the Nicene and Post-Nicene Fathers of the Christian Church. Grand Rapids: William B. Eerdmans (rpt.). Although these translations were made in the nineteenth century, this remains the most extensive collection in English of the Church Fathers.

Sources of Civilization in the West. Englewood Cliffs, N.J.: Prentice-Hall.

Works of Bonaventure. Paterson, N.J.: St. Anthony Guild Press.

II. REFERENCE WORKS

The most important bibliography for students of the Middle Ages is the following:

Paetow, Louis. *A Guide to the Study of Medieval History.* Millwood, N.Y.: Kraus International, rpt. 1980.

This work lists works published before 1930. It has been brought up to 1975 in the following:

Boyce, Gray. *Literature of Medieval History 1930–1975*, 5 volumes. Millwood, N.Y.: Kraus International, 1981.

Bibliography 337

A. Standard Texts

Hollister, C. Warren. *Medieval Europe: A Short History*, 5th ed. New York: Wiley, 1982.

Hoyt, Robert and Chodorow, Stanley. *Europe in the Middle Ages*, 3rd ed. New York: Harcourt, Brace, Jovanovich, 1976.

Lopez, Robert S. *The Birth of Europe*. New York: Evans, World, 1967.

Oakley, Francis. *The Medieval Experience*. New York: Scribners, 1974.

Peters, Edward. *Europe: The World of the Middle Ages*. Englewood Cliffs, N.J.: Prentice-Hall, 1977.

Stephenson, Carl and Lyon, Bryce. *Mediaeval History*, 4th ed. New York: Harper and Row, 1962.

Tierney, Brian and Painter, Sidney. *Western Europe in the Middle Ages, 300–1475*, 3rd ed. New York: Knopf, 1978.

B. Multiple-Volume Histories

The Cambridge Medieval History, 8 volumes in 9. Cambridge: Cambridge University Press, 1911ff.

Carlyle, R. W. and Carlyle, A. J. *A History of Medieval Political Theory in the West*, 6 volumes. London: William Blackwood and Sons, rpt., 1962.

The Christian Centuries. Princeton: Princeton University Press. The first two volumes cover the Church in the Middle Ages.

Hay, Denys, Ed. *A General History of Europe*. New York: Holt, Rinehart and Winston. Several volumes deal with the Middle Ages. The volumes dealing with the end of the ancient world and with the Renaissance and Reformation are also valuable to the medievalist.

Handbook of Church History. Montreal: Palm Publishers. The first four volumes deal with the early Church and the Middle Ages; extensive bibliographies.

History of European Civilization Library. New York: Harcourt, Brace, Jovanovich. About a dozen volumes deal with the Middle Ages; these are all well illustrated.

A History of Christian Spirituality. New York: Seabury Press.

The Making of European Civilization. New York: McGraw-Hill. This series contains several volumes dealing with the Middle Ages, each with excellent essays and lavish illustrations.

Major Issues in History. New York: Wiley. Several volumes deal with the Middle Ages, each containing documents as well as interpretive essays.

The Pelican History of Art. New York: Penguin.

The Pelican History of the Church. New York: Penguin. The volumes on the early Church, the medieval Church, and the Reformation all contain valuable information and insights.

Problems in European Civilization. Boston: D. C. Heath. Each volume contains several essays on a particular topic; some include source material as well.

C.   Other Useful References

Barraclough, Geoffrey, Ed. *The Times Atlas of World History.* Maplewood, N.J.: Hammond, 1979.

Cross, F. L., Ed. *The Oxford Dictionary of the Christian Church.* Oxford: Oxford University Press, 1966.

Dictionary of National Biography. London: Oxford University Press, 1921–22.

Hammond, N. G. L. and Scullard, H. H., Eds. *The Oxford Classical Dictionary,* 2nd ed. Oxford: Oxford University Press, 1970.

McEvedy, Colin. *The Penguin Atlas of Medieval History.* Baltimore: Penguin, 1961.

The New Catholic Encyclopedia. New York: McGraw-Hill, 1967. An extremely valuable source for many medieval topics.

Powell, James M., Ed. *Medieval Studies: An Introduction.* Syracuse: Syracuse University Press, 1976. Each chapter is an orientation to a field of specialized study within the Middle Ages. Included are branches of history, paleography (the study of handwriting), philosophy, literature, art, and music. Each chapter has its own bibliography.

Schiller, Gertrude. *Iconography of Christian Art,* trans. Janet Seligman, 2 volumes. Greenwich, Connecticut: New York Graphic Society, 1971. Although only two volumes have been translated from a much more extensive German series (still being published), this is nevertheless an important and valuable source for medieval iconography.

Storey, R. L. L. *Chronology of the Medieval World, 400–1491.* New York: D. McKay, 1973.

III.   SECONDARY WORKS

A.   General Intellectual Histories

Artz, Frederick B. *The Mind of the Middle Ages,* 3rd ed. Chicago: University of Chicago Press, 1980.

Boase, T. S. R. *Death in the Middle Ages.* New York: McGraw-Hill, 1972.

Brooke, Christopher. *The Structure of Medieval Society.* Garden City: Doubleday, 1971.

De Molen, Richard, Ed. *One Thousand Years: Western Europe in the Middle Ages.* Boston: Houghton Mifflin, 1974.

Erickson, Carolly. *The Medieval Vision.* New York: Oxford University Press, 1976.

Evans, Joan, Ed. *The Flowering of the Middle Ages.* London: Thames and Hudson, 1966.

Gilson, Etienne. *Reason and Revelation in the Middle Ages.* New York: Scribner's, 1966.

———. *The Spirit of Medieval Philosophy.* New York: Scribner's, 1940. These two volumes are both general studies by the greatest historian of medieval philosophy.

Heer, Friedrich. *The Medieval World.* New York: Mentor Books, 1961.

Knowles, David. *The Evolution of Medieval Thought.* New York: Random House, 1962. The best single-volume discussion of medieval thought.

Leff, Gordon. *Medieval Thought: St. Augustine to Ockham.* Baltimore: Penguin, 1958.

Lewis, C. S. *The Discarded Image.* Cambridge: Cambridge University Press, 1964. Although written as an introduction to medieval and renaissance literature, this is a beautifully written introduction to medieval cosmology as well.

Morrall, John B. *The Medieval Imprint.* Baltimore: Penguin, 1970.

Pelikan, Jaroslav. *The Christian Tradition 1 The Emergence of the Catholic Tradition (100–600).* Chicago: University of Chicago Press, 1971.

———. *The Christian Tradition 2 The Spirit of Eastern Christendom (600–1700).* Chicago: University of Chicago Press, 1974.

———. *The Christian Tradition 3 The Growth of Medieval Theology (600–1300).* Chicago: University of Chicago Press, 1978. These three volumes, together with the fourth volume when published (covering 1300–1700), are important studies in the development of Christian doctrine.

Rice, David Talbot, Ed. *The Dark Ages.* London: Thames and Hudson, 1965.

Southern, R. W. *The Making of the Middle Ages.* New Haven: Yale University Press, 1953.

———. *Western Society and the Church in the Middle Ages.* Baltimore: Penguin, 1970.

Strayer, Joseph R. *On the Medieval Origins of the Modern State.* Princeton: Princeton University Press, 1970.

Taylor, H. O. *The Medieval Mind,* 2 volumes, 4th ed. New York: Macmillan, 1925.

Ullmann, Walter. *Medieval Political Thought* (formerly *A History of Political Thought: The Middle Ages*). Baltimore: Penguin, 1970.

White, Lynn, Jr. *Medieval Technology and Social Change.* New York: Oxford University Press, 1966.

Wolff, Philippe. *The Awakening of Europe.* Baltimore: Penguin, 1968.

Wood, Charles T. *The Quest for Eternity: Medieval Manners and Morals.* Garden City: Doubleday, 1971.

B. *The following works are also comprehensive in scope, but from the standpoint of a single discipline or point of view.*

Auerbach, Erich. *Mimesis: The Representation of Reality in Western Literature.* Princeton: Princeton University Press, 1953. One of the most influential books of literary criticism ever written, it is also a penetrating study of the relationship between literature and culture, describing the concept of "reality" that undergirds works from Homer to the twentieth century. Six chapters deal explicitly with the Middle Ages.

Boswell, John. *Christianity, Social Tolerance, and Homosexuality.* Chicago: University of Chicago Press, 1980.

Cipolla, Carlo, Ed. *The Fontana Economic History of Europe: The Middle Ages.* London: Fontana, 1972.

Crombie, A. C. *Medieval and Early Modern Science,* 2 volumes. Garden City: Doubleday, 1959.

Curtius, Ernst R. *European Literature and the Latin Middle Ages.* Princeton: Princeton University Press, 1953. Traces, with exceptional scholarly precision, the continuity of literary commonplaces, or "topoi," from antiquity through the Middle Ages.

Friedman, John Block. *The Monstrous Races in Medieval Art and Thought.* Cambridge: Harvard University Press, 1981.

Jackson, W. T. H. *The Literature of the Middle Ages.* New York: Columbia University Press, 1960.

Kantorowicz, Ernst. *The King's Two Bodies.* Princeton: Princeton University Press, 1957.

Katzenellenbogen, Adolf. *Allegories of the Virtues and Vices in the Middle Ages*. New York: W. W. Norton, 1964.

Lackner, Bede, Ed. *Essays on Medieval Civilization*. Austin: University of Texas Press, 1978.

Lord, Albert B. *The Singer of Tales*. New York: Atheneum, 1965.

Murray, Alexander. *Reason and Society in the Middle Ages*. New York: Oxford University Press, 1978. More oriented toward social history than intellectual history.

Panofsky, Erwin. *Renaissance and Renascences in Western Art*. New York: Harper and Row, 1969.

Pounds, N. J. G. *An Economic History of Medieval Europe*. New York: Longman, 1974.

Power, Eileen. *Medieval Women*, ed. M. M. Postan. Cambridge: Cambridge University Press, 1975.

Raby, F. J. E. *A History of Christian Latin Poetry from the Beginnings to the Close of the Middle Ages*. Oxford: Oxford University Press, 1927.

————. *A History of Secular Latin Poetry in the Middle Ages*, 2 volumes. Oxford: Oxford University Press, 1934.

Russell, J. B. *A History of Medieval Christianity: Prophecy and Order*. New York: Crowell, 1968.

Scholes, Robert and Kellogg, Robert. *The Nature of Narrative*. Oxford: Oxford University Press, 1966.

Seay, Albert. *Music in the Medieval World*. Englewood Cliffs, N.J.: Prentice-Hall, 1965.

Shapiro, Meyer. *Late Antique, Early Christian, and Mediaeval Art*. New York: Braziller, 1979.

Smalley, Beryl. *Historians of the Middle Ages*. London: Thames and Hudson, 1974.

Ullmann, Walter. *The Growth of Papal Government in the Middle Ages*. London: Methuen, 1955.

————. *A Short History of the Papacy in the Middle Ages*. London: Methuen, 1972.

Wolff, Philippe, *Western Languages* A.D. *100–1500*. New York: McGraw-Hill, 1971.

Zacour, Norman. *An Introduction to Medieval Institutions*, 2nd ed. New York: St. Martin's Press, 1976.

C. Periodicals

Much of the important scholarly work done on the Middle Ages appears in articles published in journals rather than in booklength studies. We list a few of the most important periodicals that deal exclusively with the Middle Ages, but it is equally important to remember that most of the important journals in literature, philosophy, history, theology and religion, church history, music, and art are all likely to include medieval subjects. In fact, literally hundreds of periodicals touch upon medieval subjects. *Variorum Reprints* is a series of volumes containing collected articles by distinguished medievalists such as Brian Tierney and David Herlihy.

Speculum, Traditio, Medium Aevum, Mediaevalia et Humanistica, Medieval Studies, Viator, and *Journal of Medieval History* are among the most important medieval journals published in English. Foreign journals often have articles published in English as well.

Publication of the Modern Languages Association (PMLA) publishes a yearly bibliography of all work done in literature; *Revue d'histoire ecclésiastique* publishes a comprehensive bibliography on all subjects related to theology and religion.

D. Works on Specific Subjects

These deal in more detail with subjects covered in each of the chapters, as well as with aspects of the Middle Ages not covered explicitly in the book, especially social and economic history. Perhaps a reminder is needed that these secondary sources should not be looked upon as a substitute for primary sources. Peter Brown's masterful biography of Augustine will be of most use to a student who has already read some Augustine, or to a student looking for a guide to the available writings of Augustine. Another reminder that may prove useful is that often the best summary of a figure or topic is to be found in the introduction to primary sources. For example, the volume on the twelfth-century mystical writer Richard of St. Victor, in the *Classics of Western Spirituality* series, is an excellent introduction to the mystical tradition.

1. THE BIBLE

Ackroyd, P. R. and Evans, C. F., Eds. *The Cambridge History of the Bible*, vol. 1. *From the Beginnings to Jerome*. Cambridge: Cambridge University Press, 1970.

Alter, Robert. *The Art of Biblical Narrative*. New York: Basic Books, 1981.

The Anchor Bible. Garden City: Doubleday. A 44-volume commentary, many volumes of which have already been published.

Brown, Raymond et al., Eds. *The Jerome Biblical Commentary.* Englewood Cliffs, N.J.: Prentice-Hall, 1968.

Bruce, F. F. *Paul: Apostle of the Heart Set Free.* Grand Rapids, Mich.: Eerdmans, 1979.

de Lubac, Henri. *Exégèse Médiévale: Les quatres sens de l'écriture,* 2 volumes in 4. Paris: Aubier, 1959–64. Although this magisterial work has not yet been translated into English, it is important to be mentioned both as the most significant guide to the Bible in the Middle Ages and as one of the outstanding studies ever written on medieval culture.

de Vaux, Roland. *Ancient Israel,* 2 volumes. New York: McGraw-Hill, 1961.

Fowler, David. *The Bible in Early English Literature.* Seattle: The University of Washington Press, 1976.

Harvey, A. E. *Companion to the New Testament.* New York: Oxford University Press, 1970.

Jeremias, Joachim. *Jerusalem in the Time of Jesus.* Philadelphia: Fortress Press, 1969.

Lampe, G. W. H., Ed. *The Cambridge History of the Bible,* vol. 2. *The West from the Fathers to the Reformation.* Cambridge: Cambridge University Press, 1969.

Laymon, Charles M., Ed. *The Interpreter's One Volume Commentary on the Bible.* Nashville: Abingdon Press, 1971.

Noth, Martin. *The History of Israel,* rev. ed. New York: Harper and Row, 1960.

Smalley, Beryl. *The Study of the Bible in the Middle Ages.* Notre Dame: University of Notre Dame Press, 1964.

von Rad, Gerhard. *The Message of the Prophets.* New York: Harper and Row, 1962.

2. THE CLASSICAL HERITAGE

Africa, Thomas W. *Rome of the Caesars.* New York: Wiley, 1965.

Bailey, Cyril, Ed. *The Legacy of Rome.* Oxford: The Clarendon Press, 1923.

Bolgar, R. R. *The Classical Heritage.* New York: Harper and Row, 1964.

Clarke, M. L. *The Roman Mind.* New York: Norton, 1968.

Cochrane, C. W. *Christianity and Classical Culture.* Oxford: The Clarendon Press, 1940. A standard study of the subject.

Dodds, E. R. *Pagan and Christian in an Age of Anxiety.* New York: Norton (rpt.), 1970.

Guthrie, W. K. C. *The Greek Philosophers.* New York: Harper and Row (rpt.), 1960.

Klibansky, R. *The Continuity of the Platonic Tradition in the Middle Ages.* London, 1939.

Laistner, M. L. W. *Christianity and Pagan Culture in the Later Roman Empire.* Ithaca: Cornell University Press, 1951.

Marrou, H. I. *A History of Education in Antiquity.* New York: Sheed and Ward, 1956.

Mattingly, Harold. *Roman Imperial Civilization.* New York: W. W. Norton, 1957.

Reynolds, L. D. and Wilson, N. C. *Scribes and Scholars: A Guide to the Transmission of Greek and Latin Literature*, 2nd ed. Oxford: The Clarendon Press, 1974.

Seznec, Jean. *The Survival of the Pagan Gods.* Princeton: Princeton University Press, 1954.

Syme, Ronald. *The Roman Revolution.* New York: Oxford University Press, 1939.

Van Steenberghen, Fernand. *Aristotle in the West: The Origins of Latin Aristotelianism.* Louvain: Nauwelaerts, 1970.

Watson, Alan. *The Law of the Ancient Romans.* Dallas: Southern Methodist University Press, 1970.

3. EARLY CHRISTIANITY

Chadwick, Henry. *The Early Church.* Baltimore: Penguin, 1967.

Daniélou, Jean. *The Bible and the Liturgy.* Notre Dame: University of Notre Dame Press, 1956.

Delehaye, Hippolyte. *The Legends of the Saints.* Notre Dame: University of Notre Dame Press, 1961.

Grabar, André. *Christian Iconography: A Study of Its Origins.* Princeton: Princeton University Press, 1968.

Jaeger, Werner. *Early Christianity and Greek Paideia.* Oxford: Oxford University Press, 1961.

Jones, A. H. M. *Constantine and the Conversion of Europe.* Baltimore: Penguin (rpt.), 1972.

Jungmann, Joseph. *The Early Liturgy.* Notre Dame: University of Notre Dame Press, 1959.

4. THE LATIN FATHERS: JEROME AND AUGUSTINE

Brown, Peter. *Augustine of Hippo.* Berkeley: University of California Press, 1967. This masterful biography is also an excellent guide to the writings of Augustine in English.

Copleston, F. C. *A History of Philosophy*, vol. 2, *Medieval Philosophy, Part I: Augustine to Bonaventure.* Garden City: Doubleday, 1962.

Emmerson, Richard K. *Antichrist in the Middle Ages: A Study of Medieval Apocalypticism, Art and Literature.* Seattle: University of Washington Press, 1981.

Gilson, Etienne. *The Christian Philosophy of St. Augustine.* New York: Random House, 1960.

Kelly, J. N. D. *Jerome: His Life, Writings and Controversies.* New York: Harper and Row, 1975.

Ladner, Gerhart B. *The Idea of Reform.* New York: Harper and Row (rpt.), 1967.

Sumption, Jonathan. *Pilgrimage: An Image of Mediaeval Religion.* London: Faber and Faber, 1975.

Turner, Victor and Turner, Edith. *Image and Pilgrimage in Christian Culture.* New York: Columbia University Press, 1978.

5. The Transition from Ancient to Medieval

Auerbach, Erich. *Literary Language and Its Public in Late Antiquity and in the Middle Ages.* Princeton: Princeton University Press, 1965.

Bark, William C. *Origins of the Medieval World.* Garden City: Doubleday, 1958.

Bowder, Diana. *The Age of Constantine and Julian.* New York: Barnes and Noble, 1978.

Brown, Peter. *The Making of Late Antiquity.* Cambridge: Harvard University Press, 1978.

————. *The World of Late Antiquity* A.D. *150–750.* New York: Harcourt, Brace and Jovanovich, 1971.

Burns, Thomas. *The Ostrogoths: Kingship and Society.* Wiesbaden: Franz Steiner, 1980.

Dawson, Christopher. *The Making of Europe.* New York: Meridian Books, 1956.

Duckett, Eleanor S. *The Gateway to the Middle Ages*, 3 volumes. Ann Arbor: University of Michigan Press, 1961.

Ellis Davidson, H. R. *Gods and Myths of Northern Europe.* Baltimore: Penguin, 1964.

Goffart, Walter. *Barbarians and Romans* A.D. *418–584: The Techniques of Accommodation.* Princeton: Princeton University Press, 1980.

Hodgkin, Thomas. *Italy and Her Invaders 376–814*, 8 volumes. New York: Russell and Russell (rpt.), 1967.

King, P. D. *Law and Society in the Visigothic Kingdom.* Cambridge: Cambridge University Press, 1972.

Knowles, David. *The English Mystical Tradition.* New York: Harper and Row, 1961.

Lewis, Archibald R. *Emerging Medieval Europe* A.D. *400–1000.* New York: Knopf, 1967.

Llewellyn, Peter, *Rome in the Dark Ages.* New York: Praeger, 1970.

Lyon, Bryce. *The Origins of the Middle Ages: Pirenne's Challenge to Gibbon.* New York: Norton, 1972.

MacMullen, Ramsey. *Constantine.* New York: Harper and Row, 1969.

Mathew, Gervase. *Byzantine Aesthetics.* New York: Harper and Row, 1963.

Musset, Lucien. *The Germanic Invasions.* University Park: Pennsylvania State University Press, 1975.

O'Donnell, James J. *Cassiodorus.* Berkeley: University of California Press, 1979.

Patch, Howard R. *The Goddess Fortuna in Medieval Literature.* New York: Octagon (rpt.), 1967.

Rand, E. K. *Founders of the Middle Ages.* Cambridge: Harvard University Press, 1928.

Richards, Jeffrey. *Consul of God: The Life and Times of Gregory the Great.* London: Routledge and Kegan Paul, 1980.

———. *The Popes and the Papacy in the Early Middle Ages.* Routledge and Kegan Paul, 1979.

Riché, Pierre. *Education and Culture in the Barbarian West.* Columbia: University of South Carolina Press, 1976.

Runciman, Steven. *Byzantine Civilization.* New York: Meridian, 1956.

von Simson, Otto. *The Gothic Cathedral.* New York: Harper and Row, 1956. Although the main theme of this work deals with the high Middle Ages, it also contains an extremely valuable discussion of the influence of Pseudo-Dionysius on medieval thought.

Wallace-Hadrill, J. M. *The Barbarian West*, rev. ed. New York: Harper and Row, 1962.

———. *The Long-Haired Kings.* New York: Barnes and Noble, 1962.

White, Lynn, Jr., Ed. *Transformations of the Roman World.* Berkeley: University of California Press, 1966.

Wickham, Chris. *Early Medieval Italy.* London: Macmillan, 1981.

6. MONASTICISM

Brooke, Christopher. *The Monastic World 1000–1300*. New York: Random House, 1974. Lavish photographs and a readable text makes this a good introduction to monasticism.

Chadwick, Owen. *John Cassian*, 2nd ed. Cambridge: Cambridge University Press, 1968.

Chitty, Derwas. *The Desert a City*. London: Mowbrays, 1966.

Knowles, David. *Christian Monasticism*. London: Weidenfeld and Nicholson, 1969.

———. *The Monastic Order in England*, 2nd ed. Cambridge: Cambridge University Press, 1963.

———. *The Religious Orders in England*, 3 volumes. Cambridge: Cambridge University Press, 1948–59.

Leclercq, Jean. *The Love of Learning and the Desire for God*. New York: Fordham University Press, 1974. A masterful summary of monastic culture, beginning with the heritage of the fathers and antiquity and culminating in the twelfth century. The best single book on the monastic experience.

Rousseau, Philip. *Ascetics, Authority, and the Church in the Age of Jerome and Cassian*. New York: Oxford University Press, 1978.

Ryan, John. *Irish Monasticism*. Ithaca: Cornell University Press (rpt.), 1972.

Zarnecki, George. *The Monastic Achievement*. New York: McGraw-Hill, 1972.

7. THE CAROLINGIAN EMPIRE AND ITS AFTERMATH

Barraclough, Geoffrey. *The Crucible of Europe*. Berkeley: University of California Press, 1976.

Bloch, Marc. *Feudal Society*, 2 volumes. Chicago: University of Chicago Press, 1961. The standard treatment by one of the great historians of the twentieth century.

Boussard, Jacques. *The Civilization of Charlemagne*. New York: McGraw-Hill, 1968.

Bowsky, William. *A Medieval Italian Commune: Siena under the Nine, 1287–1355*. Berkeley: University of California Press, 1981.

Duby, Georges. *The Early Growth of the European Economy*. Ithaca: Cornell University Press, 1974.

Duckett, Eleanor Shipley. *Carolingian Portraits: A Study of the Ninth Century*. Ann Arbor: University of Michigan Press, 1962.

Fichtenau, Heinrich. *The Carolingian Empire: The Age of Charlemagne.* New York: Harper and Row, 1957.

Folz, Robert. *The Concept of Empire in Western Europe from the Fifth to the Fourteenth Century.* London: Arnold, 1969.

———. *The Coronation of Charlemagne: 25 December 800.* London: Routledge and Kegan Paul, 1974.

Geary, Patrick. *Sacra Furta: Thefts of Relics in the Central Middle Ages.* Princeton: Princeton University Press, 1978.

Hardison, O. B. *Christian Rite and Christian Drama in the Middle Ages.* Baltimore: The Johns Hopkins University Press, 1965.

Henderson, George. *Early Medieval.* Baltimore: Penguin, 1972.

Laistner, M. L. W. *Thought and Letters in Western Europe,* A.D. *500–900.* Ithaca: Cornell University Press, 1957.

Lopez, Robert. *The Commercial Revolution of the Middle Ages, 950–1350.* Englewood Cliffs, N.J.: Prentice-Hall, 1971.

Martines, Lauro. *Power and Imagination: City-States in Renaissance Italy.* New York: Knopf, 1979. The first section of this book is an excellent discussion of the development of cities in medieval Italy.

Pirenne, Henri. *Medieval Cities.* Princeton: Princeton University Press, 1925.

———. *Mohammed and Charlemagne.* New York: Meridian, 1957.

Rörig, Fritz. *The Medieval Town.* Berkeley: University of California Press, 1971.

Stephenson, Carl. *Mediaeval Feudalism.* Ithaca: Cornell University Press, 1942.

Strayer, Joseph R. *Medieval Statecraft and the Perspectives of History.* Princeton: Princeton University Press, 1971.

8. Church, State, and Society

Boase, T. S. R. *Boniface VIII.* London: Constable and Company, 1933.

Brentano, Robert. *Rome Before Avignon.* New York: Basic Books, 1974.

Erdmann, Carl. *The Origin of the Idea of Crusade.* Princeton: Princeton University Press, 1977.

Evans, Joan. *Monastic Life at Cluny 910–1157.* New York: Anchor Books (rpt.), 1968.

Hallam, Elizabeth. *Capetian France 987–1328.* New York: Longman, 1980.

Hunt, Noreen, Ed. *Cluniac Monasticism.* London: Macmillan, 1971.

Kern, Fritz. *Kingship and Law in the Middle Ages.* New York: Harper and Row, 1956.

Lackner, Bede, O. Cist. *Eleventh-Century Background of Cîteaux.* Kalamazoo: Cistercian Publications, 1972.

Lekai, Louis, O. Cist. *The Cistercians: Ideals and Reality.* Kent, Ohio: Kent State University Press, 1977.

Morrison, Karl, Ed. *The Investiture Controversy.* New York: Holt, Rinehart, and Winston, 1971.

Runciman, Steven. *A History of the Crusades,* 3 volumes. New York: Harper and Row, 1951–54.

Setton, Kenneth, Ed. *The Crusades,* 5 volumes. Madison: University of Wisconsin Press, 1969ff.

Tellenbach, Gerd. *Church, State and Society at the Time of the Investiture Contest.* New York: Harper and Row, 1970.

Tierney, Brian. *The Crisis of Church and State 1050–1300.* Englewood Cliffs, N.J.: Prentice-Hall, 1964.

9. TWELFTH-CENTURY RENAISSANCE

Baldwin, John W. *The Scholastic Culture of the Middle Ages 1000–1300.* Lexington, Mass.: D. C. Heath, 1971.

Brooke, Christopher. *The Twelfth-Century Renaissance.* New York: Harcourt, Brace, Jovanovich, 1969.

Chenu, M.-D., O. P. *Nature, Man and Society in the Twelfth Century.* Chicago: University of Chicago Press, 1968.

―――. *Toward Understanding St. Thomas.* Chicago: Henry Regnery, 1964.

Clagett, Marshall et al., Eds. *Twelfth-Century Europe and the Foundations of Modern Society.* Madison: University of Wisconsin Press, 1966.

Clanchy, M. T. *From Memory to Written Record: England 1066–1307.* Cambridge: Harvard University Press, 1979.

Cobban, A. B. *The Medieval Universities.* London: Methuen, 1975.

Copleston, F. C. *A History of Philosophy,* vol. 2. *Medieval Philosophy, Part II: Albert the Great to Duns Scotus.* Garden City: Doubleday, 1962.

De Wulf, Maurice. *Philosophy and Civilization in the Middle Ages.* New York: Dover, 1953.

Duby, Georges. *The Europe of the Cathedrals, 1140–1280.* Cleveland: World, 1964.

―――. *Medieval Marriage: Two Models from Twelfth-Century France.* Baltimore: The Johns Hopkins University Press, 1978.

The two case studies presented are useful not only in terms of the subject but also as examples of historical method.

Gilson, Etienne. *Heloise and Abelard*. Ann Arbor: University of Michigan Press, 1960.

Haskins, Charles H. *The Renaissance of the Twelfth Century*. Cambridge: Harvard University Press, 1927.

————. *The Rise of Universities*. Ithaca: Cornell University Press (rpt.), 1957.

Henderson, George. *Gothic*. Baltimore: Penguin, 1967.

Kolve, V. A. *The Play Called Corpus Christi*. Stanford: Stanford University Press, 1966.

Künstler, Gustav, Ed. *Romanesque Art in Europe*. Greenwich, Conn.: New York Graphic Society, 1968.

Kuttner, Stephan. *Harmony from Dissonance*. Latrobe, Penn.: St. Vincent Archabbey, 1960.

Lewis, C. S. *The Allegory of Love*. Oxford: Oxford University Press, 1936. Though much of this book has subsequently come under question, it is a beautifully written introduction to courtly literature.

Mâle, Emile. *The Gothic Image: Religious Art in France of the Thirteenth Century*. New York: Harper and Row, 1958.

————. *Religious Art in France, the Twelfth Century: A Study of the Origins of Medieval Iconography*. Princeton: Princeton University Press, 1978.

Morris, Colin. *The Discovery of the Individual 1050–1200*. London: SPCK, 1972.

Packard, Sidney. *Twelfth-Century Europe: An Interpretive Essay*. Amherst: University of Massachusetts Press, 1973.

Painter, Sidney. *French Chivalry*. Ithaca: Cornell University Press, 1957.

Panofsky, Erwin. *Gothic Architecture and Scholasticism*. New York: World, 1957.

Pieper, Joseph. *Scholasticism: Personalities and Problems of Medieval Philosophy*. New York: McGraw-Hill, 1969.

Rashdall, Hastings. *The Universities of Europe in the Middle Ages*. Eds. F. M. Powicke and A. B. Emden, 3 volumes, 2nd ed. Oxford: The Clarendon Press, 1936.

Robertson, D. W., Jr. *A Preface to Chaucer*. Princeton: Princeton University Press, 1962. The title is misleading in that Chaucer is dealt with only indirectly. This is a stimulating and controversial study of medieval literary aesthetics.

Sauerländer, Willibald and Hirmer, Max. *Gothic Sculpture in France, 1140–1270.* New York: Harry Abrams, 1972.

Shapiro, Meyer. *Romanesque Art.* New York: Braziller, 1977.

Southern, R. W. *Medieval Humanism and Other Studies.* New York: Harper and Row, 1970.

————. *St. Anselm and His Biographer.* Cambridge: Cambridge University Press, 1966.

Tierney, Brian. *Foundations of the Conciliar Theory.* Cambridge: Cambridge University Press, 1955.

Ullmann, Walter, *Law and Politics in the Middle Ages.* London: The Sources of History Limited, 1975.

————. *Medieval Foundations of Renaissance Humanism.* Ithaca: Cornell University Press, 1977. Misleading title in that this work is more a study of the High Middle Ages than the Renaissance.

Vaughn, Richard. *Matthew Paris.* Cambridge: Cambridge University Press, 1958.

Wakefield, Walter L. *Heresy, Crusade, and Inquisition in Southern France, 1100–1250.* Berkeley: University of California Press, 1974.

Weisheipl, James, O. P. *Friar Thomas d'Aquino.* Garden City: Doubleday, 1974.

10. Francis of Assisi and the Mendicants

Bougerol, J. Guy. *Introduction to the Works of Bonaventure.* Paterson, N.J.: St. Anthony Guild Press, 1964.

Brooke, Rosalind. *Early Franciscan Government.* Cambridge: Cambridge University Press, 1959.

Daniel, E. R. *The Franciscan Concept of Mission in the Middle Ages.* Lexington: University of Kentucky Press, 1975.

Esser, Cajetan. *Origins of the Franciscan Order.* Chicago: Franciscan Herald Press, 1970.

Fleming, John V. *An Introduction to the Franciscan Literature of the Middle Ages.* Chicago: Franciscan Herald Press, 1977.

Fortini, Arnaldo. *Francis of Assisi.* New York: Crossroad, 1981.

Hinnebusch, William. *The History of the Dominican Order,* 2 volumes. New York: Alba House, 1966–73.

Jeffrey, David L. *The Early English Lyric and Franciscan Spirituality.* Lincoln: University of Nebraska Press, 1975.

Little, Lester K. *Religious Poverty and the Profit Economy in Medieval Europe.* Ithaca: Cornell University Press, 1978.

Moorman, John. *The Franciscans in England.* London: Mowbrays, 1974.

————. *A History of the Franciscan Order from its Origins to the Year 1517*. Oxford: The Clarendon Press, 1968.

Reeves, Marjorie. *The Influence of Prophecy in the Later Middle Ages*. Oxford: The Clarendon Press, 1969.

————. *Joachim of Fiore and the Prophetic Future*. New York: Harper and Row, 1976.

Tierney, Brian. *Origins of Papal Infallibility 1150–1300*. Leiden: Brill, 1972.

Vicaire, M.-H., O. P. *St. Dominic and His Times*. London: Darton, Longman, Todd, 1964.

Index

(Note: Page references in italics indicate illustration)

Aachen, *47,* 183, 196, 198
Abbey Church of Cluny, *228*
Abbey Church of St. Denis, 164
Abbey Church of Souillac, *213*
Abbey Church of Pontigny, *228*
Abelard, Peter, 240, 273
   conflict with Bernard of
      Clairvaux, 268–69
   writings
     History of My Misfortunes,
      267
     Sic et Non (Yes and No),
      267–68
Abraham, 23, *24*
Acts of the Apostles, 10, 14, 17–18,
   50–51, 53, 60–61, 159, 230
Adalbert, St., 203
Admonitio Generalis (Char-
   lemagne), 180–81, 186
Adrianople, Battle of, 118
Aelred of Rievaulx, 37
Aeneid (Vergil), 39–40, 45–46

Aeschylus, 36
Agrigento, *58*
Aix-la-Chapelle. *See* Aachen
Alanus, 284
Alan of Lille, 286
   Anticlaudianus, 287
   Complaint of Nature, 287
Albigensian Crusade, 236, 251
Albigensian heresy, 53, 313
   Crusade against, 236, 251
Alcuin of York, 134, 182, 185–88
Alexander the Great, 45
Alexander III, Pope, 229, 249–50
Alexandria, 57
Alfred the Great, King, 149, 202
allegory, biblical use of, 59
Alypius, 92–94
Amalfi, 220
Ambrose, St., 73–64, 81–82, 100, 123
Amiens Cathedral, *278,* 289
Amos, 7
Anastasius, Emperor, 128

Andrea, da Firenze, 46
Angles, 120
Anglo-Saxons, 135, 202, 204–5
  conquest of Britain, 120
  conversion of, 129, 131
Anselm, St., 267
  Why God Became Man, 265–66
Anthony of Padua, 314
Antichrist, 312
Anticlaudianus (Alan of Lille), 281
anti-Semitism, 235–26
  in early Christian writings, 51–52
Antony of the Desert, St., 91–92,
  166–70, 238
Apocalypse. *See* Revelation of St.
  John
Apocalypticism, 104, 312
Apocrypha. *See* Old Testament
Apollinaris, Sidonius, 126
apostolic succession, principle of,
  53–54, 56
Aquinas, Thomas, St., 34, 48, 255–
  56, 265, 269, 282, 314
  commentaries of, 272
  influence of Aristotle on, 33, 35
  philosophical system of, 372–75
  Platonic elements in, 36
  writings
    Summa Theologiae, 161, 271–
    72, 275–77
architecture, 164
  Gothic, *278–80*
  Gothic, and Scholasticism, 276–
  78
  Romanesque, *228, 246*
Ardo Smaragdus, 194
Arianism, 69–71, 129
Aristophanes, 36
Aristotle, *34*, 112, 119, 271, 318
  concept of the state, 255–56
  influence of, on the Middle Ages,
  30, 33, 35
  philosophy of, 32–33
  rediscovery of, 255, 272, 283
  scientific works of, 35
Arius, 68, 70. *See also* Arianism
Armenian Church, 78
Arthur, King, 120, 290
Arthurian romances, 287, 290
asceticism, 72, 167
Assyrians, 5

Athanasius, St., 91, 166
Athenogoras, Patriarch, 229
Athens, 30, 37
Attila, 118
Augustine, St., 18–20, 28, 30, 40, 52,
  59, 123, 132, 146, 160, 163, 168,
  187, 272
  analysis of St. Paul's epistles, 108–
  10
  conversion of, 81, 91–92, 94, 96–97
  death of, 81, 115
  influence of, on political theory
  of Middle Ages, 111
  opposition of, to Donatism, 68
  theory of history of, 103–6
  writings
    City of God, 82, 101, 103, 105–
    11, 187
    Confessions, 82, 90–94, 96–98,
    100–101, 276
    On Christian Doctrine, 82–88
Augustus, 41, *47*
Auerbach, Erich, 92, 94
Avars, 179–80
Averroës, 271
Avicenna, 271
Avignon, papacy in, 238, 317

Babylonians, 8
Bacon, Roger, 314
baptism, 22, 137
Basil, St., 169–70
Basques, 192
Baugulf, Abbot, 188
Bavarians, 179
Bayeux Tapestry, *204*
Bede, Venerable, 44, 133–35, 155
  *History of the English Church
  and People*, 132–34, 156
Benedict IX, Pope, 227
Benedict XI, Pope, 257
Benedict of Aniane, St., 194–96, 226
Benedict of Nursia, St., *172*
  Rule of, 6–7, 10, 109, 137, 147, 171,
  173–77, 195–96, 225–27, 238–40
Beowulf, 122, 125, 132, 135, 287–88
Berlinghieri, Bonaventura, *305, 307*
Bernard of Chartres, 103, 269–71,
  319
Bernard of Clairvaux, St., 60, 65, 82,
  146, 160, 234, 236–37, 286

on canon law, 247, 249
and the Cistercian Order, 240
conflict with Peter Abelard, 268–
    69
diatribe against the Cluniacs, 243–
    44
preaches Second Crusade, 234,
    236–37, 241
on the purpose of art, 245
sermons on Song of Songs, 240–
    43, 291
Bernart de Ventadorn, 292
Bernward of Hildesheim, 200
Bible. *See* New Testament; Old
    Testament
Bishop of Rome. *See* papacy
Boethius, 35, 121, 148, 263, 271–72
    Consolation of Philosophy,
        148–54
Bohemians, 203
Bologna, 283
    University of, 285–86
Bonaventure, St., 65, 160, 286, 294,
    296–97, 303, 312, 314
    Soul's Journey Into God, 160, 312
Boniface, St., 139–41, 147–48, 179
Boniface VIII, Pope, 258, 260
    Unam Sanctam (bull), 256–57
Britain, 119, 121
    Anglo-Saxon conquest of, 120
Bruno of Cologne, 238
bubonic plague, 317
Burgundians, 71, 120
Byzantium, 117–18
Byzantine civilization, 118–19

Caedmon, 135
Camaldolese Order, 238
Cambridge, University of, 286
Canaanites, 4
canonization, 63
    of St. Francis, 310
canon law, 45, 247, 249, 283–84
Canterbury Tales (Chaucer), 146,
    177, 214, 287, 315
"Canticle of Creatures" (St.
    Francis), 309–10
Capella, Martianus
    *Marriage of Mercury and
        Philology*, 154–55

Carloman, 180
Caroline miniscule, 187
Carolingian Renaissance, 180, 185,
    187–88, 199, 262
Carthusian Order, 238–39
Cassiodorus, 121, 155, 177
Cathar movement, 53, 251
cathedral, 222
    Gothic, and Scholasticism
        compared, 276–77, 282
Cathedral of Amiens, *278–80*
Cathedral of Angoulême, *193*
Cathedral of Autun, *230*
Cathedral of Chartres, *11*, 26, 155
Cathedral of Hildesheim, *200*
Cathedral of Reuns, *24, 281*
Cathedral of St. John in the
    Lateran, 73
cathedral schools, 186–87, 199, 245,
    267, 269, 285
Catherine of Alexandria, St., 66
Catullus, 36
Celestial Hierarchies (Pseudo-
    Dionysius), 160
Celtics, 115, 120
    Christianity of, 136
cenobitic monasticism, 169
chanson de geste, 192
Charlemagne, Emperor, 43, 46–47,
    120–21, 140–41, 165, 178, 205,
    225–26, 290–91
    concept of empire of, 179–81,
        184–5
    coronation of, 182–83
    educational reforms of, 180, 185–
        86
    efforts to preserve Germanic
        heritage, 190
    legends about, 191–92, 194
    liturgical reforms of, 187–89
    vassals of, 206–7
    and the Viking invasions, 199
    writings
        Admonitio Generalis, 180–81,
            186
Charles of Anjou, King of Sicily,
    253–54
Charles the Bald, King of the West
    Franks, 207
    coronation of, 196

Charter of Charity (Cistercian), 240
Chartres, 32
  Cathedral of, *11*, 26, 155
Chaucer, Geoffrey, 39, 43, 48, 65, 111, 138, 146, 149, 222, 318
  Canterbury Tales, 146, 177, 214, 287, 315
  Troilus and Criseyde, 149, 152, 282
Chrétien de Troyes, 287, 290
  Cligès, 289–90
  Erec and Enide, 288–89
  Lancelot, 290–91
  Percival, 290
  Yvain, 290
Christ, 6–8, *11*, 17, *27*, 41, 51, 55–56, 75, *89*, *102*, *144*, 163
  birth of, accounts of, 12–13
  crucifixion of, 14–15, 60
  feeding the five thousand, 16
  Last Supper of, 12, 14
  nature of, disputes concerning, 68–69, 75, 77
  as new Adam, 23
  as priest, 23–25
  and the principle of apostolic succession, 54, 56
  and St. Peter, 16–17
  second coming of, 22–23
  Sermon on the Mount, 13
  temptation of, 10
Christian communities, 17, 19
  ecclesiastical hierarchy in, 53–55
Christianity
  ascetic movement in, 72
  beginnings of, 50–53
  and the concept of extreme realism, 264–65
  and the concept of nominalism, 265
  establishment of, in England, 133, 135, 139
  and the Goths, 71
  Gnosticism and, 52–53
  imperial support for, 72, 74
  importance of women in, 21
  influence of Cicero on, 37–38
  influence of Ovid on, 42
  influence of Vergil on, 40–41
  mysticism in, 159–60

  and paganism, 56–60, 130–32, 291
  and the practice of infant baptism, 137
  See also Church; heresy; monasticism; papacy
Church
  anti-Semitism in, 51–52
  canon law of, 45, 247, 249, 283–84
  Donatist beliefs concerning, 68
  early, 17–18
  ecclesiastical hierarchy in, 53–56
  in England, 134
  glorification of violence by, 123
  impact of Arian heresy upon, 70–71
  Irish monasticism in, 135, 137–38
  Justinian Code applied to, 259
  Latin as language of, 48
  liturgical drama in, 287
  involvement of, in imperial coronations, 197–98
  persecution of, 60–64, 66
  political influence of, 73
  principle of apostolic succession and, 53–54, 56
  reform of, 226–27, 229
  role of the laity in, 251–52
  and the lord/vassal relationship, 209–10
  See also monasticism; papacy
Church of St. Austremoine, *89*
Church of Ste. Foi, *178*, *248*, 249
Church of St. Mary Magdalen, 157, *158*, 236, *246*
Church of St. Peter (Rome), 73
Church of St. Trophime, *27*
Church of San Biagio, *58*
Church of San Francesco (Assisi), *295*
Church of San Francesco (Piscea), *305*, *307*
Church of Santi Quattro Coronati, 76
Cicero, 36, 48, 88, 264
  and the Christian concept of natural law, 37
  style of, 37
Cimabue, *295*, 310
Cistercian Order, 196, *228*, 238–39
  Charter of Charity, 240
Cîteaux, 239

cities, 217
  as centers of intellectual activity, 286
  Italian, 220–22, *221*, 236
City of God (Augustine), 82, 101
city-states, 254
Clareno, Angelo, 312
Clare of Assisi, 298
Clement V, Pope, 256
Cligès (Chrétien de Troyes), 289–90
Clovis, King, 120, 128, 140
  conversion of, 129–30
Cluny, monastic reform movement at, 195, *225*, 226–27, *248*
Code of Justinian. *See* Justinian
Coimbra, University of, 286
Columbanus, St., 135–36
Commodus, Emperor, 116
common law, English, 45, 255, 283
communes, 219–20
Complaint of Nature (Alan of Lille), 287
conceptualism, 265
Concordat of Worms, 231, 252
Concord of Discordant Canons, A (Decretum) (Gratian), 283–85
Confessions (Augustine), 40, 82, 90–94, 96–98, 100–101
Conrad II, Emperor, 208
Consuetudines, Carthusian, 238
Consolation of Philosophy (Boethius), 135, 148–54
Constantine, 76, 116–18, 122
  baptism of, 70, 130
  condemns Donatism, 68
  conversion of, 67, 72, 74–75, 129
  Donation of, 75, 76, 180
  Edict of Milan of, 66–67
  summons First Ecumenical Council, 69
Constantinople, 46, 48, 117, 141, 220, 236
Conventual Franciscans, 311
Copernicus, 319
Coptic Church, 78
Corinthians, The First Epistle of Paul the Apostle to, 20–22
Corinthians, The Second Epistle of Paul the Apostle to, 159
Corpus Christi, feast of, 253

Cortes (Aragón), 260
Council of Chalcedon, 55, 77
courtesy, ideal of, 288
Crusade, Albigensian, 236
Crusade, First, 4, 232–36
Crusade, Fourth, 235
Crusade, Second, 234, 236–37, 241
Crusade, Third, 234–35
Crusades, 4, 123
  anti-Semitism of, 235–36
  brutality of, 234
  and the concept of holy war, 232
  effects of, 235–37
  against heretics, 236
  impact on literature, 236–37
  theology of, 237
Cyprian, 79

Dacia, 200
Damasus I, Pope, 79
Daniel, 7
Dante Alighieri, 28, 36, 43, 46, 48, 75, 97–98, 104, 138, 146, 222, 244, 318
  influence of Aristotle on, 33
  influence of Vergil on, 39
  writings
    Divine Comedy, 104, 149, 160, 282, 287; "Inferno," 33, 97; "Paradiso," 156, 164, 315
    On World Government, 39, 46, 258–59
David, King, 5, 8, *102*
  psalms of, 6–7, *102*
Dares, 36
Decius, Emperor, persecution of Christians by, 63–64, 66
Decline and Fall of the Roman Empire, The (Gibbon), 116
Decretum (Gratian), 283–85
Defense of the Mendicants (Bonaventure), 312
De Monarchia (Dante), 39, 46
Deuteronomy, 4
diaconate, 53
Dialogues (Gregory the Great), 147
Dictys, 36
Diocletian, Emperor, 116–17
  persecution of the Christians by, 66–67

Dionysius the Areopagite, 159
Divine Comedy (Dante), 104, 149, 160, 282, 287
Divine Names (Pseudo-Dionysius), 161–63
Dominican Order, 60, 251, 254, 131–14
Dominic, St., 313. *See also* Dominican Order
Donation of Constantine, 76, 180
Donation of Pepin, 180, 226
Donatism, 67–68
Donatus, 67
"Dream of Scipio, The" (Cicero), 37–39
"Dream of the Rood, The," 125

East Franks, 196–97, 199, 203–9
ecclesiastical courts, 247, 249
Ecclesiasticus (Wisdom of Jesus Son of Sirach), 7
Eclogues (Vergil), 40
Ecumenical Council, First 69
Ecumenical Council, Fourth, 55, 75, 77
Ecumenical Council, Second, 70
Ecumenical Council, Third, 75, 77
Edict of Milan, 66–67
Edward I, King, 254–55
Edward the Confessor, 203–4
Einhard, 43, 182, 187, 190–91, 199, 202
Elizabeth I, Queen, 149
England
    common law of, 45, 255, 283
    conversion to Christianity of, 133–34
    "feudalization" of, 209, 211
    Latin culture in, 134–35
    Norman conquest of, 133, 203–5
    and the papacy, 133–34
    Viking invasions of, 202
    yule log ceremony in, 132
Erec and Enide (Chrétien de Troyes), 288–89
eremitical monasticism, 169
Estates General, 260
Ethelbert of Kent, King, 133, 135, 156
Etymologies (Isidore of Seville), 156–57

Eucharist, 12
Euclid, 271
Euripides, 36
Eusebius, 187
Eustace, St., *65*
excommunication, 229
Exodus, 4, 88
extreme realism, 264–65
Ezekiel, 7, 26, 145
Ezra, 5

fealty, ceremony of, 211–12
Felix, Bishop, 66–67
feudalism, 122, 209, 215
"feudal system," 209, 216
fief
    defined, 206–7
    inheritability of, 208
Flanders, 211
Formosus, Pope, 226
Four Books of Sentences (Lombard), 269
Franciscan Order, 60, 251, 254, 310–11
    influence of, 313
    Spirituals and Conventionals within, 311–12 *See also* Francis of Assisi, St.
Francis of Assisi, St., 138, *295, 305, 314, 319*
    attitude toward money and poverty, 299–302
    biographies of, 294, 296–97
    canonization of, 310
    founds Franciscan Order, 298
    love of nature of, 3–4, 306–10
    Rule of, 301–2, 311–12
    sermon to the birds, 306, *307*
    stigmata of, 303–4, *305*
    writings
        "Canticle of Creatures," 309–10
        "Last Testament," 302–3
Franks, 120, 127–28, 140–41, 148, 209
    conversion of, 129–30
    and the papacy, 140–41, 179–80
Frederick I, Barbarossa, Emperor, 215, 221–22, 234, 249, 254, 283
Frederick II, Emperor, 253
Friar's Tale (Chaucer), 315
Fulbert of Chartres, Bishop, 210–11

Fulcher of Chartres, 233
Fulda, monastery of, 188

Galatians, 22
Galbert of Bruges, 211, 216
Gallican rite, 187–88
Gaul, 120, 135, 271
  Viking raids on, 199, 202
General Prologue to the Canterbury Tales (Chaucer), 146
Genesis, 4
  Augustine's explication of, 90
Gentiles, 51
Geoffrey of Monmouth, 44, 290
George, St., 123
Gerald of Aurillac, 212
Gerard of Borgo San Donnino, 312
Gerbert of Aurillac. *See* Sylvester II, Pope
Germans, 115–17, 135, 140, 148
  art, 125
  conversion of, to Christianity, 129–30
  cruelty of, 127–28
  culture and society of, 119–23
  invasions of, 118–19, 126
  language of, 125
  law of, 123–25
  mythology of, 125
Gibbon, Edward, 116
Giotto, 310, 318
Gnosticism, 52–53
Golden Epistle (William of St. Thierry), 238
Golden Legend, 95, 157, 159–60
Gospels, 8, 10, 12–17. *See also individual gospels*
Gothic Architecture and Scholasticism (Panofsky), 276
Gothic Cathedral, The (von Simson), 164
Gothic style, 278–81, 288–89
Goths, 71, 106, 118
Granada, 119
Grande Chartreuse, La, monastery, 238–39
Gratian, 247
  Concord of Discordant Canons, A (Decretum), 283–85
Greece, 29
  influence of, on Middle Ages, 36

Greenland, 203
Gregorian chant, 147
Gregorian rite. *See* Roman rite
Gregory I, the Great, Pope, 6, 135, 176, 180, 319
  admonition on conversion, of, 139–40
  and the claim of universal papal jurisdiction, 142
  codification of liturgy and music by, 147
  on paganism and Christianity, 131–32
  reform of papacy of, 227
  on the use of art in Christian instruction, 143
  writings
    Dialogues, 147, 171, 173
    Moralia on Job, 146–47
    Pastoral Care, 143–46
Gregory II, Pope, 147–48
Gregory VI, Pope, 227
Gregory VII, Pope, 227, 229, 231–32
Gregory IX, Pope, 301, 310
Gregory of Nyssa, 159
Gregory of Tours, 44, 71, 127, 129–30, 148
  History of the Franks, 155–56
Guibert de Nogent, Abbot, 219–20, 267
Guigo, Fifth Prior of La Grande Chartreuse, 239
Guillaume de Lorris, 287

Habakkuk, 7
Haggai, 7
hagiography, 64–66, 94
Harold, King, 203
Hebrews, 3
  exile of, 5
  monarchy of, 4
Hebrews, Epistle to the, 23–25
Henry II, King, 204, 249, 254–55, 283
Henry III, Emperor, 227
heresy
  Albigensian, 236, 251, 313
  Arian, 69–71
  Cathar, 53, 251
  Donatist, 67–68, 231

Herod, King, 12–13
Herodotus, 30, 36, 49
Hildebrand. *See* Gregory VII, Pope
Hildibert of Mainz, Archbishop, 197
History of My Misfortunes (Abelard), 267
History of the English Church and People (Bede), 156
History of the Franks (Gregory of Tours), 155–56
History of the Kings of Britain (Gregory of Monmouth), 290
Holy Roman Empire, 46, 48, 260
   revival of, 254
homage, ceremony of, 211–12
Homer, 36, 39
Horace, 36
Hosea, 7, 145
Hugh Capet, 199
Hugh of St. Victor, 160
Hugh the Great, Abbot, 227
Hugolino, Cardinal. *See* Gregory IX, Pope
Huguccio of Pisa, 285
Humbert, Cardinal, 68, 229, 231
Hundred Years War, 106, 205, 317
Huns, 118
Hus, John, 75

Iceland, 203
iconoclasm, 148
Ignatius, St., 52, 54
   martyrdom of, 62
Iliad, (Homer), 36, 39
Inferno (Dante), 33, 97
Innocent III, Pope, 235, 298
   and the Crusade against the Albigensian heretics, 236
   reforms of, 251–52
   and the theory of papal supremacy, 250–51
Innocent IV, Pope, 285
Institutes (John Cassian), 170–71
Ireland
   monasticism in, 135, 137, 177
   penitential system in, 137–38
Irenaeus, St., Bishop of Lyons, 55
Isaiah, 7–8, 49, 145
Isidore of Seville, St., *Etymologies*, 156–58

Islam, 119. *See also* Moslems
Isocrates, 155
Italy, cities of, 220–22, *221*

Jacobite Church (Syria), 78
Jacobus de Voragine, 64
James, St., martyrdom of, 61
James, the Epistle of, 10
Jean de Meun, 43, 48, 149, 287
Jeremiah, 7–8, 49
Jerome, St., 3, 58–59, 187, 267
   on the relationship between classical writings and Scripture, 80–81
   as translator of Scripture, 79–80
Jerusalem, 234
Jesus. *See* Christ
Joachim of Fiore, 311–12
Job, 6, 212
   Gregory the Great's exegesis on, 146–47
Joel, 7
John, King, 216, 255
John XII, Pope, 198
John, St., 25–26
John, The Epistles of, 10
John, The Gospel of St., 10, 14–16, 163
   "bread of life" passage, 15–16
   parable of Christ as the Good Shepherd, 15, *102*, *144*
   and St. Peter, 17
   themes of, 14–15
John the Baptist, 8
John Cassian, St., 169–71
   Institutes, 170–71
John Gerson, 265
John of Paris, 258
John of Parma, 312
John of Salisbury, 269–70, 285
Jonah, 7, 135
Joshua, 4
Josias, King, 180
Judah, kingdom of, 8
Judaism, and Christianity, 51–52
Jude, The Epistle of St., 10
Judges, 4
Julian the Apostate, Emperor, 72
jurisprudence, Roman, 44
jury system, 124

Justinian, Emperor, 45, 118–19, 121, 141
  Code of, 45, 259, 282–84
Justin Martyr, 56
Jutes, 120

Kings, First Book of, 4
Kings, Fourth Book of, 5
Kings, Second Book of, 4, 180
Kings, Third Book of, 5
Knowles, David, 30

Lancelot (Chrétien de Troyes), 290–91
language, Latin, influence of, on Middle Ages, 48
Laon, 219–20
Last Supper, 12, 14
Lateran Council, Fourth, 251–52, 260
law
  canon, 247, 249, 283–84
  common, English, 45, 255, 283
  Germanic, 123
  Justinian Code, 45, 259, 282–84
  Roman, 45, 256, 259–60, 282
  Roman and Germanic, compared, 123–25
Lawrence, St., martyrdom of, 64
Lazarus, 200
Lechfeld, battle of, 203
Leclercq, Jean, 247
Leo I, the Great, Pope, 55–56, 77, 142
Leo III, Emperor, 148
Leo III, Pope, 181–82
Leo IX, Pope, 231
  reforms of, 227, 229
leprosy, 130
Leviticus, 4
liberal arts, 155, 187, 285–86
Life of St. Francis (Bonaventure), 312
Life of St. Godric, 217–18
literature
  effect of Crusades on, 236–37
  Roman, influence of, on Middle Ages, 44–45
  Scholastic elements in, 282
Little Flowers, 306
Livy, 36, 43, 187

London, 222
Lombard, Peter, 272
  Four Books of Sentences, 269, 284
Lombards, 71, 121, 129, 142, 148, 179–80
lord, defined, 206
lordship, 208–9, 212, 214–16
Lorenzetti, Ambrogio, *172*
Lothar, Emperor, *47*, 196
Lotharingia, 196
Louis VII, King, 234, 254
Louis IX, King, 235, 254
Louis the German, King of the East Franks, 207
Louis the Pious, Emperor, 183–84, 199, 202, 205
  monastic reforms of, 194–95
  reign of, 196
Louis of Toulouse, 314
Love of Learning and the Desire for God, The (Leclercq), 247
Lucan, 36
Lucy, St., 66
Luke, St., 26, 60
Luke, The Gospel of St., 10, 12
  nativity narrative, 13
  and St. Peter, 17
  themes of, 13–14
Luther Martin, 244, 318
lyric forms, 292–93
lyric poetry, 286

Maccabees, First and Second Books of, 5
Maccabaeus, Judas, 5
Macrobius, 37–38
Magyars, 203
Malachi, 7
Mâle, Emile, 82
Mani (Gnostic teacher), 53
Manichees, 52, 100–101
Marcus Aurelius, Emperor, 117
Margaret, St., 66
Mark, St., 26
Mark, The Gospel of St., 10, 12
Marriage of Mercury and Philology (Martianus Capella), 154–55
Martel, Charles, 120
Martin of Tours, St., 123

martyrs, Christian, 60–64, *65*, 66, *99*
Mary, mother of Christ, 13, 77
Matthew, The Gospel of St., 8, 10, 12–13, 26, 55–56, 189
  nativity narrative, 12–13
  add St. Peter, 16–17
Maxentius, 67
Melchizedek (priest-king), 23, *24*, 25
Menander, 36
mendicant orders. *See* Dominican Order; Franciscan Order
Meno (Plato), 32
Merovingian dynasty, 120, 128, 184
Metamorphoses (Ovid), 41–42
metaphor, use of, in Psalms, 9–10
Michael Kerularios, 229
Micah, 7
Milvian Bridge, Battle of, 117
Mimesis (Auerbach), 92
Mirror of Perfection, 301
monasteries, 136–37, 225
  as centers of learning, 177–78
  Louis the Pious' reforms of, 194–95
  rules of, 171
  schools in, 186–87, 285
  at Cluny, *225*, 226
  at Fulda, 188
  Grande Chartreuse, La, 238–39
  at Monte Cassino, 173, 175–77, 226–27
  of St. Benôit-sur-Loire, *281*
  at St. Gall, 188
  of St. Philibert, 200
  of St. Remigius, 229
  at Vivarium, 177
monasticism, 135
  beginnings of, 166
  Carthusian, 238–39
  cenobitic, 169
  Cistercian, 238–40
  Cluniac, 226–27, 238
  decline of, 195
  eremitical, 169
  Irish, 135, 137, 177
  reform of, 226–26
  and the Rule of St. Benedict, 171, 173–77
  and scholarship, 177–78
monk(s)
  activities of, 174–75

Cluniac, 226–27, 229
  discipline of, 168–70
  sacrifices of, 170
  as scholar, 177
  vows taken by, 173–74
Monophysites, 75, 77–78
Monte Cassino, monastery at, 173, 175–77, 226–27
Montpellier, University of, 286
Moralia on Job (Gregory the Great), 146–47
Moscow, 48
Moses, 4, 159
Moslems, 68, 77, 119–20, 180, 191–92, 202–3, 299, 314
  crusades against, 232–34
mysticism, Christian, 159–60

Nahum, 7
narrative poetry, 6, 287
nation-states, 254
Nehemiah, 5
Neoplatonists, 31–32
Nero, Emperor, 61
Nestorius, Bishop, 77
New Testament, 3–4, 10, 12–28, 159
  Augustine's interpretation of, 100–101
  Gnostic interpretation of, 52
Nicene Creed, 69–70
Nicholas I, Pope, 196
nominalism, 265
Normandy, 202, 216
Normans
  conquest of England by, 203–5, *204*
  and the lord/vassal relationship, 208–9
Notker the Stammerer, 149, 191
Numbers, 4

Obadiah, 7
Odoacer, 120
Odo of Cluny, 212
Odyssey (Homer), 36, 39
Old Testament, 3–9, 21–22, 51–52, 159
  allegory in, 59
  Augustine's interpretation of, 100–101

Olivi, Peter John, 312
On Christian Doctrine (Augustine), 82–88
On Friendship (Cicero), 37
On Spiritual Friendship (Aelred of Rievaulx), 37
On World Government (Dante), 39, 46, 156, 164, 258–59, 315
Origen, 57–60, 79
Orosius, 187
Ostrogoths, 121
Ottonian Renaissance, 118, 199, *200*
Otto I, the Great, King
  coronation of, 197
  and the restoration of the Carolingian Empire, 198
Otto II, Emperor, 198
Otto III, Emperor, 118, 198–99, 203
Otto of Freising, 221–22
Ovid, 36–37, 290
  influence of, on Middle Ages, 41–43
Oxford, University of, 286

Padua, University of, 286
paganism, 74, 130–33
  and Christianity, 56–60, 130–32
Palestine, 51, 132, 233
Panofsky, Erwin, 276
pantheism, 264–65
papacy
  at Avignon, 258, 317
  canon law and, 247, 249
  Charlemagne as protector of, 181
  and the coronation of Charlemagne, 182–83
  decline of, 225–26, 253–56
  development of, 54–56
  election to, 229
  and the Franks, 140–41, 179–80
  involvement of, in imperial coronations, 196–97
  and the issue of lay investiture, 231–32
  reform of, 227, 229, 231–32
  and the theory of papal supremacy, 250–51
Paradiso (Dante), 315
Paris, 222
  University of, 285–86
Parliament, English, 260

Parliament of Foules (Chaucer), 39
Parzival (Wolfram von Eschenbach), 287
Pastoral Care (Gregory the Great), 135, 143–46
Patrick, St., 135
Paul, St., 49, 52, 54, 84, 159
  attitude toward women, 20
  conversion of, 17–18, 91
  martyrdom of, 61
  ministry of, 51
  political theory of, 20
  spirituality of, 19–20
  travels of, 19
Paul, Epistles of St., 8, 10, 18–23, 50
  Augustine's analysis of, 108–9
Paul VI, Pope, 229
Paulinus, 73
Peking, 77
  Christian community in, 314
Pelagia, St., 95–97
Pentateuch, 4, 49
Pentecost, 17–18
Pepin, King of the Franks, 120
  Donation of, 180, 226
Percival (Chretien de Troyes), 290
Peter, St., 54, *193*, *230*
  and Christ, 16–17
  martyrdom of, 61
  and papal supremacy, 55–56
Peter, The Epistle of St., 10
Peter Damian, 229, 231
Peter Martyr, 314
Peter the Venerable, 243
Peter Waldo. *See* Valdes
Petrarch, 318
Phaedo (Plato), 32
Pharisees, 15
Philip II, Augustus, King, 235, 254–55, 283
Philip IV, King, 254, 256–58, 260
Philo, 57
Piers Ploywman, 104, 150
Pindar, 30, 36
Pisa, *34*, 220
Plato, 30, 35, 264, 318
  dialogues of, 32
  influence of, on Middle Ages, 30–31
  philosophy of, 31
Pliny, 157–58
Plotinus, 31

poetry
   lyric, 286, 292–93
   narrative, 6, 287
Poles, 203
Polo, Marco, 77
Polycarp, St., 62–63
Pomposa, 65
Poor Clares, 298
population, 217, 222
Porphyry, 264
Prague, University of, 286
primogeniture, 208
priesthood, 53
Proverbs, 7
Provençal, 292
Psalms, 6–7, 9–10, 212
   and the Rule of St. Benedict, 6–7,
      10
Pseudo-Dionysius, 31, 159–60, 164,
      272
   Celestial Hierarchies, 160
   Divine Names, 161–63
Ptolemy, 35, 271

quadrivium, 155, 262

Ravenna, 121, *144*
Reconquista, 232
relics, 63
Revelation of St. John the Divine,
      10, 25–26, *27*, 104–5
   description of heaven in, 27–28
   number symbolism in, 26
Richard I, the Lion-hearted, King,
      235
Richard of St. Victor, 160
Rimini, Francesca da, 97–98
Robert of Molesmes, 239
Rolf (Rollo), 202
Romance of the Rose (Jean de
      Meun), 43, 149, 287
romances, Arthurian, 287, 290
Roman Empire, 56, 63, 66–67, 69–
      73, 115, 121, 123, 132
   Christianity as official religion of,
      74
   decline of, 106, 116–18, 126, 141,
      148, 165, 318
   division of, 117
   law of, 282
Romanesque art, *231*, *281*, 288

Roman influences on Middle Ages
   concept of empire, 45–46
   language, 48
   law, 44–45, 256, 259–60
   literature, 36–44
Roman rite, 187–88
Romans, The Epistle of Paul the
      Apostle to the, 19–21, 84, 97,
      163, 168
Rome, 217
   influence of, on Middle Ages, 36
   sack of, 118
Roncesvalles, 192, 214
Roscelin, 265
Rothair, 124
Rudolf of Habsburg, 254
Rule of St. Benedict, 137, 147, 148,
      169–71, 173–76, 195–96, 225,
      227, 238–40, 244
Ruth, 4

St. Denis, Abbey Church of, 164
St. Gall, monastery of, 188
St. Philibert, monastery of, 200
St. Remigius, monastery of, 229
Saladin, 234
Salamanca, University of, 286
Sallust, 36, 43–44
Santa Sophia, 229
Sappho, 36
Saracens, 234
Saul, King, 4–5
Saxons, 120, 179–80
Scholasticism
   elements of, in literature, 285
   and Gothic architecture, 276–78
Scholastic method, 273
Scholastics, 273
schools
   cathedral, 186–87, 199, 245, 267,
      269, 285
   established by Charlemagne, 186–
      87
   monastic, 178, 186–87, 285
   of St. Victor, 160
Scipio Africanus, 37–38
Scotus Eruigena, John, 160, 164
"Seafarer, The," 125
Sebastian, St., 66, *99*, 123
Seneca, 36
Sermon on the Mount, 13

Sic et Non (Yes and No) (Abeland), 267–68
Siena, *172, 221*
Silvestris, Bernardus, 40
Simeon (prophet), 13
Simon the Magician, *230*
simony, 229–31, 251
Simson, Otto von, 164
Sir Gawain and the Green Knight, 150–51
Slavs, 203
Socrates, 57
Solomon, 5
Song of Roland, 104, 122, 192, *193,* 214, 236, 287–88, 290–91
Song of Songs (Song of Solomon), 7, 241, 292
Sophocles, 36
Soul's Journey into God (Bonaventure), 160, 312
Spenser, Edmund, 290
Spiritual Franciscans, 311–312
Statius, 36
Stephen, King, 203
Stephen, St., 17–18, 60–61
Stephen II, Pope, 148
Strayer, Joseph, 215
subinfeudation, 207
Suetonius, 36, 43–44
Suger, Abbot, 164
Summa Theologiae (Thomas Aquinas), 35, 161
Summoner's Tale (Chaucer), 315
Sylvester I, Pope, 76
Sylvester II, Pope, 203, 262–63
Synod of Whitby, 135, 156

Tacitus, 43, 121–22, 187
Terence, 36
Tertullian, 59–60, 79
Theodore of Tarsus, 134
Theodoric the Ostrogoth, 121, 128, 148, 155
Theodosian Code, 45
Theodosius, Emperor, 73–74, 183
Theophano, Princess, 198
Theophilus, *213*
Thomas à Becket, 249
Thomas of Celano, 296
Thucydides, 30, 36
Thuringians, 127

Timaeus (Plato), 32
tonsure, *172*
Torah, 4
trade, 217, 220
   stimulated by Crusades, 236
Traini, Francesco, *34*
Trajan, Emperor, 61–62, 200
transubstantiation, doctrine of, 252
trivium, 155, 263
Troilus and Criseyde (Chaucer), 149, 282
troubadours, 292–93

Ubertino da Casale, 312
Ulfilas, 71
Unam Sanctam (Boniface VIII), 256–57
universities, rise of, 285–86
Urban II, Pope, 232–33, 235

Valdes (Peter Waldo), 251
Valens, Emperor, 118
Valerian, Emperor, 64, 66
Valla, Lorenzo, 75
Valladolid, University of, 286
Vandals, 71, 81, 119
vassal, defined, 206
vassalage, 206–9, 212, 214–16
Vatican, 61, 72
Vatican Council, Second, 252
Venerable Bede. *See* Bede
Venice, 217, 220, 235
Vergil, 36, 39–40, 45, 49, 282
Vikings, 121, *204*
   conversion of, to Christianity, 202
   invasions of, 199–203
Vincent, St., 66
Visigoths, 119–20, 129, 156
Vivarium, monasteries at, 177

"Wanderer, The," 125
wergild, 124
West Franks, 196, 199, 203
Westminster, 222
Westminster Abbey, 204
Why God Became Man (Anselm), 265–66
Widukind of Corvey, 197
William of Champeaux, 265

William the Conqueror, 203–4, 208, 215

William of Ockham, 265, 318

William of St. Thierry, *Golden Epistle*, 238

Winchester Bible, *102*

Wisdom of Solomon, 7

Wolfram von Eschenbach, 287

Worms, Concordat of, 231, 252

Wyclif, John, 68, 146, 265

Yvain (Chrétien de Troyes), 290

Zacharias, Pope, 148

Zara, 235

Zephaniah, 7